MAP OF MEMBER COUNTRIES OF ASEAN

SOUTHEAST ASIAN AFFAIRS 2006

The **Institute of Southeast Asian Studies (ISEAS)** was established as an autonomous organization in 1968. It is a regional centre dedicated to the study of socio-political, security and economic trends and developments in Southeast Asia and its wider geostrategic and economic environment.

The Institute's research programmes are the Regional Economic Studies (RES, including ASEAN and APEC), Regional Strategic and Political Studies (RSPS), and Regional Social and Cultural Studies (RSCS).

ISEAS Publications, an established academic press, has issued more than 1,000 books and journals. It is the largest scholarly publisher of research about Southeast Asia from within the region. ISEAS Publications works with many other academic and trade publishers and distributors to disseminate important research and analyses from and about Southeast Asia to the rest of the world.

SOUTHEAST ASIAN AFFAIRS 2006

Edited by
Daljit Singh
Lorraine C. Salazar

INSTITUTE OF SOUTHEAST ASIAN STUDIES
Singapore

First published in Singapore in 2006 by
ISEAS Publications
Institute of Southeast Asian Studies
30 Heng Mui Keng Terrace
Pasir Panjang
Singapore 119614
E-mail: publish@iseas.edu.sg
Website: http://bookshop.iseas.edu.sg

All rights reserved. No part of this publication may be reproduced, stored in a retrieval system, or transmitted in any form or by any means, electronic, mechanical, photocopying, recording or otherwise, without the prior permission of the Institute of Southeast Asian Studies.

© 2006 Institute of Southeast Asian Studies, Singapore

The responsibility for facts and opinions in this publication rests exclusively with the authors and their interpretations do not necessarily reflect the views or the policy of the publisher or its supporters.

ISEAS Library Cataloguing-in-Publication Data

Southeast Asian Affairs.
1974–
Annual
1. Asia, Southeastern.
I. Institute of Southeast Asian Studies.
DS501 S72A

ISSN 0377-5437
ISBN 981-230-372-3 (soft cover)
ISBN 981-230-373-1 (hard cover)

Typeset by International Typesetters Pte Ltd
Printed in Singapore by Seng Lee Press Pte Ltd

Contents

Foreword *K. Kesavapany*	vii
Introduction *Daljit Singh and Lorraine C. Salazar*	ix

THE REGION

Southeast Asia in 2005: Strength in the Face of Adversity *Michael Vatikiotis*	3
Southeast Asian Economies: A Year of Exogenous Shocks *Cassey Lee, Boon-Huat Quah, and Marc Foo*	15
Terrorism: Evolving Regional Alliances and State Failure in Mindanao *Kit Collier*	26
Japan in an Insecure East Asia: Redefining Its Role in East Asian Community-Building *Tsutomu Kikuchi*	39

BRUNEI DARUSSALAM

Brunei Darussalam: Consolidating the Polity *Pushpa Thambipillai*	57

CAMBODIA

Cambodia: Positioning for 2008 *Verghese Mathews*	73

INDONESIA

Indonesia: Accomplishments Amidst Challenges *Irman G. Lanti*	93
Indonesian Military Reform: More Than a Human Rights Issue *John B. Haseman*	111

LAOS

Laos: The State of the State *Kyaw Yin Hlaing*	129

MALAYSIA

Malaysia: The Challenge of Money Politics and Religious Activism — 151
K.S. Nathan

Mahathir as Muslim Leader — 172
Ooi Kee Beng

MYANMAR

Myanmar: Challenges Galore but Opposition Failed to Score — 183
Tin Maung Maung Than

Myanmar's Human and Economic Crisis and Its Regional Implications — 208
Bruce Matthews

THE PHILIPPINES

The Philippines: Crisis, Controversies, and Economic Resilience — 227
Lorraine C. Salazar

The Abu Sayyaf Group: From Mere Banditry to Genuine Terrorism — 247
Rommel C. Banlaoi

SINGAPORE

Singapore: Globalizing on Its Own Terms — 265
Terence Chong

THAILAND

Thaksin's Political Zenith and Nadir — 285
Thitinan Pongsudhirak

Thailand's Independent Agencies under Thaksin: Relentless Gridlock and Uncertainty — 303
Alex M. Mutebi

TIMOR LESTE

Timor Leste: On a Path of Authoritarianism? — 325
Jacqueline Siapno

VIETNAM

Vietnam: Laying the Path for the 10th National Congress — 345
Danny Wong Tze Ken

Foreword

Southeast Asia was on the cusp of major changes in 2005. At year's end in December 2005, the long-awaited East Asian Summit was held in Kuala Lumpur. It marked the beginning of region-building that encompasses East, Southeast, and South Asia, as well as Australia and New Zealand, a process that heralds looking beyond narrow sub-regionalism. At the same time, ASEAN launched the process of preparing an ASEAN Charter, with the guidance of an Eminent Persons Group. Both events signalled the strengthening of ASEAN and the wider region.

Furthermore, the democratic processes were strengthened by the successful organization of regional elections in Indonesia following the legislative and presidential elections in the previous year. In Thailand and the Philippines, the political processes delivered different results: Prime Minister Thaksin came under pressure which led to his resignation in April 2006, whilst President Arroyo retained her post despite street demonstrations. Vietnam continued to achieve rapid economic growth. Bird flu appeared, but was contained, at least for the time being. Most ASEAN economies benefited from the high growth sustained by India and China. The good economic performance plus the central role of ASEAN in the driver's seat of the East Asian Summit has restored some of the shine back to ASEAN.

Southeast Asian Affairs 2006, like the previous 32 editions of this flagship publication of ISEAS, provides an informed and readable analysis of developments in the region.

K. Kesavapany
Director
Institute of Southeast Asian Studies

April 2006

Introduction

At the end of 2005 Southeast Asia looked in a better condition than at any other time since the 1997 Asian crisis. The economies had recovered and there was steady growth as countries continued to pursue economic reform. The world economy was resilient in 2005, notwithstanding a modest cyclical slowdown during the year. Moreover, Southeast Asia's economic prospects were buoyed by the growing linkages with the rising economies of China and India and a recovering Japanese economy. Apart from a few cases, regime stability characterized the political landscape of the region.

There were two other positive factors: Indonesia and the Association of Southeast Asian Nations (ASEAN). As the largest country of Southeast Asia located in a huge maritime swathe between the Philippines on the east, Australia in the south, and the Bay of Bengal in the northwest, Indonesia's stability or lack of it, has had an important bearing on perceptions of Southeast Asia. Under the administration of President Susilo Bambang Yudhoyono, the country was back on the right track, working to achieve domestic stability, improve governance, build institutions, and attract investments.

Meanwhile, ASEAN was regaining some of the importance it used to enjoy a decade earlier. It was again in the centre of moves to shape a new Asian regional architecture as it organized the first East Asian Summit that included not only the 13 members of the ASEAN+3 process but also India, Australia, and New Zealand. It was being courted by the major powers as each tried to maintain or extend its influence.

ASEAN's complexion also seemed to be undergoing subtle changes as a result of the democratization of Indonesia and the growing realization that the principle of non-intervention needed to be used flexibly to enable cooperation on transnational challenges. The decision to draw up an ASEAN Charter raised hopes of a more rules-based organization with a better sense of common values.

Yet, despite the more promising outlook for Southeast Asia, many challenges remained. Indonesia needs to achieve and sustain close to 7 per cent economic growth to make a dent on unemployment and poverty. It was difficult to see this happening unless the fragile investment climate is improved. Indonesia's democracy also needed consolidation as the country struggled to build the institutions and the rule of law without which democracy may not be sustainable. Street demonstrations in Bangkok and Manila to oust the leaders of the two countries, while reflective of political ferment and contestation in the process of democratization, also highlighted its weaknesses. In Myanmar there was no indication when the work of the National Convention, a landmark on the roadmap of reform, would be completed. Terrorism remained a threat, especially in Indonesia and the Philippines. ASEAN still needed to demonstrate that it had the will to move forward boldly to achieve greater internal cohesiveness. Its economic integration agenda remained well short of implementation.

Meanwhile the major powers were more active in Southeast Asia. In recent years China has significantly increased its influence through skilful political and economic diplomacy, eclipsing that of Japan, at least in the perception of Southeast Asian states. There were signs that US attention to the region was becoming more broad-based, and not just confined to counter-terrorism. Noteworthy in this respect was the renewed attention to Indonesia, including the resumption of military aid to Jakarta. India's economic links with Southeast Asia were still far behind the other three major powers but were growing rapidly.

In the broader Asian geopolitical environment, the uncertainties caused by the shifting alignments between the major powers were heightened by tensions in Sino-Japanese relations, which remained at a low ebb in 2005. Meanwhile US-Japan security relations continued to strengthen and Japan was on the path towards becoming a more "normal" power. Strategic cooperation between India and the United States was deepening, even as economic links between China and India were expanding rapidly. China's military modernization was causing anxieties in the United States and Japan. Overall, in strategic terms, the United States remained distracted by and preoccupied with Iraq and the war on terrorism, a state of affairs that continued to provide China more freedom of manoeuvre and latitude to expand its influence in Asia.

Southeast Asia had little or no influence on these developments even though they could have major implications for the region. ASEAN desires cooperative relations between the major powers and their balanced engagement with Southeast Asia. With this in mind, the Association has established a multiplicity of dialogue and cooperative mechanisms with them.

In the regional section of this volume, the first two articles provide the political and economic overview of Southeast Asia in 2005, with Michael Vatikiotis writing on the former and Cassey Lee, Boon-Huat Quah, and Marc Foo on the latter.

In the third article, "Terrorism: Evolving Regional Alliances and State Failure in Mindanao", Kit Collier provides a valuable reminder that, contrary to some mainstream analyses, the Jemaah Islamiyah (JI) terrorist organization is not simply a franchise of Al Qaeda or an integral part of it. Nor does it have clearly demarcated command structure and organizational boundaries. The original JI is now splintered and the immediate threat to Western targets in particular comes more from freelancers who may not answer to JI at all. The roots of JI, says Collier, are thoroughly Indonesian but its extended family is much more than an Indonesian phenomenon. It is often overlooked that the Philippines has been as much a target of JI-related bombings as Indonesia and that the sanctuaries in Southern Philippines remain the weakest link in the entire regional counter-terrorist effort.

In the fourth and final article of the regional section, "Japan in an Insecure East Asia: Redefining Its Role in East Asian Community-Building", Tsutomu Kikuchi offers a Japanese perspective on East Asian regionalism, emphasizing the importance of norms and values for deeper regional cooperation. Differences on these as well as differences of geopolitical and geoeconomic interests are likely to make the task of community-building in East Asia a challenging one. He would like Japan to be more pro-active in engaging Asia instead of retreating into the comfortable cocoon of the US-Japan alliance, though the alliance should remain the bedrock of Japan's security and Asian stability.

After the regional section, 11 country reviews as well as five special theme articles on specific countries follow.

In the article "Brunei Darussalam: Consolidating the Polity", Pushpa Thambipillai examines the political and governmental scene, including the establishment of a new Legislative Council of 30 selected members, and a major cabinet reshuffle. A new political party was set up and there seemed to be more tolerance of civil society. However, there was no indication yet when the Legislative Council would meet and the issue of election of some of the Council members had not been clarified. Thambipillai's examination of economic events focuses on the impact of the high price of oil and the government's efforts to diversify the economy to move away from dependence on hydrocarbons. Unemployment remained an issue of some concern while the government maintained its vigil against terrorism and deviant teachings of Islam. Finally, the Brunei government's activities in promoting bilateral and regional relations are recounted.

In "Cambodia — Positioning for 2008" Verghese Mathews reviews the major events of 2005, starting with the economy. He looks at the extent and implications of the country's dependence on donor assistance, especially in poverty alleviation and improvements in infrastructure and education. Next, Mathews examines the main political developments, starting with the progress made in establishing the

Khmer Rouge Tribunal, which has kept alive the hope of justice and closure for the victims and the community in general, and then going on to analyse the main political events and the fortunes of the key political players in the country. Mathews concludes by drawing attention to the continuing challenges that Cambodia faces, especially the need to strengthen democratic institutions, ensure that good governance is firmly rooted in the country, curb corruption, and dismantle the deeply entrenched patronage system.

Irman G. Lanti's "Indonesia: Accomplishments Amidst Challenges" examines the extent of the devastation caused by the tsunami in Aceh and the challenges facing the rehabilitation and reconstruction efforts, before going on to discuss the peaceful resolution of the decades-long separatist insurgency in the province. He cautions that the agreement between GAM and the Indonesian government, though an impressive achievement, has to be fully implemented before durable peace can be attained. The article discusses the significance of the regional elections held during 2005 that allowed the public to directly elect governors, *bupati* (district chiefs), and mayors. There was progress in the fight against terrorism, and steps were taken by the government to combat the growth of radical ideology of the kind that leads to terrorism. In foreign policy, the year saw the return of some activism, as signified by the holding of the 50th Anniversary of Asian-African Conference, the signing of strategic partnership agreements with China and India and moves leading to the resumption of military aid by the United States. Yet, despite the achievements of the year, Indonesia's main challenges remained the same as in the recent past: how to achieve good governance with reduced corruption and how to create a domestic environment conducive to investment and faster economic growth. "While ... the foundations for better development seemed to be in place", says Lanti, "many things that would define the future of the nation still remained in doubt."

In the companion article "Indonesian Military Reform: More Than a Human Rights Issue", John B. Haseman argues that important reforms have been implemented under a reform-minded president but there is still some way to go before Indonesia's military can attain the status the government and the people expect in a democratic society. Changing the military's institutional mindset is perhaps the most difficult of the remaining challenges.

In "Laos: The State of the State", Kyaw Yin Hlaing points out that economic reforms over the years have resulted in Laos becoming a less totalitarian and repressive state. Based on interview data, Kyaw concludes that the technical, institutional, and administrative capacities of the Laotian state are improving, even though serious shortcomings remain. Grievances do exist among the general public, but the political situation is stable and there is no real threat that the government's reform programmes will be interrupted by social protests.

K.S. Nathan's "Malaysia: The Challenge of Money Politics and Religious Activism" focuses on the problems of corruption, cronyism, and nepotism that the Abdullah government inherited from the past administration. They constitute the main challenges facing the Premier despite his efforts to solve them. In 2005, religious intolerance, especially on the part of the more activist, fundamentalist, and extremist Islamic elements within and outside the official bureaucracy, posed an additional test to Abdullah's "Islam Hadhari" project. In the realm of economics, Nathan maintains that Malaysia has done reasonably well in maintaining balanced growth and competitiveness in the face of oil price hikes and a challenging international environment. Finally, the article examines events in Malaysia's foreign relations, in particular its role in ASEAN and its hosting of the inaugural East Asia Summit.

In the theme article "Mahathir as Muslim Leader", Ooi Kee Beng shows that in the later part of his long political career, Mahathir used the same arguments in his call for "Muslims" to develop that he had used earlier in his career to push for "Malay" economic progress, with the West remaining the constant antithesis. In 1981, when he became Prime Minister, he turned into policies the ideas about uplifting the Malays he first articulated in his controversial book *The Malay Dilemma*. But he also encouraged Islamization, and in the later part of his premiership, shifted to emphasize "Muslimness" in line with international developments and his increasing prominence, as well as self-perception, as a global Muslim leader. Mahathir's understanding of Islam is that of a knowledge-seeking faith and teaching that had lost its way. This evolved view emphasizes the importance of acquiring scientific and functional knowledge and applies the same method of scolding his "patients" — now the Muslims — in order to nudge them to develop.

Tin Maung Maung Than's "Myanmar: Challenges Galore but Opposition Failed to Score" draws attention, among other things in 2005, to the domestic media blitz and mobilization of support for the National Convention (NC) and the unprecedented highlighting of it to members of the international community as a showcase of political progress. But the legitimacy of the NC was still not accepted by the political opposition and Western governments. The lack of progress in instituting political reforms in Myanmar became a bone of contention in ASEAN's relations with its dialogue partners and even within ASEAN itself. There was an increase in attempts by the international community to press for changes in the regime's conduct. But these pressures seemed to have little or no effect on the regime. Even with the support of powerful players in the international community the opposition failed to score any success in its campaign against the military regime. The National League for Democracy, displaced from the mainstream political process and deprived of its top leadership, was ineffectual. The ethnic-based political parties, save for one, continued their cooperation with the government and participated in the NC's deliberations. Far from being a failed state, Myanmar in 2005 seemed to represent the apex of state power in the nearly six decades of political independence since 1948.

In the special theme article "Myanmar's Human and Economic Crisis and Its Regional Implications", Bruce Matthews speaks of a gathering crisis in the country which could have serious regional consequences. He first reviews the internal situation in Myanmar based on fieldwork conducted in June 2005, and taking into consideration events in the later part of the year, before examining the regional and international implications of Myanmar's authoritarian polity and its failure to adequately address key matters of human security. Issues discussed include the continuing displacement of thousands of dispirited ethnic peoples, especially in the Arakan and the Shan and Karen states bordering Bangladesh and Thailand respectively; challenges associated with heroin production and other narcotics; and the increasingly significant economic and possibly strategic relationships between Myanmar, India, and China. The article ends with reflections on what strategies might best assist Myanmar in its long struggle to emerge as a fully modern Southeast Asian state.

Lorraine C. Salazar's "The Philippines: Crisis, Controversies, and Economic Resilience" examines the turbulent politics in the country and its effects on the economy in 2005. The year saw yet another attempt to remove the President through street politics which was unsuccessful because of lack of support from key social sectors. Allegations of electoral fraud and corruption caused the President's legitimacy and popularity to diminish. However, she refused to resign and, instead, deftly called for a change in the Constitution to establish a parliamentary system of government and to push ahead with economic reforms. At the end of the year the President was struggling to rebuild her credibility and giving priority to political reforms. Peace talks with the Moro Islamic Liberation Front were temporarily suspended because of the political crisis in Manila, but will resume in 2006, thus keeping alive hopes for a negotiated end to that conflict. On the other hand, the government's relations with the Communist Party of the Philippines turned for the worse. The economy remained resilient despite the political turmoil, in part because of the huge flow of remittances from Overseas Filipino Workers and the introduction of new revenue measures.

In his theme article "The Abu Sayyaf Group: From Mere Banditry to Genuine Terrorism", Rommel C. Banlaoi analyses the origins, ideology, organizational structure and capabilities of the Abu Sayyaf Group (ASG), perhaps the most lethal armed Muslim group in the Philippines today. After a period in which it earned notoriety as a bandit group, the ASG has now revived its radical Islamic agenda and returned to terrorism as a political weapon in the service of this agenda.

Terence Chong's "Singapore: Globalizing on Its Own Terms" sees a dilemma facing Singapore in its openness, on the one hand, to economic globalization and its wariness, on the other, about certain liberal democratic and cultural processes and values. Chong wonders whether a small nation-state like Singapore whose survival depends upon becoming a vibrant global city can continue with ideological and cultural protectionism. A global city, he argues, "cannot be willed into being but becomes one only when others recognize it as such ... all global cities require the cultural legitimacy from the international community of transnational professionals, creative classes, and international opinion-shapers who have the power to confer it recognition. The competition to distinguish oneself as a global city is, in reality, the competition to win legitimacy and recognition from this international community."

In "Thaksin's Political Zenith and Nadir", Thitinan Pongsudhirak reviews the remarkable turn of events in Thailand that brought its popularly elected Prime Minister from unprecedented political heights to political depths in less than a year. The article examines Thaksin's huge election victory in February 2005 and the key events following it. It then goes on to deal with the worsening insurgency in the Muslim provinces of Southern Thailand and Thaksin's mishandling of it. Anti-Thaksin public protests that started in Bangkok in September gathered momentum, becoming a significant force of street politics by the end of the year. The sale of Shin Corporation to Singapore's Temasek Holdings in January 2006 provided the final spark and impetus to galvanize the anti-Thaksin movement. Yet, this attempt to remove the Prime Minister from office remained confined largely to the urban sectors, with the bulk of rural Thais continuing to support Thaksin. Thitinan concludes with a look at Thaksin's legacy and the country's near-term prospects, including the implications of these extraordinary events for Thailand's young democracy.

Alex M. Mutebi's "Thailand's Independent Agencies under Thaksin: Relentless Gridlock and Uncertainty" examines how the various independent institutions mandated by the 1997 Constitution have struggled to establish both their authority and their credibility under Prime Minister Thaksin's tenure in office. The article looks at cases of political interference in four of Thailand's independent agencies, arguing that such interference renders ineffective the system of checks and balances and also accords undue influence to vested interests both within and outside government.

In "Timor Leste: On a Path of Authoritarianism?" Jacqueline Siapno argues that a few years into independence, the government is treading on the path towards authoritarianism as it attempts to introduce an anti-defamation law and moves to restrict public space for free comment and discussion. The article then looks at issues in East Timor's foreign relations, in particular with its two immediate neighbours, Indonesia and Australia, before discussing poverty reduction and human security. Finally, the article examines the in-between spaces in the politics of culture, memory, and identity, and the resilience of the East Timorese.

Danny Wong Tze Ken's article "Vietnam: Laying the Path for the 10th National Congress" focuses on the actions and responses of the ruling Communist Party of Vietnam (VCP) as it pursued its reform programme in the run-up to the 10th National Congress in 2006. The challenges posed by endemic corruption and the government's efforts to overcome it, questions relating to religious freedom, and the government's handling of political dissidents continued to feature in Vietnam's domestic politics. The pace of reform of state-owned enterprises and Vietnam's pending entry into the World Trade Organization were the two central economic issues. Also of great importance was the threat posed by avian flu. Finally, the article also considers Vietnam's successes in its foreign relations and raises questions on how these could be translated by the VCP government to strengthen its position domestically.

The articles in this volume promise to be timely and relevant as they address regional and domestic political, economic, security, and social developments during 2005 and their implications for countries in the region and beyond.

Daljit Singh
Lorraine C. Salazar
Editors
Southeast Asian Affairs 2006

The Region

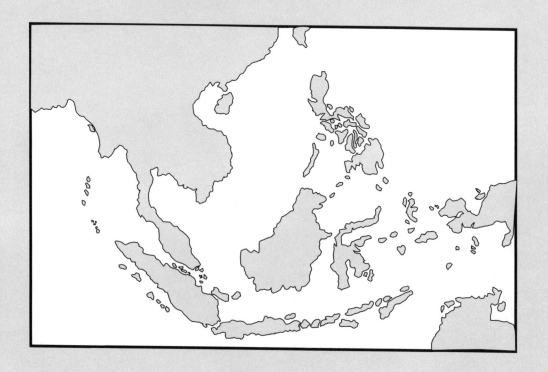

SOUTHEAST ASIA IN 2005
Strength in the Face of Adversity

Michael Vatikiotis

Southeast Asia greeted 2005 in a sombre mood, as the full scale of devastation in the wake of the tsunami triggered by a massive earthquake that sent giant waves crashing into the coastlines of north Sumatra, southern Thailand, northwestern Malaysia, and Myanmar became apparent. Almost a quarter million people were killed across the region, a loss of life almost too great to comprehend. In Aceh alone as many as 180,000 people died as a wall of dark water 10 metres high travelling at speeds of almost 400 miles an hour rushed onshore crushing everything in its path. From the air, it still looks like the aftermath of an atom blast.

The tsunami was a particular blow for Indonesia, which had just crowned a protracted and messy democratic transition with successful multi-party elections and the first direct presidential election at the end of 2004. The new government led by President Susilo Bambang Yudhoyono was poised to inaugurate a new era of confidence and stability for Indonesia. Hopes ran high. Southeast Asia badly needed its largest component state to get back on track or face the prospect of unfavourable comparison with the booming economies of China and India.

Since 2001, Southeast Asia has been badly buffeted by the global war on terror. A string of bombings in Indonesia and the Philippines, as well as the uncovering of local terrorist cells and networks over the past four years has dragged the region into the terror spotlight. Southeast Asia's most wanted terror suspect, Hambali, was arrested in central Thailand in 2003. Indonesia's resort island of Bali had been the scene of the most devastating and audacious terrorist attack since 2001, when bombs exploded outside nightclubs frequented by Western tourists in Kuta in October 2002 — and another in October 2005. The Philippines

---

MICHAEL VATIKIOTIS is a Visiting Fellow at the Institute of Southeast Asian Studies and former editor of the *Far Eastern Economic Review*.

is widely suspected to be a haven for Islamic militants who train in remote camps in the southern province of Mindanao. A terrorist attack perpetrated by Islamic extremists was perceived as the principal threat to security in Southeast Asia throughout the year.

Taken together, Indonesia's political fragility, the wider region's vulnerability, and then the ravages of natural disaster, did not exactly make for a cheery start to the year. Yet the legacy of the tsunami marked the region in significantly positive ways and influenced events throughout the year. Dire predictions of social chaos and political upheaval proved far-fetched. Instead, the tsunami, which left such a devastating trail of human and physical destruction, stimulated better government, enhanced regional cooperation, and offered a measure of peace across a region that badly needed all of these things.

The Tsunami

No one could have imagined that Indonesia's most conflict-prone province, a region closed to foreign scrutiny and governed under martial law would become the scene of Southeast Asia's biggest international relief effort, almost overnight. According to the World Bank, more than 20 international non-governmental organizations (NGOs), 430 local NGOs, dozens of bilateral and multilateral donors, and many central and local government agencies rushed to Aceh to help rebuild the shattered lives of more than 500,000 displaced by the waves. "Never before have non-government actors played such a central role in the long-term reconstruction," commented the World Bank's chief in Indonesia, Andrew Steer.[1] An estimated US$9 billion has been pledged in aid for Aceh and Nias, of which less than US$1 billion has been spent. In a report issued in December the World Bank reported: "Most children are now back in school, health centers have largely reopened, some two-thirds of farmers are back working their land, and three-quarters of the fishing boats lost have been replaced or are being built."[2]

Perhaps more remarkable than the generous outpouring of aid was the extent of regional and international participation on the ground. This was no time for Indonesia to proudly stand aloof, or worry about foreign scrutiny. President Yudhoyono was quick to grasp this fact and Aceh went from being the least accessible province of Indonesia to outsiders to one overrun by military teams from the United States, Australia, Singapore, and many other countries, including China, Spain, and Germany. Under the astute leadership of General Endriartono Sutarto, the Indonesian military made way and quickly adapted to the new order of things on the ground.

The longer-term political ramifications of the relief and reconstruction operation are significant. For all the talk of an ASEAN security community, very little has been done to execute the idea of a common and cooperative framework. The role of the armed forces from around ASEAN in the tsunami relief effort helped make the concept seem more realistic. For the United States in particular, the humanitarian operation in Aceh helped alter perceptions of the world's biggest superpower in the world's largest Muslim nation. For tiny Singapore, long viewed with suspicion by neighbours, the stamina and devotion of its doctors and military specialists on the ground in places like Melabeuh in Aceh, has not just altered the island republic's image but also convinced its military planners to look at building capacity for international relief and peacekeeping. When Hurricane Katrina hit Florida in October, Singapore's heavy-lift Chinook helicopters moved swiftly into action.

Much remains to be done. By year's end some 70,000 people were still living in tents in Aceh and Nias. Some 70,000 children below the age of 15 in Aceh were still not back in school. The pace of reconstruction was slow, but the verdict was that the relief and reconstruction operation had not succumbed to the rampant corruption and inefficiencies everyone feared. Safeguards were in place and the Indonesian government had lived up to its promise not to squander the world's generosity.

Peace Comes to Aceh

Even more remarkable, perhaps, have been the ripple effects of this relief operation. A 30-year conflict between the Aceh Independence Movement (GAM) and the Indonesian government was resolved with a peace deal signed in August after just five months of negotiation. Although the Yudhoyono government was planning to address the issue, the Aceh peace agreement concluded in August would probably have taken much longer to hammer out were it not for the tsunami. The giant waves knocked the fight out of the Aceh rebels; popular priorities focused on survival and rehabilitation rather than independence. Moral and physical constraints were imposed on the Indonesian military's proclivity to seek profit from conflict. "Here in Aceh we already have an example of how a new hope for peace can emerge out of the ruin of destruction," President Yudhoyono said at a ceremony marking the first anniversary of the tsunami.[3]

The agreement, brokered by former Finnish President Marti Ahtisaari and signed in Helsinki, provides for a generous measure of autonomy for Aceh. It gives Aceh the right to use regional symbols, including a flag, crest, and a hymn.

The establishment of Aceh-based political parties was also agreed to. In economic terms, under the agreement Aceh is entitled to retain 70 per cent of the revenues from all current and future hydrocarbon deposits and other natural resources in the territory of Aceh. There are some other provisions on the right to raise funds with external loans, right to impose taxes for internal activities, development of sea ports and airports in the province and free trade with all other parts of the country. The Indonesian government swiftly granted amnesty to jailed GAM members and hundreds of detainees were released. To oversee the implementation of the agreement and the phased demilitarization and surrender of weapons, an Aceh Monitoring Mission (AMM) was established by the European Union and ASEAN contributing countries. The AMM was given wide-ranging powers for resolving disputes. By year's end the AMM had overseen the surrender of all the agreed weapons in the possession of GAM and the withdrawal of all the agreed number of inorganic troops from the TNI side.

More importantly, perhaps, the notion of conflict resolution based on special autonomy that lies at the heart of the Aceh agreement has broken a mould in Southeast Asia's prickly nationalist environment. It could lead to a greater acceptance of forms of autonomy and federalism and help resolve other conflicts in the region.

Indonesia: Stability Amidst Adversity

In the face of such adversity, it would have been remarkable enough for Indonesia to come through the year with just the tsunami to deal with. But this was only one of many challenges that the fledgling Yudhoyono government had to deal with. The soaring global oil prices made it more and more difficult for Indonesia to justify the heavy subsidies that made domestic fuel prices the cheapest in the world. But it took the Yudhoyono government most of the year to overcome the stiff political and popular resistance to raising fuel prices, which in the end he was forced to do in the face of a serious currency crisis.

Next there was the issue of terrorism, which continued to plague Indonesia. Suicide bombers attacked popular restaurants in Bali on 1 October, killing 22 people. It was the first serious terror attack in Indonesia for a year and re-opened the whole issue of Indonesia as a crucible for Islamic extremism. These fears were eased somewhat on 9 November after a police operation in East Java resulted in the death of terrorist mastermind Azahari bin-Husin. Documents uncovered at the scene revealed that Malaysian-born Azahari and his gang were planning more attacks.

As if all this was not enough, there were a series of scandals and upheavals, including the investigation into the October 2004 death of human rights activist, Munir Thaleb; ongoing religious tensions in Central Sulawesi; and, no sooner had peace been agreed upon in Aceh, than the Papuans started clamouring for special autonomy as well. A further earthquake on the Sumatran island of Nias in March added an additional burden on the government. There were also serious health challenges with the outbreak of poliomyelitis, several areas where children suffered from malnutrition, and latterly the threat of a serious avian flu epidemic.

Yet, as well as dealing with all this, Yudhoyono pressed forward with his ambitious political agenda, cracking down on widespread corruption in the bureaucracy, as well as consolidating democracy. Local elections that occurred in stages throughout the year saw a further strengthening of regional autonomy whilst a cabinet reshuffle in early December strengthened the economic policymaking team.

Few countries in the world, let alone Southeast Asia, could have been expected to survive so much upheaval and yet press ahead with reform. Indonesia's remarkable stability in the face of adversity did much to bolster its image in the region and beyond. By year's end, the United States had restored military aid to Indonesia, lifting a ban imposed by Congress over the alleged involvement of senior Indonesian officers in human rights abuses committed before East Timor achieved independence.

Thailand: A Turn for the Worse

If Indonesia was a bright spot, in Thailand events took something of a turn for the worse. The year opened with a stunning electoral victory for Prime Minister Thaksin Shinawatra, who embarked on his second term of office armed with a landslide majority after polls held in February. No Thai Prime Minister in history has managed to amass such a commanding majority in parliament with 385 seats in the 500-seat parliament. But Thaksin embarked on his second term burdened by a worsening conflict in the three southern provinces of Narathiwat, Pattani, and Yala that are home to Thailand's Malay Muslim minority. The long-running insurrection flared up in January 2004 after a well-organized raid on a Thai army camp in Narathiwat. By the end of 2004, popular anger had been stirred up by the government's mishandling of public sentiment and the death of more than 85 Malay Muslim youths who had been demonstrating outside a police station in the border town of Tak Bai.

The year began with a series of bombings and shootings that targeted civilians as well as government officials. The sporadic tempo of violence soon transformed into a daily reality for the people of the South, whilst the government changed its policy towards the region almost as often. In March, after prodding from the influential Privy Council, Thaksin declared that the government would take a more conciliatory approach to managing the conflict. He set up a National Reconciliation Commission headed by respected former Prime Minister Anand Panyarachun. By mid-July the policy flipped again. One day after insurgents launched a major attack on the town of Yala, managing to knock out power and pin down security forces in their barracks, Thaksin declared an emergency decree that imposed martial law on the troubled region.

Much of the violence in southern Thailand over the course of 2005 showed more sophisticated planning and execution than a year earlier. In late October, for example, more than 300 insurgents launched simultaneous attacks on military and civilian official targets across the South, killing four people and stealing a quantity of weapons. There were bomb attacks on military convoys followed by coordinated ambushes and a series of car bombings of government buildings, including a bomb that exploded in the major regional airport of Had Yai. So far, the insurgents have refrained from moving their campaign of violence to Bangkok or elsewhere in the country, but some analysts believe it is only a matter of time before the violence escalates.

All the same, by year's end the government was declaring a measure of success in resolving the situation. Troubled relations with Malaysia were back on track after delicate diplomacy and the handover of a suspected separatist to Thai authorities ensured that Prime Minister Thaksin would attend the year-end ASEAN summit in Kuala Lumpur. But most observers doubted that the conflict was anywhere near contained. The shadowy insurgency, with its well-hidden leadership, seemed capable of launching attacks on Thai government targets at anytime. In a rare statement to the media, an alleged member of the insurgency told an international news agency that the goal was to declare an independent state in 2006.[4] Indeed, no sooner had the heavy monsoon flooding that killed dozens in the south subsided at the beginning of January 2006, than the killing resumed.

The conflict in southern Thailand was one of a number of problems that created political difficulties for Thaksin as he embarked on his second term. An alleged corruption scandal involving the sale of airport security scanners to the new Suwannaphum Airport undermined popular trust in the government. Capitalizing on the badly handled airport issue, Thaksin's critics started to expose other alleged wrongdoing. This helped create the perception that government policies were aimed at lining the pockets of government ministers. In August Thaksin announced a major cabinet reshuffle to address the mounting pressure on his government. Rumours of a rift between the Prime Minister and the palace swirled around Bangkok. By the end of the year, thousands of people started to gather at weekly open-air commentary sessions hosted by media mogul Sondhi Limthongkul and a government that began the year at the peak of its popularity started to look distinctly threatened.

Philippines: Democracy Challenged

Thaksin's political problems were matched in the region only by the challenge to Philippine President Gloria Macapagal Arroyo's power in the course of 2005. Arroyo's difficulties started when a former deputy director of the country's National Bureau of Investigation revealed audiotapes of a wire-tapped conversation between President Arroyo and an official of the Commission on Elections. The contents of the tape allegedly proved that Arroyo had rigged the 2004 national election. On 27 June, Arroyo admitted to inappropriately speaking to an election official, claiming it was a mere "lapse in judgment". She apologized but denied influencing the outcome of the election. "I was anxious to protect my votes and during that time had conversations with many people, including a COMELEC official," Arroyo said in a television broadcast. "My intent was not to influence the outcome of the election and it did not."[5]

Nonetheless, a loose but determined coalition of opposition figures, including elements in the armed forces and allies of former president Joseph Estrada, pushed for the president's resignation and ouster. Arroyo's brash management style does not engender loyalty and by the beginning of July ten cabinet officials resigned and asked the president to do the same. The momentum built up and a hastily assembled case for impeachment was brought before the Congress.

Amid rumours of a military coup and a massive show of people's power similar to the EDSA (Epifanio de los Santos Avenue) movement that brought down Estrada in 2001, Arroyo's position looked precarious. But she held firm and with the help of former president Fidel Ramos, who remained an ally, Arroyo rejected calls for her resignation.

In September the House of Representatives knocked down the impeachment case against Arroyo, citing it as "insufficient in substance". But Arroyo's woes are not over. Opinion polls show that the majority of the public mistrust her government and believe she won the 2004 election fraudulently. Most observers believe the only reason she remains in office is that no one in the country's fractious political elite can decide on a successor. Nor is there a consensus on the notion of changing the political system in the Philippines from an elected presidency to a prime minister and cabinet system, as proposed and backed by Ramos.

As the year drew to a close there were indications that the 58-year-old president was contemplating a move to use political reform as cover to extend her term in office without going to the polls. This prompted Ramos to signal a shift of allegiance suggesting that 2006 would see continuing political difficulties for the Arroyo administration.

Political turmoil in Manila made it no easier to make peace in the restive southern region of Mindanao. In February a disturbing outbreak of violence on the island of Sulu signalled a serious breakdown in the decade-old peace agreement between the government and the Moro National Liberation Front. The government meanwhile signalled progress in a long-running negotiation with the Moro Islamic Liberation Front, brokered by Malaysia.

Talks have been ongoing for the past four years. Newly appointed Secretary for Peace Processes Jesus Dureza announced that he hoped an agreement could be signed in 2006. Malaysian observers were less sanguine, citing ongoing military operations in Mindanao driven by the hunt for terrorist suspects that hardly built an environment for peace. Goaded by US forces in the region, the Armed Forces of the Philippines was under pressure to track down suspected JI militants responsible for helping to train extremists in Mindanao who were bent on attacking targets in Philippines and beyond.

Myopia in Myanmar

For Myanmar the year was dominated by fallout from the dismissal and arrest of former military intelligence chief and Prime Minister Khin Nyunt, which had occurred in October 2004. He had amassed considerable power and acted as an interface with the outside world. Khin Nyunt was widely seen as someone prepared to make political concessions in return for aid and development from foreign donors.

With Khin Nyunt out of the way, Senior General Than Shwe consolidated his grip on power, supported by Deputy Senior General Maung Aye. Many of those associated with Khin Nyunt, including officials, diplomats, and military officers, were detained, tried on charges of corruption or abuse of power, and given long prison sentences. But by April, Than Shwe was already talking about succession. He mentioned to Indonesia's President on a visit to Bandung that he was preparing to hand over the reins of power to Thura Shwe Man, a younger officer said to be considered like a son by Than Shwe and his powerful wife Kyaing Kyaing.

For ASEAN, Myanmar's looming chairmanship of the regional body was a serious headache. ASEAN officials feared that if Myanmar assumed the chairmanship, ASEAN's major allies and dialogue partners would stay away from annual meetings. Then in late July, as ASEAN foreign ministers gathered in Vientiane for their annual meeting, Myanmar announced it would defer assuming the ASEAN chair. It justified its giving up of the chairmanship by saying it was preoccupied with "national reconciliation", a reference to its "Road Map to Democracy".

But while the move helped ease some of the immediate discomfort in ASEAN circles, it hardly signalled a change of political direction in Myanmar, or much progress along the road map. The ruling military junta resumed a constitution-drafting national Convention in February, but the body was slammed in international circles for not including representatives of the political opposition. In December the junta renewed a detention order that keeps opposition leader Aung San Suu Kyi under house arrest for another year.

Observers searched in vain for signs of popular resistance. A series of bomb explosions were attributed to disaffected remnants of the old Khin Nyunt military intelligence clique. A top-ranking diplomat in Washington defected and sought asylum in the United States. But otherwise the junta held firmly onto power. Then suddenly in November the government was moved to a new capital some 300 km. from Rangoon. The abrupt move to Pyinmana (a new city being developed by a company owned by former drug lord Lo Hsing Han) was attributed by some to advice from a soothsayer.

The move to Pyinmana did not help relations with fellow ASEAN states because they had not been informed of the move. ASEAN members adopted a sterner line towards Myanmar at the year-end summit in Kuala Lumpur. ASEAN leaders set something of a precedent when they raised the issue of political reform during their meeting with Myanmar President General Soe Win at the summit in Kuala Lumpur, and told him that the regime must release its political prisoners.[6]

Meanwhile, there was a more concerted attempt by the international community to ratchet up the pressure on Myanmar's military rulers. In September former Czech President Vaclav Havel and Nobel Laureate Archbishop Desmond Tutu penned a report calling for UN Security Council Action on Myanmar. Significantly, the Philippines, serving a term on the UN Security Council, supported the inclusion of Myanmar for debate. In December the Council heard a general debate on Myanmar that did not result in any binding resolutions.

Regional Growth and Stability

Elsewhere the region was relatively quiet. For Laos and Cambodia there was another year of relative stability. For Vietnam, another year of stellar 8 per cent economic growth and gradual reform. For Malaysia and Singapore it was a year of consolidation for fairly new governments on both sides of the causeway.

Malaysian Prime Minister Abdullah Badawi was in a secure position after winning 198 out of 220 seats in the Malaysian parliament for the ruling National Front coalition in 2004. In the course of 2005, Abdullah demonstrated a deft touch in dealing with alleged frictions within the ruling United Malays National Organization (UMNO) party. He appeared to work well with Deputy Prime Minister Najib Tun Razak and deflected charges that his young son-in-law Khairy Jamaluddin was being groomed as a successor. Victory over the Islamic party PAS in a by-election in December brought UMNO a step closer to winning back the state of Kelantan.

Malaysians have started grumbling less about their affable new Prime Minister, now that the memory of Mahathir Mohammad has begun to fade. There are still concerns about Abdullah's unassertive and consensual style. But he has shown a consistency in policy — pressing forward with reform of the police force and the anti-corruption campaign he fought the election on. In the course of the year several prominent Malaysians were investigated for corruption and more significantly in October a senior UMNO leader, Mohammed Isa Abdul Samad, the party chief from Malacca, was removed from his post.

Next door in Singapore, Prime Minister Lee Hsien Loong was also consolidating, although he took a daring step. In November 2004, Lee sparked a national debate when he revealed a proposal to build two Integrated Resorts (IRs) — holiday resorts with casinos. In April 2005, despite substantial opposition expressed by the public, Lee announced the decision to approve the proposal. The two IRs are to be built in Marina Bay and Sentosa. To limit the negative social impact of casino gambling, Lee suggested that safeguards would be implemented, such as prohibiting minors from entering the casinos and a S$100 entrance fee for Singaporeans and permanent residents.

Dawn of an East Asian Community

It was a landmark year for regional diplomacy, with the decision to hold an inaugural East Asian Summit. Much of the year was spent arguing about the composition of the proposed East Asian community to be launched at the summit in Kuala Lumpur. As the year wore on, the United States grew more and more concerned about the exclusive nature of the summit — to which ASEAN, China, Japan, and Korea were invited. Some ASEAN members also questioned whether an East Asian Community (EAC) could afford to exclude India, Australia, and even the United States. The pressure eventually resulted in India, Australia, and New Zealand being admitted.

Looming in the background was China's obvious desire to secure an exclusive sphere of influence in Southeast Asia, one that at least marginalizes the United States and its allies in the region. Yet rather than show displeasure over the enlargement of EAC, China opted instead to make the ASEAN+3 process, which groups China together with Japan, South Korea, and ASEAN, the working core of its regional strategy.

In the end it was China's row with Japan over war memories that almost derailed the EAC. At the summit in Kuala Lumpur, Chinese officials angrily cancelled all meetings with their Japanese counterparts and it was left to the mild-mannered Malaysian hosts to ensure that Japanese Prime Minister Junichiro Koizumi and Chinese Premier Wen Jiabao managed a smile for the cameras.

Yet for all the belated concern expressed in Washington about the EAC, there was no real sign of the Bush administration taking Southeast Asia more seriously. Badly distracted by events in the Middle East, few top US officials ventured to the region in the course of 2005. US Secretary of State Condoleezza Rice opted to stay away from the annual meeting of the ASEAN Regional Forum, sending her deputy Robert Zoellick instead. The region took this as a snub, even if it probably was the result of honest delegation.

Whilst the general sense of security and well-being in the region was enhanced by greater success in tracking down terrorist suspects and healthier economic performance in the region as a whole, there were concerns all year about a possible pandemic of avian flu. The H5N1 strain of avian flu had killed almost 70 people in the region by year-end. Most of the victims died in Vietnam, where the outbreak started in the course of 2003. But in July 2005 Indonesia had its first confirmed avian flu death, and more followed. Experts were divided about the prospects of a pandemic. The conventional wisdom was that if the virus was able to transmit from human to human, it could prove lethal and kill millions. Others were more sanguine, suggesting that once the virus mutated into a human form it would most likely become less virulent.

Towards a Rules-based ASEAN

As 2006 dawned, Southeast Asia looked in better shape than at any other time since 1997. Economies have fully recovered and new synergies with China are generating new sources of growth and investment. Political stability has also been achieved, with Indonesia being the primary cause for optimism. In this context perhaps the most important, but little noticed, decision taken in 2005 was the agreement among ASEAN leaders to frame and implement an ASEAN Charter.

The decision to embark on a search for common values in the region was timely. The consolidation of democracy in Indonesia, ASEAN's largest state, has finally set an irreversible political course for the region; most members states — with one or two notable exceptions — are now firmly democratic. There is weakening support for the once hallowed principle of non-interference as forest fires raging in one country bring debilitating haze to another and calls for collective action. The tsunami forged a new willingness among neighbours to help one another in times of crisis, and reinforced the need for some kind of common security policy.

All these developments offered encouraging signs that ASEAN societies have matured and are ready for a rules-based system, rather than what former ASEAN Secretary General Rodolfo Severino has described as "diplomacy by feel". The current ASEAN Secretary General Ong Keng Yong is confident that the leaders will listen to what they have to say. "ASEAN society has matured," he said. "There is a recognition on the part of our leaders that the monopoly of ideas in government can no longer be sustained."[7] If that is true, then there is hope for an ASEAN Charter.

Notes

[1] Andrew Steer, "Reflections on One Year of Reconstruction in Aceh", *Jakarta Post*, 24 December 2005.
[2] "Aceh and Nias One Year After the Tsunami: The Recovery Effort and Way Forward" (Washington, DC: World Bank, December 2005).
[3] "Tsunami Helped End War in Indonesia's Aceh — President". Associated Press report, Banda Aceh, Indonesia, 26 December 2005.
[4] "Thai Insurgents Want New State Next Year", Agence France Presse, 26 June 2005.
[5] "Pressure Mounts on Philippine Leader", Agence France Presse, 28 June 2005.
[6] "Myanmar Takes the Shine Off ASEAN Summit Diplomacy", *Jakarta Post*, 13 December 2005.
[7] Michael Vatikiotis, "Put People First in ASEAN Charter", *Straits Times*, 14 October 2005.

SOUTHEAST ASIAN ECONOMIES
A Year of Exogenous Shocks

Cassey Lee, Boon-Huat Quah, and Marc Foo

The year 2005 will likely be remembered by most Southeast Asian countries as the year of negative exogenous shocks. Exogenous shocks to the economy often receive less analysis in textbooks than they deserve. Nevertheless, such shocks can have significant and long-term economic effects, as the oil shocks in 1970s did. The most important of these shocks in 2005 was the tsunami that occurred on 26 December 2004 and claimed more than 100,000 lives across several countries. The slowdown in the global economy and the rise in oil prices further weakened growth in Southeast Asia during 2005.

This article begins with an analysis of overall economic growth in the region in 2005.[1] It is followed by a more detailed analysis of the macroeconomic performance of Southeast Asian economies. Towards the end of the article the impact of the tsunami as well as the risk of a pandemic avian flu is discussed.

Overall Growth

The global economy went into a moderate cyclical slowdown in 2005 due to a number of factors — rising US interest rates, lower US and euro area growth, the rise in oil prices, and the catastrophic effects of Hurricane Katrina. Compared with the world's growth rate of 5.1 per cent in 2004, a record high in the last three decades, the global economy grew at a rate of 4.3 per cent in 2005.[2] While the slowdown affected both developed and developing countries, growth in the developing world continued to be strong, at 5.9 per cent. This growth rate was twice as fast as that estimated for developed countries.[3] Growth in the Asia-Pacific region, at 6 per cent, was expected

---

Cassey Lee, former Associate Professor at University of Malaya in Kuala Lumpur, is now Associate Professor, Nottingham University Business School, University of Nottingham Malaysia Campus. Boon-Huat Quah is Lecturer at Metropolitan College in Kuala Lumpur. Marc Foo is Lecturer at Taylor's Business School in Kuala Lumpur.

to be higher than growth in the developing world as a whole. This was partly due to vigorous exports and strong domestic demand in China and India.[4]

Southeast Asian economies grew at an estimated average rate of 5 per cent in 2005. This was lower than the economic growth rate of 6.3 per cent in the previous year.[5] The export-driven nature of most of the Southeast Asian economies makes them sensitive to growth in the developed economies. The decline in Southeast Asia's gross domestic product (GDP) growth in 2005 was partly due to the decline in real GDP growth and real total domestic demand observed in the developed economies.[6] Of the ten member countries of the Association of Southeast Asian Nations (ASEAN), only four — Indonesia, Brunei, Cambodia, and Laos — were expected to show improved real GDP growth rates in 2005.[7]

Indonesia showed an estimated real GDP growth rate of 5.5 per cent in 2005 compared with the previous year's 5.1 per cent. The sources of this improvement were the fairly robust growth rates in the manufacturing, construction, and services sectors as well as the revival in investment spending (due in part to a broad government campaign to improve the local investment climate).

Despite earlier gloomy IMF projections, Cambodia was expected to improve on its 2004 real GDP growth rate by 1.75 percentage points to 6.3 per cent in 2005. Higher-than-expected garment exports — the country's single largest foreign exchange earner — were expected to contribute substantially to improvements in the economy. However, the expiry of the Multifiber Arrangement (MFA) had almost no impact on Cambodian garment exports as they no longer compete solely on the basis of price. Surges in tourism, construction, and telecommunications sectors and a less-than-severe drought also helped.[8]

Singapore's real GDP grew by 5.7 per cent in 2005 — a massive 2.7 percentage points below its performance in the previous year. The country's export sector encountered some difficulties at the beginning of 2005 but managed to stage a comeback towards the year-end to ensure an upward revision from the Trade Ministry's 17 November 2005 forecast of around 5 per cent. Growth was broad-based, with manufacturing and the services sector doing particularly well.

As in other oil-importing countries, Thailand's growth suffered from higher world oil prices. The country's 2005 real GDP growth was estimated at 4.5 per cent versus the 6.0 per cent achieved the previous year. Other negative factors that played a part in weakening its economic growth included: (a) a drought during the first half of 2005; (b) decreased tourist arrivals because of the previous year's tsunami; (c) political unrest in three southern provinces; and (d) a new outbreak of the avian flu.[9]

Both Malaysia and the Philippines were affected by the initial slowdown in export demand, rising US interest rates, and the rise in oil prices. Malaysia managed better towards the year-end after its exports got back on track but its estimated real GDP growth rate for the year was still down 1.8 percentage points, at 5.3 per cent. In the Philippines, which has a substantial agriculture sector, weak farm output dragged down the GDP growth rate to 4.7 per cent in 2005.

Table 1 shows the annual real GDP growth rates of ASEAN member countries during the period 2001–2005 while Table 2 shows the year-on-year percentage changes in exports of goods and services in the ASEAN-5 for the same period.

TABLE 1
ASEAN: Real GDP growth
(Percentages, year-on-year)

	2001	2002	2003	2004	2005
ASEAN-5					
Indonesia	3.8	4.4	4.9	5.1	5.5[a]
Malaysia	0.3	4.4	5.4	7.1	5.3[b]
Philippines	1.8	4.3	4.6	6.0	4.7[a]
Singapore	−2.0	3.2	1.4	8.4	5.7[c]
Thailand	2.2	5.3	7.0	6.0	4.5[a]
Brunei	3.0	2.8	3.2	1.7	3.6[a]
Cambodia	5.5	4.0	4.5	4.55	6.3[a]
Laos	5.8	5.9	5.8	6.65	7.2[a]
Myanmar	5.3	5.3	−2.0	−1.3	1.3[d]
Vietnam	6.9	7.1	7.3	7.7	7.6[a]

[a] Estimated (*Asia Economic Monitor 2005*, ADB).
[b] Estimated (Regional Economic Compass 2006, CIMB Securities).
[c] Estimated (Ministry of Trade and Industry, Singapore).
[d] Forecast (Economist Intelligence Unit).
Sources: Asian Development Bank, *Asia Economic Monitor 2005*; Department of Foreign Affairs and Trade, Australia; World Markets Research Center of Global Insight Inc.; *Southeast Asian Affairs 2005* (Singapore: Institute of Southeast Asian Studies, 2005).

TABLE 2
ASEAN-5: Goods and services exports
(Percentages, year-on-year)

ASEAN-5	2001	2002	2003	2004	2005*
Indonesia	0.6	−1.2	8.2	8.5	7.8
Malaysia	−7.5	4.5	5.7	16.3	7.6
Philippines	−3.4	4.1	3.6	14.1	3.0
Singapore	−5.1	7.9	14.3	20.8	10.2
Thailand	−4.2	12.0	7.0	9.6	3.8

*Estimated.
Source: CLSA Asia-Pacific Markets, *Eye on Asia* (19 December 2005).

Macroeconomic Performance

Higher oil prices, tighter monetary policies, and slower increases in disposable income were a damper on consumer spending in East Asia in 2005. On the average, private consumption rose at a slower pace of 4.9 per cent during the first three quarters of 2005 versus 7.2 per cent during the whole of 2004.[10] Within the ASEAN-5, the impact of the aforementioned factors on private consumption was mixed though estimates show that all would have experienced declines in 2005.

In the Philippines, private consumption remained relatively stable. Even though consumption spending in both Indonesia and Malaysia did start to pick up towards the end of the year, its growth rate in both countries declined for the year as a whole — to 3.9 per cent in Indonesia and to 9.6 per cent in Malaysia. Other countries also showed a decline in private consumption — a 1.6 percentage point decline in Thailand and a 6.4 percentage point decline in Singapore. Table 3 shows the private consumption growth rates of the ASEAN-5 economies during the period 2001–2005.

TABLE 3
ASEAN-5: Private consumption
(Percentages, year-on-year)

ASEAN-5	2001	2002	2003	2004	2005*
Indonesia	3.5	3.8	3.9	4.9	3.9
Malaysia	2.4	4.4	6.6	10.5	9.6
Philippines	3.6	4.1	5.3	5.8	5.1
Singapore	3.2	3.0	0.6	8.6	2.2
Thailand	4.1	5.4	6.4	5.9	4.3

*Estimated.
Source: CLSA Asia-Pacific Markets, Eye on Asia (19 December 2005).

Within the ASEAN-5 economies the current accounts of both Indonesia and Thailand weakened in 2005, with the latter chalking up a deficit for the first time since the 1997 Asian financial crisis. The causes were the higher oil prices, drought, and the 2004 tsunami which significantly affected tourism (especially in Thailand). In both Singapore and Malaysia, however, current account surpluses were estimated to have increased, with the latter benefiting much from higher oil and non-oil commodity export prices. Table 4 shows the current account balances (as a percentage of nominal GDP) of the ASEAN-5 economies for the period 2001–2005.

TABLE 4
ASEAN-5: Current account balance as a percentage of nominal GDP
(Year-on-year)

ASEAN-5	2001	2002	2003	2004	2005*
Indonesia	4.1	3.9	3.4	1.3	0.8
Malaysia	8.3	8.4	12.9	12.6	14.5
Philippines	1.9	5.7	1.8	2.4	3.7
Singapore	16.8	17.7	29.2	26.1	32.5
Thailand	5.4	5.5	5.6	4.1	–2.7

*Estimated.
Source: CLSA Asia-Pacific Markets, Eye on Asia (19 December 2005).

The impact of rising world oil prices on domestic energy prices, rising domestic food prices and the pass-through effects into core inflation contributed towards inflationary trends in most of the ASEAN-5 economies in 2005. Inflation in Indonesia, the only ASEAN-5 economy to record a higher real GDP growth rate in 2005 compared with 2004, increased further in 2005 to 10.6 per cent from the previous year's already high 6.1 per cent. Rising inflationary trends were observed in Malaysia, the Philippines, and Thailand despite the decline in real GDP growth rates. Singapore was the only country to report a moderation in inflation rate. Table 5 summarizes the inflationary trends in the ASEAN-5 during the period 2001–2005.

Continuing inflationary tendencies and weakening local currencies vis-à-vis the US dollar in the ASEAN-5 economies made it necessary for central banks in the region to tighten their monetary policies in 2005 despite slower growth.

TABLE 5
ASEAN-5: Inflation
(Percentages, year-on-year)

ASEAN-5	2001	2002	2003	2004	2005*
Indonesia	11.5	11.9	6.8	6.1	10.6
Malaysia	1.4	1.8	1.1	1.4	3.1
Philippines	6.1	3.1	2.9	6.0	7.6
Singapore	1.0	–0.4	0.5	1.7	0.5
Thailand	1.7	0.6	1.8	2.8	4.6

*Estimated.
Source: CLSA Asia-Pacific Markets, Eye on Asia (19 December 2005).

In Thailand, Indonesia, and the Philippines, interest rates were raised a number of times in 2005. Malaysia increased its policy interest rate to 3.0 per cent on 30 November 2005, the first since 1998. Singapore, which uses the nominal effective exchange rate as the intermediate target of monetary policy, kept in place the tighter monetary policy stance that it had adopted since 2004.

The fiscal position of economies in the ASEAN-5, hard hit during the Asian financial crisis, has been improving since 2000 when the authorities began rectifying their imbalances. 2005 was not an easy year for some ASEAN-5 countries due to the higher oil prices and slower domestic growth. Indonesia's fiscal position in 2005 worsened marginally because of increased fuel subsidies. Both Malaysia and the Philippines recorded deficits in 2005 despite slight improvements from 2004. Thailand has managed to maintain a surplus position since 2003. The country's fiscal balance remained positive in 2005. Singapore improved even further on its surplus in 2005. Table 6 shows the fiscal balance of the central government in the ASEAN-5 countries during the period 2001–2005.

The pattern of investment growth in the ASEAN-5 was fairly mixed in 2005. The ADB estimated declining investments throughout the year in the Philippines and Singapore, and slowing investment growth in Indonesia and Thailand. In the case of Malaysia, estimates showed investments picking up, mostly in the private sector, as the cutback on large-scale infrastructure spending continued.[11]

On 21 July 2005 the People's Bank of China (PBoC) replaced its US dollar peg with a more flexible managed currency-basket.[12] The most apparent reason for the re-pegging was that China wanted to improve its trade relationship with its major trading partners, particularly the United States, which had persistently

TABLE 6
ASEAN-5: Central government fiscal balance
(Percentage of GDP)

ASEAN-5	2001	2002	2003	2004[b]	2005[c]
Indonesia	–3.2	–1.5	–1.9	–1.4	–1.6
Malaysia	–5.5	–5.6	–5.3	–4.3	–3.5
Philippines	–4.6	–5.6	–5.0	–4.2	–3.9
Singapore	4.8	4.0	5.8	3.9	4.5
Thailand[a]	–2.1	–2.3	0.4	0.3	0.5

[a] Fiscal year ending September.
[b] Estimated.
[c] Projected.
Source: IMF, Asia-Pacific Regional Outlook (September 2005).

claimed that the undervalued renminbi had exacerbated its trade deficits. The PBoC's announcement was almost immediately followed by the announcement by the Malaysian central bank, Bank Negara Malaysia (BNM), that it would be replacing its US dollar peg with a managed currency-basket system. Since both Malaysia and low-cost China compete for foreign direct investment, Kuala Lumpur had obviously waited for Beijing to make the first move. Since the de-pegging of the undervalued ringgit, however, BNM has put the ringgit on a very tight leash — a hint that the new exchange rate system will continue to be tightly managed against the dollar. Capital outflows from Malaysia turned out to be the more eventful part of the ringgit de-pegging exercise. When there was no sign of any major ringgit appreciation which the foreign investors had expected, some began unwinding their ringgit positions in both the equity and bond markets to repatriate both profits and dividends.

Tsunami

On 26 December 2004 an earthquake with a magnitude of 9.0 on the Richter scale occurred under the ocean about 150 km. west of northern Sumatra. It unleashed a tidal wave that devastated the coastlines of Indonesia, Thailand, India, Sri Lanka, and Malaysia. Six provinces along the Andaman coast of Thailand were badly hit and more than 8,000 persons died. In Aceh, Indonesia, a 800 km. coastal strip was devastated and approximately 130,000 people were killed while 37,000 remained missing. Malaysia was also not spared this calamity, but the damage and loss of lives were nowhere close to those experienced in Thailand and Indonesia.

Even though the tsunami occurred in late December 2004, much of the impact continued to be felt throughout 2005. The tsunami had significant impact on the tourism and fishery industries in Thailand. Of the 8,000 people that died in the coastal region of southern Thailand, a third were foreign tourists. The tourism industry in this region, however, proved to be quite resilient. By the end of 2005 it had almost fully recovered. However, the tsunami caused a projected loss of revenue approximating US$1.4 billion or 0.8 per cent of its GDP.[13] The tsunami also damaged fishing boats and equipment in the fishery industry in Thailand. The total losses and damage incurred in this industry was estimated at US$138.0 million. Other sectors that suffered losses included the agriculture sector (US$2.5 million) and the infrastructure sector (US$25.9 million in capital stock and US$20.9 million in revenue). The total economic losses in Thailand alone were estimated to be around US$2.09 billion.[14]

To promote long-term recovery, economic policy is now focused on rebuilding businesses in the fishery and agricultural sectors. Psychological and social support services have also been extended to those whose lives were affected. The tsunami also raised several other issues related to property rights and disputes, housing availability, assistance to poor communities, rights of migrant workers, social protection of children, and most importantly, community-based disaster awareness.

Aceh in Indonesia was even more severely devastated. Unlike the affected areas in Thailand, Aceh did not have a large tourism industry and its per capita income was generally lower. As much as a third of Aceh's population was living in poverty when the tsunami struck. The tsunami raised this proportion to half. As for the economic sectors, most of the damage was incurred by fisheries, with lesser impact on the farming and manufacturing sectors. The total economic loss inflicted by the tsunami was estimated to be around US$1.2 billion.[15]

At the end of the year, efforts to rebuild Aceh were focused on the provision of housing, health and the rehabilitation of its agricultural sector. In spite of these efforts, many were still frustrated by the slow pace of recovery. The dispensing of governmental and official aid funds had been slow due to poor execution and bureaucracy.[16] As in Thailand, the tsunami also raised issues such as land rights and the recovery of the fisheries sector. One post-tsunami effect unique to Aceh was the peace accord signed between the Indonesian government and the Acehnese rebels. This has helped the recovery process.

While recovery was under way, Aceh was estimated to need at least US$5.8 billion for asset rebuilding.[17] At the end of the year, only US$775 million of the US$4.4 billion allocated for recovery projects had been spent. Certain areas still required attention, especially transport, flood control, and the environment. The Indonesian government, via a ministerial-level Rehabilitation and Reconstruction Agency (BBR), intends to improve execution coordination with relevant stakeholders and identify areas for long-term developmental potential such as tourism. Going forward, the key priorities of the BBR for 2006 are to provide shelter for all, rehabilitate vital infrastructure, strengthen institutional and human capacities, and restore livelihoods.

Avian Flu

A potential exogenous shock to the region is an avian flu pandemic. At present the poultry sector in only a few Southeast Asian countries is affected. Any escalation of the current situation into a pandemic in the human population would be economically catastrophic for the whole region. Poultry production, export, and consumption, tourism, and industrial production would all be affected. Table 7 summarizes

TABLE 7
Confirmed human cases of avian influenza in selected countries

	Cambodia		Indonesia		Thailand		Vietnam		Total	
	Cases	Deaths	Cases	Deaths	Cases	Deaths	Cases	Deaths	Cases	Deaths
2003	0	0	0	0	0	0	3	3	3	3
2004	0	0	0	0	17	12	29	20	46	32
2005	4	4	17	11	5	2	61	19	87	36
Total	4	4	17	11	22	14	93	42	136	71

Source: World Health Organization, 10 January 2006.

the number of avian flu outbreaks and their locations in selected countries in the Southeast Asian region. In 2005 the majority of the cases came from Indonesia and Vietnam. While at the end of the year the threat appeared to be contained, the possibility of the avian flu becoming a pandemic remained real.

It is difficult to ascertain the precise economic impact of such a pandemic if it occurs in the region. The primary and direct effects would be felt in the poultry industry of the affected countries. Birds will be culled and thus the value chain and related industries will be affected. For example, the poultry feed and distribution business will be disrupted when culling occurs. Governments are expected to assist poultry farmers, especially low-income ones. The size of the poultry sector ranges from 0.6 per cent of GDP for Vietnam and Thailand to 2 per cent in the Philippines. The World Bank estimates the primary cost to be at 0.12 per cent and 0.2 per cent of GDP for Vietnam and Indonesia, respectively.[18] The secondary effects will be felt in the tourism sector of countries such as Thailand and Vietnam. According to the World Bank the cost of such a pandemic to the global economy (if it occurs) would be approximately US$800 billion. This estimate was obtained by studying the 2003 SARS (severe acute respiratory syndrome) outbreak in East Asia. As a result of the SARS outbreak, East Asian countries suffered economic losses estimated to be around 2 per cent of GDP. It is evident that the prevention of a pandemic avian flu should be a priority in the Southeast Asian region.

Notes

[1] At the time of writing, all figures quoted are estimates provided by different institutions.
[2] IMF, *World Economic Outlook: Building Institutions* (September 2005).
[3] World Bank, *Global Economic Prospects 2006* (November 2005).
[4] IMF, *Asia-Pacific Regional Outlook* (September 2005).
[5] ADB, *Asian Development Outlook 2005 Update*.
[6] IMF, *World Economic Outlook: Building Institutions* (September 2005).
[7] Data for Myanmar cannot be discussed due to measurement problems.
[8] "Roundup: World Bank Raises Cambodia's Growth Forecast in 2005". *People's Daily Online*, 4 November 2005, http://english.people.com.cn/200511/04/eng20051104_218931.html.
[9] World Bank, Thailand Office, *Thailand Economic Monitor* (November 2005).
[10] Asian Development Bank, *Asia Economic Monitor 2005* (December 2005).
[11] Ibid.
[12] The renminbi was re-pegged 2.10 per cent higher at 8.11 (subject to a daily change of +/−0.30 per cent) based on performance against an undisclosed basket.

13. "Tsunami Thailand, One Year Later: National Response and Contribution of International Partners", World Bank, http://www.worldbank.org.
14. Ibid.
15. "Aceh and Nias One Year After the Tsunami: The Recovery Effort and Way Forward", http://www.worldbank.org.
16. Ibid.
17. Ibid.
18. World Bank, "East Asia and Pacific Region: Spread of Avian Flu Could Affect Next Year's Economic Outlook", http://www.worldbank.org/earpupdate.

TERRORISM
Evolving Regional Alliances and State Failure in Mindanao

Kit Collier

The death of Azahari bin Husin in a shoot-out with Indonesian police near the East Java town of Malang on 9 November 2005 was widely acclaimed as the most important victory against the regional terror group Jemaah Islamiyah (JI) since the capture of Hambali.[1] But it became increasingly clear during the year that Malaysian-born Dr Azahari — known as the "Demolition Man" for his skills in assembling the first Bali bombs that killed 202 three years earlier — did not answer to the JI hierarchy and was operating as his own man. Indeed, in 2005 it became obvious that old ways of thinking about JI and regional terrorism were no longer adequate — if they ever were in the first place.

The dominant model, perpetuated in the media by prominent commentators Rohan Gunaratna and Zachary Abuza, views JI as an al-Qaeda franchise, with a clearly demarcated command structure and organizational boundaries, dedicated to the establishment of an Islamic caliphate embracing much of Southeast Asia. To the extent this image was ever valid, as Sidney Jones points out, it represents a five-year-old "snapshot" of JI with little relevance today.[2] A fluid pattern of alignment and realignment between autonomous jihadi factions characterized the terrorist threat in 2005, and this trend is likely to strengthen in the future.

What knits these factions loosely together is not "a very horizontal and exceptionally compartmentalized organization" with a "very rigid cell structure", as Abuza insisted after Bali's second series of suicide bombings on 1 October 2005,[3] but a shared world-view based on personal allegiances forged in exile, training camps on the Afghan border, or the conflict zones of Sulawesi, Maluku, and — looking forward — Mindanao. Gunaratna has even declared Mindanao

---

KIT COLLIER is Consultant to the International Crisis Group and Visiting Fellow at the Research School of Pacific and Asian Studies, Australian National University.

the "new strategic base of Jemaah Islamiyah", but like Abuza, misperceives the nature of this threat.[4]

This overview examines Mindanao's growing role as *the* regional terrorist crossroads in 2005, but from the perspective of local realities, not externally imposed organigrams. It demonstrates a kaleidoscopic interplay of foreign and domestic jihadi groups only possible in Mindanao's lawless enclaves, where for all practical purposes the Philippine state has failed.

Perspectives on Southeast Asian Terrorism

Carlyle Thayer identifies three basic ways of looking at terrorism in Southeast Asia: from a global, a regional, or a national perspective.[5] The global view rests on an "al-Qaeda-centric paradigm" that places Osama bin Laden at the centre of analysis and evaluates local political violence largely in terms of its purported "links" back to the terrorist mainspring. Gunaratna is the most widely cited exponent of this view, portraying JI as "al-Qaeda's instrument" and "al-Qaeda's Asian arm".[6]

Regional specialists like Abuza take this perspective a step further. While showing more interest in local context and specifics than globalists, Abuza agrees that al-Qaeda "established" JI as "a regional arm of its own", then extends the argument to apply a JI-centric paradigm to developments in Southeast Asia.[7] Like al-Qaeda, JI is seen as an organizational monolith, to be analysed like a wiring diagram. Regionalists are often inattentive to contingency and factionalism, and, for country specialists, their interest in local history and culture seems shallow, unsupported by the necessary learning.[8]

The dominance of global and regional perspectives is partly due to the reluctance of many country specialists to take terrorism seriously as a legitimate field of inquiry. Until the first Bali bombings, prominent Indonesianists downplayed globalists' and regionalists' assertions of an emerging terrorist threat.[9] The latter's often cavalier approach to evidence, sources, and referencing, their lack of area knowledge and languages, and suspicions of intelligence laundering by persons too close to security services for comfort, all help explain the initial scepticism of most country specialists.

But some of them question the value of the entire enterprise. "When it comes to clandestine terrorist activity," asserts Natasha Hamilton-Hart, "scholars and journalists are rarely in a position to contest or add to official information." For Hamilton-Hart, this renders fine-grained examination of terrorist networks "quite pointless".[10] As if in parody of the gross causal attributions favoured by the globalists and regionalists she critiques, Hamilton-Hart regards terrorism as just another form of resistance, best understood in terms of the grievances that — it is assumed — motivate it. Like Abuza's al-Qaeda-centric organigrams, this approach circumvents the active agency of Southeast Asian terrorists themselves, substituting US foreign policy for "militant Islam" as a crude, undifferentiated "root cause".

The worth of cataloguing individual terrorists' movements, contacts, and orders would be dubious indeed if its purpose were merely to demonstrate an author's privileged access to classified information. All the more so if the author lacked the area knowledge to interpret these connections in ways that add meaningful value to a list of names and dates — or even to render such minutiae accurately. But in the hands of appropriately qualified, open-minded country specialists, such details — derived from a variety of government, public, and private sources, and scrupulously cross-checked — become vital clues in understanding the real world, face-to-face relationships that make specific terrorist attacks possible.

JI and the Second Bali Bombings

As CNN viewers have come to expect, the triple suicide bombing of Raja's Café in Kuta and the Nyoman and Menega Cafés in Jimbaran beach, Bali, on the evening of 1 October 2005, which killed 20 innocent bystanders, was soon followed by "expert" pronouncements that JI was "the only group with the intention and the capability" to mount such attacks.[11] This phrase, which is Gunaratna's and Abuza's typical response to major bombings in Indonesia, misses the significance of both the new attack, and of others stretching back more than five years to the attempted car-bomb assassination of the Philippine ambassador in Jakarta — that JI is deeply divided over such operations, which are the initiative of a few ultra-militants drawing on diverse personal networks, not a cohesive corporate entity.

Media consumers may prefer digestible sound bites and familiar faces (bin Laden, Abu Bakar Ba'asyir) symbolizing well-defined organizations with clear international links. But appreciating the true complexity of these networks demands a longer attention span.[12] From the time Ba'asyir took over as *amir* (commander) of JI following the death of co-founder Abdullah Sungkar in 1999, ultras associated with Hambali and the Malaysia-based Mantiqi 1 group rankled at Ba'asyir's vacillating leadership and flirtations with open mass politics. The majority around JI's Java-based Mantiqi 2, on the other hand, became increasingly uneasy with the consequences of the ultras' bombing campaign, in which Ba'asyir acquiesced. These internal tensions mounted with successive attacks on Bali

(12 October 2002), the Jakarta Marriott Hotel (5 August 2003), and Australian Embassy (9 September 2004), all causing Muslim casualties and prompting a police crackdown that has crippled JI's formal structures.[13]

Like the Marriott and embassy attacks, the second Bali bombings were masterminded by the Malaysians, Azahari and Noordin Mohammed Top, who relied on personal networks to recruit operatives, not the JI command structure. The embassy suicide bomber, Heri Golun, was drawn into the plot through a West Java splinter group of Darul Islam (DI), known as the Banten Ring — as was the operation's field commander, Irwan Dharmawan, alias Rois, sentenced to death by a Jakarta court in September 2005. The three Bali II suicide bombers, identified as Salik Firdaus, Aip Hidayat, and Misno, appear to have belonged to yet another DI faction that kept its distance from more renowned leaders. The three are said to be quite unknown to JI prisoners shown their photographs.[14]

Like Rois, the suspected leaders of this faction, Muhammad Akram and his deputy, Enceng Kurnia, owe their web of contacts to shared experiences in Poso (Central Sulawesi), and Ambon (Maluku), where autonomous DI groups, notably Mujahidin KOMPAK, were quicker to exploit communal conflict after 1998 than JI's ponderous bureaucracy.[15] These continue to foment discord in alliance with JI — but not under its command. A raid on a paramilitary police post on Ceram island, Maluku, in May 2005, and marketplace bombings in Tentena (near Poso) in May and Palu, Central Sulawesi, in December, were all likely ad hoc attacks drawing on men with a variety of organizational affiliations.[16] Here, too, a rigid hierarchical model provides little insight into dynamics on the ground.

The distinction between Azahari and Top's bombers and the mainstream JI leadership crystallized in January 2006, when Indonesian national police chief General Sutanto announced that Top had formed an organization of his own — Tanzim Qaedat al-Jihad.[17] This is probably a formalization of the pair's existing network hitherto known as *Thoifah Muqatilah*, composed of younger militants inspired by direct action against Western targets.[18] Mainstream opinion in JI questions the legitimacy of such attacks outside Indonesia's conflict areas, focusing instead on the need to build up the organization's ideological and military strength for a decisive confrontation with the Indonesian state in 25 to 30 years' time.

What the bombers and the mainstream group do share is a commitment to passing on the lethal skills of a generation of Afghan veterans decimated by the regional wave of arrests since late 2001, when JI was first unveiled in Singapore. Communal conflicts in eastern Indonesia were intended to create a secure base area (*qoidah aminah*) where sharia law could be applied in an embryonic Islamic state, and more fighters could be trained. During the short post-Soeharto transition to democracy, some armed forces elements had enough interest in destabilization to allow jihadis a free hand. As Susilo Bambang Yudhoyono continues to consolidate Indonesia's traditionally strong bureaucratic state, however, space to train is increasingly constricted. Militants must look beyond Indonesia for safe haven, to the lawless enclaves of the southern Philippines.

Finding New Partners in Mindanao

Conventional globalist and regionalist accounts of Mindanao's role in Southeast Asian terrorism provide as outdated a snapshot as their image of JI, again assuming a world of clearly bounded organizations. In fact, numerous arrests — mostly by Indonesian and Malaysian authorities — have smashed the Mantiqi 3 structure that managed JI activity in Sulawesi, Kalimantan, Sabah, and the southern Philippines, contributing to the collapse of JI's administrative apparatus in Mindanao, Wakalah Hudaibiyah (WakHud). Its surviving members were forced into closer cooperation with local insurgents in 2005, as well as with "freelance" Indonesian and Malaysian jihadis operating outside what remains of the JI command structure. The resulting pattern of blurred organizational distinctions and new alliances was further complicated by factional rivalries within Southeast Asia's strongest secessionist group, the Moro Islamic Liberation Front (MILF).

Chronic insurgency is the most visible symptom of state failure in Mindanao, a condition described by America's top diplomat in Manila in April 2005 as "the next Afghanistan".[19] As the International Crisis Group observes, the MILF rebellion is "powerful enough to limit state capacity in much of the South, yet so decentralised that what ensues is not a shadow government, but pockets of anarchy".[20] Some of these enclaves are presided over by rebel commanders who continued to shelter foreign jihadis during the year, threatening a delicately poised peace process that holds the only real hope for long-term stability in this increasingly important regional terrorist sanctuary.

While Gunaratna ignores the MILF's indigenous dynamics, portraying the movement as a corporate subsidiary of al-Qaeda, Abuza insists that it is "a more unitary organization than it is given credit for", and that internal factionalism is not significant enough to "hamper decision-making".[21] Events in 2005 take on an even more worrying cast from this perspective than in the light of Crisis Group's assessment, for it implies that the MILF's central leadership with whom Manila is negotiating actively approves of commanders' ongoing terror ties — notwithstanding those leaders' official disavowals.

JI's formal links with the MILF date back to 1994, when late MILF chairman Salamat Hashim approved a proposal to relocate JI's training facilities from Afghanistan to Camp Abu Bakar, the MILF's headquarters in Mindanao.[22] This arrangement began to disintegrate after Philippine armed forces overran Camp Abu Bakar in July 2000, but what replaced it was a more dispersed pattern of mobile facilities, more difficult for the government to pinpoint and for MILF leaders to control.[23] At the same time, WakHud head Ahmad Faisal, alias Zulkifli, sanctioned an increasingly intimate relationship with Kadaffy Janjalani's Abu Sayyaf Group (ASG), diversifying JI's refuge and operational options.[24]

In 2004–2005, these included joint training between JI, ASG, and freelance jihadis, under MILF protection, together with members of a volatile new group — the Rajah Solaiman Movement (RSM), militant Filipino converts to Islam who have carried out two successful bombings in Manila and plotted several more.[25] On Valentine's Day 2005, a bus bomb in the capital's business district was coordinated with two near-simultaneous blasts in Davao City and General Santos City, killing eight. The attacks demonstrated that "structural" elements of JI identified with WakHud could still reach out to strike urban centres even in the Philippines' northern heartland — but only with the aid of an expanding roster of local partners, exposing JI to new security risks.[26]

Dulmatin, Freelance Jihad, and Creeping US Intervention

The US announcement within a week of Bali II of a US$10 million reward for the capture of Dulmatin, a prime suspect in the first Bali bombings, drew renewed attention to Mindanao and, in particular, the growing role of freelance jihadis there. Dulmatin had fled Central Sulawesi, moving through Tawau, Sabah, to the southern Philippines in April 2003, two months after his Bali co-conspirator Umar Patek made use of the same DI contact to escape increasingly effective law enforcement in the would-be *qoidah aminah*. Once in Mindanao, the duo established an independent relationship with Kadaffy Janjalani, who had also sought refuge on the mainland from joint US-Philippine military activity in the ASG's traditional Sulu archipelago stronghold. They began instructing recruits in MILF territory in Palimbang, Sultan Kudarat province, as part of a joint DI-KOMPAK training programme.[27]

This programme was run by a former head of KOMPAK in Ambon, Abdullah Sonata, captured in Jakarta in July 2005. Sonata is indicative of the independent mindedness of the new generation of freelancers, for he is said to have declared a formal "split" with Dr Azahari over the issue of suicide attacks in non-conflict areas (thus siding with the Mantiqi 2 mainstream, though Sonata is not himself JI). Yet he also worked closely with Umar Patek to bring suicide recruits for training in the Philippines.[28] These included members of Muhammad Akram's DI faction that furnished the Bali II suicide bombers.[29]

Dulmatin's US$10 million bounty is second only to those offered for Osama bin Laden and Abu Musab al-Zarqawi, reflecting heightened US strategic concern over Mindanao in the wake of Bali II. But American intervention acquired a new assertiveness a full year before the 1 October atrocities, when a series of air strikes on jihadi targets began. Although executed by Philippine air assets, the strikes were planned jointly on the basis of shared intelligence and observed by US military advisers in the field. In November 2004, January 2005, and again in April 2005, strikes were mounted on a cluster of municipalities in southern Maguindanao province, where a maverick MILF commander, Ameril Umbra, harboured Dulmatin, Patek and Kadaffy Janjalani, as well as "structural" JI elements. Multi-battalion ground sweeps followed from July to September, with US advisers again taking part.

This escalation in the Mindanao conflict, regulated by a formal ceasefire since 2003, elicited a surprisingly restrained response from the central MILF leadership. Umbra, also known as Commander Kato, had had a strained relationship with the leadership for at least six years, and in October 2005, just two days after Dulmatin's bounty was announced, his command was publicly "deactivated". This was an unprecedented show of open dissension within the MILF, and the leadership's first indication that it took its obligations to isolate terrorists within its ranks seriously. It remains unclear what substance there is to reports that Kato and his key sub-commanders have actually been disciplined, and whether such action flowed from their known collaboration with Janjalani and Dulmatin, or from pursuing a series of violent private feuds in 2005 that also threatened the ceasefire.[30]

The diplomatic framework for separating the Mindanao conflict from the regional jihad took a leap forward in December 2004, with the long overdue creation of an Ad Hoc Joint Action Group (AHJAG) composed of government and MILF representatives who would share information on terrorist activity in Mindanao. Manila provided the MILF with a list of 32 foreign terrorists it believed were finding sanctuary in the south in April 2005: it consisted of 31 Indonesians and one Malaysian, Zulkifli bin Hir, head of the Kumpulan Mujahidin Malaysia. It is not known what, if any, reciprocal intelligence the MILF has supplied, but in a significant goodwill gesture, several hundred MILF guerrillas were temporarily cantoned in July 2005 to allow counter-terrorist pursuit operations to proceed unhampered. A number of minor skirmishes with MILF forces still occurred, however, and Dulmatin and Janjalani, now working closely together, made good their escape.

American military pressure on the ASG and its foreign jihadi allies, and by extension the MILF, continued to mount into early 2006. "Balikatan" and "Balance Piston" exercises and "Bayanihan" training, civic action and psychological operations were extended from their initial theatres on Basilan island and Zamboanga City (beginning in 2002), to include North Cotabato and the Zamboanga peninsula, and, after a false start in 2003, the island of Jolo. Jolo, cradle of the Philippines' Muslim separatist rebellion and the ASG's principal redoubt, presents an enormous challenge to counter-terrorist strategy in the region, and a crucial opportunity. Among the most volatile of Mindanao's terrorist sanctuaries, its Tausug inhabitants are fiercely independent, and resent Manila's failing 1996 peace agreement with the MNLF. Many also nurture collective memories of US colonial repression a century ago.

Tentative US civic action deployments on Jolo began in September 2005, with full-scale Balikatan manoeuvres scheduled there in February and March 2006. If the exercises follow the pattern of Balikatan '02 on Basilan — dubbed at the time the "second front" in the global war on terror — the American presence may puncture the ASG's psychological grip over the population and begin to fill the vacuum of extra-local authority at the root of state failure. If, on the other hand, the ASG and its foreign jihadi allies decide to confront the Americans, and the US response appears indiscriminate, the former colonial power risks catalysing a new coalition that embraces MNLF and MILF forces, as well as its regional terrorist foes.

Conclusion

Far from being pointless, a detailed, accurate understanding of interpersonal terrorist relationships is fundamental to avoiding the distortions that often arise from both global/regional and country specialist perspectives. These distortions persisted in much of the commentary on Southeast Asian terrorism during 2005. Among the insights generated by more careful research, particularly by Sidney Jones, the following bear consideration by scholars, journalists, and practitioners:

- JI is not "an integral part of al-Qaeda".[31] Its roots are thoroughly Indonesian, and its ultimate objective is an Islamic state in Indonesia. Its ties to al-Qaeda, like those to related offshoots of the DI movement and Moro insurgents, are incarnate in individual associations, not bureaucratic flow charts.

- The history of these individual associations — names and dates, understood in context — is an indispensable guide to the shifting, often ad hoc, alliances between autonomous jihadi factions. After kinship, the most resilient ties cutting across organizational boundaries are built during shared, formative experiences in exile, training camps, and combat.
- Terrorist and insurgent organizations in Southeast Asia resemble bundles of personal associations more than integral corporate bodies. They are riven by internal rivalries, and members of one group may be closer to like-minded members of another than to their nominal comrades. This makes for constant flux as individuals break away and recombine in new associations. Practitioners need a keen awareness of these tendencies if they hope to defeat organized terror, not inadvertently strengthen it.
- "It's not just JI".[32] Although it has become a convenient shorthand for the terrorist threat in Indonesia, JI in its strict organizational sense may be less of a danger here and now than at any other time since 2002. As more Mantiqi 2 mainstreamers fill the shoes of detained ultras, the immediate threat, to Western targets in particular, comes from freelancers who may not answer to JI at all.
- Despite its Indonesian roots, JI's extended family is much more than an Indonesian phenomenon. Media coverage often remained trapped in a parochial national framework in 2005, as the familiar litany of past outrages — Bali I, Marriott, Australian Embassy — was reinvoked as background to Bali II. Almost universally overlooked were the Filipino victims of JI-related bombings — General Santos, Davao, Superferry, Manila — who now rival in number those killed in Indonesia.[33]
- Equally artificial is a notion of state failure defined by national boundaries. Unlike Afghanistan, the Philippines is not a failed state, but it encompasses impenetrable enclaves within which transnational terrorists continue to find sanctuary, weaving their cause into those of local insurgents with widespread support.
- These sanctuaries in the southern Philippines remain the weakest link in the entire regional counter-terrorist effort. Effective law enforcement in the stronger states of the region — Indonesia, Malaysia, and Singapore — has driven their jihadis out of preferred safe havens and would-be base areas, and into the arms of Moro militants. A new generation of Indonesian terrorists bred on the battlefields of Mindanao probably already outnumbers Indonesia's Afghan veterans, and will pose a continuing danger for years to come.

Finally, fine-grained analysis of actual processes of terrorist mobilization helps to temper popular myths on both the left and right. Suicide bombings are conscious acts of human agency. They require painstaking planning, logistics, and coordination. Tracing these acts in all their deliberate murderousness should put paid to outlandish and destabilizing conspiracy theories, as well as gross causal attributions not susceptible to proof or disproof.[34] Understanding need not imply empathy, and regional governments — especially the Philippines and Malaysia — can contribute to public understanding by putting more terrorist suspects on open and transparent trial.

Notes

1. Hambali, also known as Riduan Isamuddin and born Encep Nurjaman, was arrested in Ayuthaya, north of Bangkok, by Thai police and CIA operatives in mid-August 2003, and remains in US custody. Although his testimony would aid regional police forces enormously, US officials refuse to share access to him.
2. Sidney Jones, "The Changing Nature of Jemaah Islamiyah", *Australian Journal of International Affairs* 59, no. 2 (June 2005): 169–78.
3. Zachary Abuza, "To Bali via Mindanao: What the Bali Investigations Tell Us So Far", http://counterterror.stypepad.com/the_counterterrorism_blog/2005/10/to_bali_via_min.html#more.
4. This phrase was earlier used by Maria Ressa. See "The New Strategic Base of Jemaah Islamiyah", *Newsbreak* (Manila), 25 April 2005, pp. 16–17.
5. Carlyle A. Thayer, "New Terrorism in Southeast Asia", in *Violence in Between: Conflict and Security in Archipelagic Southeast Asia*, edited by Damien Kingsbury, pp. 53–74 (Clayton and Singapore: Monash Asia Institute and Institute of Southeast Asian Studies, 2005).
6. Rohan Gunaratna, *Inside Al-Qaeda: Global Network of Terror* (London: C.Hurst, 2002), pp. 192–93.
7. Zachary Abuza, *Militant Islam in Southeast Asia: Crucible of Terror* (Boulder: Lynne Riener, 2003), p. 122.
8. It is tedious to recount the numerous errors of fact, spelling, and interpretation that plague Abuza's work. This may explain why there has been so little published criticism of it. For country specialists, these errors expose a weak grounding in the history, geography, and culture of the peoples described. Unfortunately, the errors are reproduced by other regionalists drawing on Abuza. Note, as just one example, David Wright-Neville's reference to "Taussig" speakers who "make up the bulk of the MNLF [Moro National Liberation Front]" and the "majority of the more violent Abu Sayyaf Group". Like many regionalists, Wright-Neville does not indicate the source of his information, but Abuza's earlier work consistently makes the same mistake.

Surely such a significant population — actually the *Tausug* — should be familiar to a serious analyst of Southeast Asian terrorism. See David Wright-Neville, "Dangerous Dynamics: Activists, Militants and Terrorists in Southeast Asia", *Pacific Review* 17, no. 1 (March 2004): 36.

9. Thayer, op. cit., claims Indonesianists such as Greg Fealy "went into denial". A review of Fealy's articles in the months before Bali I reveals a more nuanced position. Fealy's main complaint was the authorities' failure to back up allegations with credible evidence. See Greg Fealy, "Is Indonesia a Terrorist Base? The Gulf between Rhetoric and Evidence Is Wide", *Inside Indonesia* (July–September 2002).

10. Natasha Hamilton-Hart, "Terrorism in Southeast Asia: Expert Analysis, Myopia and Fantasy", *Pacific Review* 18, no. 3 (September 2005): 303–25.

11. "Indonesia Must Ban JI, Says Expert", 3 October 2005, http://edition.cnn.com/2005/WORLD/asiapcf/ 10/02/bali.terror/.

12. Critics of the war on terror are quick to recognize such simplifications, but usually display a similar impatience for the detail of terrorist activity themselves.

13. Sidney Jones, "The Changing Face of Terrorism in Southeast Asia: Weaker, More Diffuse, and Still a Threat", speech delivered at the Australian Strategic Policy Institute, 15 September 2005, http://www.crisisgroup.org/home/index.cfm?id=3717&I=1.

14. Darul Islam, from which Ba'asyir and Sungkar broke away in 1992–93 to form JI, was established in 1948 by S.M. Kartosoewiryo. Strongest in West Java but with offshoots in Central Java, Sumatra, Sulawesi, and Kalimantan, the movement rebelled for an Islamic state but was crushed by the mid-1960s. Revival since the late 1960s has spawned an extended family of squabbling sects with often overlapping memberships. The most important factions today are Panji Gumilang's KW9, Kang Jaja's Banten Ring, and groups led by Kartosoewiryo's son Tahmid, Ajengan Masduki, and Gaos Taufik. Related splinter groups include AMIN, RPII, and KOMPAK, the last ostensibly operating as a charity. See Greg Fealy and Aldo Borgu, *Local Jihad: Radical Islam and Terrorism in Indonesia*. Australian Strategic Policy Institute, September 2005.

15. International Crisis Group, *Indonesia Backgrounder: Jihad in Central Sulawesi*, Asia Report No. 74 (Jakarta/Brussels, 3 February 2004).

16. International Crisis Group, *Weakening Indonesia's Mujahidin Networks: Lessons from Maluku and Poso*, Asia Report No. 103 (Jakarta/Brussels, 13 October 2005).

17. Sian Powell, "Bomber in Shift from JI to al-Qa'ida", *The Australian*, 31 January 2006.

18. *Tanzim Qaedat al-Jihad* means "jihad-base organisation", and *Thoifah Muqatilah*, "combat unit". Mainstream Mantiqi 2 leaders include Ustadz Muhaimin Yahya (alias Ustadz Ziad), Ustadz Abdullah Anshori (alias Abu Fatih), Ahmad Roihan (alias Saad), and Ustadz Abdul Manan. See Fealy and Borgu, op. cit., p. 34.

19. US Charge d'Affaires Joseph Mussomeli told Australian television that "certain portions of Mindanao are so lawless, so porous … that you run the risk of it becoming like an Afghanistan situation", referring to al-Qaeda's exploitation of the failed state to export global terror. See *Philippine Star*, 11 April 2005, p. 4.

[20] International Crisis Group, *Southern Philippines Backgrounder: Terrorism and the Peace Process*, Asia Report No. 80 (Singapore/Brussels, 13 July 2004).

[21] Zachary Abuza, *Balik-Terrorism: The Return of the Abu Sayyaf* (Carlisle, PA.: US Army War College, September 2005), p. 38.

[22] International Crisis Group, *Southern Philippines Backgrounder: Terrorism and the Peace Process*, p. 14.

[23] Abuza mistakenly dates this major government offensive to 1999. See "Al Qaeda in Southeast Asia: Exploring the Linkages", in *After Bali: The Threat of Terrorism in Southeast Asia*, edited by Kumar Ramakrishna and See Seng Tan (Singapore: Institute of Defence and Strategic Studies, 2003), pp. 133–57.

[24] Faisal was captured off Sabah in September 2003, along with his deputy, Ahmad Saifullah Ibrahim. Next in command of WakHud was Qomarudin bin Zaimun, arrested in Java in 2004; his successor is Usman, but it is not clear whether survivors in Mindanao still follow directives from the centre. See International Crisis Group, *Philippines Terrorism: The Role of Militant Islamic Converts*, Asia Report No. 110 (Jakarta/Brussels, 19 December 2005).

[25] The February 2004 Superferry bombing was the worst maritime terrorist attack in recent memory, killing at least 116, while a plan to car-bomb Manila's L.A. Café was foiled in March 2005.

[26] The principal JI co-conspirator was Rahmat Abdulrahim, a Mindanao training batch-mate of Faisal's. Rahmat was convicted in the Philippines' first successful murder prosecution of a foreign terrorist in October 2005.

[27] *Philippines Terrorism: The Role of Militant Islamic Converts*, pp. 9–10.

[28] "Mengenal Jejak Noordin-Azahari", *Tempo* (Jakarta), 16 October 2005. Three of Sonata's recruits were captured arriving in Zamboanga from Sabah in December 2004, and three more in Tawau in June 2005. These arrests were instrumental in tracking down Sonata and other key bombing suspects in Jakarta in July. They also demonstrated ongoing Arab, possibly al-Qaeda, financial support. See Simon Elegant, "On the Trail of the Bali Bombers", *Time*, 17 October 2005, p. 17.

[29] Akram is also a Mindanao (and Afghan) veteran, having run DI's Camp Ash Syabab under MILF protection until the 2000 offensive. Sonata's programme picked up from Akram's. See *Philippines Terrorism: The Role of Militant Islamic Converts*, p. 9.

[30] For background, see Kit Collier, "Precarious Peace in Mindanao", *Asia-Pacific Defence Reporter*, December 2004–January 2005, pp. 16–17.

[31] Abuza, "Al Qaeda in Southeast Asia", p. 144.

[32] Jones, "The Changing Face of Terrorism in Indonesia".

[33] Even the International Crisis Group remained trapped in this paradigm, flagging a "Terrorism in Indonesia" link on its website, despite its closely related research on the Philippines. The Group maintained during 2005 that there was as yet no firm evidence of foreign terrorist involvement in southern Thailand's deteriorating situation.

See International Crisis Group, *Southern Thailand: Insurgency, Not Jihad*, Asia Report No. 98 (Jakarta/Brussels, 18 May 2005).

[34] Former Indonesian President Abdurrahman Wahid, for example, continued to court the limelight by maintaining that Indonesian police or intelligence staged the 2002 Bali bombings — despite a solid body of evidence to the contrary now ventilated in court. With regard to the common argument that bombings in Indonesia are a direct response to Western policy in Iraq — a form of globalism that needs no concrete knowledge of Indonesia, or any other Islamist conflict zone — Sidney Jones notes that "anger at the West is so widespread that it becomes less of an explanatory factor as to why some groups turn to violence and others don't". The same might be argued of another "root cause" explanation of terrorism, poverty. See Sally Neighbour, "Weird Wahid Claim May Inflame", *The Australian*, 13 October 2005, pp. 1, 6; and Sidney Jones, "Terrorism in Southeast Asia, More Than Just JI", *Asian Wall Street Journal*, 29 July 2004.

JAPAN IN AN INSECURE EAST ASIA
Redefining Its Role in
East Asian Community-Building

Tsutomu Kikuchi

This article analyses Japan's policy towards East Asia in general and East Asian community-building in particular. Japan, as a global nation, has huge stakes in strengthening global governance institutions such as the United Nations (UN), World Trade Organization (WTO), Non-Proliferation Treaty (NPT), and International Atomic Energy Agency (IAEA). To respond to transnational and global issues such as economic globalization, the spread of weapons of mass destruction (WMD), and international terrorism, Japan needs to enhance global mechanisms and make a substantial contribution to such global governance institutions. Japan's bid for a permanent membership at the UN Security Council and the amendment of the Japanese Constitution that is on the domestic political agenda must be understood in this context.

At the same time, "regions" or regionalisms are becoming a more salient concept for managing politico-security and economic affairs in today's world. We are entering an era of "A World of Regions".[1] East Asia is becoming a more important region for Japan's peace and prosperity. The great transformation of East Asia is posing great challenges and opportunities for Japan, demanding its strong commitment to East Asian community-building.

Growing trade which is linked with foreign direct investments (FDI) and foreign production is integrating the Japanese economy closely with East Asia. Japanese multinational firms have shifted to international production and reorganized their business activities accordingly. Their production networks are spread over a large number of countries. This trend has created a strong Japanese interest in

---

TSUTOMU KIKUCHI is Professor of International Political Economy in the Department of International Politics, Aoyama-Gakuin University, Japan, and Adjunct Senior Fellow, Japan Institute of International Affairs.

liberalization, guarantees for Japanese investment, and institution-building in order to manage these economic relations.

Essentially two region-wide production and distribution networks have been established by Japanese firms in East Asia since the middle of 1980s, one with Southeast Asia and the other with China. The pressing task for Japan is to connect these two production networks more closely, thereby constructing "seamless" networks of production and distribution in East Asia. The Japanese government and business community are expecting that more tightly integrated East Asia–wide production and distribution networks will greatly enhance the international competitiveness of Japanese firms in the global market.[2] Using this advantageous position, Japan could become a 21st century economic phoenix.

In fact, contrary to general perceptions, the government and the business community of Japan mostly welcome the venture by China and ASEAN to conclude their Free Trade Agreement (FTA), because Japanese firms operating both in ASEAN region and China could obtain huge benefits from the FTA between China and ASEAN. What Japan is concerned about is that China and ASEAN may fail to conclude a deeper FTA with substantial opening of the respective economies.

Politico-security issues are also becoming more salient in East Asia. There is a variety of security problems ranging from traditional ones such as balance of power among the major powers, tension across the Taiwan Strait, and in the Korean peninsula, and territorial disputes, to non-traditional ones such as international terrorism, the spread of WMD, transnational crime, and maritime security.

In spite of the recent remarkable economic development of East Asian countries and the call for enhanced regional cooperation, there is a deep-seated sense of insecurity in most countries in the region. Geopolitical and geoeconomic transformation of the region further aggravates the sense of insecurity. China is oscillating between conflicting images of itself: a rising power that has overcome the history of humiliation and a developing country with huge internal imbalances and weaknesses. It has many vulnerabilities internally and externally. On the one hand, the rapid economic growth gives it self-confidence. On the other hand, it knows how vulnerable its political, economic, and social foundations to sustain this growth are. An exaggerated image of China as the next superpower overtaking the United States is creating much concern among its neighbours. ASEAN countries are facing the challenge of transforming their domestic politics. And ASEAN is searching for a new role and identity in a broader East Asia in the face of the rising complexities in major powers relationships and the difficult task of integrating the ten members within the organization.

In spite of its enormous economic power, the decade-long economic recession deprived Japan of self-confidence. The country is struggling to sustain its status as an economic superpower and to regain its economic influence. The security environment of Japan has worsened. Japan is also struggling to define its relations with its neighbours, especially China as the old mantra of "Japan-China friendship" does not work any more. To deal with these challenges, Japan requires both traditional instruments such as military alliances and more broadly based regional coalitions among the countries in the region. Also, Japan is finding that history is becoming a serious stumbling bloc in its relations with some of its neighbours, but it has failed to find a solution acceptable to both the neighbours and an increasingly nationalistic Japanese public opinion. Japan must take an honest look back at its own history. Only by honest self-reflection by the Japanese themselves can Japan overcome the legacy of the war, and deprive the use of history as a diplomatic card aimed at eroding Japan's political influence. But the road ahead is bumpy.

Organizing East Asian International Relations: Competing Norms and Principles

East Asian countries will further expand their functional cooperation under the auspices of ASEAN+3 and/or East Asian Summit. However, the crucial question for community-building is whether normative premises for organizing such cooperation are appropriate enough to address the pressing issues facing the

DIAGRAM A
Organizing norms/principles of international relations

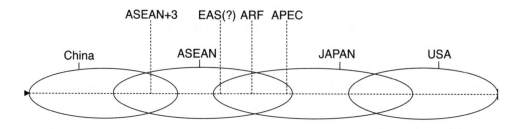

"External" Norms/Principles
National sovereignty
Non-intervention in internal affairs
Different nation-building processes

"Internal" Norms/Principles
Democracy, human rights
Harmonization of domestic institutions

region. Increased interactions (functional cooperation) among East Asians will not necessarily contribute to building an East Asian community. The question to be addressed therefore is the "quality of cooperation": that is, whether East Asia can develop regional institutions effective enough tso tackle the pressing issues facing the region. Existing premises must be reconsidered and modified.

In this regard, put simply, there are four distinct concepts on how we organize the international relations of the region.

ASEAN+X and the extension of "ASEAN Way"

The first is the "ASEAN way". Fearing that Southeast Asia could become a strategic buffer zone, pulled in one direction or the other by the struggle among the big powers, ASEAN has tried to establish for itself a steering role in East Asian community-building.[3] Competition among the major powers has allowed ASEAN to seize the opportunity to draw Tokyo, Beijing, New Delhi, and Canberra into a bidding competition for the hearts and minds of ASEAN. Again, ASEAN is coming back to the central stage of regional institution-building in East Asia.

Active approaches by the major powers to establish more comprehensive partnerships with ASEAN have been leading to the construction of ASEAN-centred institutional arrangements, namely, the ASEAN+X institutional arrangements. We now have ASEAN+3 (Japan, China, and South Korea), ASEAN+2 (Australia and New Zealand), ASEAN+1 (India and Russia, respectively). The East Asia Summit is regarded as a part of the ASEAN-centred institutional arrangements.[4]

Based upon the "ASEAN+X" institutional framework, ASEAN has been "transplanting" its basic principles and norms (the "ASEAN way") to East Asia as a whole. This can be seen in ASEAN's endeavours to invite non-ASEAN countries to sign the TAC (the Treaty of Amity and Cooperation). Signing the TAC is regarded as a pre-condition to joining the East Asia Summit.

It should be noted that ASEAN countries are modifying to some extent their long-held normative premises of cooperation because they now recognize that these premises are not conducive to addressing transnational security threats and the problems generated by economic globalization which all regional countries are currently confronted with. The "Myanmar problem" provides additional stimulus to this process. ASEAN countries are now having another look at democratic governance, civil society, human security, and human rights as binding common guiding principles among the members. The ASEAN Charter currently under consideration will be the first test as to whether ASEAN can succeed in modifying the normative premises that have been contributing to stabilizing state-to-state relations among the members.

China and the modern version of the Westphalian norms/principles

The second is a Chinese way. The "New Security Concept" and the concept of "Peaceful Rise/Development" were recently added to the Five Principles of Peaceful Coexistence.[5] Although these concepts emphasize various new forms such as mutual trust/benefit, dialogue, consultation, confidence-building, and cooperation, they are basically Westphalian.

China's norms and principles mostly relate to "external" dimensions that define inter-state relations. As for "internal" matters, China sticks firmly to the traditional concepts of national sovereignty and non-intervention principles. In fact, if we examine the Chinese concepts such as "Peaceful Development" and "New Security Concept" closely, we find that there are no references to collective engagement to "internal" matters. China's new concepts are applied only to inter-state (not intra-state) affairs. China's recent approach to neighbouring countries has been to share these basic norms and principles. Through joint declarations and statements with the neighbouring countries, China tried to reinforce them with these Westphalian principles.

United States and "internal" norms/principles

The third is an American way, which emphasizes "internal" norms and principles and harmonization of domestic institutions under liberal doctrines. As is clearly shown in the speech by US President Bush in Kyoto, Japan, in November 2005, democracy, freedom, human rights, and good governance are the key principles that should underline international relations in the region.[6]

According to US principles, not only economic but also political liberalization is important in forging a regional cooperative framework. And future regional economic cooperation is no longer defined as simple mutual liberalization of trade but as harmonization and possibly coordination of economic policies and domestic institutions. Enhanced confidence-building among the countries requires regionally common democratic and transparent domestic institutions.

Japan and the "hybrid" type of norms/principles

Japan's position represents the fourth way. We may call this a "hybrid" type of concept. On the one hand, Japan has been supporting ASEAN's way: informal confidence-building through intensive dialogue. On the other hand, Japan is pursuing more intrusive and binding regional arrangements that touch upon internal matters such as democracy, human rights, transparency, and harmonization of internal regulatory systems. It is in this context that Japan has been pushing

India, Australia, and New Zealand to join the East Asia Summit processes. The participation of those three countries is expected to facilitate the construction of more intrusive arrangements in the region.

East Asia today needs stronger and more intrusive regional institutions that touch upon domestic affairs to address the pressing political, security, economic, and social issues facing the region. Achieving common rules of conduct and entering into reciprocal commitments and obligations needs some degree of "like-mindedness" among the states concerned. Similarity of social organizations and values, and convergence of political and security interests all make it easier to accept the necessary levels of intrusive management.

What Japan is most concerned about is that East Asian cooperation might be organized under mixed principles and norms of China's way and the old-fashioned ASEAN way, mostly dealing with the "external" dimensions of state-to-state relations and leaving internal matters out of the agenda of regional cooperation. In its cooperation with ASEAN, China has tried to avoid facing such sensitive issues as human rights, political liberalization, military transparency, and deeper integration issues touching upon domestic institutional adjustments.

The complexity of a modern economy requires a detailed set of common laws and regulations for global market relations to function smoothly. The focus has shifted from border measures towards the harmonization of business rules and domestic institutions. Political openness and liberalization are critical for increasing transparency in domestic affairs, which is one of the keys for confidence-building among countries. In the East Asian context, many countries in the region have been actively engaged in bilateral FTAs with each other and with extra-regional countries.[7] The emergence of the complex web of bilateral FTAs in East Asia will make regional community-building extremely difficult. Of course, there are arguments that the various bilateral agreements will contribute to consolidating a single East Asian FTA. They are viewed as procurators to the formation of a broader FTA covering the entire East Asia. But these arguments are based upon wishful thinking. Each bilateral FTA is tailor-made (in scope, agenda, and so forth), making it difficult to amalgamate them into a single region-wide agreement at a later stage.[8] Therefore a further fragmentation is currently being observed in East Asia.[9]

There is a need to develop some common modality to regulate bilateral FTAs. This must include guidance for deeper integration that would facilitate domestic institutional transformation. It is quite important for Japan to review its ongoing bilateral FTA negotiations with neighbouring countries by approaching them from this perspective. The Japan-Singapore Economic Partnership Agreement presents one of the models for Japan to observe.

Transparency is critical in military confidence-building. We must let others know more accurately and openly what we are thinking and doing. The lack of transparency causes misunderstanding and mutual suspicion, further aggravating the security dilemma. We need more intrusive arrangements in this regard. East Asia must go beyond ongoing cooperative activities based on the existing premises.

Responding to Uncertainty: Engaging, Risk-Hedging, and Soft-Balancing

Geopolitical and geoeconomic considerations further complicate the process of regional community-building. East Asia is now in a period of great transition. The distribution of power among the countries is unstable. Rapid military modernization is under way in the name of protecting national sovereignty. The relationships among the major powers are not stable and serious security dilemmas exist among them.

Several East Asian countries are facing the challenge of transformation of the political regimes from authoritarian to democratic ones. Democratic transformation is often accompanied by domestic instability. Terrorism further aggravates internal instability. Regional cooperation very much depends on the coherence and viability of the states. The absence of stable and viable states makes the process of region-building difficult as states remain the essential building blocks on which regional cooperative exercises are based.

Furthermore, citizens are not always fully ready to adjust themselves to the internal and external changes that have been brought about by such factors as rapid economic globalization and the changing power relations among countries. Rapid change is causing concern about the future among them and such concerns are feeding nationalism. We have seen the danger of the convergence of nationalism and populism.[10]

The Asian economic future is also uncertain. The regional economic structure has been becoming more competitive. China and ASEAN (and India) are competing with each other for foreign direct investment and new markets. Japan, for the first time in the modern era, is facing serious economic challenges from other Asian nations. Further, how the United States rectifies the huge economic imbalance across the Pacific, which will have an enormous impact on Asian economies, is uncertain.

Sustainability of Chinese economic growth, which is one of the driving forces of East Asian cooperation, is uncertain.[11] Indeed there are grave concerns stemming from the distorted composition of China's aggregate demand, in which consumption represents only 40 per cent and investment accounts for just as much, while the total export and import values are equal to approximately 60 per cent of GDP. Apparently this is not sustainable. Furthermore, the sustainability of the market mechanism under the authoritarian one-party system is also uncertain.[12] The Chinese economy could turn out to be less a miracle than a mirage.

All these feed a sense of insecurity and uncertainty, which have led East Asian countries to adopt a variety of strategies to protect their interests, and in the process further complicating the international political economy of region-building and in East Asia. They are entering into various bilateral deals with intra- and extra-regional countries/regions through strategies simultaneously ranging from "engaging" to "risk-hedging" and "soft-balancing", especially towards the major powers.[13]

China

China responded quickly to the emerging US-led unipolar world after the end of the Cold War by trying to make the world more multipolar in which US power is constrained by other major powers. However, China's strategy has not produced a tangible effect. Thus, fearing US intervention in China's internal and external policies, China has established various institutions with neighbouring countries to strengthen China's bargaining positions *vis-à-vis* the United States.

China established a "strategic partnership" with Russia, took the initiative in establishing the Shanghai Cooperation Organization (SCC), and normalized its relations with India and Vietnam. It has been strengthening its relations with its southern neighbours in ASEAN. There have been some marked changes in China's approach to Southeast Asia over the past decade. ASEAN's approach (the ASEAN way), which emphasizes consensus-decisions, informality, inclusiveness, and voluntarism, has been quite advantageous to China in the sense that it has spared China ASEAN's collective pressure.[14]

China's "new" thinking on Japan, which advocates a policy of upgrading its relationship with Japan to a strategic one, might be another manifestation of China's eagerness to enhance the relationships with its neighbours in the face of US hegemony.[15] The Six-Party Talks that were established to resolve the North Korean nuclear crisis are also expected to serve as an additional regional multilateral mechanism to constrain US unilateral actions.[16]

China has skilfully utilized the anxieties and concerns shared by Asian countries about US unilateral "hegemonic" behaviour. It has been skilfully constructing institutions with neighbours to softly balance US global hegemony.

The US preoccupation with Iraq and the war against global terrorism have given China an opportunity to expand its role in Southeast Asia. On the surface, China's regional diplomacy is not directed against the United States and/or Japan. But by enlarging its political and economic space in the region through multilateral institutions, China will make it more difficult for the United States to enlist regional support against China in the future. In the long run, China may have a larger ambition of forging and leading an East Asia community. China's enhanced relations with ASEAN will serve as a foundation for forging such a broader regional community.

ASEAN

ASEAN countries have also been adopting complex strategies of engaging, risk-hedging, and soft-balancing vis-à-vis the major powers.[17]

Many countries are engaging China and the United States economically to obtain economic gains. At the same time, they are diversifying their respective economic relations to avoid undue dependence and to hedge the risks of economic uncertainty. This is clearly demonstrated in the recent conclusion of the bilateral FTAs with both intra– and extra–East Asian partners. ASEAN concluded an FTA with China but, at the same time, it started negotiations with other countries such as Japan, Australia, and India.

ASEAN countries are engaging China in the security area. But, at the same time, they are enhancing their respective security relations with the United States to hedge the security risks that may arise from the "rise of China". Malaysia and Singapore provide military facilities and access to US naval and air forces and also engage in bilateral and multilateral joint military exercises with the United States.

At the same time, they are deeply concerned about US unilateralism and US "intervention" in their internal affairs in the name of promoting freedom, democracy, human rights, and good governance. Therefore, they are enhancing their relations with neighbours to protect themselves against US unilateral behaviour. Some ASEAN members view East Asian cooperation as an instrument to protect themselves from US "hegemonic" behaviour.[18]

The United States

The United States has also been engaging China in international and regional fora. Economic relations between the United States and China have been expanding dramatically. Today the US government is pushing China to be a "responsible stakeholder" in the international system, going beyond just being a member of the international society.[19] At the same time, however, the United States seems to be concerned about the increase of Chinese influence in Asia that may reduce the influence and power of the United States. So the United States has been expanding its economic and security relations with various countries in Asia, including its alliance relations with Japan and Australia. It has been expanding security cooperation with some of the ASEAN countries through joint exercises, military training programmes, the provision of military hardware and access agreements for US forces. In the economics area, the United States has been seeking FTAs with some of the Southeast Asian countries under the Enterprise of ASEAN Initiative. The negotiations with South Korea for an FTA will resume soon.

Japan and the region

Of critical importance for Japan is how to deal with China, the United States, and ASEAN.

Japan has been expanding its relations with China and actively engaging it in international and regional societies. At the same time, Japan has been hedging the risks inherent in the uncertainties about China's future, given such developments as military modernization, possible domestic instability, and "assertiveness" in Chinese foreign policies towards Japan. China still attracts huge Japanese investment, but Japanese companies are now also looking for other appropriate sites for investment in other regions. "Risk-hedging" is a critical factor for Japanese business.

The most significant change in relations with China is that Tokyo has adopted a more assertive stance towards Beijing, abandoning its long-held policy of seeking to avoid open confrontation with China under the banner of "Japan-China friendship". Both Japan and China are yet to get used to the idea that, for the first time, they are both major powers in East Asia simultaneously. Japan suspects that China is seeking to erode Japanese power and influence in the region.

Japan views the "rise" of China not as a threat but as an opportunity and a challenge. Economically, China is not a threat to Japan but gives Japan plenty of opportunities. China is not an economic competitor to Japan in the foreseeable future. The argument that Japan is concerned about and even jealous of China's economic development is fundamentally flawed, ignoring the fundamental changes of economic relations in East Asia over the recent decades.

CEPII, the French economic research institute, has been publishing interesting research papers recently that are based upon detailed analysis of intra-regional trade in East Asia. The findings of the CEPII papers reveal the real picture of China's economic development that cannot be obtained by just reading ordinary trade statistics.

China's export of high-technology products has expanded in recent years. According to the research done by CEPII, however, this growth is attributable to China's integration into the East Asia–wide regional production and distribution networks formed through extensive FDI by foreign firms. Japanese firms have been playing a key role in constructing this region-wide production network. Most of China's trade in high-tech products is related to processing activities and is handled by foreign affiliates, including Japanese ones.[20] In the mean time, China's contribution in terms of added value has been limited to its function in the assembly sector that is heavily dependent upon the supply of abundant cheap labour. Put differently, what China has been doing is importing expensive parts and intermediary goods from Japan and the NIEs (and from foreign multinational companies operating in ASEAN countries), and then assembling them into finished products for export to the United States and Europe.

These days "made in China" products are mostly made elsewhere by multinational companies including Japanese ones that are using China as the final assembly station in their cross-border production networks. "Made in China" should be correctly called "assembled in China". Japanese and other multinational companies are largely "invisible" behind the "Chinese" factories producing a large amount of tradable goods. And about 60 per cent of China's exports are controlled by foreign companies. They are reaping the bulk of profits from the exports from China.[21]

With the coming of an ageing society, Japan must generate profits overseas by effectively using the assets it has accumulated. It needs good overseas markets for investment from which it must obtain profit.[22] China's growth provides Japan with excellent opportunities for investment. Furthermore, Japan can relocate industries that have lost international competitiveness to China and restructure the Japanese economic structure, thereby further enhancing Japanese economic competitiveness. There is no reason for Japan to be worried by China's economic growth. What Japan is concerned about is domestic instability and economic confusion in China caused by social unrest and poor economic governance.

At the same time, Japan does not take it for granted that China's rise will be peaceful. China is young as a nation-state with a strong desire to regain pre-eminence in the world. China remains a potential destabilizing factor until it matures as a nation-state, developing political institutions and culture to resolve disputes peacefully and allowing pluralistic political values.

In response to the growing Asian strategic complexities and uncertainties, Japan has been enhancing its alliance with the United States. The defence cooperation between the two countries has expanded enormously. The US-Japan 2+2 Ministerial Security Consultative Committee meeting between the defence and foreign ministers of the respective governments in February 2005 issued a joint statement which showed that the two governments had forged a common strategic agenda for the alliance. The joint statement also recognized Taiwan as "a mutual security concern", for the first time since Japan's normalization of relations with China in 1972.

Japan and the United States have agreed to share military bases in Japan by US troops and the Japanese Self-Defense Forces, improve bilateral interoperability, and increase joint exercises. The new and engaged Japan, emerging as a more confident power alongside the United States, would be a key in shaping the future of Asia.

Through active engagement with the United States, Japan has also been strengthening ties across the Pacific. The present regional political, economic, and security structures support Japan's pan-Pacific orientation. The United States has been playing and will continue to play the critical role for peace and prosperity in Asia.

Militarily, the US forward military presence, supported by a web of alliance networks, continues to provide a basic foundation of regional peace and stability, containing political and military tensions arising from the rivalries in East Asia, and contributing to shaping the future of Asia.

Economically, the United States continues to play a critical role for Asian development. Certainly the trade between China and the rest of Asia has increased tremendously, generating a new image of an East Asia that is economically self-sufficient and self-sustaining. The US market is still vital for Asia's growth, however. East Asian production networks led by multilateral companies have given rise to a "triangular trade pattern": Japan and NIEs export capital goods and sophisticated intermediate goods (parts and components) to the less-developed countries (ASEAN and China), which process them for export to the United States and Europe. China's huge surplus in its trade with the United States and trade deficit with the rest of Asia is a just reflection of this triangular trade relationship.[23] China's surplus vis-à-vis the United States is offset by China's huge deficit in trade (components and parts) with other Asian economies. In this regard, it can be pointed out that the massive US trade deficit is held against East Asia as a whole, which has grown into a giant factory with economies interlinked through extensive, region-wide production and distribution networks run by foreign firms.

So the trade statistics showing huge surplus in China's trade with the United States are misleading indicators of China's economic power. The situation wherein East Asian economies were heavily dependent upon the US market has not changed in spite of China's remarkable economic growth.[24]

The above analysis implies that structural changes have not taken place in the relationships between East Asian economies and the United States for the last few decades, in spite of the dramatic increase of intra-Asian trade. The concept of "the Asia-Pacific" as a region is still valid both economically and militarily.

Given the role of the US-Japan alliance as a public good that provides stability in this turbulent region, it is quite appropriate for Japan to enhance its alliance relationship with the United States. At the same time, however, Japan has to be sensitive to different perceptions among the countries of the region on the unipolar world or US hegemony. Overall, Japan is comfortable to live with a US-led uniplolar world. In a sense, Japan is seeking to jointly manage US power and influence in East Asia.

The attitudes of other Asian nations are more ambivalent in this regard. Such ambivalence exists in ASEAN countries and in South Korea. On the one hand, there is a common understanding that the continued engagement and commitment of the United States to Asia is essential for the region. Given the uncertainty associated with change in China, many countries of East Asia need the US military and economic presence in the region to hedge against risks posed by China.

On the other hand, however, they are concerned about possible intervention by the United States in what they regard as their domestic affairs, in the name of protecting human rights, promoting democracy and good governance and fighting terrorism. The US military doctrine advocating preventive strike as a legitimate sovereign right further aggravates these concerns. They are critical of US unilateral "hegemonic" behaviour. Thus, some of the ASEAN countries feel that they need some collective mechanism to protect them from "undue intervention" by the United States. In South Korea anti-American nationalism and a populist leadership mutually reinforce each other. There is also concern in South Korea about the rising tensions between China and Japan and about the recent enhancement of military cooperation between Japan and the United States in response to strategic complexities in East Asia mainly caused by China. Japan should not take it for granted that ASEAN countries and South Korea fully support the US-Japan alliance. Japan should be aware that the US global power creates a lot of local resistance and it does not automatically translate into US influence in a specific region.

Last, but not the least, is Japan's approach to ASEAN. ASEAN has been one of the most important partners of Japan of decades. Japan has been enhancing cooperation with ASEAN and with individual ASEAN members. A resilient, confident, outward-oriented, and open ASEAN is in Japan's interest. As before, Japan is ready to support ASEAN to move towards a regional institution that can tackle pressing issues. But this would not be possible without being accompanied by a modification of existing premises underlining ASEAN cooperation. Even if painful and difficult, only a renovated ASEAN is eligible to lead East Asian cooperation.

Conclusion

East Asia needs agreed norms and principles to promote much deeper collaboration to respond to the various challenges. But this is not easy to achieve. Deep-seated differences on the organizing norms and principles of international relations and geopolitical and geoeconomic factors prevailing in East Asia prevent regional countries from fully committing themselves to the cause of community-building. Given the complicated diplomatic strategies adopted by the regional countries, the progress of East Asian cooperation will be slow at best.

In the mean time, after having suffered from a deep sense of insecurity and uncertainty, Japan must recognize that it has capability and responsibility to make East Asia a stable and prosperous region. Japan's future is closely connected with that of East Asia, given the political, economic, and security interdependence. The alliance with the United States is critical not only for Japanese security but also for the entire East Asia. But Japan should not just escape into the comfortable shelter of the alliance. It must face and respond to the challenges in East Asia, even if this demands a painful rethinking of Japan's past and future role in the region.

Notes

[1] Peter J. Katzenstein, *A World of Regions* (Ithaca: Cornell University Press, 2005).
[2] See the Annual White Papers published by the Japanese Ministry of Economy, Trade and Industry (METI) for the last few years.
[3] Michael Vatikiotis, "Three Cheers for East Asian Summit: A Bullish View of Asian Regionalism, *Jakarta Post*, 20 December 2005.
[4] The East Asia Summit was originally designed as a forum where East Asian countries participate on an equal footing, not as an ASEAN-centred one.
[5] Speech by Zheng Bijian, "China's New Road of Peaceful Rise and China-US Relations", 16 June 2005, Washington, The Brookings Institution. See also *China's Peaceful Development Road* (Information Office, China's State Council), 22 December 2005.

6. President Bush Discusses Freedom and Democracy in Kyoto, Japan, 16 November 2005, http://www.whitehouse.gov/news/releases/2005/11/20051116-6html#.
7. Teofilo C. Daquila and Le Huu Huy, "Singapore and ASEAN in the Global Economy", *Asian Survey* 43, no. 6 (2003): 908–28.
8. Hadi Soesastro, "Indonesia and FTAs in East Asia", *Japan Spotlight*, 17 March 2004.
9. Hadi Soesastro, *Building an East Asian Community through Trade and Investment Integration*, CSIS Working Paper WPE067 (Jakarta, April 2003), p. 10.
10. Peter Hays Gries, *China's New Nationalism* (Berkeley: University of California Press, 2005).
11. For the argument that the massive flow of FDI that fuelled China's growth reflects China's economic weakness rather than strength, see Yasheng Huang, *Selling China: Foreign direct Investment during the Reform Era* (Cambridge: Cambridge University Press, 2003).
12. One leading scholar on the Chinese economy who is based in Japan is now giving a strong message to China that without substantial democratization of its political system China may lose not only its future economic growth prospects but also the economic assets that it has accumulated during the recent decades. See C.H. Kwan, Chugoku Keizai Kakumei Saisyuusyo [The final chapter of Chinese economic revolution], *Nihon Keizai Shinbun* [Japan Economic Journal], 2005.
13. On "soft-balancing" in realist theory, see *Balance of Power: Theory and Practice in the 21st Century*, edited by T.V. Paul, James J. Wirtz, and Michael Fortmann (Stanford: Stanford University Press, 2004).
14. Kuik Cheng-Ghwee, "Multilateralism in China's ASEAN Policy: Its Evolution, Characteristics, and Aspiration", *Contemporary Southeast Asia* 27, no. 1 (April 2005): 102–22.
15. On the debates over China's new thinking on Japan, see Peter Hays Gries, "China's New Thinking on Japan", *China Quarterly* 184 (2005): 831–50.
16. Tsutomu Kikuchi, "Institutional Linkages and Security Order in Northeast Asia" (paper presented at the United Nations University and the Aoyama-Gakuin University workshop on "Institutionalizing Northeast Asia: Making the Impossible Possible", held from 20 to 22 September 2005 at the UNU headquarters in Tokyo.
17. Yuen Foong Khong, "Coping with Strategic Uncertainty: The Role of Institutions and Soft Balancing in Southeast Asia's Post–Cold War Strategy", in *Rethinking Security in East Asia: Identity, Power, and Efficiency*, edited by Allen Carlson, Peter Katzenstein, and J.J. Suh (Stanford: Stanford University Press, 2004); Evelyn Goh, *Great Powers and Southeast Asian Regional Security Strategies: Omni-Enmeshment, Balancing and Hierarchical Order*, Working Paper No. 84 (Singapore: Institute of Defence and Strategic Studies, July 2005).
18. Singapore is a good example of a country adopting complex diplomatic strategies. On the one hand, it is seeking to enhance economic relations with China. However,

Singapore has also concluded bilateral FTAs with the United States, Japan, Australia, India, EFTA, and others to diversify its economic relations. In security, Singapore has military contacts with China, but at the same time, has enhanced its security relations with other countries including the United States, Japan, and Australia.

[19] See Robert Zoellick' speech "Wither China: Membership or Responsibility?" at the US-China Commission on 21 September 2005.

[20] *China's Integration in East Asia: Production Sharing, FDI and High Tech Trade*, CEPII (Centre D'etudes Prospectives et D'informations Internationales) Working Paper No. 2005-09, p. 40.

[21] David Barboza, "Some Assembly Needed: China as Asian Factory", *New York Times*, 9 February 2006.

[22] Japanese income profits transferred from overseas to Japan are approximately equal to its trade surplus. Japan is becoming a mature economy where gains from overseas investment is crucial for economic prosperity.

[23] "China in the International Segmentation of Production Processes", CEPII Working Paper No. 2002-02. See also Hiroya Tanikawa, "The Pitfalls of the Ideas of East Asian Economic Integration", *Column 0132* (Research Institute of Economy, Trade and Industry, Japan), June 2004.

[24] See also Edward J. Lincoln, *East Asian Economic Regionalism* (Washington, DC: The Brookings Institution, 2004).

Brunei Darussalam

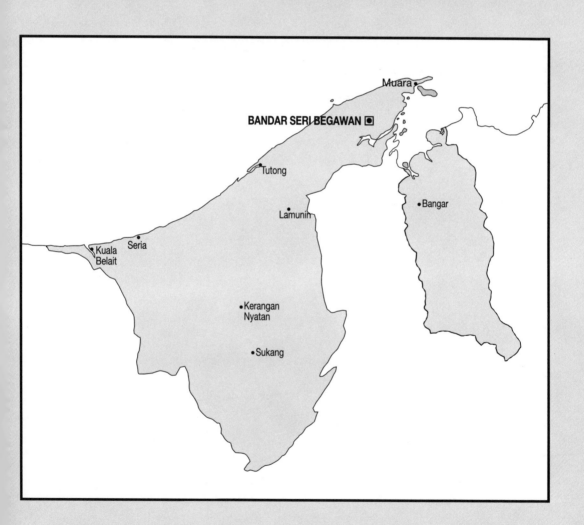

BRUNEI DARUSSALAM
Consolidating the Polity

Pushpa Thambipillai

The year 2005 was another crucial year for Brunei Darussalam, setting in motion its policy directions for the next decade or so. In fact, it was a strengthening of the strategies introduced the previous year. Consolidation and reform were the key targets of the government as it gained confidence and momentum in forging ahead with political and economic development. The society, in the mean time, took the opportunity to participate in public affairs as signs of openness and transparency increased.

Politics and Governance

The major event of the previous year had been the reconvening of the Legislative Council after an absence of over 20 years as it had been suspended since independence in 1984. One of the main tasks of that assembly, composed of 21 appointed members, was to discuss and pass various amendments to the 1959 Constitution. A high-level committee had been established a few years earlier to review the constitution and related legal matters. His Majesty Sultan Haji Hassanal Bolkiah as Head of State, signed the Proclamation of Brunei's Constitution (Amendments) on 29 September 2004 during the sitting of the legislature. While the constitution reinforced Brunei as a Malay Islamic Monarchy, the legislative process was given prominence as a means for the people to take part in the development of the state, even though the numbers of those participating were limited. It was projected as an official forum to voice opinions and raise issues. Some of the discussions in the Assembly supported that notion. It was also announced that the legislature would be enlarged to 45 members, with provisions for a maximum of

---

PUSHPA THAMBIPILLAI teaches in the Department of Public Policy and Administration, Faculty of Business, Economics and Policy Studies, University of Brunei Darussalam.

15 representatives to be elected from the four districts of Brunei-Muara, Tutong, Belait, and Temburong.

Contrary to the announcement made the previous year, the legislature did not convene in 2005. By decree, the previous Legislative Council was dissolved as of 1 September and a new one was constituted to take effect as of 2 September.[1] The new body consists of 30 members: 14 ex-officio (it is essentially the newly appointed cabinet), three titled persons, seven individuals of distinction, and six district representatives, who had earlier been elected as village heads (*ketua kampong*) or subdistrict heads (*penghulu*) by their constituents. Prior to the announcement, earlier in the year, work on an elaborate Legislative Council building costing about B$62 million had begun. It is scheduled for completion in 2007. However, there is no indication when the current assembly will meet or when it will be increased to 45; the issue of direct elections has also not been clarified. It is probable that the elected 15 might constitute district representatives. Anyway, there have been no outward signs of preparations that the infrastructure for holding elections to the assembly is under way.

In a bid to strengthen the government machinery and focus on issues of stability and development, the Sultan announced a cabinet reshuffle in May 2005.[2] It saw the retirement of some of the senior ministers (notably the Minister of Home Affairs, the Minister of Culture, Youth and Sports, and the Minister of Education) and the inclusion of some new appointees. There had been no major reshuffle in the past 17 years (except for the replacement of three ministers for various reasons), and thus the action was seen as significant, though the announcement came unexpectedly. The Sultan, who is head of state and government, heads the cabinet of 14, and retains his positions as prime minister, defence minister, and finance minister. A major restructuring of the cabinet was the addition of Prince Al-Muhtadee Billah, the Crown Prince, as senior minister in the Prime Minister's Office. Two ministers who retained their portfolios were the Minister of Foreign Affairs and the Minister of Religious Affairs. Some of the other ministers were reshuffled, promoted from deputy to full minister or appointed from the ranks of the senior permanent secretaries. A retired major-general (who had headed the Brunei Economic Development Board, or BEDB) was a newcomer to the cabinet; so were two deputy ministers selected from the private sector (for their experience in the oil and gas industry) to assist in the development and industry ministries. Newly created posts in the cabinet included the minister of energy (located in the Prime Minister's Office), minister for finance II and minister for foreign affairs II. All the other ministries were accorded deputy ministers. The posts of the state mufti (the highest authority on Islam) and the attorney general were also accorded ministerial status. In announcing the new structure, the Sultan revealed that the appointments were for a five-year period (the first of its kind), and expected the team to lead Brunei towards the desired society of peace and development. The complete list includes 16 ministerial positions (including the mufti and attorney) and ten deputy ministers who took their oath of office at the end of May.[3] With the specific term of reference for their appointments, it is expected that each ministry has a more definite plan of action to be completed before the minister's term is completed.

Two other observations on the cabinet appointments are significant. One is that the Crown Prince (and Deputy Sultan) was allotted the post of senior minister in the Prime Minister's Office. Lately he has assumed a more prominent role, deputizing for the Sultan, visiting government offices, officiating at important gatherings and meeting with ambassadors and other foreign visitors. As the future Sultan, he is being given greater responsibilities and exposure to the broader fields of government. Another outcome of the reshuffle is the newly created energy post, which signifies the central role that oil and gas play in Brunei's economic life and thus the need to consolidate and coordinate energy-related policies and actions.

A related change in integrating the developmental tasks (announced later) was the transfer of the Department of International Relations and Trade (which dealt with economic issues pertaining to ASEAN, BIMP-EAGA [Brunei, Indonesia, Malaysia, Philippines–East ASEAN Growth Area], APEC [Asia Pacific Economic Cooperation], and WTO [World Trade Organization]), from the Ministry of Industry and Primary Resources to the Ministry of Foreign Affairs. The latter came to be known as the Ministry of Foreign Affairs and Trade as of August 2005. All forms of external economic and diplomatic links now come under a single ministry.

Good governance was one of the main themes at the core of the administrative changes undertaken. The expectation is that the ministerial and higher-level appointments would spur dedication and commitment. The various criteria of good governance were extolled in the numerous training programmes and seminars held regularly for civil servants. A senior civil servant had earlier emphasized the role of the Civil Service in the 21st century and efforts to revamp certain policies, organizational structures, and behaviour were regularly reviewed.[4] Discussions on the Strategic Vision for all departments and ministries were also under way in 2005. Each government agency has prepared its respective vision for the next two decades so that collectively the country's ideals could be achieved. Each year on 29 September the country observes Civil Service Day. The theme for 2005 was "Public Service Excellence", extolled in an address by the Crown Prince.[5] The Sultan had expressed concern over the undue red tape prevalent in the administrative system and introduced certain financial reforms to expedite development-oriented procedures.[6] The reforms in the insurance, banking, and other areas were necessary to meet international standards. There is general acknowledgment that Brunei needs to upgrade its services so that it can better meet the challenges of globalization as well as attract foreign investment. Internal appraisals are not uncommon, mainly as a result of working visits by the Sultan and the Crown Prince. At one of those visits, the Audit Department revealed that various agencies and departments owe the government a cumulative sum of B$380 million at the end of 2004 due to inadequate collection procedures.[7] In that year alone, about B$5 million was lost through embezzlement, wastage, and excess payments in government departments, statutory boards, and government-owned companies. The Auditor General noted that the lack of a professional and trained workforce was one of the problems encountered by the department, an issue not peculiar to that office alone.

Developmental Issues

Brunei continued on a development trend similar to that in the previous year. Gross domestic product grew at an average of 1.7 to 2 per cent. Economic growth was fairly low despite the favourable oil prices that had increased to over US$50 a barrel over the period. However, in order to conserve its resources, Brunei had been extracting less oil and gas than the optimum. Nevertheless, with high oil prices, income from the hydrocarbons accounted for 90 per cent of its total revenue. The country has also been enjoying a budget surplus since the second half of 2004. Total non-oil exports declined, mainly as a result of a decline in garment exports, which had faced a severe downturn after a good decade of growth. The removal of special access under the WTO rules meant the loss of Western markets. The industry was unviable given the unfavourable setting of high prices for land and capital. Also, it relied exclusively on foreign labour for its factories. Some of the factories closed shop. In fact, one of the major textile producers, a joint venture between local and foreign investors, did not pay its foreign labour force of a few hundred workers for about six months. Legal proceedings commenced, which forced it to shut down operations.

Brunei's main export destinations continue to be Japan and ASEAN, each accounting for about a third of its exports. China, while accounting for only 5 to 7 per cent of the exports, appears to be the most rapidly expanding market as compared with previous years when it averaged 4 per cent. Similarly, imports from China have also increased. However, ASEAN still accounts for about half the imports.[8]

Brunei Shell Petroleum Company, the largest oil company in the country, continues to explore for oil offshore and has recorded success in areas as close as a kilometre from the coast in the Seria fields. Production in the new wells is expected to begin in another year or two. Onshore potentials for oil resources have also been encouraging. The government-owned Brunei National Petroleum Company (Petroleum BRUNEI was established in 2002) opened bids for exploration by local and foreign companies in onshore areas covering a few thousand square kilometres.[9] The successful companies are to be notified in early 2006. It will then take another three to four years before the exploration leads to actual production. It is envisaged that the exploration alone will generate a number of related business activities and employment, and widen the number of energy players in the country's hydrocarbon sector. This will further boost the role of the new cabinet post in charge of energy matters. (The Minister for Energy is also the chairman of Petroleum BRUNEI.) In late 2005 the Department of Electrical Services, which was under the Ministry of Development since 1984, was transferred to the Minister for Energy.[10] The Petroleum Unit (already under the Prime Minister's Office), together with the Electrical Department, is expected to provide an integrated energy policy; the former in formulating hydrocarbon-related policies and the latter in providing the energy services. This is a crucial public sector service as all sources of energy for the county are derived from hydrocarbons. There have also been calls to consumers by the Minister for Energy to conserve energy and reduce their high electricity bills. A related issue was that the outstanding energy bills not paid by consumers (both individuals and organizations) amounted to several million dollars.

The high consumption of gasoline and diesel had prompted the authorities to introduce cost-saving measures. In order to avert any excess purchase or illegal trade in gasoline from outside the country, new directives were issued on restrictions on gasoline and diesel to begin in January 2006. Automobiles could only fill up to a full tank and could not purchase in bulk, which were now restricted to locally registered companies. As gasoline is heavily subsidized in Brunei, its retail price is the lowest in the region, and the government wants to ensure that only citizens and residents are entitled to enjoy this subsidy. However, it would not prevent drivers from neighbouring countries from filling up their tanks as long as this was within the 250-litre capacity. Private purchases in large containers (which happened frequently before) are now prohibited.[11]

The government, being the main player in the economic life of the state, has had to prioritize its spending in order to boost economic growth. The often-heard slogan that the private sector is the engine of growth is yet to be realized. The business sector is hopeful that government spending would increase. Public sector injection of funds, for example, in the construction of buildings and infrastructure, in transportation and in the information technology (IT) sector, was expected to boost private businesses, wholesale, and retail trade. The government has allocated B$900 million for the final year of the 8th National Development Plan.[12] Part of the fund is to cover payments for 249 completed or ongoing projects and the rest is for 286 new projects yet to be implemented. The new projects are in the transport and communication, social services, public utilities, security, ICT, and infrastructure sectors.[13]

The government has also targeted the financial sector as a possible source of economic activity. The Brunei International Financial Centre (BIFC) was established under the Ministry of Finance in 2000 to promote the country in areas of banking, finance, securities, and insurance. A number of legislations have been introduced to regulate the various areas of international finance and to make it attractive for investors. Islamic finance and banking is also seen as a niche area in attracting funds. It is worth noting that the Overseas Chinese Banking Corporation Limited (OCBC Bank of Singapore) has been granted an international Islamic Banking Licence, the first foreign bank to have obtained such a licence. The Malaysian-owned Commerce International Merchant Bank (CIMB) has also established a branch under the BIFC. In other moves to strengthen Islamic financial institutions, the Ministry of Finance announced in July 2005 that the two local banks, Islamic Bank of Brunei (IBB) and Islamic Development Bank of Brunei (IDBB), are to merge, making the new entity the largest financial institution in the country. There are also plans to establish an Islamic Capital Bond Market, including the issuance of short-term bonds so that local institutions could gain access to local funds under the Islamic jurisprudence.[14] The Brunei LNG (liquefied natural gas) and IDBB have agreed to finance the company's projects through the *Sukuk Al Ijarah* (Islamic bonds).

Three years earlier, the government established the BEDB to independently charter the country's industrialization programme. It has succeeded, to an extent, in drawing up a master plan, and in creating interest among potential foreign investors. The BEDB provided revised projections of investments of up to US$5.291 billion by 2008 and job creation for 12,000 in direct and indirect activities.[15] It has earmarked an island, Pulau Muara Besar, at the entrance to the Muara harbour, to be developed into a "mega port" and economic processing zone with investments that could reach US$1 billion. Large foreign investors are targeted to facilitate the projects. Downstream activities from the oil and gas sector are planned for an industrial estate in Sungai Liang, near the oil town of Seria. The next two years will reveal how much of the interest shown is realized as investment. One of the confirmed projects will be a methanol plant in Sungai Liang in 2008, a joint venture between Petroleum BRUNEI and two major Japanese companies.

Diversifying the economy and encouraging the development of manufacturing as an economic base is a major concern of policymakers. A number of specialized industries have recently been attracted to Brunei. For instance, an agreement has been initiated between a subsidiary of the government-owned bank IDBB and a local company to set up a hi-tech spectacle lens manufacturing plant that would create 300 jobs. However, the micro and small industries (identified as those employing between five and one hundred) are still the backbone of the business sector as more than 90 per cent of the registered businesses fall under that category. Local entrepreneurs have been urged to look into niche markets in expanding their activities, especially in foreign markets. A niche area that Brunei is actively considering is the "halal" food production and certification, given the global market of a billion Muslims who consume halal products. Other countries, notably Malaysia, have already embarked in this direction. Brunei is anxious to establish its own credentials but has been slow in realizing its intentions.

Agriculture, aqua culture, and animal rearing have also seen increased interest from local entrepreneurs. These sectors constitute a high percentage of the local consumption and contribute to economic growth. Tourism is another area that has been targeted over the past decade as a potential source of income. However, tourist arrivals per capita are still low in comparison with neighbouring countries including the Borneo states of Sabah and Sarawak. Hotel occupancy is also usually low, unless there is an international convention. Efforts are being made to promote the "Borneo package" in collaboration with the two Malaysian states. In addition, the upgrading of the tourism unit to a Department of Tourism Development, and the establishment of a national Tourism Board, would contribute to a more sustainable tourism industry over the next decade. The Board, constituting relevant stakeholders from the public and private sectors, has been meeting to plan its strategies for the next decade.

A sector that is rapidly expanding is the telecommunications sector. In keeping up with global trends in IT, concepts of e-government and e-education are becoming catch phrases. However, it will be a few years before there are direct results. Brunei has a high per capita ownership of mobile phones — about 170,000 for a population of 350,000. A second mobile phone company entered the market in 2005. B-mobile Communications provides the country's first 3G telephone service. Apparently Brunei is one of only three countries in the region (besides Singapore and Malaysia) that enjoy such service.

Societal Features

Unemployment is a worrisome issue as it lingers at around 5 to 7 per cent. For a small country of under 300,000 citizens and permanent residents, it is a potential socioeconomic problem especially since the majority are young job seekers. In a speech on the issue, the Sultan urged his subjects to work hard and earn a decent living (citing some of the teachings of Prophet Mohammad, as it was the occasion of the Prophet's birthday celebration). He queried why there were more than 7,000 registered job seekers when there was a foreign workforce of more than 75,000. As there was no shortage of opportunities to acquire the required skills and experience, he acknowledged that part of the problem probably lay in the attitude of local job seekers. Thus, changing people's attitude towards employment would be important in locals being gainfully employed.

Currently there are several institutions that provide skills training, including entrepreneur skills. For instance, the Entrepreneur Centre was established under the Ministry of Industry and Primary Resources to provide start-up training for would-be small businesses. The University of Brunei also has an Entrepreneur Development Unit that offers courses to students keen on embarking on a business career. In addition, the Brunei Shell Company has been a sponsor of a programme for youths called "Live Wire" where they are inducted into opportunities in the private sector. There is an encouraging indication that more locals are starting up their own businesses, or taking up much lower-paid employment in the private sector, rather than waiting for public sector employment. Government employment has traditionally been the premier choice because of its higher salaries and perks. Again, the Sultan's concerns constituted a major part of his New Year address given on the last day of 2005, emphasizing the role of the private sector in diversifying the economy and in creating more employment opportunities for the local population.[16] Social stability hinged on an economically vibrant society and Brunei was fortunate to enjoy peace and stability and thus, emphasized the Sultan, its continuity should be ensured.

The Department of Labour has introduced several measures to address the local unemployment situation. According to its survey, only 25 per cent of the workforce in the private sector is local. Thus, localization has become the priority. Fourteen job categories have been reserved for locals in the private sector (such as clerks, drivers, and sales personnel) while the establishment of a database would help degree and diploma holders, who make up 5 per cent of those registered with the labour office, in seeking jobs.[17]

Education and the appropriate type of training for the young continue to be a major concern for the policymakers. In a reversal of a decision taken two years earlier, the responsibility for the teaching of religious education, which had been transferred to the Ministry of Education, was returned to the Ministry of Religious Affairs. The Sultan also announced that the second university that he had mentioned the previous year would be an Islamic university. This university is currently in its planning stages. However, it was not clear whether it would be purely a theological-based centre or if it would incorporate various disciplines, for instance, engineering. In the mean time, the University of Brunei celebrated its twentieth anniversary in 2005.

Brunei continues to provide free medical and dental services to its citizens and public sector employees, but an announcement circulated to government staff reiterated that such services would only apply to government hospitals and not to the Jerudong Park Medical Center (JPMC) or the Gleneagles JPMC Cardiac Centre, which were considered private institutions even though the Brunei government was the joint owner.

The avian flu epidemic, though not found in Brunei or Borneo Island, has been given due attention by the health authorities. The potential of a global flu pandemic is a serious threat. Local experts have participated in national preparedness exercises and international meetings on the issue. A district hospital has been identified as the isolation centre if a bird flu outbreak occurs. The fact that the Crown Prince heads the national committee on that issue signifies the importance attached to it.[18]

In order to maintain its domestic peace and uphold its Islamic ideology, enforcement officers have continued their surveillance on social ills such as corruption, drug use and peddling, contraband smuggling, and illegal immigration. Those who overstay their visa or work illegally comprise the largest category of immigration offenders. They are usually fined, jailed, or deported. Most offenders appear to be from Bangladesh, India, Indonesia, and the Philippines, as reported in the media. A new legislation makes it an offence to hire an illegal worker. This addresses a finding that a number of small establishments hire cheap foreign labour without valid papers. It has also been disclosed that over the years the number of unlicensed businesses had risen to over 1,000. Relevant departments such as labour, land, and district offices as well as the town municipal board were taking measures to rectify this problem.

A measure of transparency and tolerance of civil society is also gradually appearing. The Sultan has also publicly acknowledged its appreciation of the activities of non-governmental organizations (NGOs) in their work in the community, especially those working with the poor and underprivileged. Although small in number, the NGOs fall into various categories. The ones most active are associated with the government or receive financial assistance from public authorities.

What was of some interest to the community was when a new political party appeared on the scene. It was registered in August 2005 as Parti Pembangunan Bangsa (National Development Party, or NDP). Several public meetings to explain its objectives (towards nation-building) were held, leading to the grand opening of its party headquarters three months later. It was significant that a member of the Brunei Privy Council was the guest of honour while the presence of about ten foreign envoys was also an unusual event.[19] The birth of the new party has also given a boost to the other two political parties, Parti Kesedaran Rakyat Brunei (PAKAR), and Parti Perpaduan Kebangsaan Brunei (National Unity Party, or PPKB). The latter is the more active of the two and is currently expanding its membership; the former has been split by internal disputes and is in the process of rebuilding itself.

The political parties have pledged their loyalty to the ruler and government and thus are not seen as detrimental to the state's monarchical system. In fact, the appearance of the NDP has attracted the visits of diplomats from the British, Canadian, and American embassies, something not publicly seen before. The media reported that the US Deputy Chief of Mission has also met the leaders of the PPKB and the Consumers Association of Brunei Darussalam, a consumer advocate that has generally kept a low profile. Two leaders from the PPKB attended the International Conference on the "Political Parties' Role for Prosperity and Democratization in ASEAN Countries" organized by Golkar (Golongan Karya) in Jakarta in November. It is probably the first time that a small party from Brunei (apparently with approval), interacted on the international podium with the likes of UMNO (United Malays National Organisation), PAP (People's Action Party), ANC (African National Congress), and CPC (Communist Party of China) among others. However, the PPKB's national role in the Brunei context is clearly quite different from that of the other political parties at the meet.[20] To maintain stricter control, a revised Societies Order came into effect in early 2005. Under its provisions all clubs and associations are required to register or face stiff penalty. To date there have been no reports of any violations.

One should not be under the impression that the state is softening its vigil against terrorism and deviant teachings of Islam. A former member of the banned Al-Arqam movement was freed after his rehabilitation. He had been arrested two years earlier after he had attempted to revive the religious movement banned in 1991 both in Malaysia (where it originated) and in Brunei.

As an Islamic country where most residents can afford the month-long haj pilgrimage to Mecca, the year was no different from previous occasions. About a thousand pilgrims left on the pilgrimage, preceded by a special audience with the Sultan and members of the royal family.[21]

Diplomacy and Security

Brunei continues its strong commitment to ASEAN and in its relations with neighbours. As always, priority is given to ASEAN cooperation in the political, economic, and socio-cultural areas. The 2005 ASEAN Summit in Kuala Lumpur also included a summit of the leaders of BIMP-EAGA, the growth area that Brunei is a member of. With AFTA already in place, and an EAGA road map set up, the government is hoping that the private sector, both national and regional, would get more involved in the trade and industrialization of the state. A number of local symposiums with the participation of foreign experts were held to explore the role of small and medium enterprises in BIMP-EAGA and ASEAN.

In international diplomacy, the United Nations, APEC, Organization of Islamic Conferences (OIC), and the Commonwealth saw the participation of Brunei's leaders in their annual summits. The Asia Africa Summit in Jakarta where more than 100 leaders met to commemorate the first meeting in 1955, and the G77's Second South Summit in Doha also saw the participation of the Sultan and the Foreign Minister as Brunei closely associates itself with the group.

At the bilateral level, close ties continued with its neighbours, especially with Singapore and Malaysia where official visits were undertaken. The Sultan was conferred the honorary doctorate of law by the National University of Singapore in recognition of his role in nurturing strong ties between the two countries. As part of the bilateral exchange with Malaysia, a working visit by Prime Minister Abdullah Ahmad Badawi explored new areas of cooperation, for example, in Islamic banking and insurance, while continuing the dialogue on resolving the long-standing disputes over the Brunei-Malaysia maritime boundaries.

Another significant state visitor was the Chinese President, Hu Jintao. Relations between Brunei and China, especially in the economic field, have been steadily increasing, aided by the ASEAN-China Free Trade Agreement. A joint statement issued during the visit predicted that with increased opportunities bilateral trade could reach US$1 billion by 2010.[22] Currently, trade between the two countries reached US$250 million, an increase of about 9 per cent from 2004.

In a visit to Russia, the Sultan and President Putin held discussions on expanding the currently negligible bilateral relations. Brunei does maintain a permanent mission in Moscow although there is no reciprocal presence in Bandar Seri Begawan. It was reported that President Putin invited Brunei to participate in the hydrocarbon industries in Siberia and the Far East.

The Sultan's official visit to Australia confirmed the two countries' cooperation not only in the economic spheres, but also in combating transnational crimes such as terrorism. The visit reinforced Australia as a growing partner in Brunei's education and trade sectors. By the end of 2005, bilateral trade had reached B$1 billion, with Brunei exporting about 21 per cent of its crude oil to Australia while importing mostly live animals and processed food. Meanwhile, Japan, another important partner, is in discussion with Brunei to establish an Economic Partnership Agreement. This was revealed during a meeting between the leaders of the two countries at the sidelines of the ASEAN Summit in Kuala Lumpur. Brunei is also actively pursuing its international political and economic interests. It has signed a multilateral free trade pact involving Singapore, New Zealand, and Chile.

Brunei is contributing its share to ensure regional stability through ASEAN cooperation in defence and security matters. Brunei's armed forces are participating in bilateral military exercises in order to acquire the necessary defence skills. For example, there was a joint exercise against maritime piracy between the Japan Coast Guard vessels and the Brunei Air Force and Marine Police. Another joint exercise was with the US navy under the Cooperation Afloat Readiness and Training (CARAT) exercise series. Personnel are also regularly sent to foreign venues such as Singapore, Malaysia, and the United Kingdom for training. Foreign forces wishing to train under tropical conditions have undertaken joint military exercises with their local counterparts, as was the case of the infantry regiment from New Zealand. Also, the police representatives attended the Interpol General Assembly in Berlin in September and the ASEAN Chiefs of Police Conference (Aseanpol) in Bali in May 2005.

Over the past year, Brunei has participated in two peace-monitoring missions. The first began in 2004, as part of the 64-man International Monitoring Team in Mindanao to observe the truce signed in 2002 between the Philippine government and the Moro Islamic Liberation Front (MILF). A 12-month tour of duty for the first group of eight army personnel ended in September 2005 and another group was sent to replace it. The second, the Aceh Monitoring Mission, comprised 20 armed forces and police personnel. The ASEAN Ministerial Meeting in Laos in July 2005 had agreed to the sending of monitors from Singapore, Malaysia, Thailand, the Philippines, and Brunei after the peace accord was signed. The Brunei team joined about 200 other observers from ASEAN and the European Union to monitor the peace deal between the Indonesian government and the Free Aceh Movement (GAM) signed in Helsinki in August 2005. These missions have been acknowledged as providing valuable experience to the Brunei personnel. Brunei has a small but well-integrated armed force of about 4,000 men and it continues to upgrade its resources. The foundation laying for the infrastructure for the Royal Brunei Land Forces' third battalion commenced in Kampong Lumut in August. The new battalion would strengthen the existing size of the armed forces.

Brunei has been a generous donor to international relief. The state and the people often contribute generously to disaster funds. The beginning of the year 2005 saw the establishment of the Tsunami Relief Fund that collected more than B$3 million by the end of July under the coordination of the Ministry of Culture, Youth, and Sports. The funds were designated mainly for Aceh, though some were for Sri Lanka and the Maldives. Various groups in Brunei, including the Indonesian Association, also organized additional collection of relief funds and supplies for Aceh. In addition, the Yayasan Sultan Haji Hassanal Bolkiah (a charity foundation) collected a large amount of donations and is in the process of rebuilding mosques, schools, and other infrastructure in Aceh. Soon after the tsunami, medical and relief personnel were sent to help in the relief operations. The Sultan visited areas in the Aceh province where a 50-strong Brunei military and civilian contingent was operating. This was the country's first experience in a global relief effort, gaining recognition from the World Health Organization (WHO) for the services it provided. The Brunei government had pledged B$6 million to all affected countries in Southeast and South Asia. Similarly, the northern Pakistan earthquake later in the year has also generated activities to collect donations by public and private organizations.

It has indeed been a busy year for Brunei Darussalam, with several celebrations, official ceremonies, national sport events such as the first international golf meet, the first Brunei marathon, and on a quiet level, the marriage of His Majesty Sultan Haji Hassanal Bolkiah to Yang Teramat Mulia Azrinaz Mazhar binti Hakim Mazhar of Malaysia.

Notes

[1] *Borneo Bulletin*, 1 September 2005.
[2] *Borneo Bulletin*, 25 May 2005.
[3] *Pelita Brunei*, 1 June 2005.
[4] Pehin Haji Hazahir bin Pehin Haji Abdullah; see *Borneo Bulletin*, 21 May 2004.
[5] *Pelita Brunei*, 5 October 2005.

6 *Borneo Bulletin*, 16 July 2005.
7 *Borneo Bulletin*, 18 August 2005.
8 *Brunei Economic Bulletin* 4, no. 2 (September 2005): 6–10.
9 *Borneo Bulletin*, 30 August 2005.
10 *Borneo Bulletin*, 2 December 2005.
11 *Borneo Bulletin*, 29 December 2005.
12 Brunei Darussalam, *Eighth National Development Plan 2002–2005*.
13 *Brunei Economic Bulletin* 4, no. 2 (September 2005): 12–14.
14 *Borneo Bulletin*, 4 November 2005.
15 *Borneo Bulletin*, 29 November 2005.
16 *Borneo Bulletin*, 1 January 2006.
17 *Borneo Bulletin*, 28 April 2005, 7 November 2005.
18 *Pelita Brunei*, 30 November 2005.
19 *Borneo Bulletin*, 2 December 2005.
20 *Borneo Bulletin*, 1 December 2005, 7 December 2005.
21 *Pelita Brunei*, 30 November 2005.
22 *Borneo Bulletin*, 22 April 2005.

Cambodia

CAMBODIA
Positioning for 2008

Verghese Mathews

There is truly never a dull day in Cambodia and 2005 was no exception. What started off as an uncertain year ended much better than expected, but only to subsequently witness renewed excitement and condemnation of the government for the detention of some high-profile political activists towards the end of the year and in early January 2006.

Truly, too, some things hardly ever change. In contemporary Cambodian politics any issue is fair game for both the opposition and the government — as one tries to make the country ungovernable while the other tries to make its adversary impotent. The country's friends and detractors alike assess the post-conflict Cambodian political culture as not having yet imbibed Western concepts of power sharing, loyal opposition, and open dissent.[1] Politicking, it would appear, is both in the blood and in the roots of the hairs of Cambodian politicians who practise it with great enthusiasm and blatant impunity.

The Economy in 2005

Interestingly enough, Cambodia has managed to record a fairly impressive economic growth rate the past few years. In 2005 the economy grew more than 6 per cent. While this was less than the 7 per cent of 2004, it exceeded World Bank projections three times over. The garment industry continued to spearhead growth, followed by the tourism and construction sectors.[2] Nonetheless, Cambodia remains one of the poorest countries in the world with a per capita income of only US$320.[3]

The growth was due, in no small measure, to increasingly prudent fiscal policies and to overall sustained political stability.[4] In this context, in late December 2005,

---

Verghese Mathews is Visiting Research Fellow at the Institute of Southeast Asian Studies and a former Singapore Ambassador to Cambodia.

the Royal Cambodian Government (RCG) was delighted with the announcement of the International Monetary Fund (IMF) that it would grant Phnom Penh a 100 per cent debt relief, amounting to approximately US$82 million — the amount that Cambodia had amassed before 1 January 2005.

The cherry on the cake of the announcement was the IMF observation that Cambodia, one of a handful of countries to be thus rewarded, had qualified for the debt relief because "of its overall satisfactory recent macroeconomic performance, progress in poverty reduction, and improvements in public expenditure management". The IMF further noted that since 1999 Cambodia had enjoyed robust economic expansion, with annual growth rates averaging over 7 per cent, inflation well under control, and improvements in its public administration — in particular, public expenditure management.[5]

While this was a rare and sweet vindication of Cambodian efforts in the last few years, the country still has other debts to worry about. When presenting the 2006 budget, Finance Minister Keat Chhon emphasized that despite the IMF relief, Cambodia still had great difficulties in repaying debts, accumulated since 1992, of US$500 million to the Asian Development Bank (ADB) and US$570 million to the World Bank. Meanwhile, Cambodia was negotiating with Russia and the United States over old debts owed to the two countries.[6]

Likewise, the well-regarded Director-General of the Finance Ministry, Hang Chuon Naron, a man with both his feet firmly on the ground, admitted that even though Cambodia had achieved high economic growth, the poverty levels had also remained high because growth had been very narrow, concentrated on the garments and tourism sectors.[7]

Both these warnings are a reminder that while there are undoubtedly ongoing attempts by both the RCG and the non-governmental organizations (NGOs) to reduce poverty levels in Cambodia, the harsh reality is that there is so much more to be done.

Donor Assistance

There is no doubt that Cambodia's progress in poverty reduction and improvements in infrastructure and education, however modest, was to a large extent because of the generous annual foreign aid, which the country continues to depend on. In 2005, donors pledged US$504 million in aid, raising the post-1993 total to over US$5 billion.[8]

In recent years, donor countries have become more insistent that in return for aid, Cambodia had to demonstrate adequate progress in the mutually agreed reform targets. At the 2005 meeting of the donor countries and the RCG, this message was clearly spelt out. As one observer noted, the World Bank "took its strongest stand to date in support of political reform in Cambodia, suggesting that future aid pledges be conditioned on improved governance". The next meeting is set tentatively for March 2006 at which donor scrutiny of the reform programme can be expected to prominently factor. Likewise, donors can be expected to raise the question of human rights, even though the recently jailed four activists have been released.

The RCG, conscious of heightened donor frustration at reform delays, has reiterated that donor concerns are taken seriously. However, the donor community is obviously no longer satisfied with just ministerial reassurances without concrete outcomes. Senior Cambodian officials readily recognize that the country cannot hope to accelerate economic growth nor enhance the lives of its people without donor aid for several more years to come. What is unsaid is that bread-and-butter issues increasingly factor in the elections, the next one being in 2008. A better informed and a more politically aware electorate is fast moving from voting for political personalities to voting for clear and tangible political programmes.

A senior RCG minister, soon after the 2003 elections, privately conceded that unlike in the previous elections he could no longer tell which party a voter would support — as voters now readily accepted gifts from all the parties! The minister was certain that by 2008 the electorate would be far more conscious of the power of the ballot.[9]

The Khmer Rouge Tribunal

In 2005 a much-welcomed forward movement in the long-awaited Khmer Rouge Tribunal took place despite the doubts and disappointments intermittently expressed by detractors that the whole exercise was a mere façade and that the RCG, supposedly pressured by China, had no real intentions of proceeding with the trial. In the past, the RCG would have ignored such allegation or merely scoffed at it. However, in recent times, partly because of the desire to project itself as a responsible regional player, both the RCG and the Cambodia People's Party (CPP) had taken to robustly rebutting the more outrageous allegations.

In that spirit the CPP saw it necessary for party president Chea Sim to publicly declare that the CPP unequivocally supported all efforts of the United Nations and the RCG "to jointly organize" the trial to seek justice for an estimated 1.8 million people who died of starvation, disease, forced labour, or execution during the three years, eight months, and twenty days of the Pol Pot regime. It is both interesting and significant that the CPP came out with such a firm stand on the proposed trial as it may be recalled that when the idea of the Tribunal re-surfaced in the Cambodian political arena around 2001, there was open talk in Phnom Penh of significant resistance both at the CPP leadership and grassroots levels. In particular there was much confusion at the grassroots level on the crucial question of who would be summoned for the trial. The issue was a serious enough problem for Hun Sen to address it during his various stops while criss-crossing the country from 2001 to 2003. At one such stop in Anglong Veng, at the opening ceremony of a new facility, he assured a large assembled group of ex-Khmer Rouge (KR) soldiers and their families that they would not be tried. "Don't go back to the jungle, you and your children belong here," he pleaded.

A senior civil servant subsequently explained to ambassadors who were present at the ceremony that many of the former KR soldiers had a "distorted view" about who would be brought to trial. Party strategists had therefore proposed that the only way to assure the unsettled ground was for Hun Sen to directly talk to them and for his speech to be broadcasted to other villages.[10]

Time and much persuasion were also needed to win over those in the party leadership who feared that the tribunal could impact on the fragile peace and the normality that was slowly returning to Cambodia. Then there were those who were finally reassured only when it was made clear that just six or seven of those "who were most responsible" for the atrocities would be tried. This prolonged internal negotiations unfortunately escaped some international officials and commentators who had, at one time or other, alleged that the RCG was deliberately delaying the process.

The march towards the KR Tribunal has come a long way since then. According to the latest UN report, "there has been substantial progress towards the establishment of Extraordinary Chambers for the Prosecution under Cambodian Law of Crimes Committed during the period of Democratic Kampuchea".[11] Both the RCG and the United Nations have named their respective coordinators, the venue for the tribunal has been agreed upon, and the process of selecting the international and local judges and prosecutors is almost completed. The only remaining logistical, though not insurmountable, problem is to secure the RCG share for financing the Tribunal.

The Tribunal is estimated to cost US$56.3 million over three years. The United Nations has raised its share of US$43 million while the RCG is yet to come up with the remaining US$13.3 million. In March 2005 the RCG announced that it could only manage to raise US$3 million in cash and services and sought international assistance for the remaining US$10 million. This has been slow in coming. India, an old ally of Cambodia, was the first to come forward in October with a US$1 million grant, while the European Commission (EC) followed suit in December with a US$1.2 million contribution under the European Initiative for Democracy and Human Rights (EIDHR). The EC funds will be disbursed via the United Nations Development Program (UNDP) as soon as the starting date of the Tribunal is officially announced.[12] Hun Sen, who insisted that the process could not be delayed any further, quickly overruled a suggestion by the Cambodian coordinator for the KR Tribunal that the start of the Tribunal depended on securing all the funds first.[13] This allayed the fears of the critics, many of whom were concerned that some of the potential candidates for trial may die well before the legal process starts.

Thus, there can be no doubt that any delay, given that hopes have now been raised, will be unacceptable both domestically and internationally.

A positive and much welcome spin-off of the Tribunal issue was that concerned donors, NGOs, and pressure groups succeeded in focusing local and international attention on the Cambodian judiciary and the need for urgent and comprehensive reforms in at least three key areas of the judicial system — corruption, competence, and independence. The December/January detention of the human rights activists generated strong criticism against the judiciary. More agitation can be expected if the names of the Cambodian judges and prosecutors, when announced, are considered unacceptable.

Meanwhile, two notorious KR leaders in detention are in poor health. There is genuine concern especially in the international community that they may die before appearing in court. The two are Ta Mok, former KR military chief who is now 78, and Kang Kek Ieu, who is better known to friends and enemies alike as Duch, 59, the head of the infamous Tuol Sleng interrogation and torture centre from where few emerged alive and where boy-soldiers acted as heartless interrogators. Outside of prison and living and moving freely are the infamous trio, "Brother Number Two" Nuon Chea, former head of state Khieu Samphan, and former Foreign Minister Ieng Sary, who are all expected to appear before the bench of international and Cambodian judges, towards the end of 2006. To date, no Khmer Rouge leader has yet faced trial for the atrocities they committed.[14]

There is greater expectation now that the long-awaited process of justice is, at last, about to take off even though there is no certainty that it will proceed as planned. Many Cambodians are too young to have had first-hand knowledge of the suffering under the Khmer Rouge but very few of them would not have had at least a relative who perished.

Youk Chhang, the dynamic head of the Documentation Center of Cambodia, which houses the world's largest collection of documents about the Pol Pot era, has consistently pointed out that the trial is not about the past, not about aged perpetrators, not about revenge or compensation for those who lost their lives but about the aftershocks of genocide, which still fracture the foundations of Cambodian society, family, community, health, and social well-being.[15]

There are different expectations but at the end of the day, the general hope is that the Tribunal, the first of its kind in Asia, will bring justice to the victims, a closure for the community, and a lesson for the future.

The Political Acrobatics

While in several areas Cambodia had done well in 2005, these were not what made the headlines. It was once again the never-ending political acrobatics that captured the centre-stage and preoccupied the local and international media. Over the last decade in particular, Cambodian politicians have raised debilitating politicking and disruptive one-upmanship into a fine art.

Notwithstanding the political gymnastics, there has been a gradual maturing of the political styles in the past year. The post-conflict "culture of violence" has decreased dramatically to the extent that violence is no longer an integral part of Cambodian political culture. The Cambodian elite has still a long way to go to achieve the central elements of the accepted norms of the Western democratic process, but there are perceptible steps in that direction.

Old-fashioned politicians who were rewarded for past services, for example, are being gradually replaced by more educated and competent young politicians, technocrats, and businessmen who are able to address complex challenges and relate equally well to the increasing numbers of potentially troublesome unemployed youths deserting the villages and moving to the cities and the towns.

This evolving change in the political party scene, slow as it may be, has gone largely unnoticed, as the major focus has been on the manoeuvres of the main players. Not surprisingly, despite the infusion of the new blood, the infighting and the factionalism of Cambodian politics continued unabated in 2005.

The main players have remained the same for years — the political parties, the monarchy, the civil society, and international groups. However, the political dynamics in 2005 have resulted in significant changes in the fortunes of the political players and their outreach to international sympathizers and allies.

By and large, it was not a good year for the opposition Sam Rainsy Party though it turned out to be much better than expected for the dominant CPP of Prime Minister Hun Sen and its coalition partner in government, the royalist FUNCINPEC (Front Uni National pour un Cambodge Indépendant, Neutre,

Pacifique, et Coopératif, or National United Front for an Independent, Neutral, Peaceful, and Cooperative Cambodia), headed by Prince Norodom Ranariddh.

Meanwhile, newly crowned King Norodom Sihamoni manifested a regal decorum and a quiet charm that quickly endeared him especially to the common folk, "the little people", as his father, ex-King Norodom Sihanouk, was wont fondly to refer to them. Unlike his father, Sihamoni clearly indicated from the very start that he would not directly involve himself in the political arena. He has kept his word and is becoming a rallying point for national unity and national reconciliation. This has, however, not prevented aggrieved and desperate parties seeking his direct intervention even on issues that are clearly beyond his constitutional prerogative. Still the Palace must be a lonely place for the reluctant king given the sometimes unfair demands by pressure groups to support one cause or another.

Looking back at 2005, King Sihamoni has undoubtedly emerged as the best-loved figure. Hun Sen is clearly the strongest of the leaders while Ranariddh has surprised his detractors as a deft survivor.[16] However, he has to be constantly on his toes to ensure his party's survival in the run-up to the 2008 elections.

Rainsy is indisputably the main loser. The downward slide of his fortunes was evident when the loose alliance between him and Ranariddh following the July 2003 elections crumbled. To some of Rainsy's critics, while he demonstrated charisma and passion in the electioneering period, he was found wanting in the post-election horse-trading.

The subsequent removal of his parliamentary immunity from prosecution in February weakened him further and this was compounded on 22 December when a Cambodian court found him guilty on two counts of criminal defamation and sentenced him in absentia to 18 months in prison for remarks he made against Hun Sen and Ranariddh. Rainsy, who has been in self-exile in Paris following the removal of his parliamentary immunity, refused to attend the trial.

Rainsy was alleged to have accused Hun Sen of being involved in a 1997 grenade attack on an opposition rally that resulted in 19 deaths. He was also alleged to have accused Ranariddh of having accepted substantial bribes from the CPP as an inducement for FUNCINPEC to join the government.

Rainsy has described the judicial decision "farcical" and repeated his allegation that the Cambodian courts were not independent, a contention that even some impartial observers have shared.

The US State Department expressed concern at what it called "the continuing deterioration of democratic principles such as free speech".[17] Likewise, Rainsy's friends overseas, including human rights organizations, have come out in strident support. Yet back home where the votes count, his glamour is gone and his party is steadily losing credibility.

While Rainsy's extended stay outside the country had presented unprecedented elbow room for other aspirants in his tightly run party, no clear alternative leader has emerged except for some muted but growing support for Kem Sokha, the human rights activist. With the latest court ruling, Rainsy's options have been further limited.

Rainsy, not one to sit idly by, quickly called for a pardon from the King, which if granted would enable him to return to public life in Phnom Penh. His friends and supporters, especially the anti–Hun Sen Cambodian diaspora in the United States and France, have picked up this call and have flooded Internet newsgroups with similar demands to the King. Rainsy realizes the precariousness of his situation as party leader unless some form of compromise is arrived at with Hun Sen. For the moment, Hun Sen is playing hardball — something that he excels in — and has publicly stated that there will be no pardon until Rainsy serves two-thirds of his jail term.

Some months ago, there was a similar flood of appeals by almost the same groups for the King not to sign a supplementary border agreement between Cambodia and Vietnam.[18] The young King was under tremendous pressure for weeks, even when it was clear to many that his hands were tied as a constitutional monarch. Sihamoni could have, as some had suggested then, chosen the easy way out and gone on a holiday, leaving it to the acting Head of State to sign the bill into law. In the event Sihamoni boldly chose to stay and signed the bill knowing that it would upset some people.

Once again, the pressure is building up — this time for Sihamoni to pardon Rainsy and others. Once again, the Cambodian elites play their strategic games around the King who maintains a regal silence on the issue and remains above the fracas.

The pressure was much less last year on Hun Sen. At the 24 November annual CPP congress, he was named the undisputed prime-ministerial candidate in the 2008 election,[19] a far cry from the situation before the 2003 election when rumours of disquiet in the party leadership was rife and the confirmation was not so readily forthcoming until much nearer the polling date. To prevent a repeat of this situation from happening, many analysts observed that Hun Sen moved to enlarge the membership of the CPP Central Committee, from 153 to 268 members, and stacked it with many of his men.[20]

Hun Sen is clearly in charge, and this is not at all surprising given that he has done well both as a clear-minded and resolute Prime Minister and as a party strategist. However, the toughness he sometimes exhibits has not endeared him to some sections of the public, especially liberal groups and human rights activists at home and abroad. There are others, though, who counter that at this stage of the country's development, "properly managed toughness" can be persuasive.

Ranariddh was undoubtedly the luckiest in 2005 among the three main political players, considering the fact that in the last decade his party's fortunes had gone from bad to worse and many had written the party off after the 2003 election. His joining the government as a coalition partner presented him a much-needed lifeline and he knows it. The subsequent warming-up of personal relations between him and Hun Sen, though it has yet to percolate all the way down to the provincial structures, had been a great boost for FUNCINPEC and generally beneficial for the country.

The Arrests of Four Activists[21]

Towards the end of the year, the RCG came under severe criticism for the arrests of several activists on charges of criminal defamation. The arrests, widely seen as unwarranted, impacted differently on different players and presented the opposition an opportunity on a silver platter to fan ground unhappiness against the RCG.

Due to the arrests, the government was condemned for undermining free expression, returning to enhanced authoritarianism, the blatant misuse of the courts to stifle criticism, and of going down the "Myanmar way". The irony, though, is that there is perhaps much more free expression in Cambodia than in many other countries, both developing and developed alike. In fact, it has become part of the evolving Cambodian political culture to roundly, and often unfairly, criticize both the government and the opposition in the partisan media. The question that naturally arises is why the government, which had hitherto tolerated criticisms, should now over-react?

There are probably several reasons why the government reacted this way, but two are the most critical — first, the reaction to the signing in October 2005 of a Supplementary Border Agreement with Vietnam and second, the perceived direct involvement of foreign-influenced NGOs in Cambodia's internal affairs.

The earlier border agreements between Cambodia and Vietnam were concluded during the decade when Cambodia was under Vietnamese occupation. These agreements remain highly controversial and emotive, as a significant number of Cambodians believe that the agreements overly favoured the occupying force. Former King Norodom Sihanouk, for example, never recognized those treaties and had even openly accused Vietnam of encroaching into Cambodian territory.

Reportedly, Sihanouk stated that "the Cambodian border markers had grown legs and that they were marching inwards", a now famous quote in relation to the issue.

Government critics fear that the Supplementary Border Agreement was a highly creative back-door attempt by the two governments to legitimize the earlier unacceptable "occupation" agreements. The government's assurances that Cambodia would not lose any territory with the signing of the supplementary agreement failed to persuade the detractors.

The CPP knew it was taking a calculated risk in proceeding with the signing of the agreement, knowing well that anti-Vietnamese feelings could be easily aroused. Moreover, there was no doubt that the opposition had the capacity to rally crowds to the streets given such a touchy issue at hand. Hun Sen opted for tough action, some say with the nudging from Vietnam, to ensure that there wasn't a groundswell against him, the party, or the RCG. An especially sensitive contention was that Hun Sen and the CPP had sold Cambodian territory to the Vietnamese. Hun Sen warned in unambiguous terms that he would sue anyone who made such allegations. A regional magazine quoted him as saying that anyone who "spoke out against the agreement with Vietnam would be committing an act of treason and would be arrested for defamation".[22] In addition, government spokesman and Information Minister Khieu Kanharith said on record that the CPP "would be committing political suicide" if it allowed such incendiary charges to circulate unchallenged. An Amnesty International official aptly commented that there was "perhaps no more sensitive charge for a Cambodian leader than to be 'soft on Vietnam'. This has the potential to unite not only the opposition, but to create dissent in his own ranks. That's why he is overreacting now".[23]

This brings to us to the second reason for the alleged over-reaction. In the last few years the RCG had been monitoring with increasing concern the activities of certain civil society groups, in particular the US-based International Republican Institute (IRI) and the call of some of its supporters for regime change in Cambodia.

Sources in Phnom Penh have confided that the IRI, which initially focused on strengthening democratic institutions and providing training to officials, had increasingly taken on funding to establish entities or strengthen existing organizations that were critical of the RCG and the CPP. There are several examples, though the most prominent one was Kem Sokha's Cambodian Centre for Human Rights.

The IRI's alleged direct involvement with local political and activist groups critical of the RCG was understandably not looked upon with any official favour.

Moreover, critics have claimed that the IRI, in its attempts to "democratize" Cambodia, had in particular steadfastly championed the Sam Rainsy Party (SRP) and had been generous with funding and technical assistance for pro-SRP organizations.

Another example is "The Voice of Radio 93.5 FM", which began in 2003 as a local station operating using cannibalized parts of karaoke equipment. It since expanded beyond its owner Ke Sun Kea's wildest dreams. The *Cambodia Daily* reported that with more than US$100,000 in USAID and IRI grants, the station now has the infrastructure to become a leader in the country's independent media. More importantly, the station has begun to carry the "Voice of Democracy", the human rights programme produced by Kem Sokha's Cambodian Center for Human Rights, which had been denied its own frequency by the Ministry of Information. In this situation, the IRI outwitted the Ministry.

IRI resident programme director Alex Sutton hoped that IRI's funding and expertise would help Radio 93.5 reach out to a new segment of the population. "It's very common when you go out to the villages to see that one radio is shared by many people. So the target audience is often a group of 20 people gathered around their radios", Sutton explained.[24]

Given the potent combination of the perceived external support for opposition forces and the domestic unhappiness over the signing of the treaty and the earlier calls for regime change, the security agencies quickly recognized the capacity of its detractors to rabble rouse in the country. The RCG opted for pre-emptive strikes to nip any problem in the bud and quickly detained four influential activists: radio journalist Mom Sonando, union leader Rong Chhun, and human rights activists Kem Sokha and Pa Nguon Tieng.

The much-publicized arrests began with that of Mom Sonando, Director of the popular Beehive Radio on 11 October on charges of defamation and incitement related to an interview he had conducted three weeks earlier with Sean Pengse, a former Cambodian cabinet minister and presently director of the Paris-based Committee on Border Issues. Sean argued a case against Cambodia signing the controversial Supplementary Boarder Treaty. He described as "absurd" the RCG's assertion that Cambodia had not lost any territory to Vietnam under the treaty. In this context, Sean Peangse had mentioned in several interviews that the best way to resolve the border problem was to reject the treaties signed during the Vietnamese occupation and to commence new border negotiations based on legitimate documents and maps deposited at the United Nations and elsewhere.

Similarly, in an a VOA interview Sean insisted that Hun Sen "very well knew" that the border agreements in question with Vietnam were illegal under the Paris

Peace Accords and that all those treaties should be cancelled. Both Beehive and Sean have been thorns on the government's side for quite a while and given the sensitivity of the border issue the two were seen by security officials and party strategists as a dangerous combination.[25]

Mom Sonando's arrest immediately triggered off alarm bells in Western capitals and among liberal groups. The RCG was obviously not overly perturbed by the international reaction or at least gave that impression as, on his return to Phnom Penh from Hanoi after the signing ceremony, Hun Sen publicly threatened to sue anyone who accused him of selling Cambodian territory.

On 31 December one of Cambodia's most prominent human rights activists, Kem Sokha, leader of the US-funded Cambodian Center for Human Rights, was arrested. He was charged with criminal defamation stemming from a banner displayed at a rally on 10 December to mark International Human Rights Day. The banner referred to Hun Sen as "a communist dictator who sold away [Cambodian] land to Vietnam".[26]

Kem Sokha has the reputation of being a very affable person and not one given to theatricals. Some see him as a future leader of the Sam Rainsy Party. They believe that should he take over the party, he would be more willing to work with the government and that there would be a further maturing of the Cambodian political process.[27]

The government certainly succeeded in the short term with its tough approach, realizing all the while that its actions were bound to incur universal condemnation. It was willing to take the risk and in the process cleverly shifted the focus of unhappiness from the domestically sensitive and controversial border treaty to the domestically less potent human rights issues.

The RCG, nevertheless, stoutly defended its difficult position on the basis that it had followed due process, that there was sufficient evidence of defamation, and that it would have been an abrogation of its duty if it failed to prosecute those guilty of such serious crime. Officials also took pains to point out that defamation as a criminal offence was not of the RCG's making but a legacy no less than that of the United Nations Transitional Authority, which prepared Cambodia for the 1993 elections following the Paris Peace Agreement of 1991. However, critics were not impressed and have countered, "it was a law for exceptional circumstances that should have been replaced by now".[28]

It was during this period of increased tension that Hun Sen declared on 24 January 2006 that he had reached a compromise with four of the activists, who had earlier been released on bail from prison, and that he would drop criminal defamation suits against them. Hun Sen explained that the four activists had written him letters apologizing for their defamatory comments. The media ascribed the RCG move to "a change of heart that came amid mounting pressure at home and abroad". Yet, only two days earlier Hun Sen had insisted that he had absolutely no intention of withdrawing the charges against the four.[29]

To local analysts there was no "change of heart" — it was merely another phase of a strategy in progress. A noted opposition politician commented privately that the compromise reached between the prime minister and the activists was, "by and large, a stroke of genius from a number of perspectives. All lawsuits initiated by the prime minister have been dropped after the human rights and democracy activists issued statement of gratitude, clarification, and regrets."[30]

Hun Sen's subsequent strategy of dropping the charges against the four has earned him some domestic goodwill but more importantly brought tensions down several notches. Meanwhile, those who had predicted the demise of democracy and of Cambodia going the Myanmar way, while this is arguably not impossible, may have themselves over-reacted this time.

As for the four high-profile activists, the opposition commentator mentioned earlier argued that should they be so inclined, the current ease of tension would give them the opportunity to regroup, "and possibly, embark upon a political defiance strategy that is well planned to enrich democracy and human rights in Cambodia".

Continuing Challenges

As the year 2005 ended, the varied and complex challenges Cambodia faced a decade ago still remained — the major ones being the need to further strengthen democratic institutions and to ensure that good governance is firmly rooted in the country. This calls, in particular, for a determined and comprehensive attempt at curbing corruption and dismantling the deeply entrenched patronage system.

On the issue of corruption, it continues to be a matter of grave regret that an anti-corruption law drafted in 1994 is stuck on the drawing board. While it will, no doubt, take a long time for tangible results to emerge in the fight against corruption and cronyism, the RCG has little excuse now for not tabling the Anti-Corruption Bill in 2006. Many agencies and donor countries have either publicly or privately called for the tabling of the Bill. One example will suffice. The European Parliament in November 2005 called on Cambodia "to engage in political and institutional reforms to build a democratic state government by a rule of law", "to combat effectively the endemic scourges of corruption", and "to refuse the current culture of impunity".[31]

The EC demands will definitely be a factor when the donor countries meet Hun Sen and his government in 2006 but are unlikely to overshadow the discussions on the reform agenda. A senior government official was privately delighted at the news of the release of the activists and the dropping of the charges against them as the donor meeting could focus on substantive economic and reform issues. More importantly, he said, the government had much to report to the donors about the progress it had achieved during 2005.

Another issue that NGOs and international organizations have brought to the attention of the donor community is the increasing number of instances of large-scale land grabbing by powerful people. Interestingly, Hun Sen warned that a "revolution" could erupt among rural Cambodians if the practice did not cease.[32] There is also the issue of a growing number of youths from the rural areas and from the smaller towns moving to the cities in search of jobs.

These are but some of the many issues the RCG will have to adequately and expeditiously address in 2006.

Cambodia is midway between the last elections in 2003 and the next in 2008 — a point not lost on the three major parties when they held their annual congresses in the last quarter of 2005. Political parties took stock of their respective chances for what many believe will be a watershed election. Sam Rainsy, who was not present for his party's congress in Phnom Penh, later met about 30 of his leaders in Manila in November to discuss election plans and party reforms.[33]

The CPP, more than the other two parties, has been working the ground. The party has little fear of 2008. However, it will need to enhance the livelihood of the rural people, who form the backbone of its support, to retain its present edge over the two other parties. Nevertheless, the realistic consensus in the party leadership is that it would again be unlikely to gain a two-thirds majority in the polls to form the government by itself. Thus, it would again need a coalition partner in 2008. The CPP's preference so far has been to continue its coalition with FUNCINPEC as it considers the Sam Rainsy Party both unreliable and difficult to negotiate with. In addition, personal chemistry at the leadership level is also lacking. However, nothing is cast in stone and the coalition partners in 2008 could be either FUNCINPEC or SRP or, maybe even both.

In this context it must be pointed out that the CPP plans well ahead and during 2005 some of its moves were calculated to bolster FUNCINPEC's sagging position and to give Ranariddh the time to consolidate his own position, renew the party and prepare for the elections. It has been privately argued by CPP insiders that one major motivation for the CPP campaign against Sam Rainsy was precisely to help FUNCINPEC.

As for Sam Rainsy, the latest arrests have further whittled away at his domestic political standing — as the four activists were seen to have earned their colours by going to jail for their beliefs whereas Sam Rainsy had opted to remain safely overseas. In addition, there is a strong prevailing view that Sam Rainsy will not be bundled to jail should he return to the country as that would not only be unacceptable but also counter-productive for the CPP. Rainsy will have to face trial, though, for the defamation charges like the four activists. But then, some compromise can always be worked out.

Hun Sen is stronger now than he has ever been before. Today he is also the longest-serving prime minister in ASEAN. In the past few years he has gained confidence and stature as a leader. Now that there are no visible challenges at home, he appears to be inclined to spend more time on regional issues and to be recognized as a regional player. Insiders suggest that Hun Sen is ready to shed the public image of a tough-speaking, tough-acting, no-nonsense prime minister given to bouts of uncontrolled temper. They predict a new public persona, which they claim is the Hun Sen they know, emerging in the coming months.

There is also concern within the RCG that despite all its efforts and some significant success in several fields, Cambodia continues to get a bad press. 2005 was no exception as it did not succeed "to alter the image that Cambodia has acquired as a country where the rule of law means little when the interests of the government are involved; and as a country where the rich are powerful and the powerful are rich".[34] Nevertheless, officials, many of whom believe that the international media unfairly continues to be either unkind or biased, see the need for Cambodia to have a softer public image and are looking at ways to achieve this.

A silver lining for Cambodia is Hun Sen's capacity to attract and surround himself with competent young technocrats — people who could have easily obtained lucrative jobs in the private sector or stayed in their well-paying comfortable jobs overseas. There are now several such technocrats who are dedicated to advancing the interests of the country and the well-being of the people. Hun Sen has protected these people from the claws of vested interests and given them increasing responsibilities. It is now for Hun Sen to focus on and to promote this younger generation of technocrats and politicians to leadership levels so that they may address the increasingly complex challenges facing the country. If anyone can bring about this change, Hun Sen can — and Cambodia will emerge the winner.

Notes

1. Ronald Bruce St John, "Cambodia's Failing Democracy", *Foreign Policy in Focus*, 23 January 2006.
2. Lee Berthiaume, "For Cambodia, a Year of Hope and Controversy", *Cambodia Daily*, 29 December 2006.
3. David R. Sands, "Cambodia Human Rights Progress Slips", *Washington Times*, 13 January 2006.
4. National Poverty Reduction Strategy Progress Report, Cambodia, 25 July 2005.
5. "IMF to Extend 100 Percent Debt Relief to Cambodia", *IMF Press Release*, 22 December 2005.
6. Vong Sokheng, "Debt Burden Clouds the Silver Lining", *Phnom Penh Post*, 30 December 2005.
7. Ibid.
8. Ronald Bruce St John, "Cambodia's Failing Democracy", *Foreign Policy in Focus*, 23 January 2006.
9. Private conversation with the author in Phnom Penh in July 2003.
10. The writer was present when the senior official briefed the ambassadors.
11. Report of the Secretary-General on Khmer Rouge trials, A/60/565, 25 November 2006.
12. "Europe Pledges $1.2 Million for KR Tribunal", *Cambodia Daily*, 29 December 2005.
13. Yun Samean, "Soldiers Make Way for KR Tribunal Force", *Cambodia Daily*, 20 December 2005.
14. "Khmer Rouge Trials Move a Big Step Closer", Reuters, 9 December 2005.
15. Comments by Youk Chhang in an e-mail to the writer.
16. Observers of Cambodian politics considered FUNCINPEC, Ranariddh's political party, a political "has been" because it was badly factionalized and thus performed poorly in the 2003 elections. However, the coalition with Hun Sen's CPP breathed a new lease of life to the party.
17. Statement by Sean McCormack, Spokesman, Department of State, 23 December 2005, http://www.allamericanpatriots.com.
18. There is a wide spectrum of people who are against the border agreement, such as SRP members, some royalists, the Cambodian diaspora overseas, many of whom are anti–Hun Sen. Still others are plain anti-Vietnamese.
19. "Cambodian Ruling Party to Strengthen Cooperation with FUNCINPEC", *People's Daily Online* (Beijing), 25 November 2005.
20. Vong Sokheng, "Governing Parties Cement Their Reign", *Phnom Penh Post*, 2 December 2005.
21. An earlier version of this section was published at the *New Straits Times*, 8 February 2006.

[22] Nathaniel Myers, "Hun Sen Undermines Cambodia's Stability", *Far Eastern Economic Review*, January/February 2006.
[23] "Cambodia Human Rights Progress Slips", *Washington Times*, 13 January 2006.
[24] Samantha Melamed, "Independent Radio Station Makes Waves with Aid", *Cambodia Daily*, 23 December 2005.
[25] Reasey Poch, "Sean Pengse Discusses Cambodian Border Issues", *Hello VOA*, 20 October 2005.
[26] Kem Sokha's lawyer, quoted in "Government Detains Human Rights Activist", *Los Angeles Times*, 1 January 2006.
[27] Conversation with senior Cambodian government official in Singapore in January 2006.
[28] Guy De Launey, "Cambodia Clamps Down on Dissent", BBC (British Broadcasting Corporation), 7 January 2006.
[29] Sopheng Cheang, "Cambodian Leader to Drop Defamation Suits", Associated Press, 24 January 2006.
[30] Limited Circulation Private Note, 25i06, dated 25 January 2006.
[31] European Parliament resolution on the human rights situation in Cambodia, Laos, and Vietnam (P6_TA-PROV(2005)0462), 1 December 2005, http://www.llamericanpatriots.com.
[32] "Cambodian PM Warns Land Seizures Could Spark 'Revolution'", *ABC Radio Australia*, 8 December 2005.
[33] Ethan Plaut, "Sam Rainsy, SRP Members Meeting in Manila", *Cambodia Daily*, 16 November 2006.
[34] Milton Osborne, "Plus ca Change", *Asian Analysis*, October 2005.

Indonesia

Indonesia

INDONESIA
Accomplishments Amidst Challenges

Irman G. Lanti

For Indonesia 2005 was marked by a number of achievements, especially in politics and security. The experiment with democracy that had been initiated with the fall of Soeharto in 1998 seemed to be stabilizing, albeit perhaps temporarily. The direct regional elections were by and large successful in electing governors, mayors, and district heads. The government of Susilo Bambang Yudhoyono (SBY) and Jusuf Kalla enjoyed some degree of success in dealing with the restive provinces, most notably Aceh. The tsunami disaster that struck the province on 26 December 2004 provided the impetus for peace talks between the rebel group GAM (Gerakan Aceh Merdeka, or Free Aceh Movement) and the Indonesian government. In foreign policy, strategic partnership agreements were signed with China and India, the two rising powers in the world. Jakarta was also successful in lobbying the US government to lift the arms embargo that had been put in place after the riots following East Timor's referendum in 2000. The death of terrorist leader Dr Azahari and the subsequent capture of members of the domestic terror cell network were the highlights of the fight against terrorism in Indonesia. The country's law enforcement agencies also made significant advances in the fight against corruption, one of Indonesia's foremost woes.

Despite these successes, the country still faced a number of tribulations, especially in the economic domain. The sky-rocketing of oil prices on the world market pushed the government to slash the subsidy for petroleum in the domestic market. This move created significant pressure on the population, and sharply reduced the popularity of Yudhoyono's administration. Additionally, in spite of the serious drive by the government to reduce corruption and bureaucratic red

---

IRMAN G. LANTI is a Member of the Board of Advisers of The Indonesian Institute; a member of the Board of Directors, Center for Information and Development Studies (CIDES); and Senior Fellow at the Habibie Centre, Jakarta.

tape, foreign investors were still shying away from Indonesia, citing a lack of legal clarity and predictability as the reason.

On the whole, 2005 will be marked in Indonesia's history as the year of positive accomplishments, raised expectations, and continued challenges. While the country stabilized significantly compared with the previous few years and the foundations for better development seemed to be in place, many things that would define the future of the nation still remained in doubt.

The Tsunami and Peace in Aceh

The tsunami disaster that struck Aceh and Nias on 26 December 2004 caused tremendous destruction and human loss. Table 1 lists the extent of the devastation.

The tsunami also destroyed the capacity of the local government, especially in the subdistrict (*kecamatan*) and village (*gampong*) levels. Many local government officials either perished in or were severely traumatized by the disaster. The diminished capacity of the local government hampered the rehabilitation and reconstruction programmes in Aceh.[1] The central government, therefore, commissioned a special body to oversee and manage reconstruction in Aceh. The BRR (Badan Rehabilitasi dan Rekonstruksi Aceh dan Nias, or Aceh and Nias Rehabilitation and Reconstruction Agency) was established on 16 April 2005, and chaired by a former minister, Dr Kuntoro Mangkusubroto. The BRR coordinates the reconstruction effort funded by 15 donor nations to the tune of US$525 million, and also assists the Asian Development Bank in implementing its US$300 million programmes. In addition, various aid agencies and non-governmental organizations (NGOs) also have programmes in Aceh and Nias.

However, there were many complaints that the progress in the disaster areas was very slow. According to BRR's own account, a year after the disaster only around 16,200 new houses were completed. 50,000 displaced persons were still temporarily lodged in barracks, while a greater number (67,500) were still living in tents. Critics said that the aid for Aceh, organized just like other aid programmes in other parts of the world, did not use enough local components and knowledge. Aid agencies did not have sufficient knowledge of the psychological and sociological texture of the Acehnese, who have been tormented by a decade-long conflict. Some even suspected that aid agencies spent a lot of money paying consultants, and foreign ones at that.[2]

Aceh has traditionally been one of the restive provinces of Indonesia. Armed secessionist rebellion took root in Aceh from 1976. The Indonesian government has traditionally taken a heavy-handed approach to suppress the rebellion. The

TABLE 1
The tsunami and post-tsunami damage in Aceh and Nias

Sector	Damage
People	• 167,000 dead or missing as a result of the tsunami • 500,000 displaced from homes in Aceh • 900 dead from the March earthquake and 13,500 families displaced from their homes in Nias
Housing	• 80,000–110,000 new houses needed • About 50,000 housed in barracks; • About 67,500 remain in tents
Infrastructure	• 3,000 km. of roads impassable • 14 of 19 seaports badly damaged • 8 of 10 airports damaged • 120 arterial bridges and 1,500 minor bridges destroyed
Education	• More than 2,000 school buildings damaged • Approximately 2,500 teachers died
Health	• More than eight hospitals damaged or destroyed • 114 health centres and sub-centres damaged or destroyed
Economy	• US$1.2 billion damage to the productive sector • Projected economic decline of 5 per cent in Aceh, 20 per cent in Nias
Fisheries	• 4,717 coastal fishing boats lost • 20,000 hectares of fish ponds destroyed or were not functioning
Agriculture	• 60,000 farmers displaced • Over 60,000 hectares of agricultural land damaged
Enterprise	• 100,000 small business persons lost their livelihoods

Source: *Aceh and Nias One Year After the Tsunami: The Recovery Effort and Way Forward* (BRR Publication, December 2005), table 1, p. 5.

introduction of DOM (Daerah Operasi Militer, or Military Operation Zone) in Aceh had increased the resentment of the local population towards Indonesian rule.[3] The fall of Soeharto changed the government's approach. DOM was scrapped in August 1998, three months after Soeharto stepped down. However, the violence continued. Sensing an opportunity, GAM stepped up armed action. The government then responded with a Military Emergency in late 2003, followed by a Civil Emergency, which lasted until May 2005. Some efforts were made to solve the conflict, such as the Humanitarian Pause Agreement in 2000 and Cessation of

Hostility Act (CoHA) in 2003, but all had come to naught; and the conflict had intensified by the day.

Ironically, it took no less than a demonstration of tremendous human suffering after the tsunami disaster to get the contending parties back to the negotiating table. The tsunami provided the rude awakening to the need to find a solution to the Aceh conflict. The signing of a memorandum of understanding (MOU) in Helsinki between the Indonesian government and the rebel GAM on 15 August 2005 marked a historic milestone in the elusive quest for peace in Aceh.

The signing of the peace agreement was preceded by five rounds of peace talks after the tsunami disaster. They were held in Helsinki under the auspices of the Crisis Management Initiative, an NGO led by former Finnish president Martti Ahtisari. The negotiations in each of the five rounds were very tough, as both GAM and the Indonesian government held on to their respective demands.

Among the points of agreement were: (a) GAM would give up the demand for independence and cease its armed struggle; (b) in return, the Indonesian government would provide a general amnesty to all GAM combatants, and an avenue for GAM members to participate in local politics in Aceh. Additionally, the Indonesian government also reconfirmed that it would not revoke the special autonomy status that had been enjoyed by the Acehnese for four years.

But the signing of the agreement does not necessarily guarantee peace in Aceh. There are still many potential obstacles. The Helsinki rounds of peace talks have generated wide controversy in Indonesia. Those who oppose the talks say that the government is giving GAM too many concessions. The hardliners in the TNI (Indonesian military) and in the parliament argue that by talking to rebel leaders based in Sweden, who had renounced Indonesian citizenship, and by holding the talks outside of Indonesia, the government risked "internationalizing" the Aceh question. Some of these hawks even see a resemblance between the inclusion of international observers from the European Union and ASEAN and the involvement of the international community in the East Timor referendum in 1999, which they still see as a "loss" to Indonesia.

The other point of controversy is GAM's request for its members to be allowed full participation in the politics and governance of Aceh. The general amnesty will allow GAM members to vote and run as candidates for governor, district heads, mayors, as well as members of local parliaments. GAM had insisted on being allowed to transform itself into a local political party, which would field candidates for local elections. But the law on political parties in Indonesia only allows parties that are nationally based. The 24 parties that contested in the

2004 Indonesian election have their national headquarters in Jakarta, and were represented in at least two-thirds of Indonesia's 33 provinces and around 400 districts and municipalities. With its local character, GAM will probably only have appeal in Aceh.

Indonesians are divided on this issue. Those who are for peace at any cost suggest that there should be an exception to the Aceh case. Local parties should be allowed only in Aceh. Those who are opposed see the opening of a "Pandora's box". They fear that the consent for GAM to transform into a local party will inspire other separatist-minded groups, especially in other trouble-spots in Indonesia such as in Maluku and Papua, to pursue a similar path. There is also a suspicion that GAM will use the local party as a platform to launch the separatist agenda through the ballot box. There are others who prefer to take a middle approach by allowing GAM members to stand as independent candidates in local elections, but not allowing them to organize themselves in a local political party.

By the close of 2005, both sides had followed up faithfully on the dictates of the peace agreement. GAM had surrendered 1,018 weapons to the Aceh Monitoring Mission (AMM), a joint mission established by the European Union and five ASEAN member countries to monitor the implementation of the peace agreement. The TNI responded by redeploying some 30,000 of non-organic troops (troops from units that are normally based outside Aceh) stationed in Aceh. However, given the great potential for failure arising from possible actions from both sides, peace in Aceh remains precarious.

Regional Direct Elections: Democratic Consolidation or Experiment?

In politics, Indonesia completed the full circle of electoral reform in 2005. Following the direct presidential elections in 2004, and the creation of the non-political party DPD (Dewan Perwakilan Daerah, or Council of Regional Representatives), in 2005 voters all over the country cast their votes in a massive series of regional elections to elect governors, *bupati* (district heads), and mayors. 226 regional elections were held in 2005, of which a whopping 190 were held in the month of June alone. These elections marked a clear break from the past system in which regional chiefs were elected by local parliaments. During Soeharto's New Order era, the election by local parliaments was often regarded as a mere formality, as the central government always decided who it wanted to install as governors, *bupati*, or mayors. But now all political appointments were going to be decided through popular elections.

The *pilkada* (*pemilihan kepala daerah langsung*, or "direct regional chiefs elections"), as it is known in the Indonesian language, achieved mixed results. Accusations of money politics and vote-rigging were plenty. There were some riots, mostly instigated by disgruntled defeated candidates.[4] But most of *pilkada* took place peacefully and successfully and resulted in a smooth power transition.

Three significant observations can be made on *pilkada* which have implications for the future of Indonesian democracy. First, political party machineries did not function effectively. Some candidates nominated by parties that won in the 2004 parliamentary elections came out as losers in the *pilkada*. The case of West Sumatra gubernatorial election is probably the most indicative of this trend. Table 2 lists the candidates in West Sumatra in the 27 June 2005 elections, their nominating parties, the percentage of votes received in the legislative election a year before and the percentage of votes received by the gubernatorial candidates.

It is apparent from the table that the achievement of political parties in the legislative election did not match the performance of their candidates in *pilkada*. Gamawan Fauzi, the candidate nominated by the PDI-P (Partai Demokrasi Indonesia–Perjuangan, or Indonesian Democratic Party–Struggle), which among the major parties won the smallest number of votes in the parliamentary elections, won overwhelmingly in the *pilkada*, while Leonardy Harmainy, the candidate nominated by Golkar, which won the largest number of votes in the parliamentary elections, lagged far behind the other candidates.

Second, by extension of the first observation, individual candidates mattered more than their political party affiliations. Again, the case of West Sumatra gubernatorial election was the most telling in this respect. Gamawan Fauzi was a seasoned local bureaucrat, who while in office as the *bupati* of one of the districts in West Sumatra was known for being clean, honest, and professional. The other candidates were either local politicians whose credentials were hardly known or Jakarta-based politicians or businesspersons whose roots and support bases in the province were questionable.

Third, *pilkada* had produced pragmatism and moderation among political parties. The coalition pattern showed inconsistency across hundreds of *pilkada* cases. There were no fixed coalition partners among certain parties. Coalition partners at the national parliamentary level were not relevant at the local level. The West Sumatra case also demonstrated this inconsistency. At the national level, the PDI-P stood in opposition to the SBY administration, while the PBB (Partai Bulan Bintang, or Crescent Star Party) was one of the three parties that nominated SBY during the presidential election. But in the West Sumatra *pilkada*,

TABLE 2
Results of gubernatorial elections in West Sumatra

Pairs of Candidates (for Governor and Vice Governor)	Nominating Parties	Nominating Parties' Percentage of Votes in Legislative Election of 2004	Candidates' Percentage of Votes in *Pilkada*
Gamawan Fauzi & Marlis Rahman	PDI-P, PBB	9.57	41.50
Irwan Prayitno & Ikasuma Hamid	PKS, PBR	15.86	24.50
Jeffrie Geovanie & Dasman Lanin	Coalition of 16 parties, PAN	29.14	16.06
Leonardy Harmainy & Rusdi Lubis	Golkar	28.72	10.27
Kapitra Ampera & Dalimi Abdullah	PPP, PD	16.71	7.67

Source: Results compiled from the website of the KPU (Komisi Pemilihan Umum, or General Elections Commission): http://www.kpu.go.id/suara/dprkursi.php?fprop=13&fpml=1 and http://kpu.go.id/suara/dprkursi.php?fprop=13&fpml=2, and the website of an election watch organized by the National Democratic Institute (NDI): http://www.jurdil.org/pilkada05/Content%20Hasil%20PILKADA%20%202005%20%20(by%20date).pdf.

both parties joined hands in nominating Gamawan Fauzi. Likewise, the PKS (Partai Keadilan Sejahtera, or Prosperous Justice Party) supported SBY's government in the national parliament, while the PBR (Partai Bintang Reformasi, or Reform Star Party) supported Megawati during the presidential election. But both coalesced in nominating Irwan Prayitno in West Sumatra's *pilkada*. The inconsistency was also apparent in the lack of a discernible pattern in the coalitions along ideological lines. Nationalist parties were having coalitions with the Muslim parties in nominating candidates. Muslim parties were also coalescing with the nationalist and in some cases, even with Christian-based parties.

The lack of a visible coalition pattern in *pilkada* may be beneficial for Indonesian democracy. In the democratic setting in the 1950s and after *Reformasi*, the Indonesian political scene was always dominated by the *aliran* (streams of political thinking) parties.[5] The rivalry among the *aliran* parties sometimes made it difficult for Indonesia to move forward. So the loss of *aliran*-ism in *pilkada*, and the flexibility of all parties to cooperate with each other may provide a template for a more moderate Indonesian political outlook. On the other hand, the lack of a coalition pattern along ideological lines may also mean the lack of competitive platforms among candidates. As could be seen during the *pilkada* campaign, almost all candidates were trumpeting the same very general platforms. No serious debates on societal and development issues were heard. As a result, candidates usually received votes for their popularity rather than for any distinctive platform.

Stepping Up the Fight against Terrorism

Terror attacks have plagued Indonesia since *Reformasi*. Terror bombs have exploded annually since 2000 in various parts of the country, targeting foreign interests, as well as non-Muslim Indonesians. Table 3 lists the major terror attacks that Indonesia has had to endure for the last five years.

On 1 October 2005, a series of bombings struck restaurants frequently visited by foreign tourists in the Kuta and Jimbaran areas in Bali. This second Bali bombing killed 23 and injured more than one hundred. The attacks were carried out by suicide bombers who had wrapped bombs around their torsos. While this type of attack is common in Israel and Iraq, it was new to Indonesia. The suicide bombers seemed to take advantage of an opportunity offered by the fuel price hikes announced by the government on the same day. That announcement distracted a lot of Indonesians. The security apparatus was geared to anticipate student demonstrations in major cities, and its attention was thus diverted from possible terror attacks.

TABLE 3
Major terror attacks in Indonesia, 2000–2005

Location	Date	Victims
Jakarta Stock Exchange	13 September 2000	15 killed
15 churches in Medan, Jakarta, Bandung, Sukabumi, Ciamis, and Mojokerto	24 December 2000	20 killed
Plaza Atrium Senen, Jakarta	23 September 2001	6 injured
US Consulate in Renon, Bali, and Paddy's Cafe and Sari Club, Kuta, Bali	12 October 2002	202 killed, 88 of whom were Australian citizens
J.W. Marriott Hotel, central business district, Jakarta	5 August 2003	13 killed
Australian Embassy, Kuningan, Jakarta	9 September 2004	10 killed, hundreds injured
Tentena central market, Poso, Central Sulawesi	28 May 2005	22 killed
Raja's bar and restaurant, Kuta Square, Nyoman's and Menega cafes, Jimbaran, Bali	1 October 2005	23 killed, 102 injured

Following the attack, the police stepped up the search for terror network cells. Two masterminds, Malaysian nationals Dr Azahari Husin and Noordin M. Top, were on the top of the list of wanted men. The police had been after both for quite some time, but they had proven to be very elusive. The hunt bore fruit on 9 November 2005, when Azahari was killed in a police raid on a rented house in the outskirts of Malang, East Java. Azahari's death was hailed as a landmark in Indonesia's fight against terrorism and it boosted the morale of the police. The police continued the hunt for Noordin in various towns in Java. Even though Noordin narrowly escaped capture in the raid that led to Azahari's death, the police nabbed a number of suspected members of the terror network, as well as several unused bombs, bomb-making manuals, documents detailing plans of future attacks, and videos containing the confessions of the would-be second Bali suicide bombers. The discovery of these materials, especially the videos, has served as an eye-opener on the presence of a perverted ideology among a tiny number of Indonesian Muslims. The government, through Vice-President Jusuf Kalla took the initiative to show the videos to a number of Muslim clerics to point out the existence of such groups holding a jihadist view. Many Muslim leaders then came out into the open to condemn the foulness of such ideology. Leaders of Nahdlatul Ulama (NU) and Muhammadiyah, two largest Muslim organizations in the country, and of other organizations, have voiced their concerns over the ideology promoted by some fringe Muslim elements. Even some leaders from Islamist groups, during a gathering held by the MUI (Majelis Ulama Indonesia, or Indonesian Ulema Council), declared that suicide bombing is not a correct form of jihad.[6] Previously, Indonesians, especially Muslim leaders, had been in a state of denial regarding the existence of terror cells in Indonesia.[7] The videos have provided clear evidence to the contrary. Thus they have served as an important tool in the fight against terrorism in Indonesia.

But again, as in the past, the effort of the government to curb the growth of the terrorist cells was met with some resistance, largely due to the failure of the government to conduct effective communication with the public on the need for stronger action. This was apparent when Vice-President Jusuf Kalla announced that the security apparatus would collect the fingerprints of the *santri* (pupils) in Islamic boarding schools (*pesantren/madrasah*). This needed doing because in documents uncovered during police raids it was revealed that the terrorists had recruited some alumni of the *pesantren*. The *pesantren* reacted vehemently against such a move, because they felt that it would stigmatize them as a breeding ground for terrorists. This particular government initiative was soon in complete disarray when the chief of the National Police (Polri) General Sutanto in effect rebutted the Vice-President's announcement by denying that the security agencies would carry out the fingerprinting.[8] The lack of coherence on the part of the government as well as its failure to communicate with the *pesantren* once again put at risk the prospects of stronger action against terrorist groups in Indonesia.

The Return of an Active Foreign Policy

Even though, like his predecessors, SBY's agenda is predominantly domestic in scope, his government may be better remembered for its performance in foreign policy. From the fall of Soeharto in 1998, Indonesia had not recovered its position of influence and respect as the largest nation in the region, which used to be the hallmark of Soeharto's foreign policy. Successive administrations that never actually ruled effectively had put foreign policy on the backburner because of pressing domestic concerns. Even though public attention in 2005 was still focused on domestic issues, foreign policy received more public exposure than before.

The single most important reason for this could be the 50th Commemoration of the Asian African Conference held in Jakarta and Bandung in April 2005. Indonesia had worked closely with South Africa and Japan in the preparation of the summit. While the commemoration might not have produced anything tangible beyond the official declaration, it invoked a nostalgic sense of longing among the people for the Soekarno days when Indonesia used to play a much more active role globally.

But perhaps the more important outcome from the commemoration was what happened on the sidelines following the event. The signing of the "strategic partnership" agreement between President Hu Jintao and President Susilo Bambang Yudhoyono in Jakarta on 25 April 2005 was probably the most significant achievement in Indonesia's foreign policy in 2005.[9] Three months later it was followed by President Yudhoyono's state visit to Beijing on 27–30 July 2005, during which five additional agreements were signed, and the two countries expressed their intention to more than double the trade volume in five years, from US$14 billion to US$30 billion.[10] The strategic partnership agreement also indicates Indonesia's desire to play a foreign policy role that is more independent of the West. Indonesia's more active outsourcing for new foreign policy partners is also apparent in the conclusion of a similar strategic partnership agreement with India, which was signed by Indian Prime Minister Manmohan Singh and President Yudhoyono during SBY's visit to India in 21–23 November 2005.[11] Indonesia's Foreign Ministry even stated that Indonesia, China, and India have the intention of establishing a triangular partnership that will serve to counter possible US unilateralism in South and East Asia.[12]

The strategic partnership with China signified a major turn-around in Sino-Indonesian relations. Indonesia's perception of China has now been transformed from one of a primary threat source to that of a "strategic partner". It has also signified a success in China's diplomatic offensive to its southern neighbours. The Chinese media hailed the partnership agreement as a sign that China has eventually made inroads into a region that was traditionally suspicious of China and its intentions.[13] From the Indonesian perspective, the partnership is refreshing because it provides a template for future Indonesian foreign relations that are more independent of pressures from the West.

But at the same time the SBY government has cleverly carried out all these manoeuvres without alienating the Western powers, most notably the United

States. President Yudhoyono's good credentials in Washington's eyes stem from a strong link he has had with the United States as an Army officer in the past.[14] The United States viewed SBY as a strong ally, especially in the global fight against terrorism. And SBY knew how to capitalize on the strong relationship in Indonesia's interests, especially on two important points: the easing of the arms embargo that had been applied by the United States following the violence in the aftermath of the East Timor referendum in 2000, and support for the integrity of Indonesia in the face of regional rebellions in Aceh and Papua.

The arms embargo had put considerable strain on the Indonesian military. This was because most of the military hardware of the TNI came from Western sources, most notably, the United States. 34 per cent of TNI's arms came from the United States, 12 per cent from France, 12 per cent from Germany, 10 per cent from Russia, and 9 per cent from the United Kingdom. In aggregate, some 79 per cent of TNI's hardware came from countries of the North Atlantic Treaty Organization (NATO). The level of dependence was greatest in the air force: 88 per cent of its armaments came from NATO countries. For the army and navy, the figures were 77 and 73 per cent, respectively.[15] The embargo hit the technology-heavy air force and navy the hardest. The level of readiness in these forces was only around 40 per cent. Many air force fighters and navy ships were unable to operate because of lack of spare parts resulting from cannibalization. The effect of the embargo on the diminishing capacity of the TNI was clearly evident during the handling of the tsunami disaster in Aceh. Early response capacity of the military, which is to be expected in the event of a large-scale natural calamity, was weak. Appreciating this consequence of the embargo, US Secretary of State Colin Powell announced during his visit to Aceh on 4–5 January 2005 that the United States would resume supply of spare parts for military transport planes.[16] The SBY administration continued to build on this momentum by launching several diplomatic offensives, which included two meetings between SBY and President Bush in May 2005 during a state visit to the United States and again in November 2005 on the margins of the APEC forum in South Korea. As a result, by the end of November 2005 the United States decided to lift the arms embargo and allowed for a resumption of military-to-military relations.[17]

Indonesian diplomacy in 2005 was also quite successful in resisting the campaign for international support carried out by the regional separatist movements in Aceh and Papua. Apart from the tsunami factor described above, the signing of the peace MoU between rebel GAM and the Indonesian government in Helsinki in August 2005 could be seen as a result of GAM's realization of the diminishing support it received from abroad. The support for Papua's independence, however, remained substantial. For instance, there have been renewed calls among European politicians, especially in the Netherlands, to annul the result of the plebiscite (known in its Indonesian acronym as *penentuan pendapat rakyat*, or pepera) in 1969, in which the majority of the Papuans were said to have voted for integration with Indonesia. But during the state visit to the United States, President Yudhoyono managed to get the reaffirmation of the US President's support for Indonesia's territorial integrity and the US opposition towards secessionist movements in any part of Indonesia.[18]

The Challenges of the Future: Corruption and the Economy

Despite the progress that Indonesia made in 2005, the country was still beset by the old problems relating to the economy and corruption. These problems are in turn related to the issue of the rule of law and will likely remain in the years ahead.

For many years Indonesia has consistently been placed among the lowest ranks on the Corruption Perception Index (CPI) issued by Transparency International, an authoritative institution carrying out surveys on corruption and transparency all over the world. In 2005, Indonesia ranked 137 out of 159 countries and territories surveyed. Chart 1 depicts Indonesia's CPI, according to Transparency International, for the past ten years. As can be seen from the chart, Indonesia registered only a slight improvement from 2004 to 2005. In 2004 Indonesia's CPI was 2.0, while in 2005 it was 2.2. Over the years, Indonesia has only made incremental, very slow improvement in its CPI. In six years, from 1999 to 2005, the country has only improved by 0.5 in the index.[19]

Slight as it might be, the latest improvement was the fruit of a serious drive in the fight against corruption that Indonesia launched in 2005. The KPK (Komisi Pemberantasan Korupsi, or Corruption Eradication Commission), which was set up in 2002, had shown impressive results in dealing with corruption cases in 2005. It investigated and prosecuted many high-profile cases, including a corruption case involving the commissioners of the KPU (Komisi Pemilihan Umum, or General Elections Commission), including the chief of the KPU Nazaruddin Syamsuddin, as well as the case of the Governor of Aceh, Abdullah Puteh. To complement the KPK, the President has also established a special unit called Timtastipikor (Tim Terpadu Pemberantasan Tindak Pidana Korupsi, or Corruption Criminal Act Eradication Joint Team) in May 2005. Among others, Timtastipikor has dealt with major corruption cases in the Department of Religious Affairs.

CHART 1
Indonesia's Corruption Perception Index (CPI), 1995–2005

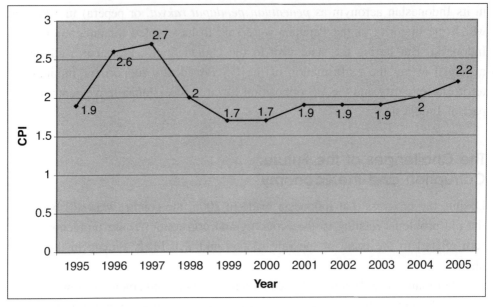

Source: Publications of Transparency International (various years).

Despite these achievements, corruption remained a serious problem in the country. After a long period of authoritarian rule, in which corruption was tolerated and even became the tacit rule of the bureaucracy, it has become an endemic and cultural problem. The fight against corruption could occupy the attention of Indonesians for many years, but at least Indonesia has taken the initial steps in the right direction.

Another issue that will remain a challenge in the future is the state of the economy. Like many governments in the world, in 2005 the SBY government had to face difficult choices stemming from the big rise of oil prices on the world market. The spot price of crude oil shot up almost three times in two years, from US$27.43 per barrel in July 2003 to more than US$70 per barrel in August 2005. In the last few years, Indonesia has been unable to fulfil its OPEC quota of around 1.1 million barrels per day. With rising domestic consumption of petroleum, the country has been transformed from an oil-exporting country to a net-importer of oil. The problem was made more acute by the fact that for a long time the government had subsidized petroleum prices sold in the domestic market. But the steep rise of the international oil prices made this practice no longer tenable, since the subsidy came to Rp 130 trillion (around US$13 billion) annually. The SBY government was left with practically no choice but to cut back the subsidy. Otherwise, the state budget would have to endure a significant burden.

After a long process of tinkering with the idea, the government finally announced its decision on 1 October 2005. It was met with public uproar, mostly due to the size of the fuel price hike, which was more than 100 per cent on average. Politically, the SBY administration was secure. No serious political move was taken as a reaction towards the policy. This was due to the support that the government enjoyed in parliament, particularly after Vice-President Jusuf Kalla took over the leadership of Golkar, the largest party in parliament, at the end of 2004. But the socioeconomic effect of the policy might not be easy to ameliorate. The inflation rate in October and November 2005 shot up to 17.89 per cent and 18.38 per cent, respectively, and then decreased slightly in December. Chart 2 illustrates the rise of inflation in Indonesia in 2005.

The inflationary effect of the policy will make life tougher for everyone, especially the urban poor or lower middle class. The compensation fund provided

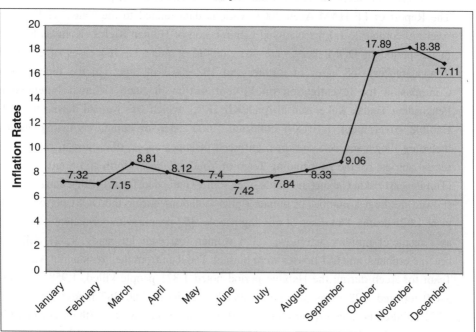

CHART 2
Indonesia's monthly inflation rates, 2005

Source: Publications of Bank of Indonesia (various months).

by the government, amounting to Rp 100,000 per family, per month will not be given to these people because the government has established a set of criteria that makes only the rural poor eligible for it, even though they are less affected by the fuel price hike as they practically live out of the land. The higher inflation rate will increase poverty in Indonesia and significantly slow down economic growth. Indonesian workers are going to be the most affected. Not only will they have to endure rising living expenses, but also face the potential of being laid off. Since industries will bear the brunt of the fuel price hike, they will probably have to take efficiency measures, such as laying off some of their workers. This would add to the already high rate of open unemployment in Indonesia, which reached 10.3 per cent in 2005. The spectre of social problems arising from the increasing unemployment is quite daunting, and might exacerbate the social unrest in Indonesia. This is the challenge that Indonesia has to face in the years ahead.

Notes

[1] Rizal Sukma, "Prospects for Conflict Resolution in Post-Tsunami Aceh" (paper presented at Cornell University, Ithaca, New York, 23 February 2005).
[2] See, for instance, Cypri Jehan Paju Dale, "Bisnis Bantuan di Aceh dan Nias" [The aid business in Aceh and Nias], *Kompas*, 26 December 2005, p. 6.
[3] The Report of FP HAM Aceh 2001: various data related to the state's violence in Aceh. According to (a) the National Commission of Human Rights (Komnas HAM), in the period of DOM there were 781 victims of murders, 163 cases of enforced disappearances, 368 cases of torture, and 102 cases of rape; (b) the Independent Commission for Investigation on Violent Action in Aceh (Komisi Independen Pengusutan Tindak Kekerasan di Aceh/KIPTKA), which was formed during the B.J. Habibie government, KIPTKA collected 5,000 cases of human rights violations, including illegal murders, tortures, enforced disappearances, illicit arrest, rapes, and sexual abuses; (c) the Fact-finding Team of Youth of Pidie, North and South of Aceh (Tim Pencari Fakta Gabungan Pemda Aceh Pidie, Utara, dan Timur) with a database that showed the largest number of human rights violations during the DOM period, there were 1,021 deaths, 864 cases of missing people, 357 people with permanent disability, as a result of military activities; 1,376 women lost their husbands, 4,521 children became orphans, and 681 houses were burned. The data from the Presidential Advisory Team for Aceh during the Habibie period noted 1,321 people killed, 1,958 missing, 3,430 tortured, 128 cases of rapes, 1,244 houses burnt, and 287 houses destroyed. 4,521 children became orphans, and 1,850 women became widows (the preceding bit of data on the widows came from Muhammad Qodari in *Kompas*, 12 May 2003). These figures are nowhere close to those of an International Amnesty report in 1993,

which noted 10,000 cases of human rights violations in Aceh from 1989 to 1992, which were classified as cases of murders and enforced disappearances. Hasan Tiro's GAM side even claimed that there were 20,000 victims of ABRI killings during DOM and DI/TII. See Teuku Kemal Fasya, *Ritus Kekerasan dan Libido Nasionalisme* [Violent rituals and nationalism libido] (Yogyakarta: Buku Baik-ELSAM, 2005), pp. 245–46.

4. For a survey on some of the *pilkada* conflicts, consult Moch. Nurhasim, eds., *Konflik Antar Elit Politik Lokal dalam Pemilihan Kepala Daerah* [Conflicts among the local political elite in the election of regional chiefs] (Yogyakarta: Pustaka Pelajar, 2005).

5. For a discussion on *aliran* politics, consult Herbert Feith and Lance Castles, eds., *Indonesian Political Thinking, 1945–1965* (Ithaca: Cornell University Press, 1970).

6. See http://www.sciencedaily.com/upi/?feed=TopNews&article=UPI-1-20051205-07083900-bc-indonesia-islamists.xml.

7. Irman G. Lanti, *How to Secure Indonesia's Cooperation in the Fight Against Militants*, IDSS Commentaries, no. 1/2002, February 2002.

8. *Jakarta Post*, "Kalla Defends Plan to Fingerprint Students of Religious Schools", 8 December 2005.

9. Eric Teo Chu Cheow, "Assessing the Sino-Indonesian Strategic Partnership", *PacNet* (Pacific Forum CSIS), no. 25, 23 June 2005.

10. "Indonesia and China Forge Strategic Partnership", *Straits Times*, 29 July 2005.

11. See "Joint Declaration between the Republic of India and the Republic of Indonesia", 23 November 2005. The text can be found at http://www.meaindia.nic.in/declarestatement/2005/11/23jd01.htm.

12. Based on an interview with an authoritative figure in Indonesia's Foreign Ministry, Jakarta, May 2005.

13. See, for example, "A Good, Safe, and Enriched Neighbour", *China Daily*, 28 April 2005.

14. Yudhoyono underwent several military training courses in the United States. As a young officer, in 1976 he attended the US Army Airborne and Ranger Course in Fort Benning, Georgia. He returned to Fort Benning in 1982 to attend the Infantry Officer Advanced Course, and then went to Fort Bragg, California in 1983. He attended the US Command and General Staff College at Fort Leavenworth, Kansas in 1991. He also received a Masters degree in Management from Webster University, Missouri.

15. Figures taken from Andi Widjajanto, "Arms Procurement, Russia, and the Defense Industry", *Jakarta Post*, 3 January 2006, p. 6.

16. Glenn Kessler, "Powell Pledges Continued Support to Asia", *Washington Post*, 4 January 2005; "US Hopes Planes Won't Be Used Against Rebels", http://www.laksamana.net, 7 January 2005.

17 Peter Gelling, "U.S. to Allow Sale of Arms to Indonesia", *International Herald Tribune*, 24 November 2005.
18 "Joint Statement between the United States of America and the Republic of Indonesia", http://www.usindo.org/Briefs/2005/Joint%20Statement%20US-Indonesia%202005.htm.
21 Interestingly, the highest figure that Indonesia has ever reached since Transparency International launched the CPI in 1995 was in 1997 (CPI = 2.7). This was the final year under President Soeharto before he stepped down in 1998. Ironically, one of the major factors that spurred the *Reformasi* movement was the corruption accusation levelled against Soeharto and his cronies. But successive post-Soeharto governments have still not been able to bring Indonesia's CPI to the pre-1998 level.

INDONESIAN MILITARY REFORM
More Than a Human Rights Issue

John B. Haseman

Military reform in Indonesia is an ongoing but long-term process. The armed forces are making remarkable progress in transforming itself into its new role in a vigorous democratic society.[2] Since the resignation of President Soeharto in May 1998 the armed forces establishment has implemented important reforms to bring about this transformation.[3] While the military is still the most powerful element of Indonesian society, it is no longer the monolithic arbiter of political power in Indonesia that it was for the three decades of Soeharto's New Order.

Military reform in Indonesia is important to many players. Three institutional elements stand out in this regard. Obviously the greatest impact is on the Indonesian military itself. Military reform is also of consummate importance to the people of Indonesia, most of whom favour reform of the TNI in some substantial form. Finally, reform of the TNI is a key element in the foreign policy with Indonesia of several important friendly countries, including Australia, the United States, and the United Kingdom.

The TNI has not yet implemented all of the reforms its critics desire, but it must be given credit for the changes it has made to date. The TNI gave up its blocks of reserved appointed seats in parliament and regional assemblies. Military personnel now must retire before taking civilian government posts, whether electoral positions in parliament or at the province level and below, or in non-defence-related positions in the government civil service. This is a huge contrast to the Soeharto years, when thousands of military personnel occupied civil government and societal posts at all levels and active duty officers routinely filled

---

JOHN B. HASEMAN is a retired US Army Colonel who served ten years in Indonesia, including four years as US Defense Attache, 1990–94, and has written extensively on Indonesian and Southeast Asian political-military affairs.

cabinet posts. There are no active duty officers in the current national cabinet, a significant change from the Soeharto years.[4]

The TNI has withdrawn, as an institution, from day-to-day political activities. The TNI does not support any political party — no more wearing the yellow jacket of Golkar, for example, as senior officers did during the Soeharto years. While an important reform, this is also somewhat misleading because, in an ironic reversal of form from the Soeharto years, civilian political parties and politicians now seek support from the TNI and from influential individual senior military officers. It is therefore inaccurate to say that the TNI has withdrawn from politics. What it *has* done is to refuse institutional support to any political party. The TNI is still an influential force in Indonesian society, but it no longer dominates politics as it did during the Soeharto era.[5]

An American observer summed up the progress of military reform in these words:

> The military gave up much of their political power under pressure from civil society and voters and with a speed that is striking when compared with situations in some other post-authoritarian states. Though there is still a pressing agenda for further civil-military reform, it must be acknowledged that the military are now out of parliament, secondments to civilian posts have ended, there is the very beginning of a degree of defense budget transparency unimaginable a few years ago, and the military is increasingly under civilian control. While much remains to be done to further entrench a professional armed forces in the context of a democratic Indonesia, but clearly [sic] a lot of the hard work has begun, and begun to take root.[6]

Recent Trends in Military Reform

Military reform was slow to develop in the immediate aftermath of Soeharto's fall. Reform did not have widespread political and financial support during the first three post-Soeharto governments so it fell short in many respects. The late Lieutenant General Agus Wirahadikusumah, the most vociferous reformist of that time, pushed hard for major military reform early during the administration of President Abdurrahman Wahid. He was vocal in pointing out areas of what he considered blatant corruption in military finances, and many senior officers viewed him as an insubordinate upstart and a threat to lucrative off-budget income and the Byzantine political machinations designed to destabilize the Wahid government. Hardliners and sceptics in the military hierarchy scuttled General

Wirahadikusumah's efforts; and he and a small group of like-minded supporters were sidelined to powerless postings. President Wahid ended his push for deep military reform as a result. President Megawati Soekarnoputri actively courted military support and during her term in office military reforms were relegated to lower priority.

The election of President Susilo Bambang Yudhoyono in 2004 marked an important milestone in military reform. For many years he was seen as a leader of a large group of officers quietly opposed to the prominence of Soeharto's cabal of protégés and family that led the military for more than 30 years. The controversial *dwi-fungsi* doctrine, which Soeharto used to justify the military's involvement in virtually every aspect of civil society for more than four decades, was jettisoned in 1999. In charge of the TNI's social and political affairs at the time, then Lieutenant General Yudhoyono was a principal architect of the New Paradigm (*Paradigma Baru*), the formal military doctrine that replaced *dwi-fungsi*. The New Paradigm doctrine is the first formal exposition of the missions of the armed forces in a democratic society.[7] It is still subject to review and criticism and should not be assumed to be in its final form.

Now the spirit of reform has regained momentum, with President Yudhoyono having not only a mandate for change but also two equally reform-minded senior cabinet ministers to help him. Dr Juwono Sudarsono holds the defence portfolio for the second time. A respected academic and a former minister for education under President Habibie and minister for defence under President Megawati (the first civilian to hold that post for decades), he returned from assignment as Indonesia's ambassador to London with the assurance that he would have more presidential support in reordering the military than he had the first time. Retired Admiral Widodo Adi Sucipto is Coordinating Minister for Political, Justice, and Security Affairs, the position President Yudhoyono held in the government of President Megawati. Admiral Widodo succeeded the hardliner General Wiranto as TNI chief, and as the first naval officer to run the entire military he rode the initial wave of *reformasi* under President Abdurrahman Wahid.

Strategic Military Reform

The Yudhoyono administration already has placed a high priority on several agenda items that might be dubbed strategic military reform. These reflect the complexities of reform within the political environment of the country, with all of its developments and weaknesses. These strategic reforms require institutional changes beyond "mere military" reform, and are long term in their scope and goals.

Three important issues in strategic military reform are evolution to civilian control, the broad concept of defence budget transparency, and a reduction in the TNI's dependence on off-budget funding — the military business empire has long been the cause of corruption, rogue behaviour, and other weaknesses in the chain of command.

The TNI is directly subordinate to the president, not the minister for defence. The military chain of command runs directly from the president to the TNI commander-in-chief and then to the tactical and territorial military commands. The minister for defence currently coordinates doctrine and strategy, long-range planning, and budget affairs, but little else. Bringing the military under a civilian minister for defence is a new and controversial concept for Indonesia, and will likely be implemented slowly and in small increments.

One area in which civilian control has begun to be felt is that of budget and military procurement. Dr Sudarsono has already implemented a policy to centralize all military arms purchases in the Department of Defence, taking that power away from TNI headquarters and the three military services. Parliament has mandated the transfer of many military businesses to civilian control. To begin implementation of parliament's intent, Dr Sudarsono announced that all military businesses grossing at least five billion rupiah (about US$540,000) annually would be placed under civilian control.[8] The 2004 defence law requires the government to fully fund the TNI in five years, and includes support for Dr Sudarsono's plan to civilianize large military businesses. TNI commander-in-chief General Endriartono Sutarto went a step further by declaring that the TNI will turn those businesses over to civilian control by 2007, retaining only cooperatives providing for the basic needs of soldiers and their dependents.[9]

The most significant weakness of this military business civilianization policy is that it will affect only a small number of the "legal" military businesses and does not touch the huge array of illicit businesses allegedly controlled by the TNI, such as illegal logging, protection rackets, prostitution, and trafficking in smuggled goods and narcotics. No known public source has ever delineated the magnitude of those "black" businesses, which are the primary targets of reformists in any case.

The government and parliament have already begun to codify procedures to subordinate the TNI under the Department of Defence, including proposed amendments to the defence law that will strengthen civilian oversight of the military.[10] This may well be the most contentious element of military reform. There is an ongoing combined Defence Department–TNI study group exploring ways in which a transition to civilian control might take place, but no time schedule has been applied. The military as an institution has never been under civilian control and there is no history of subordination to any figure other than the president (who also holds the rank of TNI supreme commander). A certain degree of hubris is deeply ingrained in the army in particular, because of its history as the virtual co-founder of the republic when it fought on against the Dutch after Indonesia's civilian leaders had surrendered. It could take another generation before army officers mentally as well as formally accept their subordination to civilian authority.[11]

A major structural weakness in achieving the goal of civilian control over the military is that there is currently no cadre of civilians with defence and security experience who could fill policy formulation, strategic planning, and decision-making posts in a more powerful Department of Defence. The defence minister and a key parliamentarian, Mr Theo Sambuaga, who chairs Commission I overseeing foreign affairs, defence, and security matters, agree on priorities for developing human resources in the military as well as the creation of a civilian cadre of officials with defence credentials. Their goals include sending abroad as many mid-grade military officers and civilians (perhaps from think tanks and university faculties) as possible for training, and thus to create a new generation of civilian experts in defence planning, budgeting, and management who can fill key jobs in government, parliament, and civilian research institutions.[12]

Dr Sudarsono has often called attention to the continued weakness of civilian oversight over the military. He ascribes this weakness almost entirely to the immaturity of political parties and other civilian institutions. Indonesia's political parties are largely "disjointed, disorganized and often in disarray", he has written. "In consequence, instilled with the doctrine of military supremacy over the civilians for more than half of their lives, TNI officers remain reluctant to respect civilian control as long as the civilian politicians have little inclination or ability to assert their authority".[13]

Arguably the most important reform the Yudhoyono government can make in the security area is to relieve the TNI of its need to pay for most of its costs — perhaps as much as 70 per cent of all its costs by some estimates — from off-budget sources. The TNI's dependence on non-budgetary funds is the major factor shaping the TNI's notoriety for corrupt and criminal behaviour. Pay all of the TNI's bills, some critics argue, and perhaps it would not be so dependent on drug smuggling in Aceh and illegal logging in Papua.

This is far more than a corruption issue. It will require major improvements to national tax laws and implementation of them, as well as attention to allocation of national resources. The simple fact is that Indonesia does not collect enough national revenue to fully fund its security forces. Inadequate state funding can also seriously compromise the chain of command if soldiers place their loyalty with local commanders, who take responsibility for their welfare, rather than on central headquarters. An armed force that gets only one-third of its financing from its central government is more likely to prioritize loyalty to its other sources of income, and the system thus lessens state control over the military establishment.

President Yudhoyono is as aware of this problem as anyone in his administration. In early 2005 he spoke about raising the defence budget to about 3 to 5 per cent of the gross national product from the current level of below 2 per cent. If successful, this action would be closer to the proportion being spent by other countries at a comparable level of development.[14] This is not an unreasonably large increase, and would come close to a realistic budgetary requirement to cover the TNI's expenses without undue reliance on income from the military business empire. Defence Minister Sudarsono is doing his best to narrow the budget shortfall — something his predecessors never even tried. He proposed a defence budget of 59 trillion rupiah (about US$5.9 billion) for 2006, but he is not likely to get near that amount. The Defence Department sought the equivalent of US$4.7 billion for fiscal year 2005, but got only US$2.3 billion — an amount, Dr Sudarsono noted, that is only half of what Singapore normally spends a year to defend a country with 2 per cent of Indonesia's population and a territory about the size of Indonesia's island of Bali.[15]

A major target of reform-minded critics of military power in Indonesia is the army's huge territorial structure. This organization extends military commands at every level of the government and places military personnel from province down to the village level: organized into 12 Military Regional Commands that have as their area of control major geographic expanses comprising both single provinces (on Java) and regions of several provinces (in the Outer Islands). Below the military regional commands are several layers of commands at the province, regency, district, and village levels. Well over half of the army's personnel strength is assigned to the territorial structure.[16]

The territorial structure's historical basis dates back to the revolution against the colonial Dutch army, when fledgling military personnel and units dispersed throughout the countryside and laid the basis for the Indonesian army's doctrine, which even today stresses mobile guerrilla warfare against outside invasion. Today the security issues are far different, but the army retains the territorial structure to provide a cohesive security apparatus, gather intelligence, and maintain contact with the population.

A number of critics have urged dropping at least the bottom three rungs of the structure: the non-commissioned officers at the village level (*babinsa*), the subdistrict commands (*koramil*), and the district commands (*kodim*). Other commentators want the entire structure abolished altogether and the army reorganized in conventional divisions so that it can be fully devoted to external defence.[17] The counter-argument is that in most of the countryside — particularly in the Outer Islands — the civilian infrastructure is a long way from attaining the level of expertise and authority that the territorial structure exercises for security and management.

In any case, major changes in the territorial structure and missions are not likely for many years to come. Most recently, reflecting President Yudhoyono's directive for all national security and intelligence forces to upgrade their counter-terrorism activities, in October 2005 TNI commander-in-chief General Sutarto announced that the *babinsa* level of the territorial structure would be re-invigorated. The rationale for re-establishing the "sergeant in the village" is to expand the national intelligence infrastructure to assist police and other counter-terrorist efforts in tracking and locating known and suspected terrorists and their extremist supporters. Critics will watch closely, determined to oppose any actions that might foreshadow a regression to the unwanted abuses of the Soeharto era.

An additional important but unspoken rationale for the army's territorial structure is its dominant role in supporting the military business empire, especially in the Outer Islands where economic development is less robust. Regardless of the degree to which military reform gradually moves key businesses to civilian government control, the tentacles of the remaining military cooperatives and the deniable but extant illicit business activities will remain in place.[18]

Professionalism and Reform: The TNI's "Software"

A key element of military reform in Indonesia is to continue with efforts to improve the military professionalism of the armed forces. This encompasses a wide range that includes training and education, maintenance and repair of equipment and weapons systems, and selective upgrade of weaponry through new acquisitions. It also includes a requirement to upgrade military discipline and accountability by strengthening the chain of command and assuring punishment for misdeeds, whether lax professional performance or deliberate human rights abuses.

President Yudhoyono emphasized his determination to continue this aspect of military reform through his selection, in February 2005, of new chiefs of staff for the three military services. These officers are untainted by past human rights abuses. Significantly, the president retained on active duty the TNI commander-in-chief, General Endriartono Sutarto, who kept the military out of politics and committed it to reform for more than four years. General Sutarto retired in March 2006 and was succeeded by Air Chief Marshal Djoko Suyanto. The selection of an air force commander-in-chief reaffirmed a policy of rotating the top post among the three military services. The President has made an important statement on military reform through his actions and by choosing able officers to the top positions in the TNI.

For decades Indonesia relied on a series of bilateral military-to-military ties to assist in improving its professionalism through acquisition of military equipment and weapons, overseas training, and cooperative military exercises. Indonesia has maintained a variety of bilateral military-to-military relations with many countries over the years. The thrust of those programmes has been to assist the TNI to improve its professional capabilities through maintenance and repair of ageing weapons systems, purchase of more modern weapons and equipment, and cooperative education, and training programmes. The degree and nature of such programmes varied from year to year and from country to country, and were largely dependent on the political relationship between Indonesia and the other countries involved.

Apart from the natural partnerships between Indonesia and its fellow members in the Association of Southeast Asian Nations (ASEAN), a number of countries have maintained security assistance programmes with Indonesia over the years. The United States, the United Kingdom, Germany, and Australia are among the most involved. But those countries began to curtail their cooperation and assistance programmes with Indonesia in 1992, as their own domestic political pressures and policies reacted to human rights violations in East Timor. Virtually all such military-to-military programmes were suspended after the violence surrounding the 1999 referendum in which East Timorese voted overwhelmingly for independence.[19] Since then Indonesia has begun to explore alternative sources of weapons and equipment.

Human rights issues were the primary concern in the military-to-military relations between Indonesia and the United States and, to a lesser extent, Australia and the United Kingdom in the decade between 1992 and 2001. But since the September 2001 terrorist attacks in the United States and subsequent terrorist attacks in Indonesia, the United Kingdom, and elsewhere in the world, it is clear that new strategic priorities elsewhere in the world have directly affected Indonesia and the process of international support for reform and professionalization in the TNI.

The reversal of the decade-long American arms embargo in November 2005 reflected new strategic priorities — not only the international war on terrorism but also America's belated recognition that the Soeharto era autocracy had ended and Indonesia had become the world's third-largest democracy. The American policy change is not without controversy in US political circles, and has aroused the anger of human rights and political organizations in Indonesia and overseas. American congressional critics of Indonesia placed restrictions in 2006 legislation on military relations, but advocates of resumed relations gained a compromise that allowed the administration to waive those restrictions in the interest of national security. President George W. Bush took advantage of that compromise to change America's policy by waiver. The policy change also puts pressure on Indonesia and the TNI to continue progress in military reform. If not, there is always the possibility that Congress could again impose restrictions at some time in the future.

Objectives of military reform by improving professionalism are obviously a matter for the Indonesian government to determine, but some general comments outline areas in which cooperative international military relations can contribute. The least controversial objectives are probably the pressing need to repair and upgrade Indonesia's deteriorated strategic transport capability, both air and sea, and the need to restore the readiness of its tactical sea and air fleets either through upgrade and repairs or by new acquisitions. The end of the US arms embargo provides immediate opportunities to address these priorities.

Indonesia has already announced plans to repair as many of its C-130 transport aircraft as possible, as well as possibly to purchase additional aircraft. Before the US arms embargo 24 of Indonesia's C-130 aircraft were operational but that number is now down to six.[20] A programme for refurbishment of these aircraft will likely get quick approval in the United States. In fact the embargo on military sales was partly lifted in January 2005 to allow purchase of spare parts for the C-130 fleet in the aftermath of the Aceh tsunami, and advocates of a restored military relationship with Indonesia frequently cite the use of the C-130 for humanitarian relief operations. Dr Sudarsono also announced plans to rotate the Indonesian air force's F-16 fleet to the United States for major repairs and upgrades, probably at a rate of two aircraft per year.[21] The United States is likely to approve this programme as well. Indonesia's determination to seek out alternate sources for its defence equipment requirements was surely a factor in the US government's change of policy. The US congressional legislation pointedly exempted the Indonesian navy from its political restraints. Thus programmes to upgrade the navy's capabilities to patrol its vast maritime resources, guard against poaching and piracy, and provide reliable strategic sealift will likely move forward.

While improvements in the hardware of Indonesia's military are of keen importance, it is the area of "software" — TNI personnel — that has in the past drawn the most criticism from reformists at home and overseas. One of the key elements in America's decision to re-engage the TNI is its belief that re-engagement with the TNI, improved training and education, coupled with changes in leadership philosophy in Indonesia's new democratic environment, will result in a better-disciplined TNI force that is more responsive to leadership in the chain of command, and fewer human rights violations. To that end the United States resumed its International Military Education and Training (IMET) programme with Indonesia in March 2005. The IMET programme provides funding and eligibility for foreign officers to attend US military schools.[22]

Since the 1950s more than 4,000 Indonesian military personnel have attended schools and on-the-job training under IMET auspices. The programme was curtailed in 1992 after Indonesian army troops killed scores of civilians in Dili, East Timor. Indonesia now benefits from several other training and education programmes. The United States also provides the so-called Expanded IMET (E-MET) programme, which allows defence-sector civilians to attend military training courses, as well as a number of other education and training programmes funded all or in part by the US government.

Other military-to-military programmes include exchange visits among senior officers, attendance at conferences and seminars sponsored by the US Pacific Command (PACOM), and a variety of field training opportunities — primarily in the fields of health care, safety, and disaster response. Indonesian officers attend a variety of conferences and symposia sponsored by PACOM components, including the International Sea Power Symposium, the Pacific Armies Management Seminar, Pacific Air Force Disaster Management Symposium, and a variety of medical conferences and training exchanges. The United States resumed a low-level military exercise programme in early 2005, and can be expected to implement a stepped-up programme of soldier-to-soldier, sailor-to-sailor, and airman-to-airman exercises and training iterations. Most of these programmes are funded as part of PACOM operational activities.

Australia has also resumed its education and training programmes with the TNI. The United States might take a cue from Australia, which has agreed to negotiate with Indonesia a non-treaty security pact covering defence, police cooperation, counter-terrorism, and people trafficking. These security relationships with Indonesia are based on the new realities of the world. Indonesia is seen as a key player in the war on terrorism. Since the 2001 attacks in the United States no country has suffered more casualties from terrorist attacks than Indonesia. As an emerging successful democracy Indonesia is an example to other Islamic countries that democracy can flourish in a Muslim society.

It will not be easy to reconnect with the TNI. The armed forces chief, Air Marshal Suyanto, is among the last TNI officers on active duty to have attended overseas schooling. When he retires there will be only a few others left in senior ranks with a history of personal friendships with foreign officers. There is a widespread feeling among the TNI ranks of disenfranchisement, reinforced by the influence of hardline senior officers whose criticism of overseas training programmes increased with each year of annual embarrassment at enforced isolation. Don McFetridge, a retired army colonel who served as US Defence Attaché in Jakarta from 1994 to 1998, sees this as a serious problem. "We don't know people in the next generation of military leaders to talk to," he says. "Most of the reformers have already retired and moved on."[23]

The culture of impunity from prosecution — for human rights abuses as well as ordinary criminal activity — that pervades the TNI is perhaps the single most criticized aspect of the military. This attitude adversely influenced US and Australian political relations with Indonesia over the past decade. It is also a major target of reformers. An important change that would address this issue would be to transfer authority to prosecute non-service connected crimes by service personnel from the military's judicial system to the civilian court system. Although the Supreme Court now has ultimate review over decisions made in the military judicial system, the TNI has strenuously opposed transfer of non-military criminal investigation and prosecution to the civilian courts. One of their arguments — which illustrates the challenges that surround all aspects of military reform — is that the civilian judicial system is blatantly corrupt and incapable of handling military judicial issues in a proper manner.

Senior US officials hope that re-engagement with the TNI will encourage continued reform. The relationship should gradually increase to span the entire gamut of security sector reform, which includes improving the Indonesian police's capability to assume a larger role in internal security, strengthening civilian authority over all the security services, and elevating the role of civil society. As one defence scholar interprets it, security sector reform "assumes the existence of a strong linkage between defense, security, and development".[24]

While increased exposure to international military education and training is an important part of professionalization, international friendship and mutual understanding is an important secondary goal. As one Indonesian officer told this author many years ago, it is important that respective militaries "know each other". Knowledge of each other's doctrine, policies, and military strategy and capability can be invaluable, as the multilateral international cooperation after the Aceh tsunami demonstrated. Indonesia also hopes to reinvigorate its participation in UN peacekeeping operations — prior to 1999 it was a frequent participant in such missions. A return to a more robust international cooperation programme will assist in achieving that objective.

It is important not to neglect basic and mid-level education in the primary branches of military service. It is precisely at levels of command headed by lieutenants, captains, and majors where lapses in human rights most often occur. It is at the junior officer and non-commissioned officer (NCO) levels, in field operational environments, that most human rights abuses occur in Indonesia. It does little good for senior officers to disseminate doctrine and instructions on the importance of human rights if junior officers implementing those instructions are untrained in these concepts. Professional military education that incorporates the latest principles of human rights, military operations in civilian environments, and civil-military relations cannot help but reduce the incidence of abuses and meet the demands of Indonesian reformists who want to see more acceptable behaviour by the military become the norm.

Indonesia has asked specifically for classroom seats to be reserved for as many of Indonesia's mid-ranking officers as possible. These are the potential military leaders in the next decade. Indonesia has asked all of the donors of military training — not just the United States — to significantly increase the number of officers able to attend courses in military law, role, and operations of the military police, budget planning and management, strategic defence planning, defence procurement and logistics management, maintenance (aircraft, ships, tactical vehicles), and resource and personnel management. Such training programmes will go a long way towards reform and professionalization of the "software" of the TNI.

Conclusion

It is important to keep in mind that military reform in Indonesia encompasses far more than the human rights issues that often dominate any discussion on the subject. Many critics of the pace of military reform — both domestic and foreign — mistakenly equate "military reform" only with improvement in addressing human rights concerns. Military reform in Indonesia is a far more complex subject that involves a variety of intertwined national-level governmental factors. The national taxation system, budgetary processes, court and judicial systems, the broader aspect of national government reforms, and political reform all play a role in military reform efforts. Also important to the issue of military reform is the impact of recent events — like the tsunami and the international relief effort, terrorist attacks and responses, the Aceh peace process — and the relationship between those events, the national policies of many other countries, and those effects on Indonesia's international military-to-military relations.

Indonesia's defence leaders — military and civilian — have stressed that military reform is a long-term activity that has no defined start and end points, a process that will continue to evolve in parallel with Indonesia's continued political and social evolution from autocracy to democracy. Much has already been changed. Some changes are deep and wide and will have lasting effect, others may be longer on form and shallow on substance. Much remains to be done. Government and military leaders appear to be committed to changing the military's role in Indonesian society and reforms that match national objectives and democratic mores. It will take time — Dr Sudarsono expects the process of acculturation and modernizing and civilianizing the defence structure to be a lengthy process that will take from 10 to 25 years.[25] But it is clear that Indonesian society and its evolving democratic system will support the process of military reform as a component of the far more complex task of governmental reform.

Notes

[1] Portions of this article are adapted from "Toward a Stronger U.S.-Indonesia Security Relationship", a monograph by John B. Haseman and Eduardo Lachica (United States–Indonesia Society [USINDO], 2005).

[2] The Indonesian armed forces is called Tentara Nasional Indonesia — TNI, or the Indonesian National Military Forces. Prior to 1998 it was called ABRI — Angkatan Bersenjata Republik Indonesia, or the Armed Forces of the Republic of Indonesia. The term TNI is used throughout this article.

[3] A more detailed examination of military reform efforts can be found in John B. Haseman and Angel Rabasa, *The Military and Democracy in Indonesia: Challenges, Politics, and Power* (Santa Monica, CA: The RAND Corporation, 2002).

[4] Three retired officers serve in the cabinet: retired Admiral Widodo Adi Sucipto, Coordinating Minister for Political, Security, and Legal Affairs; retired Lieutenant General Ma'ruf, Minister of Home Affairs and Regional Autonomy; and retired Rear Admiral Freddy Numberi, Minister of Fisheries and Maritime Affairs.

[5] Haseman and Lachica, "Toward a Stronger U.S.-Indonesia Security Relationship".

6. Douglas Ramage, "Indonesia in Transition: Recent Developments and Implications for U.S. Policy", presentation to the Committee on International Relations, Subcommittee on Asia and the Pacific, US House of Representatives, 10 March 2005.
7. Haseman and Lachica, "Toward a Stronger U.S.-Indonesia Security Relationship".
8. "Transparency Will Be Instituted in Defense Ministry", Interview with Juwono Sudarsono, *Jakarta Post*, 4 November 2004.
9. Reuters, 12 April 2005. The TNI insists that those cooperatives provide low-cost basic commodities to soldiers and their families in much the same way as military exchange organizations operate in the United States and other Western countries.
10. Juwono Sudarsono, Address at USINDO luncheon, Washington, DC, 14 March 2005.
11. Haseman and Lachica, "Toward a Stronger U.S.-Indonesia Security Relationship".
12. Haseman, interviews with Dr Sudarsono, Jakarta, 8 February 2005, and Theo Sambuaga, Jakarta, 11 February 2005.
13. Juwono Sudarsono, *Indonesian Voices*, USINDO, September 2004.
14. *Straits Times*, 26 February 2005.
15. Address at USINDO luncheon, Washington, DC, 14 March 2005.
16. The respective levels of command are the KODAM (Komando Daerah Militer), KOREM (Komando Resor Militer), KODIM (Komando District Militer), KORAMIL (Komando Rayon Militer), and the BABINSA (sergeant in the village). The best detailed analysis of the army's organization is Robert Lowry, *The Armed Forces of Indonesia* (St Leonards, New South Wales: Allen & Unwin, 1996).
17. For a review of critical opinions about the TNI's territorial system, see Rizal Sukma and Edy Prasetyono, "Security Sector Reform in Indonesia: The Military and the Police", Netherlands Institute of International Relations (Clingerdael), February 2003; and Marcus Mietzner, "Politics of Engagement: The Indonesian Armed Forces, Islamic Extremism and the 'War on Terror'", *Brown Journal of World Affairs* IX, no. 1 (Spring 1992).
18. Sukma and Prasetyono, "Security Sector Reform in Indonesia".
19. The circumstances of that period are not within the purview of this discussion — having been widely reported over the years.
20. Reuters, "Indonesia Plans to Buy U.S.-Made Hercules Planes", 25 November 2005.
21. Associated Press, "Indonesia to Buy U.S. Military Equipment", 25 November 2005.
22. Details of the programme are summarized in Haseman, "The United States, IMET, and Indonesia", *USINDO Report*, no. 3, January 1998. Colonel Haseman first served in the former Defense Liaison Group in Jakarta from 1978 to 1981, when he managed the IMET programme — at its height in 1980 Indonesia's IMET programme was the largest in the world.
23. Interview by Eduardo Lachica, 15 December 2002, cited in Haseman and Lachica, "Toward a Stronger U.S.-Indonesia Security Relationship".

[24] The concept of security sector reform was first brought out for public debate by Britain's New Labour government in 1998. It essentially argues that security assistance should not be limited to conventional military aid but should also seek to influence the performance of the police, the intelligence services, and other public institutions with a security role. The British interpretation emphasizes good governance programmes and a more active and ambitious style of defence diplomacy than is the usual US practice. See Alice Hills, "Defence Diplomacy and Security Sector Reform", *Contemporary Security Policy* 21, no. 1 (April 2000).

[25] "TNI Businesses Must Be Restructured", Interview with Juwono Sudarsono, *Tempo*, 28 December 2004–3 January 2005.

Laos

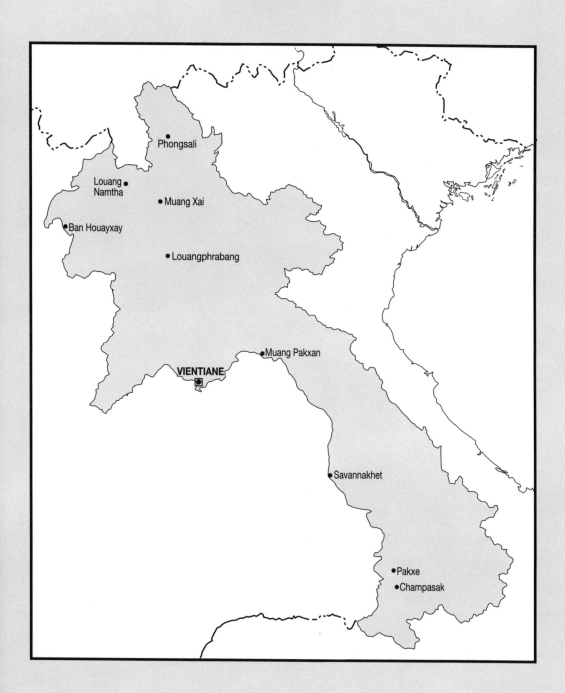

LAOS
The State of the State

Kyaw Yin Hlaing

The year 2005 marked the 35th anniversary of the People's Revolutionary Party's takeover of the Laotian government. Throughout this period, journalists and scholars have used various labels to describe the Laotian state. Some referred to it as a communist or socialist authoritarian state while others have described it as a weak state that could not even pay the salaries of many of its employees regularly. It is true that Laos is one of the five remaining communist countries in the world. It is also true that the Lao People's Revolutionary Party (LPRP) does not tolerate any form of political opposition that directly or indirectly challenges its rule. Laos remains one of the most underdeveloped and poorest countries in the world. Even in 2005, about 38 per cent of the population reportedly lived below the poverty line and the salary of senior government officials was not enough for a family of four to live decently. Furthermore, a large majority of the working people, especially those from minority areas, do not have any formal education.

In spite of these factors, this article attempts to demonstrate that the Laotian state is not static. Since the collapse of the communist bloc, the Laotian state has undertaken several reforms. Consequently, the nature of the state has changed over time. The government has also loosened control over the population. In the early 1990s, foreigner could not travel around the country freely. A Laotian businessman noted that he would not dare to talk to any foreigner as it could earn him a prison term.[1] In 2005, however, many foreigners moved around the country and interacted with people quite freely. One can see at coffee houses, restaurants and bars in Vientiane that most Laotian people are not afraid of dealing with foreigners any more. Since early 2000, the infrastructure has improved significantly.

KYAW YIN HLAING is Assistant Professor in the Department of Political Science at the National University of Singapore.

This article examines the state of the state in Laos in 2005. In so doing, the article will highlight how the nature of the Laotian state changed in the last 15 years and assess its capacity to deal with social and economic reforms.

How Socialist and Authoritarian Is the Laotian State?

In 1975 the LPRP took control of the country by toppling the monarchy and establishing a one-party dominated socialist state under the rubric of Lao People's Democratic Republic (PDR). Political organizations apart from the LPRP and its affiliated mass organizations were not allowed to exist. The LPRP was only supposed to give guidance to the government in implementing policies. In reality, however, the party and the state were intertwined, and party officials had the final say in everything. As in most other communist countries, government officials were not promoted to senior positions without attending the party's cadre training school. In trying to indoctrinate ordinary people with communist ideology, the government installed loudspeakers in public places in major cities to broadcast communist propaganda.

In its dealings with the public, the government did not tolerate any challengers. Independent civil society organizations were virtually non-existent. As in most other communist countries, the government mainly used mass organizations to control societal groups. The party-state functioned more like a bureaucratic polity in which only senior members had a say in both the policy-making and implementation processes. The government also controlled the flow of information. Developments that reflected the weaknesses of the party-state were not covered in the state media. Due to the repressive environment, most Laotians did not talk about politics in public places. A Laotian businessman who later settled in America noted:

> We felt that government agents were omnipresent and we would get into trouble if we talked about politics. It was okay if we spoke good things about the party and the government but if the government knew that we were criticizing its activities, we could get arrested. That was what we believed. We practised self-censorship.

As noted above, ordinary people dared not interact with foreigners up to the late 1990s. A Westerner who used to work for an international non-governmental organization (NGO) operating in Laos recounted:

> I came to Vientiane in the early 1990s. I was not allowed to talk to anybody. Nobody wanted to talk to me. I could not go to provinces.

> Shops and restaurants had to close around 7 pm. It was not that the country was unsafe. It was very safe but the government was just controlling the lives of ordinary people. People were too afraid to break laws openly.

Twenty Laotians I interviewed also supported this view. They all believed that the government would take brutal action against challengers. Most people tried to avoid doing things that would make them look like anti-government activists. As the Cold War wound down and assistance from the communist bloc declined, the LPRP government started changing its socialist policies. In 1986 the government undertook some economic reforms and began to downplay the importance of socialism. There was also no mention of communism or socialism in the new constitution that was promulgated in 1991. The government also stopped playing communist propaganda in public places since the mid-1990s. With the exception of the LPRP congress, senior party-state officials rarely referred to socialism or communism in their speeches. When asked in late 2005 how important communism or socialism was for the Lao PDR, a former party-state official noted:

> We can say that communism is no longer relevant to the Lao PDR. The government has stopped placing emphasis on communism since about ten years ago. Government officials don't like to talk about it. We, ordinary people, don't like to talk about it either. Although the LPRP still wears the communist mask, our leaders know that if they stuck to the communist ideology, their tenure would not last very long.

The LPRP government has also relaxed its control over the populace. Since 1998 the LPRP government has allowed some respected community leaders to form semi-autonomous professional organizations such as teachers' association. Though such organizations are not allowed to be involved in any form of anti-government activities, they are allowed to engage in some social welfare activities freely. Although they still had to affiliate themselves to government agencies or mass organizations and limit their activities to non-controversial ones, the emerging semi-autonomous social organizations have created space for ordinary people to meet government officials and engage in non-political social activities. As noted by a foreign NGO worker:

> Most people don't think much of the emerging semi-autonomous social organizations in Laos. Of course, they are still in a nascent

> stage and are nowhere near as vibrant as those in most other ASEAN countries; the fact that they are around means something to those of us who have been involved in developmental activities in Laos for several years. The government has lately allowed six local NGOs to have their own logos and seals. This is a major development in an authoritarian communist country. As you know, the government has opened up space for societal actors. This is a clear indicator of the relaxation of control of society by the government. Hopefully, the space would grow larger over time. Hopefully, in the near future, international NGOs would be able to start working with local civil society organizations and NGOs, not just with government agencies and mass organizations.

Since the early 2000s, the government has also taken less and less ruthless actions against ordinary people. For instance, in the 1990s the government confiscated without any compensation all privately owned land that was in the way of the construction of new roads. In 2005, however, many people refused to give up their land for state construction projects and the government stopped forcing people out of their properties, especially in town and city areas. A local NGO worker proudly said:

> In the past, those who refused to give up their properties for the state project could even be subject to jail terms. By 2005, however, the government did not respond forcefully against such people any more. They just continue to live on their own land. This is a big change.

This change was apparently an outcome of the government's relaxation of the restrictions over foreigners, especially foreign NGO workers, in the country. A foreign NGO worker recounted:

> In the early 1990s, it was not easy to travel around the country. We had to deal with a lot of paperwork to get permission to travel within the country. Now, we can go to anywhere we want. The government has issued a special ID for us but nobody really bothers to check us. When we could travel around the country, we understood the local situation better and, as a result, we could help local people more efficiently. When we [foreign NGO workers] heard that the government was confiscating private properties for state projects without any compensation, we advised local people not to give up their properties. At the same time, we also told government officials that it

was not proper to take away private properties without any proper compensation.

Nothing better illustrates the fact that the government has become less repressive than the lessening of restrictions on religious organizations. When the LPRP took control of the country, the government seriously restricted the activities of all religious groups, including Buddhist organizations. The government also reportedly nationalized the properties of many Christian organizations. Although the 1991 Constitution states that the government "respects and protects all lawful activities of Buddhists and of followers of other religions, [and] mobilizes and encourages Buddhist monks and novices as well as the priests of other religions to participate in activities that are beneficial to the country and the people", it does not clearly explain what unlawful activities are.[2] The resolution of the Party (1992) clarifies some of the activities of religious organizations that the LPRP government might consider unlawful.[3] However, the party-state failed to disseminate the information about the resolution to the provincial level, and many local party-state officials reportedly were not aware of the 1992 clarification and so continued to restrict religious activities in their own areas. The activities of Christian groups were subject to more restrictions, as these groups occasionally tried to help the ethnic minorities, some of whom were involved in anti-government activities. From the early 2000s, the central government started allowing religious groups to engage in their activities more freely. The Prime Minister's decree (2002) further clarified the rights and duties of various religious organizations.[4] The Lao Front for National Construction, a government-affiliated political organization, issued instructions clarifying the 1992 and 2002 decrees about religious organizations to various levels of the government and called for government agencies to disseminate the content of the decrees to lower-level government agencies.[5] Probably because of such concerted efforts of the central government and its affiliated social organizations, religious organizations have come to enjoy more and more freedom. A Christian pastor succinctly noted:

> 2005 is a better year than the 1990s or even early 2000s. In the past, it was quite difficult for us to meet government officials. Even when we wanted to make some non-religious contribution to the country, they still did not want us to do it. They did not trust us. Since early 2000s, the government has become more helpful. As long as we did not engage in suspicious activities in minority areas, we could organize religious activities quite freely.

Meanwhile, a foreign pastor noted:

> Foreign missionaries have come to this country throughout the LPRP period. But in the 1990s, they could not do much. Many of them left the country, as they could not do anything outside the rooms of the building they rented. Some were even expelled. In the late 1990s, many of us came into the country as NGOs. We helped the government in educational, environmental and other social sectors. In return, the government turned a blind eye towards our activities. In some cases, officials even indirectly advised us how we could circumvent certain existing rules. We did not have to bribe them. They helped us out of appreciation for our contribution to the state development projects.

All five Laotian Buddhists I interviewed unanimously said that Buddhist organizations also enjoyed more freedom since 2000. Although there are a few hundred Muslims residing in Laos, Buddhist and Christians alike did not seem to want to talk about them. As I did not get a chance to interview any Muslims, I am not able to judge how the changes in the government's position on religious activities have affected the activities of Islamic groups. However, a local NGO worker noted that because the government was more suspicious of the Christian groups than the Muslim groups, the latter should enjoy more freedom than the former.

All aforesaid changes in the nature of the Laotian state can be better understood in the light of changes in Vietnam and Laos' growing reliance on Western assistance. The Laotian party-state has long been a close ally, or rather a satellite state, of the Vietnamese party-state. All senior LPRP party-state officials attended training in Vietnam. When Vietnam began economic reforms, the LPRP government also started to undertake economic reforms and relaxed its control over the society. Laotian party-state officials also became more tolerant of non-political activities of the people. Since the collapse of the Eastern bloc, the LPRP government has come to rely on Western countries for financial and technical assistance. Naturally, donor countries pressured the LPRP government to abide by the Universal Declaration of Human Rights and undertake economic and political reforms. As Western countries intensified their criticism of human rights violations in the neighbouring country, Myanmar, the LPRP government tried to show that it was not a pariah state by relaxing restrictions on its people. A foreign consultant who is close to the government observed:

> Senior Laotian officials did not want their country to be put in the same category with Myanmar, for fear that Western countries might impose similar economic sanctions that have been imposed on Myanmar, on Laos. They wanted to show that they were not like their Myanmar counterparts. That is, they wanted to show that they respected human rights. As about 80 percent of the investment budget came from foreign assistance, they could not afford to upset donor countries.

To be sure, I am not suggesting that Laos is already on its way to a state-initiated democratic transition. The Laotian people are still subject to numerous restrictions. They are still afraid to discuss politics in public places. When I was interviewing some locals in early 2006, the first thing many of my interviewees said to me was that they did not want to discuss political issues in the presence of other people. Furthermore, religious organizations still have to be cautious about the kind of activities they choose to engage in. The government is still not tolerant of any form of opposition and is prepared to take brutal action against those who defy its rules. On the whole, however, it is fair to say that the Laotian state is less authoritarian than it used to be.

Is the Laotian State a Weak State?

Like their counterparts in other communist states, the Laotian state often sets goals it cannot achieve. The outcomes of the policies adopted by the LPRP government in the 1980s and early 1990s fell short of declared goals. Even though the LPRP government has been undertaking economic reforms for more than two decades, Laos remains one of the poorest countries in the world. Obviously the Laotian state lacks the capacity to develop the country. However, analysing state capacity in an aggregated manner will not let us see the complex nature of state strength. In this article, following Merilee Grindle, I will access the perceived capacity of the Laotian state in terms of technical, institutional, administrative capacities of the Laotian state as well as its perceived political capacity.[6]

Technical capacity

The level of technical capacity or the capacity to formulate appropriate policies is often determined by the expertise and calibre of the policy-makers. Because most senior Laotian government officials were trained in the ex–Soviet Union, Vietnam, Cuba, and some Eastern European countries, one could assume that their understanding of market economic reforms is limited. A foreign consultant who interacted with Laotian officials in the 1990s noted, "It was very depressing to deal with them. They did not have any idea about what they were supposed to be doing. They did not understand what I was trying to explain to them." The situation was worse at the provincial and lower levels. Unlike the officials in the central government, many provincial government officials were not properly educated and often did not understand the directives of the central government, which they were supposed to implement at the local level.[7] Only about 10 per cent of the LPRP civil servants have had access to university education.[8] A major cause of the weak technical capacity was the weak education system. Three Laotian businessmen who went to university in Vientiane in the 1980s said to me that after having undergone graduate studies in Thailand and Singapore, they came to realize that the education system in Laos was far behind that of its ASEAN neighbours. Most university lecturers lacked proficiency in English and were unable to read books in the English language. Furthermore, many lecturers did not have a good grasp of the subjects they were teaching. The reports prepared by the Australian and Japanese funding agencies also indicated that both the basic and higher education systems were not good enough to prepare Laotians for the new economic system.[9] That is why all funding or donor agencies such as the World Bank, the International Monetary Fund, the United Nations Development Program (UNDP), and the Asian Development Bank (ADB) have placed emphasis on the training of human resources before undertaking major administrative and economic reforms. The 2005 *World Bank Report* still considers human resource constraints as "a significant challenge in Lao PDR".[10]

The LPRP government understood the weak state of human resources in the country and sought assistance from Western countries. Government reports also clearly and openly outlined the problems with its education system.[11] The fact that the communist country had admitted its own weakness was an indication that its government was genuine about doing something about its problems. With the assistance of several countries of the European Union, Laotian government officials learned about economic and administrative reforms both in Laos and abroad. Many Laotian government officials also received scholarships to study at major universities in America, Japan, and West European countries. Studies conducted by the World Bank, the Governance Reform and the Livelihood Strengthening Program — a programme supported by the UNDP, World Bank, and SNV (a Netherlands development organization) — indicated improvements in the performance of government officials after their participation in training organized by donor countries and international organizations.[12] The same consultant quoted above also remarked:

> The performance of Laotian officials has improved significantly in the last three years. They now better understand the policies they are supposed to be making. It is now much easier to discuss policy issues with them. Many officials can now discuss policy issues in English.

Another foreign consultant noted:

> In the last three years, I saw a lot of improvement in Laotian government officials. They have learned a lot about how to make economic policies. There are still so many problems with the economic policies of the Laotian government. I have personally witnessed that they managed to improve their expertise in economic policy-making.

When asked to assess the technical capacity of various government agencies, a Laotian government official proudly said:

> In the last four or five years, we got several opportunities to improve ourselves. We attended various training sessions in Singapore, Thailand, Vietnam and several Western countries. Many of my colleagues did graduate studies in Western universities. We can now read the books and articles written in English. Also, thanks to foreign NGOs, ADB and the World Bank, we also have access to information, books and reports about the expertise we need to attain. Trust me, the state of our technical capacity in 2005 was very good. It has gotten much better than it used to be.

One indication of ongoing efforts to improve the economy can be seen in the economic reports and guidelines issued by the government in 2003, 2004, and 2005, which were more coherent and systemic than the ones published in the 1990s. Along with such positive indicators of the improvement in the technical capacity of the Laotian state, there is also some evidence of improvement in the Laotian universities. A local NGO worker and two foreign consultants noted that the quality of graduates from the National University of Laos has improved significantly since 2001.

A lot more can and should be done to raise the level of expertise of Laotians, however. Laos has the lowest per capita investment in education of any ASEAN country, and the qualifications of many Laotian party-state officials are not up to international standards yet. Nevertheless, there are indications that the technical capacity of the Laotian state in 2005 was significantly better than it used to be.

Institutional capacity

Traditionally, the institutional capacity (the capacity to adopt necessary rules and regulations) of the LPRP government was very weak. The LPRP government ruled the country without a constitution until 1991. In fact, Laos PDR is quite well known for being the land of decrees and directives. The government often issues decrees and directives for civil servants and the people to follow. However, partly due to the pressure and advice of foreign consultants and Western funding agencies, the LPRP government has clarified existing laws, decrees, and directives and issued new laws and decrees to attract foreign investments and to improve the efficiency of the government. For instance, in order to deal with corruption, the government has been issuing various decrees and instructions to empower anti-corruption agencies and set clear guidelines for investigating corruption cases since the early 1990s. Even though the Laotian state rarely discussed corruption issues openly until 1998, it has been well-equipped with regulatory devices to deal with them all along. The Laotian state now has clearer regulations and instructions regarding revenue collection and property rights.[13] In addition, as discussed earlier, the Laotian state now also has clearer rules and regulations for religious activities. The five foreign NGO workers and consultants that I interviewed who have worked on political, economic, and social reform projects in Laos for three to five years also noted that the Laotian state has most of the necessary regulatory devices to deal with its social, economic, and political issues.

In fact, the problem with the Laotian state's institutional capacity is that it has too many decrees, directives, and instructions. As noted by a foreign NGO worker, there are decrees to deal with certain issues, decrees to modify some of the existing decrees, and decrees to revoke some existing rules and regulations. Even though Laos has had a constitution and a parliament for more than a decade now, the Laotian state is still resorting to non-parliamentary rule-making. At present, there are reportedly thousands of decrees and directives but only about 68 laws passed by parliament. Western donors have recently called for the government to upgrade some decrees "to the level of law[s]".[14] The government itself admitted that there were problems with its decrees and directives and indicated that it would try to improve them. However, a government report noted that due to the "low capacity" of local officials, it found it very difficult to introduce new rules and regulations that were different from local traditions.[15] Though the Laotian state's institutional capacity has improved considerably, the fact is that it is still weak. As will be seen in the following section, the government has, thus far, failed to resolve problems generated by the confusing and complicating nature of its decrees and directives.

Administrative capacity

Along with economic reforms, the Laotian state has tried to improve its administrative capacity (the capacity to implement policies and to enforce rules and regulations) by undertaking civil service, administrative, and judicial reforms since the mid-1990s. Regardless of such measures, the Laotian state's administrative capacity remains very weak. Many government officials still lack the skills and expertise they need to do their jobs.[16] Local government officials often do not understand the directives and instructions they receive from the central state. There were several instances when provincial government officials misinterpreted the central government's decrees.[17] A Christian priest recounted his encounter with some local government officials who did not understand the government's decree on religious activities. In some cases, the government officials did not know about the existence of certain decrees and directives. Two of the foreign NGO workers I interviewed noted that several government officials from Vientiane and some provincial and district areas were not aware of some decrees regarding the decentralization of the government. Some government officials only came to learn about the existence of certain decrees from foreign and local NGO officials who were working on developmental projects in collaboration with the government. In some remote areas, the government officials were incapable of reading the decrees and directives from the central government.[18] But not much could be done about this as there was a shortage of qualified staff both at the central and local areas. Although the government had tried to retrain government officials with the assistance of Western donors, most government officials, especially the ones from the local areas, had yet to attend any training as of 2005. Many Western donors, such as the ADB and the World Bank, had undertaken to provide training for government officials, though this could not be extended to all officials. Furthermore, rampant cronyism and low wages have made the hiring of qualified staff almost impossible. Whenever there were vacancies at various levels of the government, officials would bring in their own relatives and friends, with scant regard to their qualifications.[19] Often, those who urgently needed help to get a job were the very ones who did not have the necessary qualifications. A former government official–turned NGO worker noted that many government agencies were filled with unqualified people who were related to senior government officials. A UNDP report on "Corruption in Lao PDR" also made the same observation.[20]

On the other hand, for many qualified people, jobs in the government are no longer attractive. As the monthly salary of mid-level government officials is a meagre US$30, most people prefer to work for international NGOs or private business enterprises. The same local NGO worker quoted above said:

> When I was working for the government, I was very poor. My family did not have enough money to live comfortably. Since I started working for a foreign NGO, I don't have to worry about money anymore. My current income is fifty times more than what I used to earn when I was working for the government. That's why you cannot expect government officials not to be corrupt. I had to accept bribes when I was working for the government. Otherwise, my family would starve.

Not surprisingly, many talented graduates of local universities prefer jobs with the NGOs and private business companies to jobs in the government. University graduates who choose to work for the government are mainly interested in positions that allow them to increase their pay packet by bribes. This inclination is discernible in that many university graduates wish to become income-tax collectors, for it is one of the most lucrative jobs in the government. Needless to say, corruption in the government is rampant. The fact that many government officials whose salaries are insufficient to meet the basic needs of a family of two, are living like rich people clearly demonstrates that many of them accept bribes. A former government official noted:

> The salaries of government officials are very low but many senior government officials and their family members live comfortably. They live in mansions. If they just lived on their own salaries, we would not see the children of government officials riding fancy motorcycles on the road.

Rampant corruption has seriously undermined the capacity of civil servants and technocrats to implement policies and to enforce rules and regulations. For instance, a foreign funding agency observed that thanks to corrupt tax collectors, the government loses about US$100 million annually.

According to a government official, the confusing nature of the government's decrees also made it harder for local officials to do their work. He also noted that even well-educated officials had difficulty understanding certain government decrees. So some provincial and district government officials sometimes continued to adhere to old decrees that the central government had already revoked because they did not understand what is required of the new decrees. This situation was compounded by contradictions within the system and the lack of trust between government officials and between various government agencies. On the one hand, the Laotian government had been undertaking decentralization reforms in the last few years, giving provincial and district-level government bodies more administrative power. On the other hand, the central government continued to practise democratic centralism, which basically requires local government bodies to strictly follow the central government's instructions. Torn between these two contradictory systems, several provincial and district officials did not know what they should do when they needed to deal with local problems on their own.[21]

The fact that the stock of social capital in the government was quite limited also made policy implementation and the enforcement of rules and regulations very difficult. Three of the NGO workers I interviewed noted that due to the training offered by some Western donors, the performance of several individual government officials had improved significantly. However, they also remarked that there was a lack of trust between Laotian government officials and this did not help when they had to work collectively, resulting in a lack of proper coordination and consultation between various government agencies.

Needless to say, the aforesaid conditions have seriously undermined the administrative capacity of the Laotian state. The shortage of qualified staff has contributed to failures or ineffectiveness of several reform programmes and policies. Due to the shortage of qualified lawyers and legal scholars, various levels of courts were understaffed, the government's legal reforms were delayed, and the legal system did not function properly.[22] Most Laotian people do not have much trust in formal rules and regulations. Instead, they believe that interpersonal linkages are more important than anything else for business transactions with government agencies. A foreign NGO worker said that he could not reject the project proposal of an incompetent construction company, for the owner of the company was a crony of a senior government official. Government officials seem to be prepared not to enforce rules and regulations in a consistent manner while well-connected people do not seem to worry about rules and regulations. A Laotian government official noted:

> Roads in Vientiane can sometimes be overrun by unruly youths with motorcycles. They break traffic rules all the time. They also create brawls in disco bars. Police officers cannot do much to tame these people, as they are children of senior government officials. All you need is connections. As long as you don't challenge the rule of the LPRP, you can break all other rules and get away with it. If you can find a way to bribe government officials, you can change the laws. It is not a difficult thing to do.

Nevertheless the administrative capacity of the Laotian state is not totally hopeless. As noted earlier, the government has undertaken several civil service and administrative reforms. At the same time Western donors have continued to give both financial and technical assistance to the Laotian government's administrative reforms. A foreign consultant was cautiously optimistic:

> EU countries have invested millions of dollars in the capacity building of the Laotian government. Senior Laotian government officials also understand that they will have to find a way to improve the capacity of government officials. They discuss it openly. I think things will get better eventually.

Political legitimacy

As a small country that relies heavily on foreign assistance, the LPRP government seeks both international and domestic legitimacy. With regard to international legitimacy, the LPRP government tries to project itself as a small peace-loving nation on good terms with other countries. This strategy appears to be working quite well. The LPRP government has managed to maintain good relations with its major donor countries: the European Union, Australia, Japan, New Zealand, and Switzerland,[23] all of whom have promised to continue providing technical and financial aid. Although the US State Department criticized the LPRP government for human rights violations in 2005, the US government continued to assist the LPRP government in areas such as drug eradication, the clearing and disposing of unexploded ordnance, health, and education.[24] The only foreign relations glitch that the LPRP government committed was the exchange of criticisms with its Thai counterpart over the disappearance of 27 Hmong people who had been deported from Thailand to Laos in December 2005.[25] Despite this incident, Laos has maintained very good relations with ASEAN member countries. Unlike its Myanmar counterpart, Laos has been viewed as a beneficial new member by ASEAN's founding members. On the whole, the LPRP government's international legitimacy in 2005 remained strong.

With regard to domestic legitimacy, the LPRP government, like other communist governments, relied on communist ideology for legitimization. Since the collapse of the communist bloc, however, the government has turned to performance-based criteria such as economic reforms and prosperity as new sources of legitimacy. The LPRP government takes pride in the success of its economic reforms: continued economic growth in 2005 which was projected at

7.3 per cent, declining inflation rate from 10.5 per cent in 2004 to 5.9 per cent in 2005, stable exchange rate at 10,613 Lao kip to the US dollar in 2004 and 10,572 kip to the dollar in 2005, increased foreign investment in hydropower plant and mining industries, increased exports, which rose 13 per cent in 2004, and the creation of employment in the private sector.[26]

Since there is no proper research on the legitimacy of the Laotian government, it is difficult to judge the outcome of the LPRP government's activities and the state of the government's legitimacy. However, some available anecdotal evidence suggests that regardless of the fact that the country remains very underdeveloped, the LPRP government does not appear to face a legitimacy crisis. All 25 Laotians I interviewed did not think that their government should be replaced. All my interviewees were aware of developments in the region and 20 of them noted that they did not want their country to go through the kind of instability Thailand and Myanmar were going through. They all said that their country was very stable under the rule of the LPRP. The two foreign NGO workers who had worked in provincial areas for a few years also said most of the local people did not question the legitimacy of the central government. They only expressed their unhappiness with local government officials and wished for the replacement of "mean local officials" by the central government. However, there was a strong potential for anti-government activities in some minority areas. A foreign former NGO worker noted that the criticisms of the government that he heard of only came from some minority people, but these people were not strong enough to engage in any major movement against the government. Those who tried to confront the government were crushed, a good example being the armed struggle launched by the Hmong minority, which was no match for the government forces.

There is also no credible Laotian opposition that is operating either inside or outside the country. Members of the previous regime did not engage in any major anti-PRP activities. Student activism in Laos is virtually dead. There is no autonomous middle class and civil society. The handful of middle-class people created by the economic reforms is not only very weak but also very close to the government. Most big businessmen who complain about the inefficiency of the government privately cannot afford to undermine the legitimacy of the government openly. It is not just because they are afraid of the government's reprisal but because their interests are often intertwined with those of several senior government officials. When asked if he or his business friend would intentionally try to undermine the legitimacy of the government, a businessman responded:

> Why should I do that? I cannot do business here if the government does not like me. There are officials who like me and have helped me. I would rather promote my friendship with officials than undermine the government. I would not gain anything from trying to undermine the government.

As a result, anti-regime discourses are very weak. Because the government controls the flow of information, people are more exposed to the regime's propaganda. To be sure, Laotian people have easy access to the news media in Thailand. However, the Thai media rarely covers news about Laos. There are also a number of Internet cafes in Vientiane and other major cities and towns. Unlike in other authoritarian countries, the Laotian government does not try very hard to block political websites. This, however, does not impact on public attitudes towards the government, for, according to some local researchers, less than 5 per cent of the population regularly use the Internet as a source of information about Laotian politics. The public, on its part, do not appear to believe everything the government tells them. However, the impression I got from interviews with 25 Laotian people is that the absence of strong alternative voices has made them think that the LPRP government is very strong.

This is not to suggest that Laotian people are politically apathetic. Since the government opened up the country, many people have studied in more developed and politically open countries and have worked with foreign NGO workers and consultants. Many of these people have compared their country with other foreign countries they know. In my conversation with them, two Laotian workers expressed their concern over the environmental degradation that might be triggered by the government's dam projects. They said they and their friends regularly read news about Laos on the Internet. They also said some of their friends also listen to the Laotian language programming of Radio Free Asia. All 25 Laotians I interviewed expressed their unhappiness and frustration with the growing corruption in the government and the inefficiency of government officials. Eighteen of them said they privately questioned how senior government officials and their family members could afford a luxurious lifestyle. It is very obvious that there are grievances among Laotian people. However, the absence of alternative political organizations and attendant political constraints has prevented the translation of public grievances into social protests. In the mean time, a large majority of Laotian people seem to have accepted that there is no better alternative to the LPRP government.

Conclusion

There is no doubt that the LPRP government has become less communistic and less repressive than it used to be. The 7.3 per cent projected economic growth for 2005, a stable exchange rate, and inflation have indicated that regardless of difficulties with its administrative and economic reforms, the LPRP government's technical, institutional, and administrative capacities are improving. Even though there are grievances among the general public, the political situation is very stable and the government does not have to worry about its reform programmes being interrupted by social protests. The main objective of the LPRP government's reforms is to graduate from being one of the poorest countries in the world by the year 2020 and achieve what is commonly known as the Millennium Development Goals. The big question then is whether the Laotian state has the capacity to achieve these goals.

As noted above, there are still many problems with various aspects of the LPRP government's capacity to develop the country. All the reports released by international organizations and the LPRP government have indicated that the pace of improvement in the efficiency of the government is unsatisfactory. The government's ability to implement policies and enforce rules and regulations is rather limited and more drastic reforms are needed to improve it. At present, EU countries, the ADB, and the World Bank seem very committed to helping the LPRP government improve its technical, institutional, and administrative capacities. The LPRP government, for its part, also appears to be committed to administrative reforms. An experienced foreign consultant noted that the LPRP government would have to be two to three hundred times more efficient than it now is before the country can graduate from its LCD (least-developed country) status. The six government officials I talked to enthusiastically said their country would certainly be able to achieve the Millennium Development Goals. Some foreign NGO workers had doubts about this, while a few others were cautiously optimistic. However, the fact that the LPRP government has managed to stay in power for more than a decade after the collapse the communist bloc alone shows that the Laotian state remains in good stead.

Notes

The author wishes to thank Woon Yong Hong, Bacharee Puengpak, and N. Ganesan for their research and editorial assistance.

[1] Because most of my interviewees were still living or working in Laos, they do not wish to be quoted by name. I therefore will not give citations to all the interviews

1. I have quoted in the article. Of the 36 people I interviewed, 9 are present or former government officials, 11 are present or former NGO workers, 4 are students, and 12 are business people.
2. Constitution of Lao PDR, Law on Government of Lao PDR, Law on Local Administration of Lao PDR (Vientiane: Public Administration and Civil Service Authority, 2005), p. 4.
3. Maha Khampeuy Vannasopha, *Religious Affairs in Lao PDR* (Vientiane: Department of Religious Affairs, 2005), pp. 18–25.
4. Ibid., pp. 28–37.
5. Ibid., pp. 38–43.
6. Merilee Grindle, *Challenging the State* (New York: Cambridge University Press, 1996).
7. Governance Reform and Livelihood Strengthening Programme, "Local Governance Self-assessment Report: Khammouane Province", 2005, pp. 26–31.
8. International Development Association, "Country Assistance Strategy for the Lao People's Democratic Republic", 10 March 2005, p. 8.
9. AusAid, Laos Australia Development Cooperation Program (2004–10) (Canberra: AusAid, 2005); Hayashida Kazuno, "Teaching Law and Political Science at the National University of Laos", Nagoya University Center for Asian Legal Exchange Newsletter (No. 3, 2001).
10. International Development Association, "Country Assistance Strategy for the Lao People's Democratic Republic", pp. 8–9.
11. Lao PDR, "Background Paper on Governance" (Vientiane, March 2003); Governance Reform and Livelihood Strengthening Programme, "Local Governance Self-assessment Report: Khammouane Province", 2005.
12. International Development Association, "Country Assistance Strategy for the Lao People's Democratic Republic", 10 March 2005; Governance Reform and Livelihood Strengthening Programme, "Local Governance Self-assessment Report: Khammouane Province", 2005.
13. Governance Reform and Livelihood Strengthening Programme, "Local Governance Self-assessment Report: Khammouane Province", pp. 37–38.
14. Patrick Keuleers, *Corruption in Lao PDR* (Bangkok: UNDP, March 2004), p. 14.
15. Lao PDR, "Background Paper on Governance" (Vientiane, March 2003), p. 8.
16. International Development Association, "Country Assistance Strategy for the Lao People's Democratic Republic", p. 8.
17. Governance Reform and Livelihood Strengthening Programme, "Local Governance Self-assessment Report: Khammouane Province", pp. 17–35.
18. Ibid.
19. Ibid., p. 27.
20. Keuleers, op. cit.

[21] Governance Reform and Livelihood Strengthening Programme, "Local Governance Self-assessment Report: Khammouane Province", pp. 17–35.
[22] Keuleers, op. cit., p. 17.
[23] The EU's Relations with Lao People's Democratic Republic, http://europa.eu.int/comm/external_relations/lao/intro/index.htm; "Lao PDR Donors' Matrix", 2005, table 1.
[24] The Bureau of Democracy, Human Rights, and Labor, "Country Reports on Human Rights Practices — 2005", 8 March 2006.
[25] "Hmong Refugees: Laos Blames Thailand for 'Inhumane Act'", *Nation*, 2 February 2006.
[26] World Bank, "Lao PDR Economic Monitor", October 2005, pp. 1–2.

Malaysia

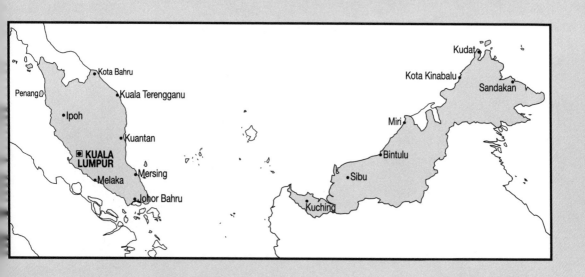

MALAYSIA
The Challenge of Money Politics and Religious Activism

K.S. Nathan

1. UMNO, Money Politics, and the Malay Agenda

In January 2005, Prime Minister Abdullah Badawi began his fifteenth month in office as leader of this multi-ethnic nation of 26 million people, with a raft of issues that remained unsettled since assuming office on 1 November 2003. Abdullah was faced with pressing problems such as money politics, cronyism, budget deficits, glaring failures of several government-linked companies (GLCs), and religious intolerance. On a personal level, 2005 was a particularly difficult year for Abdullah, as his ailing wife Endon Mahmood succumbed to breast cancer in October after battling it for two years.

The United Malays National Organisation (UMNO) General Assembly (19–23 July 2005) furnished the testing ground for Abdullah's leadership style and ability to emerge as a conciliator and problem solver for intra-UMNO politics and the general management of the ruling Barisan Nasional (BN). The BN is a 14-member coalition government in which two ethnic-based parties — the Malaysian Chinese Association (MCA) and the Malaysian Indian Congress (MIC) are senior partners representing numerically significant minorities in the country. The Prime Minister was conscious of the fact that he was not only UMNO President — the political party with 3.4 million Malay members — but was also the Prime Minister of a multiracial country. Abdullah squarely addressed the issue of money politics, which figured largely in the month-long run-up to the General Assembly. In his keynote speech, he remarked: "there can be no pride in winning an election through corrupt means and subsequently accepting money to bribe others".[1] Adding that it would be a tragedy for the Malays if wealth was used

---

K.S. NATHAN is Senior Fellow at the Institute of Southeast Asian Studies, Singapore.

to barter power and power was used to sell out the race, Abdullah stressed that efforts to enhance integrity and eradicate corruption would cover both the public and private sectors, including statutory agencies and GLCs.

The premier was evidently referring, in his speech, to the recent suspension of Isa Ahmad, the UMNO Vice-President and Federal Territories Minister, who secured the largest number of votes for the three vice-presidential posts in the September 2004 party elections. The party's disciplinary committee suspended Isa for six years, effectively ending his political career. A former Chief Minister of Negeri Sembilan, Isa was found guilty of bribing delegates by paying them between RM300 and RM1,000 for their votes. Yet, there is a certain measure of public disquiet over whether Isa was the sacrificial lamb in the scandal of money politics in the ruling ethnic Malay party. Although Isa's suspension was halved to three years on appeal, he was forced to resign his ministerial post in October. Was Isa the victim of a political conspiracy to remove him and to conceal the more serious disease afflicting the entire UMNO mindset of buying votes to attain high political positions in the party and government? Was Isa only the tip of the iceberg? Earlier in January, a Negeri Sembilan state executive councillor, Waad Abu Mansor, had his Court of Appeal decision overturned by the Federal Court, which sent him to jail on corruption charges. The latter even went as far as criticizing the Court of Appeal's decision in substituting fines for jail terms as this was not a sufficient deterrent to corruption and money politics.[2]

Although ISA's suspension was a stern reminder against indulgence in money politics, Abdullah still has a long way to go in curbing the disease. UMNO's drive, especially during Mahathir's tenure, to rapidly create a corpus of world-class Malay entrepreneurs through the political machinery of the party and the government invariably led to abuse. To achieve Vision 2020 via Malay economic empowerment. According to a specialist on Malaysia's political economy, "the government picked potential entrepreneurs and conferred on them — without open tender — concessions like licenses, contracts and privatized projects financed by loans from banks owned by the government".[3] This method of racial targeting and selective patronage eventually became so entrenched and institutionalized in the body politic that even the well-intentioned efforts of Mahathir's successor to eradicate this endemic disease has achieved only minimal results.

No doubt some measure of success has been achieved in the battle against corruption since Abdullah assumed power. In 2004, Kasitah Gaddam, then Cooperative and Land Development Minister, faced corruption charges in court as did several top businessmen and senior civil servants. Yet the premier's Integrity

Institute of Malaysia, set up in 2004 with the aim of educating the public and promoting the fight against corruption, has plenty of work ahead to cause even a dent in the corruption cycle. According to a survey, only 30 per cent of Malaysia's overwhelmingly Malay civil servants were prepared to report incidents of graft to the relevant authorities such as the Anti-Corruption Agency (ACA), while 30.5 per cent of undergraduates in public universities said that they would accept kickbacks if they were in a position of power.[4] More recent evidence of scandals and economic failures in GLCs tend to undermine Abdullah's initiatives in revitalizing the bureaucracy and his anti-graft campaign.

Trade and Industry Minister Rafidah Aziz was at the centre of a controversy surrounding the issue of permits for the importation of foreign cars. The Approved Permits (AP) issue came to the fore when former premier Dr Mahathir called for full disclosure of the list of AP recipients. As adviser to Proton, Mahathir questioned why of the 67,000 permits issued in 2004, 54,400 went to just 20 companies while the remaining 12,600 went to 82 companies. Mahathir was obviously disturbed by the dismissal of his protégé, Proton chief executive Tengku Mahaleel Tengku Ariff, who had himself earlier attacked the government's policy as hurting Proton. Mahathir argued that the sharp drop in Proton's market share from 65 to 45 per cent following the opening of the car market under the ASEAN Free Trade Area (AFTA) was not due to low quality. A partial reason was the AP policy, which he claimed contradicted the original spirit of creating a *bumiputera* industrial and commercial community.[5]

The APs, which were given only to *bumiputera* (literally, "sons of the soil", referring primarily to Malays and other indigenous races) to enable them to import cars, were initially intended to help create a group of Malay car businessmen. The policy of nurturing Malays to succeed in business was an integral component of the New Economic Policy (NEP) launched in 1970, and then replaced by the New Development Policy in 1990. While the original objective was noble in intent, the APs soon degenerated into a get-rich-quick scheme dominated by politically well-connected businessmen. In her defence, Rafidah, whose ministry issues the APs, argued that in 2004, only 17,455 permits representing 3.2 per cent of the total car production of 530,035 vehicles for that year were issued to import cars of between 1,500 cc and 1,800 cc — the only category of cars in direct competition with Proton, the national car and Mahathir's brainchild. Rafidah argued that all AP holders had to meet stringent criteria set by the ministry before being issued an AP. Yet many, including Dr Mahathir, remained unconvinced of the fairness of the distribution of APs. Mahathir alleged that Proton's share of the car market had appreciably declined in the past few years, suggesting that there was gross abuse of the AP system. He claimed that the car permits were being sold to non-Malay businessmen for huge profits.[6]

Allegations of favouritism, nepotism, cronyism, and lack of transparency were levelled at Rafidah over the issuance of APs to three main holders: Nasimuddin S.M. Amin, chairman of Naza Motor Group (12,524 APs), and Syed Azman Syed Ibrahim and Mohd. Haniff Abdul Aziz who together were given 15,759 APs.[7] Mahathir strongly denied that during his tenure he had ever accorded national car status to Naza Ria, which at the time of its launch in August 2003 had only 18 per cent local parts content, compared with the minimum 40 per cent needed to qualify as a local car.[8] Mahathir's arguments must be viewed in the light of increasing competition faced by Proton from Naza, which allegedly was being favoured by Rafidah.

In the context of Abdullah's anti-graft drive, such practices were seen not only as being irregular and biased towards well-connected individuals but also defeating the redistributive goal of empowering the Malays as a whole. It was therefore no surprise that a new cabinet committee was set up to review the National Automotive Policy and the AP system, both of which were previously handled by Rafidah's ministry. This move dealt a major blow to her credibility in managing and implementing key aspects of *bumiputera* economic empowerment.

In another development over the episode involving the national car, Mahathir attacked Proton's recent sale of its 57.7 per cent stake in MV Augusta, an Italian motorcycle manufacturer, for one euro (RM4.50), saying "this sale must cause Proton to lose RM315 million less RM4.50".[9]

Yet, despite the AP controversy and rising unease over money politics in UMNO, expectations of a long overdue cabinet reshuffle did not materialize. Abdullah preferred instead to minimize political risk by continuing to operate with a team he largely inherited from Dr Mahathir.

The Malaysian police have come under increasing scrutiny in the past two years of Abdullah's tenure, following allegations of widespread corruption and human rights abuses. In November, cases involving harassment of Malaysians and foreigners who had lodged reports against police misconduct were widely reported in the media. In one case a Malaysian woman and three female Chinese tourists complained of police abuse to the parliamentary human rights caucus. Public concern over police excesses was highlighted by the release of a secretly recorded video showing a naked woman (a Malay woman initially presumed to be a Chinese national) doing nude squats ostensibly to expose any hidden contraband from her body — an issue that inflamed local Chinese sentiment and threatened to strain relations with China. In another case a policeman sued a student who lodged a report against him with the Anti-Corruption Agency after he asked the student for a bribe in a traffic violation. The cabinet directed the police to stop such harassment, as they further tarnish the police's name. They also urged the withdrawal of the defamation suit against the student, expressing concern that such types of police harassment could obstruct the battle against corruption.[10] The latest case of alleged police abuse involved the shaving of heads of 11 elderly Chinese men who were arrested and detained for illegal gambling. Prime Minister Abdullah Badawi ordered a probe on these cases to ensure that proper police procedures were followed in dealing with cases where human dignity and individual rights were involved.[11]

In the light of these incidents it is noteworthy that the Report of the Royal Commission to Enhance the Operation and Management of the Royal Malaysia Police (Polis DiRaja Malaysia, PDRM) stated that the Anti-Corruption Agency's report on corruption in government agencies between 1999 and 2003 found the PDRM to be the most corrupt, followed by the Town Councils. However, the Royal Commission report noted that corruption in the PDRM was part of a larger problem of corruption in Malaysia that was recognized as serious by both people and government alike.[12] The Commission recommended ten "strategic thrusts" to reform the police force: (1) modernize the role, functions, and organization of the Royal Malaysia Police (RMP), (2) launch a nationwide drive against crime, (3) enhance investigative policing, (4) eradicate police corruption, (5) make policing comply with prescribed laws and human rights obligations, (6) raise awareness of women's and children's rights in the RMP, (7) improve establishment, remuneration, and scheme of service of the RMP, (8) enhance human resource management and performance in the RMP, (9) upgrade the equipment and logistics of the RMP, and (10) provide better work premises and housing.[13]

These recommendations are laudable. However, they must be read in the context of an endemic culture of corruption in Malaysia's political economy, spawned partly by the zeal to fast-track the achievement of NEP targets. Such proclivities would tend to debunk reform efforts in terms of producing concrete results that could substantially change the public image of the police thereby delivering a major boost to public confidence in Abdullah's anti-graft campaign. UMNO Youth had already opposed the setting up of a police watchdog (an Independent Police Complaints and Misconduct Commission) recommended by the Royal Commission. They claimed that such a monitoring body will not solve all problems, and that the more pressing need was to listen to the views of the 93,000 members of the police force.[14] Several police associations also expressed concern over the recommendations, with three expressly rejecting the need for a watchdog.[15]

As the year 2006 began, Abdullah's battle against money politics seemed to get tougher rather than easier. Court of Appeal Judge Gopal Sri Ram, in his written judgement of a case involving a highway toll company Metramac, concluded that two Malay tycoons, Halim Saad and Anuar Othman, misappropriated RM32.5 million of Metramac's finances because of their links with former Finance Minister Daim Zainuddin. Ram also concluded that their actions were a breach of company laws and possibly an aggravated form of criminal breach of trust.[16] Daim denied his role in the scandal, claiming he quit as finance minister in 1991, and that Anwar Ibrahim was the finance minister when the supposed deal between the government and Metramac was signed in 1992.

The Metramac case, like many others before and after it, indicates how the government's pro-Malay policies have spawned a small group of well-connected *bumiputera* who have hijacked for self-aggrandisement the NEP's well-intentioned programme of national development. Yet, regardless of the setbacks in stimulating Malay efficiency and productivity and the attendant social costs of failure, the UMNO-led government has been, and remains, committed to *bumiputera* economic empowerment as the sine qua non of Malaysia's political and socio-economic stability.

At the July annual UMNO General Assembly, UMNO Youth leader Hishamuddin Hussein brandished a kris (sword) during his speech. This act was apparently intended to warn non-Malays that they would face dire consequences if ever they attempt to question the Malays' constitutionally prescribed special privileges or to demand equal rights as citizens of Malaysia.[16] In reiterating the Malay Agenda, Hishamuddin reasserted the sanctity of the Social Contract arrived at during independence in 1957, where Malay political supremacy was recognized in exchange for citizenship rights for non-Malays. Hishamuddin also demanded the re-introduction of the New Economic Policy (NEP, 1970–90) even though all post-NEP government policies, such as the New Development Policy (NDP), comply with the NEP framework. Article 153 of the Malaysian Constitution on special rights for Malays and other indigenous people (*bumiputera*), is often invoked during political party gatherings such as the annual General Assembly, to garner delegates' approval and support to ascend to top party and government positions.

Expectedly, Hishamuddin's kris-wielding act raised non-Malay anxiety. The opposition Democratic Action Party (DAP) Secretary-General, Lim Kit Siang, observed that "the time had come to focus on a national Malaysian Agenda that benefits and unites all ethnic groups to build a nation on the bedrock of needs, merit, hard work, moral and ethical values, and not appeal to kris-wielding, extremist and destructive emotions".[18]

Khairy Jamaluddin, UMNO Deputy Youth Chief and son-in-law of Abdullah Badawi, proposed the adoption of a New National Agenda (NNA), re-emphasizing the need for NEP-type affirmative action to ensure that Malays achieve targets set in the 9th Malaysia Plan to be launched in March 2006.[19] The focus of the NNA would be on distributional aspects of the country's development strategy rather than on growth. Such a proposal reflects UMNO's dissatisfaction with the success of redistribution, as Malays supposedly own only 19.3 per cent of the national wealth. This figure is, however, open to dispute depending on how Malay equity ownership is measured. According to political analyst Hng Hung Yong, the 19.3 per cent figure does not include the government's shareholding in various entities used to promote Malay employment and wealth creation — such as Petronas, Felda, Bank Rakyat, and all other GLCs. Hng notes that board representation, management control, ownership, and employment in these organizations are in the hands of Malays who have at their disposal massive resources to promote the Malay Agenda. He concludes that any attempt therefore to measure Malay participation in the economy should not ignore these linkages. Hng's central argument is that NEP targets could have been met much more effectively without disadvantaging any particular race if it had been defined and implemented as an anti-poverty programme. Detraction from the true spirit of the NEP, he argues, is the cause for racial polarization in Malaysian society today.[20]

In June the Prime Minister issued a three-month suspension to a deputy minister from the Malaysian Indian Congress (MIC), S. Sothinathan, for transgressing the principle of cabinet responsibility. The decision was unprecedented in the history of the ruling Barisan Nasional. Sothinathan criticized the government in parliament, arguing that it was the duty of the MIC as a party in the ruling government to "right a wrong when it happens".[21] The controversy began when Sothinathan, who is also MIC Secretary-General, raised the issue of discrimination against Malaysian Indian medical graduates by the Malaysian Medical Council (MMC). The latter claimed that medical graduates from the Ukraine-based Crimea State Medical University (CSMU) were poorly qualified and decided not to recognize their degrees. Most Malaysian Indians decide to pursue their medical ambition overseas because of strict racial quotas governing entry into local universities.[22] The issue resulted in heated exchanges in parliament even among members of the Barisan Nasional, which underscored the fact that racial tension can resurface when ethnic minorities begin to feel the crunch of the government's pro-Malay policies.

The issue surrounding the de-recognition and non-recognition of medical degrees from unscheduled universities overseas underscored a broader trend of ethnic polarization in Malaysian higher education as a direct consequence of the government's pro-Malay policies. Ethnic preferential programmes favouring *bumiputera* have resulted in Malay students dominating entry in public institutions of higher education, crowding out non-Malays, who end up enrolling in private colleges and universities. As one analyst notes, "the privatization and internationalization of higher education has but only perpetuated the ethnic fragmentation at the tertiary level".[23]

2. The Political Opposition:
PAS' Islamic Agenda under Pressure for Reform

The political opposition remained fractured and divided. Thus, its ability to seriously challenge the ruling coalition continued to remain very weak. The Pan Malaysian Islamic Party (PAS) — the only Malay opposition party capable of challenging UMNO's political legitimacy, is still contending with the severe setback it suffered in the March 2004 General Election when its parliamentary strength was significantly reduced from 27 to six seats. The split within the party between the conservative and hardline *ulama* including party Chief Abdul Hadi Awang and the liberal-minded and professionally qualified reformers took its toll in the Kelantan state by-election in December. PAS' control of the State Assembly was narrowed from a 24–21 majority to 23–22 after the poll. Pressures for reform are evidently emerging from the "Young Turks" in PAS who feel that the party badly needs a generational change to address the more complex problems arising from globalization. In their view, the purely textual, theological, and literal interpretations of the Koran would not suffice to face the new challenges in the 21st century. Yet it must be admitted that despite its best efforts, a religion-based party has, thus far, never been able to gain power at the national level since Malaysian independence in 1957. Of late, PAS leaders have attempted to widen the party's appeal among non-Muslims by emphasizing the establishment of an "Islamic society" rather than an "Islamic state".

This ideological setback, as well as the rather poor record of socio-economic development in the PAS-held state of Kelantan was reflected in the 6 December by-election. In a three-cornered fight for the state seat of Pengkalan Pasir, the BN's candidate, Hanafi Mamat, won with a 134-vote majority, following the death of PAS incumbent, Wan Abdul Aziz. UMNO's Hanafi Mamat polled 7,422 votes while his main rival, Hanifa Mat Yatim of PAS, garnered 7,288. The election results left PAS with just a one-seat majority in the Kelantan state parliament — the thinnest margin in the history of Malaysian politics. This could threaten the Islamist party's grip on power in its last remaining bastion after having lost control of Terengganu in 2004.[24]

Former deputy premier Anwar Ibrahim's political future remains uncertain. At the July UMNO General Assembly, Anwar was branded a traitor, followed by stern rejection of any attempts to reinstate him in the party. Dr Mahathir called Anwar a "backstabber" and accused him of being a liar for portraying the former premier as a corrupt leader.[25] Anwar has been barred from politics until 2008. His political come-back efforts by supporting PAS in the Kelantan state by-election failed to help swing voters in the Islamist party's favour. Yet Anwar remains a cause for concern in UMNO, as his return to the party in his quest for the top office in the country cannot be ruled out. He is a populist and charismatic leader, enjoying good support among Malay-Muslims who have not forgotten his earlier role as leader of ABIM (Malaysian Islamic Youth Movement) and his initiatives in promoting Islamization during his governmental tenure. He has threatened to bring defamation charges against Mahathir for branding him a homosexual if the latter failed to tender an apology and settle damages for RM100 million.[26] Anwar is fully aware that Mahathir's presence in the political scene as well as remarks about him could be a stumbling block to his efforts to make a political come-back — hence the urgency to clear his name.

In this connection, a measure of public confidence in the judiciary has been restored under Abdullah's leadership, stemming from three court victories favouring Anwar: first, an apology and payment of unspecified damages by former Police Chief, Rahim Noor, for assaulting him in 1998 while in police custody; second, clearing him on a sodomy charge; and third, a libel suit against a publisher.[27] Notably, these legal victories were preceded by Anwar's release from prison on 2 September 2004 when the Federal Court overturned his conviction on a sodomy charge. Undoubtedly, his party supporters in keADILan (National Justice Party, of which Anwar remains an ordinary member), as well as outside were encouraged and even emboldened by this reversal in fortune of the former deputy premier, thus enhancing prospects of his political resurgence.

3. Islamic Activism in the Context of Religious Pluralism

As the year drew to a close, a major debate was sparked by the death of an army commando and mountaineer, M. Moorthy, on 20 December. Following his death, the religious affairs department of the Federal Territory (JAWI) intervened to prevent Moorthy's widow from claiming his body from the hospital mortuary on the grounds that Moorthy had converted to Islam and assumed the name Mohammed Abdullah. The case was referred to the civil court where the High Court Judge, Mohd. Raus Sharif, decided that since Moorthy had converted to Islam, the matter fell within the jurisdiction of the Shariah court. However, Moorthy's widow claimed that her husband never told her of his conversion to Islam, and that he was a practising Hindu until his death. Her appeal to cremate his body according to Hindu rites was denied, and Moorthy was buried in a Muslim cemetery.

Because of its legal significance as to whether a non-Muslim has no remedy in the civil court in disputes over conversion to Islam, several non-Muslim cabinet members sent a memorandum to the Prime Minister urging a review of Article 121(1) (A) of the Federal Constitution to prevent a repeat of Moorthy's case. Abdullah declared that there was no need for review, citing another case where the Shariah court in Seremban ruled that a Malay woman died as a non-Muslim, and therefore was not entitled to a Muslim burial.[28] The Seremban court's decision in the case of Nyoya Tahir was unprecedented as it was the first time in the history of the country's Islamic courts that non-Muslims had appeared to give evidence before it. In this case, the Chinese family of the deceased appeared in an Islamic court to vouch that she never practised Islam.[29]

However, the controversy and ill feelings generated by Moorthy's case have the potential of sowing religious discord between the Muslim-Malay majority and the Hindu-Indian minority. Conscious of the ramifications and implications for religious harmony in the country, a minister in the Prime Minister's Department, Nazri Aziz, in an apparent attempt to defuse tension, observed: "When a person's faith is in question, the civil court should be allowed to hear it. The question in Moorthy's case was whether he was a Muslim in the first place. If we let the Muslim court decide this, justice might not be served because it would decide in favour of Islam".[30] In this regard, an inter-faith group, the Malaysian Consultative Council of Buddhism, Christianity, Hinduism, and Sikhism (MCCBCHS) also remarked that it was wrong for the Shariah court to have assumed jurisdiction over persons who do not profess Islam, and urged the government to amend Article 121(1) (A) of the Malaysian Constitution to preserve inter-religious harmony and promote national unity.[31]

In another case, the cabinet was compelled to hand down a decision that undergraduates should not be compelled to wear the *tudung* (headscarf worn by Muslim females). The Minister for National Unity, Maximus Ongkili, together with several other non-Muslim cabinet colleagues raised strong objections against the decision of International Islamic University Malaysia (IIUM) to bar a non-Muslim student from the convocation ceremony for refusing to wear the headscarf. The cabinet viewed this as coercion, citing the IIUM Students' Discipline Rules 2004 Guidebook, which clearly states that only Muslim female students' attire should cover the whole body except the face and palms.[32] Indeed, the very fact of cabinet intervention in such matters was indicative of how far "creeping Islamization" has gone in Malaysian society, and the obvious dangers it poses to religious and social freedom as well as inter-religious harmony in a culturally diverse society.

The rising trend of Islamic activism was also seen in the passage in December of the controversial Islamic Family Law (Federal Territories) (Amendment Bill) 2005. This parliamentary enactment caused an uproar among Muslim women over its discriminatory nature, as it tended to enhance the rights of Muslim men in cases of polygamy and their rights to divorce. Sisters in Islam executive director Zainah Anwar claimed that under Section 23(9)(b) of the Bill, Muslim men can also claim a share of their wives' matrimonial assets before taking on another wife or before they divorce. Zainah argued that the law was unjust and against the true principles of Islam, maintaining that Shariah provides that the husband has no right to his wife's property, while the wife has a right to his property for her and her children. A coalition of non-governmental organizations called Joint Action Group for Gender Equality (JAGGE) urged the withdrawal of the law, which they claimed had denied justice and equality to Muslim women.[33]

The above developments seem to contradict Abdullah's "Islam Hadhari" project, which aims to project the humane, progressive, tolerant, and peaceful aspects of Islam in a multi-religious environment.

4. The Economy: Targeting Balanced Development and Global Competitiveness

The Malaysian economy fared reasonably well in 2005, posting a 5 per cent growth in gross domestic product (GDP). The budget deficit dropped to 3.8 per cent from 4.3 per cent in 2004, helped largely by the scaling down or cancellation of mega projects approved during the Mahathir era. The deficit would have fallen further had it not been for the government's intervention to stabilize fuel prices in the wake of oil price hikes in world markets. The country's foreign reserves remained strong at RM304.3 billion (August 2005), due to the repatriation of export earnings and inflows of FDI and portfolio funds.[34]

In unveiling the 2006 budget on 30 September, PM Abdullah Badawi said the government aimed to further reduce the deficit in 2006 to 3.5 per cent so as to inject greater flexibility into its efforts to sustain the growth momentum. Beginning in 2007, a comprehensive value-added tax, known as the "goods and services tax", or GST, will be introduced to improve tax collection through indirect taxation and to ensure a more stable source of revenue.

The 2006 budget outlined several strategies to boost national resilience and improve the country's capability to meet emerging external challenges especially from escalating oil prices, higher interest rates, and increasing global competition. The fast-growing Islamic banking sector is expected to further expand, with the goal of doubling its share of total banking assets from 10.5 to 20 per cent by the year 2010.

In pursuing this goal, the government's four main strategies focus on: (a) implementing pro-active measures to accelerate economic activities, (b) providing a business-friendly environment, (c) developing the country's human capital, and (d) enhancing the well-being and quality of life of Malaysians. Strengthening *bumiputera* ownership of corporate wealth and participation in the Malaysian and global economy has always been a goal of the NEP and its successor, the NDP. To accomplish this goal under the 9th Malaysia Plan (2006–10), Abdullah who is also Finance Minister, announced that the Exim Bank would be placed under his ministry, while the bank's scope and functions will be substantially expanded to encourage and assist *bumiputera* entrepreneurs to venture abroad. In addition, a *bumiputera* property trust foundation (Yayasan Amanah Hartanah Bumiputera) will be set up with an initial capital of RM2 billion to expand *bumiputera* commercial property ownership in major towns.[35] The budget also included plans to further develop the Multimedia Super Corridor (a 750 sq. km. information and communication technology (ICT) zone near Kuala Lumpur), and the creation of a RM1 billion fund for small and medium enterprises (SMEs) to be disbursed by the SME Bank, which began operations in October.

The manufacturing sector continued to play a key role in the economy. Export-oriented industries were rapidly replacing import-substitution industries and industries based on processing output of primary produce. Significantly, export of goods and services, which constituted 14 per cent of current-price GDP in 1980, had jumped to 121.2 per cent in 2004. Manufacturing accounted for 31.4 per cent of GDP in 2004, with exports of electronic and electrical goods alone constituting 65.8 per cent of manufactured goods exports, compared with a share of only 30 per cent in the 1970s. The sensitivity of this sector to external markets has obliged the government to increase Malaysia's export competitiveness through export trade promotion.

Abdullah's commitment to modernize the agricultural sector and increase its share of the national output, which constituted 9.5 per cent of GDP in 2004, was seen in the allocation of a RM2.8 billion development fund for agriculture, animal husbandry, fisheries, and forestry, including the promotion of research and development in *halal* products for which the government envisaged an expanding market.

The services sector (including financial services) performed extraordinarily well, emerging as the major source of economic growth in 2005, with a growth rate of 5.8 per cent, and accounting for 57.4 per cent of GDP in 2004. The Treasury's *Economic Report 2005/2006* released on 30 September forecasts a 6.1 per cent growth in 2006 with the transport, storage, and communication sub-sectors benefiting from capacity expansion of airlines and investment by telecommunication companies. Performance in government services, commerce (retail trade, restaurants, and tourism-related activities) accounted for most of the earnings buoyed by the strength of domestic demand and private consumption. To encourage mergers and acquisitions, companies listed on Bursa Malaysia and approved by the Securities Commission will be given certain tax exemptions, while additional tax incentives will be provided to venture capitalists involved in high-risk projects in food production, forest plantation, biotechnology, nanotechnology, optics, and photonics. Through these measures, the government hopes to substantially increase the knowledge content of the economy using ICT and further deepen and widen Malaysia's industrial base and the services sector.

Natural gas production scored a double-digit growth year-on-year, due to rising demand from key consumers, such as Japan, South Korea, and Taiwan. In 2004, Japan took 61 per cent of liquefied natural gas (LNG) exports, while South Korea and Taiwan accounted for 23 and 12 per cent, respectively. This development encouraged the national petroleum corporation (Petronas) to further expand its LNG liquefication facility in Bintulu, Sarawak.[36]

Inflation has remained high, triggered largely by three increases in petrol and diesel prices. Petrol prices rose 20 per cent to RM1.62 per litre at year-end, while diesel was sold at RM0.80 (US$0.20) per litre.

To ease the financial burden of Malaysians, especially those in the low-income group, Abdullah announced on 7 September that there would be no further increase in the price of petrol, diesel, and cooking gas in 2005, no further increase in toll rates until the end of 2006, and a reduction in road tax effective on 12 September. However, he left the door open for a possible increase in petrol, diesel, and gas prices in 2006.

Malaysia's external trade balance for the period January–September 2005 posted a larger surplus of RM71.8 billion compared with RM60.1 billion in the same period in 2004. Total exports rose by 10.5 per cent to RM391.2 billion while imports rose by 8.6 per cent to RM319.4 billion when compared with the corresponding figure in 2004, with exports valued at RM354.0 billion and imports at RM294.0 billion. Electrical and electronic products constituted the largest export earner, expanding by 7.9 per cent and comprising RM193.3 billion or 49.4 per cent of exports. Palm oil, together with palm oil-based products, retained its position as the second largest export revenue earner, accounting for 5.5 per cent of total exports, while crude petroleum, the third largest commodity, contributed 5.4 per cent of total exports.

Malaysia's top five trading partners remained unchanged year on year: United States, Singapore, Japan, the European Union, and China, all of whom contributed 62.5 per cent of the country's total trade during January–September 2005. Nevertheless, intra-regional trade remains an important component of global trade. Malaysia's trade with other ASEAN countries totalled RM216.3 billion or 24.6 per cent of the total trade compared with 20 years ago, when the figure was well below 10 per cent.

On 21 July Malaysia removed its exchange rate peg in favour of a managed float weighted against a basket of currencies. This decision followed China's removal of the renminbi peg to the US dollar on the same day. The effect of the change in exchange rate policy, however, was not dramatic, with the ringgit's value barely rising vis-à-vis the US dollar. As of December, the exchange rate was US$1 = RM3.78. As the United States and Japan are Malaysia's major trade partners, the ringgit would be vulnerable to movements in these two currencies. Additionally, Malaysia's economic performance and ability to attract FDI were subject to external threats such as high oil prices, the strength of the US dollar, and downward pressures on investment. Although unemployment has fallen to a significantly low figure of just above 3 per cent, there are concerns about graduate unemployment, especially among Malays. A survey by the Economic Planning Agency found that there were nearly 60,000 unemployed graduates, mostly female ethnic Malays from lower-income groups. This was due to the lack of experience, poor English and communication skills, and lack of professional competencies required by the private sector. Despite past governmental efforts to establish skills training and re-training schemes for Malays, little progress has been achieved to date. Nevertheless, under the 2006 budget, the government plans to implement several schemes to enhance *bumiputera* skills and competencies, including the setting up of a Young Entrepreneur's Scheme, a Skills

Training Centre, and the Prosper Graduate Programme to encourage graduates to become entrepreneurs.

In addition, RM5 billion was allocated as development expenditure for education and training. Private institutions of higher learning are considered to play an important role in human resource development, besides contributing to the nation's objective of becoming a regional educational hub. In December 2004 there were 6,000 foreign students in public institutions of higher learning, and 26,000 students in private institutions of higher learning.

On the chronic shortage of skilled workers in the manufacturing sector, the government reversed a January decision to repatriate foreign labourers under an immigration crackdown in which 400,000 foreign workers, mostly Indonesians, left Malaysia. Since May, illegal workers on tourist visas were issued work permits. Nevertheless, the government is cognizant of the fact that while the illegal migrants, estimated at over 800,000, do not pay taxes and live in shantytowns, their services are badly needed, especially in the construction and plantation sectors.

5. Foreign Policy: Broadening and Deepening Regional Cooperation

The Prime Minister's style of diplomacy and mass communication is evidently in sharp contrast to his predecessor, who preferred to make his often controversial views known on the world stage. Abdullah Badawi is not a rhetorician nor is he a seeker of world fame. He has gone about quietly promoting Malaysia's interests at the national, regional, and international levels through his less obtrusive style of leadership.

ASEAN remains the cornerstone of Malaysian foreign policy — a pattern and trend that remain consistent with previous eras since Malaysian independence in 1957. Southeast Asia primarily, and the East Asian region in a broader context, continues to figure prominently in Malaysia's pursuit of its foreign policy interests. Efforts to fast-track the creation of the ASEAN Economic Community (AEC) were reiterated at the ASEAN leaders summit on 13 December, with the goal of bringing the target date forward from 2020 to 2015. Such optimism, however, needs to be balanced against the performance of the second-tier ASEAN members (Cambodia, Laos, Myanmar, and Vietnam). Nevertheless, the establishment of the AEC could bring enormous benefits to the grouping's 530 million citizenry, creating a single economic entity of ten countries with a free flow of goods, services, investment, skilled labour, and capital, while boasting a joint GDP of US$800 billion. ASEAN hopes that the Eminent Persons Group comprising ten wise men (one from each member country) would fine-tune the achievements of the broader ASEAN community. The challenges are indeed manifold, including the entity's firm adherence to the principle of non-interference and jealous protection of national sovereignty.

Broader regionalism in the form of the East Asian Summit (EAS), held back-to-back with the 11th ASEAN Leaders Summit in Kuala Lumpur in December, featured strongly in terms of initiatives taken to come to terms with rising China and India. Noting that East Asian cooperation had become more urgent in view of contingencies such as the 1997 Asian Financial Crisis, the SARS (severe acute respiratory syndrome), and avian flu risks, and the threat of terrorism, Abdullah outlined his vision for East Asia. In charting the way forward, he prioritized the following areas: (a) an inaugural summit, (b) a regional charter, (c) a free trade area, (d) a monetary and financial cooperation pact, (e) a zone of amity and cooperation, (f) a transportation and communications network, and (g) a declaration of human rights and obligations. The EAS banded together the ASEAN-10 plus Asia's economic giants China, Japan, and South Korea, as well as rising India and major trading partners Australia and New Zealand. The GDP of the combined economies of the 16-nation grouping is over US$8.3 trillion and account for one-fifth of global trade.[37]

However, Dr Mahathir injected a less optimistic note. The former premier predicted that the EAS will be ineffective and its views diluted to accommodate the wishes of Europe and the United States. Mahathir regards Australia and New Zealand as being neither Asian nor from the East.[38]

Nevertheless, intra-ASEAN cooperation involving Malaysia's relations with Thailand, and also Myanmar, and to some extent Singapore, showed evidence of occasional stress and strain. With Bangkok, in particular, the fate of 131 Thai Muslim refugees currently detained at a Malaysian immigration depot after fleeing the violence in Narathiwat province last August remains unsettled. Heated exchanges between the Malaysian and Thai Foreign Ministers, Syed Hamid Albar and Kantathi Suphamongkhon took place. Each has accused the other of inappropriate neighbourly conduct. The exchanges did not help to quell the situation since the outburst of Muslim religious violence in southern Thailand in the past three years.[39] Failure to resolve this simmering dispute could well affect the long-term security and prosperity of the two countries, and even the wider region.[40]

Malaysia's current chairmanship of the 57-member Organization of Islamic Conference (OIC) encompassing over 1.3 billion Muslims worldwide has obliged Prime Minister Abdullah Badawi to inject new life and chart new agendas for the grouping. Abdullah, like Mahathir, is only too aware that the OIC has been more a talk-shop than one committed to a concrete plan of action that can make a difference to the economic well-being of the Muslim world in which the majority of its citizenry are afflicted by poverty, illiteracy, and under-development. At the annual OIC summit in Putra Jaya, Malaysia's administrative capital, Abdullah proposed the setting up of a pan-Islamic trade bloc which aims to lower trade barriers and promote intra-bloc trade, establishing a US$190 billion infrastructure bond fund to develop the poorer countries which constitute nearly 50 per cent of the total membership, and mobilizing funds from the richer members for the development of Islamic financial and capital markets to reduce the use of non-Muslim intermediaries.[41] To be sure, these are ambitious targets whose achievement depends more on what the OIC members can do to promote internal reform (political, economic, and social) rather than on expectations of major changes or concessions from the global political economy.

At the regional level, the awkward atmosphere surrounding Myanmar's assumption of the ASEAN chair was cleared when a deal was struck with Yangon that it would give up the ASEAN chair in 2006 in the light of intra-regional and extra-regional concerns over its lack of internal democratization. Yangon agreed to re-occupy the chair at a later stage when sufficient progress has been made.

In the field of security cooperation, Malaysia, together with Indonesia and the Philippines, was strengthening cooperative efforts to combat piracy in the 800 km Straits of Malacca — a vital international waterway carrying half of the world's oil and a third of its commerce, and through which some 50,000 ships pass each year. Although a territorial dispute in the Sulawesi Sea has soured bilateral relations with Jakarta, the three ASEAN neighbours are seriously considering the use of "hot pursuit" into each other's territorial waters to more effectively eliminate piracy. If they succeed in this bold measure in maritime security, it would be an unprecedented step in sharing sovereignty signalling a major boost to intra-ASEAN security cooperation. Another anti-piracy measure proposed by Defence Minister Najib Tun Razak, the "Eyes in the Sky" programme involving surveillance aircraft from Malaysia, Singapore, Indonesia, and Thailand got underway, and complements the coordinated patrols which began in July 2004.[42] It is noteworthy that while coordinated patrols represent progress in regional security cooperation, joint patrols including the right of hot pursuit signifies a major departure from the traditionally held notions of national sovereignty. National sensitivities over territorial sovereignty still predominate, especially when the issue of foreign participation in patrolling the Straits of Malacca is involved. In this regard, Foreign Minister Syed Hamid Albar noted that Malaysia is open to cooperating with the United States, Australia, and Japan to combat piracy in the Straits, and even terrorism, provided the principle of territorial sovereignty is strictly upheld.[43]

Among issues that crop up as irritants from time to time is the haze problem originating from forest fires in Indonesia. A choking smog persisted over northern Malaysia in August forcing Syed Hamid Albar to remark that Malaysians were dying of the haze partly due to the lacklustre efforts of Jakarta in putting out the fires in Sumatra. Malaysia sent firefighters to Sumatra in the 1997–98 haze crisis, which blighted parts of Southeast Asia and seriously disrupted air travel that resulted in a US$9 billion loss.[44] For its part, Indonesia has blamed the forest fires on ten plantation companies, eight of them Malaysian-owned, and served notice that Jakarta will prosecute them.[45] The recurrence of this environmental problem on an almost annually basis is a potential source of strain in Kuala Lumpur–Jakarta relations.

Meanwhile, bilateral relations between Malaysia and Singapore have generally improved since Abdullah took over the reins from Mahathir, reflecting Abdullah's more cordial personal style. Yet national interests must be defended and promoted, and it is here that differences still do crop up from time to time. Malaysia's proposal to build a bridge to replace the causeway still remains unresolved. Recently, Kuala Lumpur indicated that it will go ahead with construction of its half of the bridge even in the absence of approval from Singapore.[46] The rapid expansion in capacity of Malaysian ports, especially the Port of Tanjung Peleapas in Johor and Port Klang in Selangor, has posed a significant threat to the Port of Singapore. Thus, the city-state has proposed to settle the bridge issue more comprehensively by ensuring "a balance of benefits".

6. Conclusion

In the domestic sphere, Abdullah's efforts in rationalizing government procedure especially with regard to procurements, tender for contracts, and raising the efficiency level and responsiveness of the bloated and top-heavy bureaucracy are haunted by the ghosts of the Mahathir era. Corruption, cronyism, and nepotism — the top three challenges of the Malaysian polity — continue to challenge the Abdullah administration despite the premier's best efforts to stamp them out. Indeed, in the past two years since Abdullah took over as prime minister, he has been hard put to impress local and foreign publics that the government was serious in its anti-corruption drive. According to the Berlin-based Transparency International (TI), Malaysia scored a 5.1 in 2005 out of the maximum 10 points

— reflecting only a slight improvement from the score of 5 in 2004 but still lower than the 5.2 in 2003 when Mahathir was still in power. TI's Corruption Perception Index for Malaysia showed that the country has not made much progress in controlling a disease that is a major concern among local and foreign investors. As Param Cumarasamy, president of TI's Malaysia chapter, aptly remarked: "We have not gone very far in reducing corruption although we have been busy on the battleground".[47]

Serious failures of several high-profile GLCs like Malaysia Airlines, as well as poor banking supervision highlighted by heavy losses incurred by Bank Islam Malaysia[48] reflect the extent of political penetration and manipulation exercised principally by UMNO stalwarts with the resultant effect of constraining the productivity, performance, and accountability of these enterprises. In sum, money politics is still very much a part of the Malaysian political economy, and Abdullah's efforts, thus far, have only achieved marginal results. On the religious front, Abdullah faced the additional challenge of Islamic activism that could derail his "Islam Hadhari" agenda.

At the external level, however, Malaysia can take credit for boosting ASEAN's relevance by hosting the inaugural EAS and obliging major regional and global players to be positively engaged for the development, security, and prosperity of the Asia-Pacific region.

Notes

[1] *Straits Times*, 22 July 2005, p. 16.
[2] *Straits Times*, 7 January 2005, p. 21.
[3] Edmund Terence Gomez, "The Perils of Pro-Malay Policies", *Far Eastern Economic Review* 168, no. 8, September 2005, p. 37.
[4] *Straits Times*, 30 June 2005, p. 12.
[5] *Straits Times*, 6 July 2005, p. 17.
[6] *Straits Times*, 1 June 2005, p. 14.
[7] *Straits Times*, 20 July 2005, p. 14.
[8] Reme Ahmad, "Mahathir Defends Himself over Naza Saga", *Straits Times*, 15 October 2005, p. 32.
[9] *Straits Times*, 4 January 2006, p. 12.
[10] *Straits Times*, 24 November 2005, p. 21.
[11] "Abdullah Orders Probe into Shaving Incident", *Straits Times*, 6 February 2006, p. 12.
[12] *Report of the Royal Commission to Enhance the Operation and Management of the Royal Malaysia Police* (Kuala Lumpur: Percetakan Nasional Malaysia Berhad, 2005), chap. 4, pp. 116–17.

13. *Report of the Royal Commission*, Executive Summary, p. 7.
14. Carolyn Hong, "UMNO Youth Against Plan to Set Up Police Watchdog", *Straits Times*, 6 February 2006, p. 12.
15. Reme Ahmad, "Malaysian Police Fight Back in Face of Bad Publicity", *Straits Times*, 9 February 2006, p. 10.
16. *Straits Times*, 18 January 2006.
17. R. Surenthra Kumar, "Rebranding the NEP", *Sun Weekend*, 30–31 July 2005, p. 10.
18. *Sun Weekend*, 30–31 July 2005, p. 10.
19. *Sun Weekend*, 30–31 July 2005, p. 10.
20. Hng Hung Yong, "Revisiting Malaysia's New Economic Policy", *Straits Times*, 1 September 2005, p. 33.
21. *Today*, 23 June 2005, p. 6.
22. *Straits Times*, 23 June 2005, p. 13.
23. Lee Hock Guan, "Globalisation and Ethnic Integration in Malaysian Education", in *Malaysia: Recent Trends and Challenges*, edited by Saw Swee-Hock and K. Kesavapany (Singapore: Institute of Southeast Asian Studies, 2005), p. 253.
24. Reme Ahmad, "It's Final: Barisan Wins Kelantan By-Election", *Straits Times*, 8 December 2005, p. 6.
25. *Straits Times*, 13 May 2005, p. 14.
26. Leslie Lau, "Anwar vs Mahathir: Ex-DPM Can't Lose", *New Straits Times*, 24 September 2005, p. 35. On 27 January 2006, Anwar's lawyer, Sankara Nair, filed a defamation suit against Mahathir with the High Court in Kuala Lumpur for calling him a homosexual.
27. On 3 August 2005 Anwar Ibrahim reached an out-of-court settlement with ex-police chief, Rahim Noor. On 18 August 2005 the High Court in Kuala Lumpur awarded Anwar Ibrahim RM4.5 million (US$1.2 million) in damages over a book entitled "Fifty Reasons Why Anwar Ibrahim Cannot Be Prime Minister" that triggered his sacking.
28. *New Straits Times*, 25 January 2006, p. 2; *Straits Times*, 24 January 2006, p. 11.
29. *New Straits Times*, 30 December 2005, pp. 1–2.
30. *New Straits Times*, 30 December 2005, pp. 1–2.
31. *New Straits Times*, 29 December 2005, p. 4.
32. *Straits Times*, 11 November 2005, p. 19.
33. "Don't Enforce Law, Govt. Urged", *New Straits Times*, 24 December 2005, p. 10.
34. Economist Intelligence Report: Country Profile 2005 — Malaysia, p. 36.
35. See "Malaysian Budget 2006 Highlights", http:www.readycompanies.com/Budget2005-2006.htm.
36. *Economist Intelligence Unit*, Country Report: Malaysia, December 2005, p. 28.
37. *Straits Times*, 7 December 2005, p. 12, and 15 December 2005, p. 1.
38. Carolyn Hong, "Mahathir Criticises East Asia Summit", *Straits Times*, 8 December 2005, p. 17.

39. *Straits Times*, 19 October 2005, p. 14.
40. Colum Murphy, "Friction on the Thai-Malay Fault Line", *Far Eastern Economic Review* 168, no. 10 (November 2005): 21.
41. Reme Ahmad, "Abdullah Calls for Pan-Islamic Trade Bloc", *Straits Times*, 24 June 2005, p. 14.
42. *Straits Times*, 14 September 2005, p. 3.
43. "Strait Security: KL Can Work with US and Others", *Straits Times*, 1 August 2005, p. 11.
44. *Straits Times*, 15 August 2005, p. 12.
45. *Straits Times*, 16 August 2005, p. 16.
46. *New Straits Times*, 26 January 2006, p. 1, and 31 January 2006, p. 2.
47. Carolyn Hong, "KL's Score No Better Despite War on Graft", *Straits Times*, 19 October 2005, p. 14.
48. Economist Intelligence Unit, *Country Report: Malaysia*, December 2005, pp. 20–21.

MAHATHIR AS MUSLIM LEADER

Ooi Kee Beng

From Malay to Muslim Dilemma

At the relatively mature age of 45, Mahathir Mohamad published *The Malay Dilemma*, an effective formulation of the position taken by many Malay nationalists about the unacceptability of the socio-economic state of the Malays.[1] With it came fame, and infamy. The book was written in haste after his suspension from the ruling United Malays National Organisation (UMNO) following his public criticism of Tunku Abdul Rahman, Malaysia's first premier, in 1970. After being rehabilitated in 1972 by the succeeding premier, Abdul Razak Hussein, Mahathir quickly rose within the political hierarchy. In May 1981 he became Malaysia's fourth prime minister and stayed in that position until he retired in October 2003 at the age of 77. Along the way he fought and won countless battles against political rivals on all imaginable fronts, and worked to turn Malaysia into an industrialized economy.

Alongside the impressive economic progress, an Islamization of Malaysia took place during Mahathir's watch. In 1982 he brought Islamic youth leader, Anwar Ibrahim, who was not a member of any political party at that time, into UMNO, purportedly to help him put an Islamic stamp on his modernization ideas, and to resist the Islamist party, Parti Islam SeMalaysia (PAS). That is the generally accepted interpretation of Mahathir's surprise move. Such conclusions result from the assumption that Mahathir — and UMNO for that matter — is basically a secular leader concerned with the material development of his country and his own ethnic group, the Malays, and that the "Muslimness" of the Malays was of lesser importance.

Yet, Mahathir himself had claimed that he did not accept the polarity of secularism and religion, even if this particular conviction appears to have come late in his life. In *The Malay Dilemma*, for example, Islam is not dealt with centrally.

Ooi Kee Beng is Fellow at the Institute of Southeast Asian Studies, Singapore.

While such a stance may be regarded as a rejection of what is normally considered a Western dichotomy, Mahathir's position was just as much — if not more poignantly so — a criticism of Muslim leaders through the ages who turned their backs on all knowledge that they considered not to be religious. He blames the fall of Islamic polities on these *ulamas*.

Of equal interest is the fact that from the very beginning of his political career, his idea of national politics was based on historical argumentation that also generated a global perspective on the subject. From the Malay point of view, his book amounted to a tract on Malay decolonization. From the Muslim point of view, his championing of Islam is a critique against the historical abandonment of the religion's material function and of scientific knowledge.

Much of the dynamics that informed his policies during his time in power could be traced to ideas proposed in *The Malay Dilemma*. These ideas were a desperate call for the socio-political decolonization of the Malays, and also provided guidelines for the construction of the Malay nation-state. Thus, if proper attention had been paid to the ideas expressed in this book, his "Look East" policy and "Buy British Last" initiatives at the start of his premiership would not have shocked so many. Also, Mahathir's aversion towards the Commonwealth and towards Australian political attitudes would have been expected. In short, a historical diagnosis informed by moral outrage, followed by a quick cure had been the gist of Mahathir's long period as leader of the Malays.

In the later part of his period in power, however, especially after 11 September 2001, his speeches began to touch more and more on Islam, on the backwardness of Muslims, the misunderstanding of Islam, and Western aggression against the Muslim world. This was understandable in the wake of the invasion of Afghanistan, and then Iraq. However, this shift in focus has become permanent, given his retirement and the unhappy attempts he had made over the past year to criticize the Malaysian government over various matters, especially with regard to the national car project. Mahathir had gone from being leader of Malays to the position of strident guide for progress-seeking Muslims.

His infamous speech made to the Organization of the Islamic Conference (OIC) in October 2003 in Kuala Lumpur, generally interpreted in the West as a run-of-the-mill anti-Semitic attack, was quite typical of him. He called on his Muslim listeners to pull themselves together and recognize the challenges and threats arrayed against them. This he had undoubtedly done before in *The Malay Dilemma,* with the Malays as the unhappy categorical subject of criticism. In his 2003 speech, his focus was on the Muslims as being in need of change, and with the West as the constant antithesis.

His growing conviction — especially after the 1997 financial crisis that precipitated events such as the conflict with Anwar Ibrahim — was that national pride and religious passion, to be effective, had to be exercised within the colonial and imperialistic context where Western powers were culprits in denial. Such a position has not always made him popular even among those he claims to champion. Oftentimes, he ends up scolding them, purportedly, for their own good. This he did with the Malays, when he was the champion of Malay rights and as prime minister, and this he now does with the Muslims of the world.

His decision to step down in October 2003 gained him credibility in certain parts of the Muslim world, especially where leaders have been unwilling to give up power. For example, when Mahathir mentioned to students at the Al Azhar University in Egypt that he stepped down after having been in power for 22 years, he was thunderously applauded. This surprised him, and he later confided to aides that the show of appreciation was, he now believed, a criticism of Egyptian President Hosni Mubarak, who had been unwilling to retire.

Since 2003 he has received 26 awards of various kinds from governments, prestigious bodies, and seats of learning throughout the world. These included honorary doctorates from Muslim countries such as Bangladesh, Indonesia, Pakistan, and Sudan, and from Waseda University in Japan.[2] In November 2005, Mahathir was awarded the Gaddafi International Prize for Human Rights, which seemed to indicate that his stature in the Muslim world had not disappeared with his retirement as premier. Others awarded this somewhat dubious prize included Nelson Mandela (1989), Louise Farakan (1996), and Fidel Castro (1998).[3] These awards and recognition point to his wide-ranging impact internationally.

Mahathir's position as a champion of Muslim development was secured for him by the impressive growth of the Malaysian economy, the marketing of Malaysian modernity, and the parallel branding of these achievements as Muslim successes. In the wake of Malaysia's national development, Mahathir's worldview developed to take on a civilizational expanse. Malaysia may be part of the Malay world, of Southeast Asia, of the Indic cultural sphere, and of East Asia. Yet for Mahathir, his distrust of Western international politics — and perhaps of certain non-Muslim Asian civilizations as well — led him to consider Malaysia most importantly as part of the Islamic world. His "look eastward" for inspiration from East Asia was with time complemented by his "look westward" to the Muslim world. In the latter case, however, it was to position Malaysia as a model for Muslim countries to emulate, and not as an imitator, as in the former case. In a way, he was transplanting the Flying Geese model from East Asia westward to the Middle East.

Mahathir's long term in office tended to overshadow the fact that the Malays were often split during his premiership. Already when he burst onto the political stage in 1969 with a biting criticism of Tunku Abdul Rahman, he was showing Malaysia what was to come. His appointment as deputy prime minister in 1976 also caused intra-party tension. Continuing conflicts within UMNO led to its traumatic split in 1987, Mahathir's creation of UMNO Baru (New UMNO) and the parallel formation of its unsuccessful rival, Semangat 46. Furthermore, the fact that he changed deputies four times during his 22 years in office expressed the conflicts found within the Malay community and among its leaders.

Presently, questions about Anwar Ibrahim continue to dog Mahathir as he travels the world. In September 2005, Anwar filed a legal suit against Mahathir for continuing to refer to him as a homosexual. Both men now do the lecture circuit globally, and proclaim themselves as moderates articulating visions about how the Muslim world should modernize. Both are able to enjoy such a position today mainly because the agenda of Malay nationalism in Malaysia went hand in hand with the country's Islamization during Mahathir's time in power. Malaysia's national economic success, which in reality is not tantamount to the success of Malay nationalism, alerted Third World countries to the possibility that Malaysia could be an alternative model of progress, especially for Muslim countries. Mahathir's willingness to criticize Western powers promoted him further as a spokesman for developing countries. Given the lack of a strong voice and of viable models of development in the Muslim world, it was understandable that Malaysia and Mahathir became objects of hope for many countries, at least until the financial crisis of 1997. His stature as a Muslim leader was therefore partly a function of developments in the Muslim world at large, as well as of economic success in Malaysia.

What of Mahathir's "Islamic credentials"? His successor, Abdullah Badawi, is often credited in the eyes of Malay voters as having more going for him as a Muslim leader than does Mahathir. This perception seems justified by the impressive electoral victory that Abdullah Badawi's team engineered in March 2004. However, Abdullah, despite inheriting the chairmanship of the OIC, certainly does not command the global Muslim audience that Mahathir did, and still does. To be sure, it is doubtful that Abdullah has any such ambition.

Despite the strong association between Malayness and Islam, the struggles the Malays are involved in differ greatly from those that Muslims worldwide are caught in today. While one can act as leader of Malays and as champion of Islam at one and the same time in the Malaysian context, global stature is required if one is to champion Islam beyond the national stage. Mahathir, though diminished in stature by his retirement and by his fight with Anwar Ibrahim, still commands widespread respect among Muslims throughout the world.

Also, by virtue of his stance on Western international politics and on Israel, Mahathir has always been widely regarded in Western eyes as a Muslim leader, and not always of a comfortably moderate kind either. This has helped to enhance his stature in the Muslim world.

Throughout his period as prime minister, Mahathir put much effort into projecting his regime as an Islamizing one. As early as March 1982, just before that year's April elections, he made it known on returning from a visit to the Middle East that Malaysia would house an international Islamic university. This was realized, and the institution was later named the International Islamic University. Soon after the elections, he announced that an Islamic bank would be formed. This was realized about a year later, on 1 July 1983.[4] Where Muslim values are concerned, at that point in time, Mahathir's concern was with improving the work ethics of the Malays. He thus proposed the emulation of Japanese and Korean workers. Twenty years later, his focus shifted to the need for "brain power" and "knowledge".

Resisting Knowledge Hegemony

In Khoo Boo Teik's 1995 book on "Mahathirism", nationalism, capitalism, populism, and authoritarianism are recognized alongside Islam as the impulses informing Mahathir's political praxis. In later years, however, an "anti-hegemonic" activism that paradoxically does not embrace narrow provincialism but instead pleads for effective modernization for the purpose of limiting Western hegemony became more obvious in his speeches.

If we were to pinpoint the time when Mahathir's Malay nationalism became national Islamism, it would be June 2002, nine months after 9/11, and 18 months before he retired, when he surprised everyone, including those closest to him, by stating in parliament that Malaysia was "a model Islamic fundamentalist state" and not "a moderate Muslim state" as people were wont to think. In typical Mahathir fashion, he tried to shock the world — and Malaysia's oppositional Islamic party — by declaring that being a Muslim fundamentalist did not contradict the connotations of peace normally associated with being "moderate". This attempt at a deconstruction of popular notions that he deemed incorrect was in line with a dawning realization in Mahathir of the importance of "knowledge creation" in the fight for cultural survival. Strangely, his historical model to emulate in this context was the Jews.

Two weeks before he stepped down as prime minister in October 2003, Mahathir, as the host, gave his "swan song" speech to the 10th Session of the OIC Summit in Putrajaya. The two-day conference was well attended by leaders of Muslim countries, something that could be read as a show of respect for the retiring Prime Minister. Coached in terms of warfare, Mahathir's speech called for Muslims to think opportunistically, using the history of the Jews as an example of how a small group could, with appropriate use of brain power, make the world at large work in their favour. Such a perspective did not go down well among many in the West, as can be expected, but it was well received at the forum. Thus, on the eve of his retirement, he managed to position himself squarely as a Muslim political leader and global strategist.

"Knowledge" appears to be what he thinks Muslims today require, which essentially amounts to nothing less than a call for a change of attitude towards science and materialism. In a speech made at the University in London in September 2003, titled "Islam and the *Ummah*: Reexamining and Reinventing Ourselves in the Face of New Challenges", he stated:

> In the early years of Islam, the Muslims, obeying the injunction to "Read", i.e. to acquire knowledge, studied the works of the Greeks and others on philosophy, medicine, science and mathematics ... Because of the extensive knowledge in all fields of learning and their consequent skills in the acquisition of wealth, in administration and in military defence, the Muslim civilisation thrived and grew, enabling the Muslims to live the way of life as prescribed by the Quran.[5]

The call for Muslims to seek knowledge as a civilizational defence has become a steady theme in Mahathir's thinking, as has his conviction that Islam's problem "is with the interpretation". Interestingly, in a commentary in *Project Syndicate*, which was widely carried by newspapers worldwide, Mahathir bravely praised the founder of modern Turkey, Mustafa Kamal Ataturk, for the "clearsightedness" that, according to Mahathir, "saved Islam in Turkey and saved Turkey for Islam".[6]

> Failure to understand and interpret the true and fundamental message of the Koran has brought only misfortune to Muslims. By limiting our reading to religious works and neglecting modern science, we destroyed Islamic civilisation and lost our way in the world.

In concluding a talk given in Singapore on 11 October 2004, for example, he called for Asian leaders to "assert true leadership, seize the initiative of ideas and thoughts, and restore self-respect or face the humiliation of foreign hegemony and the contempt of their own people".[7]

Mahathir is currently chairman of the 1440H Vision Commission of the Islamic Development Bank (IDB). This position has provided him, in his retirement, with a useful link to the Middle East and North Africa, where he is widely courted to speak on Islam and modernity. In the Commission's first meeting in September 2005, Mahathir argued that Muslim nations faced the common challenges of poverty, a low level of education, and the lack of women empowerment.[8]

In perceiving Mahathir as a global Muslim leader, however, one should not at the same time lose sight of the fact that there has been a certain consistency in his broader picture of post-colonial international relations.[9] This stems from a deep distrust of Western powers, which, beyond his understanding of the dire state of Muslim governance in general, informs his many initiatives to encourage the growth of intra-Asia cooperation. His attempt to create an exclusively Asian East Asian Economic Caucus (EAEC) in 1990 was overshadowed by the Asia Pacific Economic Cooperation (APEC). Many today consider the East Asia Summit (EAS) held in Kuala Lumpur in December 2005 as the realization of his EAEC idea. Mahathir himself, however, rejects such a notion, arguing that the inclusion of Australia and New Zealand made a travesty of the idea of Asia.

In September 2005, Mahathir spoke at a human rights conference in Kuala Lumpur. His speech caused a walkout by Western diplomats when he criticized the war in Iraq and branded the United States and the United Kingdom "state terrorists". Mahathir argued:

> The British and American bomber pilots came, unopposed, safe and cosy in their state-of-the-art aircraft, pressing buttons to drop bombs, to kill and maim. ... And these murderers, for that is what they are, would go back to celebrate "mission accomplished". Who are the terrorists? The people below who were bombed or the bombers? Whose rights have been snatched away?[10]

Mahathir's ambition to be a frontman for the Muslim world is therefore not so much a religious stance as it is a political statement. The difference would in any case be of no consequence to him. Thus, his latest actions are best understood as tactics designed specifically to criticize and humiliate the governments of Bush and Blair. On 15 December 2005, his Perdana Peace Foundation organized the Global Peace Forum in Kuala Lumpur where a call was made to voters in democratic countries to overrule any politician aiming to take his country to war. The initiative was pointedly aimed at the United States and Britain starting the Iraq War without popular or international support.[11]

On 3–4 February 2006, Mahathir headed a mock trial of US President George W. Bush, British Premier Tony Blair, and Israeli Prime Minister Ariel Sharon in Cairo. The three men were found guilty of war crimes by a tribunal invited by the Arab Lawyers Union.[12] The exercise, it seems, was mischievously done purely for its propaganda value.

What distinguishes Mahathir from many other global leaders of Islam are his propositions, firstly, that Islam, far from contradicting or opposing material progress, actually seeks it, and secondly, that the centuries-old humiliation of Muslims can be stopped, not so much by asking detractors to desist, but through an unbiased search for practical knowledge on the part of Muslims themselves.

So what do Muslims need to do, according to Mahathir?

> In the past, Muslims were strong because they were learned. Muhammad's injunction was to read, but the Koran does not say *what* to read. Indeed, there was no "Muslim scholarship" at the time, so to read meant to read whatever was available. The early Muslims read the works of the great Greek scientists, mathematicians, and philosophers. They also studied the works of the Persians, the Indians and the Chinese.[13]

While he regularly aims accusations at Western powers, Mahathir seems to put the blame on the Muslims themselves as well, identifying the distinction made by Muslim scholars in the 15th century between religious and secular knowledge as the crucial turning point. With that distinction, and with the ultimate preference for the former over the latter, "we destroyed Islamic civilization and lost our way in the world".[14]

This is reminiscent of the public outpouring of disappointment at the Malays before his retirement as prime minister. Whether his patients are the Malay cultural collective or the Muslim religious community, the doctor's diagnosis and his prescription have thus remained the same.

Notes

[1] Mahathir Mohamad, *The Malay Dilemma* (Singapore: Donald Moore for Asia Pacific Press, 1970).

[2] http://www.perdana.org.my/index.php?option=com_content&task=view&id=146&Itemid=378.

[3] http://library.perdana.org.my/News_Online/Malaysiakini-01122005.pdf.

[4] Khoo Boo Teik, *Paradoxes of Mahathirism: An Intellectual Biography of Mahathir Mohamad* (Kuala Lumpur: Oxford University Press 1995), pp. 174–86.

[5] http://www.pmo.gov.my/WebNotesApp/PMMain.nsf/0/aa56fb4d7f80868048256db00011b2e7?OpenDocument. 1440 is the Muslim equivalent of the year 2020.

6. Mahathir bin Mohamad, November 2005 "Islam's Forsaken Renaissance", http://www.project-syndicate.org/print_commentary/mahathir1/English.
7. The 2nd Lecture of the Ho Rih Hwa Pubilc Lecture Series. See Radio Singapore International, 11 October 2004, "Why Asia Should Not Adopt Western Models of Democracy Wholesale", http://www.rsi.sg/english/newsline/view/2004101118546/1/.html.
8. IDB News, "Vision of the Future", http://www.isdb.org/english_docs/idb_home/news_1440hVision.htm.
9. Khoo, op. cit., p. 7.
10. Scotsman.com, 9 September 2005, "Walkout Over 'Terrorist UK' Speech", http://news.scotsman.com/latest.cfm?id=1914712005.
11. Eric Garris, 19 December 2005. "World Peace Forum Moves to Create International Peace Secretariat", http://www.antiwar.com/orig/garris.php?articleid=8274.
12. "Mahathir Heads Court That 'Convicts' Bush, Blair, Sharon", http://straitstimes.asia1.com.sg/sub/asia/story/0,5562,369630,00.html?
13. Mahathir bin Mohamad, *Islam's Forsaken Renaissance* (2005), http://www.project-syndicate.org/print_commentary/mahathir1/English.
14. Ibid.

Myanmar

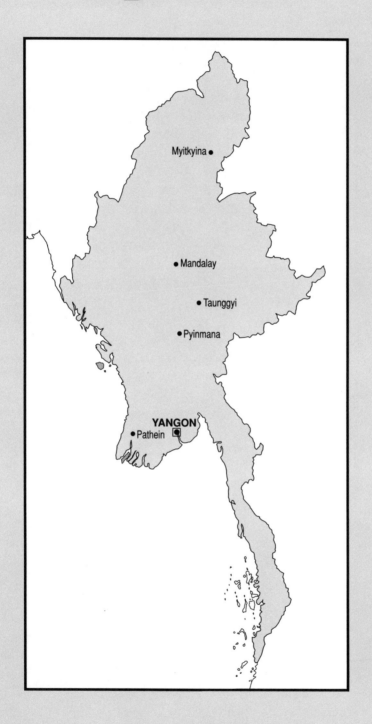

MYANMAR
Challenges Galore but Opposition Failed to Score

Tin Maung Maung Than

The main events that characterized Myanmar's political scene in 2005 were the military government's highlighting of its National Convention (NC) as a showcase for political progress and the crackdown on political activists from the Shan ethnic group. The legitimacy of the NC established by the State Law and Order Restoration Council (SLORC, the junta from 1988 to 1997) and endorsed by the State Peace and Development Council (SPDC) was still not accepted by the political opposition and the US-led Western governments while the crackdown attracted a fresh round of condemnations by the advocates of human rights, political opposition from within and without the country and Western governments. In fact, the issue of the apparent lack of progress in instituting political reforms towards democratic rule had become the bone of contention in ASEAN's relations with its dialogue partners and even within ASEAN itself and the year saw a significant increase in attempts by the international community to press for changes in the regime's conduct to conform with Western norms of human rights and democracy.

The issues of democratic reforms and the continued detention of opposition icon Daw Aung San Suu Kyi as well as allegations of forced labour, ill-treatment of political prisoners, internal displacement, and religious persecution that dogged the regime since it came to power were highlighted time and again by the regime's critics and detractors who unleashed a torrent of complaints, condemnations and warnings throughout the year, culminating in calls for a move to refer Myanmar to the United Nations Security Council (UNSC) as threat to peace and security in the region.

Meanwhile, on the economic front, the government continued its claim of double-digit GDP (gross domestic product) growth as in the previous few years,

---

Tin Maung Maung Than is Senior Fellow the Institute of Southeast Asian Studies.

despite cost-push inflationary pressures and further deterioration in the free market exchange rate of the local currency (kyat, or K) to the US dollar. The government's claim of a high economic growth rate was disputed by outside observers such as the Economist Intelligence Unit and the Asian Development Bank.

The National Convention, the New Constitution, and the Road Map

According to the military junta, a firm constitution is necessary for a stable political environment in which indigenized rules of "multi-party democracy" can be "formulated". As such, SLORC envisaged a political configuration institutionalizing the military's role in "national politics" as a solution to the problem of dysfunctional "party politics".[1]

In accordance with the announcement on 30 August 2003 by the (then) prime minister General Khin Nyunt of a seven-point "road map" that outlined a path towards constitutional rule in Myanmar, the NC assigned with the task of drafting the detailed principles of a new state constitution was reconvened on 17 May 2004, after a suspension that lasted eight years. The military government in Yangon claimed that the NC was a crucial initial step in the state's seven-step "political programme" or "road map" that entails reconvening the NC; gradually implementing the deliberative process; drafting a new constitution according to the basic principles and details endorsed by the NC; holding a national referendum to adopt the constitution; holding free and fair elections for a hierarchy (national and regional) of legislative bodies or *pyithu huttaws* (people's assemblies); convening the national assembly; and finally ushering in a "a modern, developed and democratic nation" governed by leaders elected in accordance with the new constitution.[2]

The National League for Democracy (NLD), the party that won some 80 per cent of the seats in the May 1990 general elections, stayed out of the NC, disagreeing with its aims and procedures. So did the Shan National League for Democracy (SNLD), an ethnic party that won the second largest number of seats in the 1990 elections, and the United Nationalities Alliance (UNA), a group constituting elected ethnic representatives whose parties were deregistered.

During 2005, the NC reconvened on 17 February with 1,075 out of 1,081 delegates attending the opening plenary session, while the ceasefire group, SSA-N-SR (3) (Shan State Army [North], Special Region [3]) sought an exemption from having to send delegates, citing pressing internal matters.[3] It then adjourned on 31 March, after deliberating on details for the sharing of legislative, executive, and judicial powers between the central and regional governments.[4]

During the period when the NC was in recess, the state-owned media continued to highlight the NC's aims, objectives and accomplishments and its importance, emphasizing vigilance against an assortment of domestic and foreign enemies bent on destroying the hard-earned independence and national unity. Meanwhile, junta members and ministers echoed that refrain frequently in speeches made all over the countryside. Government-sponsored associations for women, business, and war veterans as well as the Union Solidarity and Development Association (USDA), a 22 million strong social organization whose patron is the junta chairman, all joined in a show of support for the NC and the Road Map while condemning the "internal" and "external destructive elements" at rallies, meetings, and gatherings, thereby repeating the same message.

The media blitz and mobilization of support for the NC were followed by an unprecedented move by the authorities to highlight the NC to representatives of the international community just days before its resumption on 5 December. Chief Justice U Aung Toe, the Vice-Chairman of the National Convention Convening Commission (NCCC, the steering body chaired by the junta's Secretary-1 Lieutenant General Thein Sein), and members of the NCCC arranged three separate briefings on as many days for the diplomatic community, resident representatives of UN agencies, together with military attaches and representatives of local and foreign news media, whereby the NCCC team clarified matters related to the reconvening of the National Convention. Out of 1,080 delegates, 1,074 turned up on the opening day with the New Mon Stat Party (NMSP), a major ethnic ceasefire group, reportedly sending only observers in contrast to full participation on previous occasions.[5] On the other hand, the ceasefire group SSA-N-SR (3) returned to join the NC. The NC's proceedings continued throughout December and by the end of the year it was claimed that "about 70 per cent of its functions to draft an enduring State Constitution" had been completed and the implementation of the road map was on course.[6]

Government and the Military: Security Challenges and Reactions

In the military junta's perspective there appears to be no separation between national or state security and regime security. Moreover, national unity exemplified by a strong unitary state and absence of ethnic-based secession has been regarded as a cornerstone of state security. Events in 2005 perceived as security challenges elicited harsh responses from the authorities; the most notable ones were the "Shan affair" and the unprecedented bombings in Yangon. Meanwhile, prisoners who were deemed no longer a security threat or who had served their terms had been released in large numbers. The purge of General Khin Nyunt's legacy continued and the former prime minister and his family were prosecuted as well. There were more than a few changes in the personnel make-up of the government and the military command structure during the year.

The Shan affair

The first hint of the crackdown on Shan activists was the arrest of seven Shan nationalists and politicians including President Major-General Sao Hso Ten of the Shan State Peace Council (SSPC) (who was also a leader of the ceasefire group SSA-N), SNLD Chairman Hkun Htun Oo, and General Secretary Sai Nyunt Lwin by the military government after they attended a meeting of the Shan Sate Intellectual Advisory Council (SSIAC) on 7 February (Shan State Day), which included some non-Shan political personalities as well.[7] All three were charged *in camera* with high treason and were reportedly sentenced, in November, to prison terms of 53 years and two life sentences and 25 years and two life sentences for Hkun Htun Oo and Sai Nyunt Win, respectively, while Sao Hso Ten received a sentence constituting 46 years and three life sentences.[8] Six other Shan activists arrested in connection with the ill-conceived meeting in February were reportedly given equally long sentences as well.[9] Khun Tun Oo's brother Sao Oo Kya arrested separately in August with charges of defaming the state, breaching of the Hotel and Tourism Act and anti-government activities was also sentenced to 13 years' imprisonment in October.[10] The main reason for the crackdown is likely to be the attempt by local Shan nationalists to link up with expatriates, unlawful associations, insurgent factions, and external lobbies to push for a "federal" arrangement, which has been anathema to Myanmar's military leaders since the 1950s.

The next challenge came from 67-year-old Sao Hkam Hpa (Sao Surkhanpha, nicknamed Tiger Yawnghwe), the eldest son of Myanmar's late first President, Sao Shwe Thaike (the *Sawbwa* of Yawnghwe) and a couple of politically unknown Shan elders who unilaterally announced the formation of the Interim Shan Government (ISG) and declared independence for the "Federated Shan States" (FSS). This event of 17 April (Myanmar New Year according to the traditional lunar calendar) took everybody by surprise but only five fringe expatriate groups (two Mon, two Rakhine, and a hitherto unknown US-based group) among the ethnic-based opposition and a breakaway faction of SSA-South supported it.[11] It received virtually no support from the mainstream pro-democracy opposition as well as Shan activists and politicians who dismissed the action as a frustrated "last hurrah" by deluded expatriate old men trying to resurrect past glories. In fact, the NLD and SNLD publicly rejected the formation of the ISG and FSS, while ceasefire groups also put up notices of rejection in the government newspapers. Even the SSA-South that professed it was fighting for the autonomy of the Shan people refused to endorse Sao Hkam Hpa's claims. The government quickly outlawed the group led by Sao Hkam Hpa, the self-proclaimed "President", branding the members as "fugitives" and declaring the group to be an "unlawful association". Mass rallies were also organized in many townships of the Shan state to denounce the ISG and its leaders.[12] This ineffectual secessionist attempt fizzled out in the following months for lack of credibility and popular support within and without the country.

The aforementioned events put the SSNA (Shan State National Army), which had established a ceasefire in 1995 and was a member of the SSPC, in a difficult position. News that SSNA's two brigades had lain down arms on 12 April (Brigade-11) and 20 May (Brigade-19) were followed by a surprise announcement on 21 May 2005 that Colonel Sai Yee, the SSNA commander, had defected with some headquarters troops to join his friend Colonel Ywet Sit aka Yawdserk of SSA-South in the fight against the government. However, speculation among the military regime's opponents that the remaining three brigades might join Sai Yee and set off a snowball effect among other ceasefire groups in the Shan state proved unfounded in the remaining months of the year.[13] Instead, 119 members from the SSNA Brigade-6 and the Shan State Army (breakaway faction) disarmed on 24 July, further depleting the military strength of the SSNA and leaving it in a much-weakened position.

Yangon bombings

Probably the most shocking event in 2005 was the exploding of three sophisticated and powerful bombs, five minutes apart, in the afternoon of 7 May, at two crowded shopping centres in Yangon and the state-owned Yangon Trade Centre where a Thai trade fair was being held.[14] The government claimed that 11 persons were killed and 162 wounded, of which eight later died. Nobody claimed responsibility for these attacks, which were roundly condemned by both detractors and supporters of the military regime. However, the government quickly blamed four opposition groups (who supposedly acted in concert to destabilize the country) for being behind the attacks. They were the National Coalition Government of the Union of Burma (NCGUB), a group of Washington-based exiled politicians who had professed non-violence all along; the Karen National Union (KNU), which claimed to have been still observing an unofficial ceasefire agreement made with the deposed Prime Minister General Khin Nyunt; the Karenni National Progressive Party (KNPP), a ceasefire group that reverted to fighting in the late 1990s; and the SSA-S, a breakaway faction of the drug warlord Khun Sa's Mong-Tai Army that refused to surrender when the latter gave up arms in January 1996. Furthermore, on 15 May the junta's information minister, in his lengthy "clarification" at the press conference broadened the list of suspects to many more groups, organizations, and individuals abroad — ethnic groups, former student activists, labour activists, exiled elected parliamentarians, political activists, and armed groups. Accusations were levelled at an unnamed "world famous organization of a big nation" (probably alluding to the US Central Intelligence Agency, or CIA) that provided cash (US$100,000) and training in a "neighbouring country". It was also stated that the explosive involved was RDX (Research Department Explosive, a powerful high-velocity compound) "produced in big power nations".[15]

At a press conference held on 28 August 2005 by the junta's Information Committee, it was revealed that some associates of the perpetrators had been arrested. The police chief also claimed that the "Yangon bomb blasts were carried out by VBSW [Vigorous Burmese Student Warriors][16]" with the help of "ABSDF [All Burma Students' Democratic Front][17] terrorists and NDD [Network for Democracy and Development, a political organization founded by former members of the ABSDF in March 2001 and based in Thailand] mercenaries", all under the tutelage of Maung Maung (a) Pyi Thit Nyunt Wai [former government employee and general secretary of the FTUB or the Federation of Trade Unions-Burma].[18]

Conspiracy to destabilize Myanmar?

An elaborate conspiracy replete with intriguing plots and multiple agents labelled "terrorists" was exposed in the same press conference to support the claim that all those involved conspired to "synchronize" the "three-pronged attack" on the government comprising the "above-ground" political plot (the Shan affair, see above), the "underground" violent "military terrorist attacks" (the Yangon bombing and other incidents of bombing, ambushes and military attacks throughout the country) and the formation of ISG and FSS by Shan aristocrats. All supposedly done with "advice, money, material and technological assistance of their [all the pro-democracy groups named] alien masters". The Information Minister assured the nation that "[w]ith greater Political, Economic and Military Mights [sic] today, the Government can easily crush, in cooperation with the people, the terrorist destructionists who are taking refuge at the border of a neighbouring country". He said that there was no need to worry as the "Government and the Tatmadaw [Myanmar Armed Forces] are strong enough to safeguard the sovereignty and lives and properties of the people".[19]

Prisoners released

Although the government had never acknowledged the existence of "political prisoners" as such, insisting that all those incarcerated under the country's penal system were serving sentences for breaching existing laws, advocates of human rights had identified over a thousand prisoners under the "political" category. In early July the government released nearly 400 prisoners of which some 250 people from prisons in different parts of the country were political activists and dissidents.[20]

The junta, purges, cabinet changes, and military reshuffles

From September 1988 onwards, Myanmar's military leadership has controlled the state executive and oftentimes the government-controlled media refer to the government as a "Tatmadaw Government". The Myanmar Armed Forces (MAF), which called itself the Tatmadaw (literally, "royal force"), has portrayed itself as the most disciplined, cohesive, and enduring institution in Myanmar. Nevertheless, ever since the prime minister and military intelligence chief General Khin Nyunt was dismissed in October 2004 and his intelligence apparatus subsequently dismantled and replaced by the Office of Military Affairs Security (OMAS), speculation about a major shakeup in the MAF command hierarchy has surfaced time and again. Many observers, especially those sympathetic to the opposition movement, subscribed to the view that once the delicate triangular balance of power was disrupted the dyadic relationship between the two top military leaders would be fraught with tension and this could degenerate into a contest for supremacy. However, this prophecy was not borne out as the year passed. On the other hand, a short-lived piece of sensational news caused a stir on 23 August when a rumour that the junta Chairman Senior General Than Shwe was deposed by his deputy Vice Senior General Maung Aye was picked up by the BBC (British Broadcasting Corporation) Myanmar language service and promptly disseminated. The apparent scoop backfired, eliciting a scathing rebuttal from Myanmar's Information Minister on 28 August.[21]

As for the sorry saga of General Khin Nyunt, it was reported that he was given a suspended sentence of 44 years in July after a trial *in camera* for charges that included bribery and corruption.[22] Later, his two sons, businessman Ye Naing Win and former Lieutenant Colonel Zaw Naing Oo reportedly received lengthy suspended sentences as well.[23] The fallout from his removal continued throughout the year with the dismissal of, perhaps, hundreds of intelligence officers and some of other ranks whose ill-gotten gains were also confiscated. At the end of March, Myanmar's second-ranking diplomat in Washington, a former military intelligence major, sought political asylum with his family, claiming that he would be persecuted as a follower of the deposed intelligence chief General Khin Nyunt. The Directors-General of the Prime Minister's Office, a former military officer and incumbent since the 1980s, and the SPDC Office (a serving officer) were replaced in the third quarter of the year. Several ambassadors believed to be former intelligence officials or identified as belonging to the disgraced premier's camp were recalled and retired. In their place several high-ranking military officers were appointed as new ambassadors in a move that also involved some reshuffling of assignments.

In mid-2005 the new Prime Minister Lieutenant General Soe Win was promoted to the rank of full general. Meanwhile, in early August the Education Minister, who was believed to be close to Than Shwe, was dismissed and replaced by an academic who had been the Deputy Minister in the Ministry of Science and Technology. Two ministers without portfolio attached to the Prime Minister's Office were "permitted to retire" as well. A young colonel was appointed as the deputy minister for the Ministry of National Planning and Economic Development. All these changes had virtually no effect on the administration.

In the military itself, a reshuffling of six out of twelve regional commanders in late May further fuelled speculation. In August two more regional commanders, including a brother-in-law of Maung Aye, swapped commands while two junta members also exchanged staff positions in the army headquarters.[24] All these appeared to be part of a normal process, perhaps long overdue, of rotation of duty among senior officers rather than being indicators of an ongoing power struggle among the top brass, as speculated by the regime's detractors.

Finally, the regime's Information Minister announced at a press conference on 7 November that on the morning of 6 November the government had begun relocating all its ministries and government agencies to a new administrative capital that was being built at a place called Kyetpyay at the foothills of the Yoma mountain range (which formed the central spine of Myanmar) and near Pyinmana, a medium-sized town some 244 road-miles north of Yangon.[25] The announcement took almost everybody, including the civil servants involved, by surprise.[26] Speculation abounded on the reasons for the sudden move, ranging from astrological/cosmogonic explanations to fear of an Iraq-style US invasion. The real reason remains unknown but it seems likely that the junta regarded the relocation a strategic prerequisite to its relinquishing state power to an elected government at the culmination of the seven-point road map. It could be that in the junta's perception the advantage to be gained in ensuring regime control over the polity and safeguarding the integrity of the state greatly outweigh the diplomatic, economic, and social costs incurred in such a move.[27] It seemed that by physically separating the seat of power from the urban sprawl of Yangon with its population of more than 5 million, the future regime would be much less vulnerable to a repeat of the 1988 crisis brought about by proximity to discontented urban masses.

Domestic Politics

In the context of the military's grip on power and its control of the political reform process, the other major political players in Myanmar are the mainstream political parties and groups representing ethnic nationalities. The National League for Democracy (NLD) has assumed the mantle of the leading opposition party calling for the establishment of a Western-style liberal democracy and citing the mandate obtained in its victory at the May 1990 general elections. Most of the ethnic-based parties and ceasefire groups have kept their arms but have been participating in the NC.

The NLD

The NLD kept insisting that its leaders Daw Aung San Suu Kyi (General Secretary) and U Tin Oo (Vice Chairman) be released unconditionally from house arrest while also calling for the release of SNLD leaders and a dialogue with the junta. Moreover, as reiterated in its statement on the 15th Anniversary Commemoration of its election victory, the party continued to demand the release of all political prisoners, the reopening of all its offices that have been closed down since 2003, and the right to organize rallies freely. In 2005 the NLD failed to gain any concession to its demands.

Since right from the outset, the NLD has been a coalition of individuals and groups advocating different means towards the same end and has owed its cohesiveness to its charismatic and iconic leader Daw Aung San Suu Kyi. Its top leadership itself, comprising two distinct components, viz., retired military commanders (all senior to the junta leaders) and intellectuals (retired civil servants, lawyers, journalists), has not been free from tension and mistrust. There have been inherent tensions between the elderly leaders and the impatient youths as well as between those advocating a conservative and conciliatory approach towards the military and others who have preferred a more radical and confrontational stance. In fact, such tensions surfaced in February 2005 when it was announced that 18 of its members (including four elected representatives and youth members) were expelled on grounds of "disservice to party policy".[28]

In 2005 the NLD, displaced from the mainstream political process and deprived of its top leadership, appeared ineffectual and extremely cautious.[29] It had resorted to the traditional liberal democratic tactics of signature campaigns to free its leaders, issuing demands to the authorities, articulating appeals to the United Nations and advanced democracies of the West and organizing commemorative gatherings that cut no ice with the authorities and had little impact on the polity. It appeared that the ageing leaders were fulfilling a "caretaker" role and, in the absence of Daw Aung San Suu Kyi, were incapable or unwilling to make critical decisions. It saw a number of its organizers and activists detained for criminal offences and breaches of existing prohibitions. As in 2004, it seemed marginalized and there was a danger that it would be overtaken by events in the near future unless it could find creative solutions to increase capacity, enhance credibility, and renew its ageing leadership, in the face of massive constraints.[30]

Ethnic groups

The legally existing ethnic-based political parties, with the exception of the SNLD, continued their cooperation with the government, abiding by all the rules and regulations imposed by the authorities and duly participating in the NC's deliberations. The SNLD appeared to be in disarray with its top leaders in incarceration.

The major ceasefire groups like the Kachin and Mon, though politically more sophisticated than the others (altogether 17 groups had been acknowledged by the government), appeared to be suffering from internal rifts mainly due to corruption and jostling for power in anticipation of the new political order as well as problems of leadership succession as leaders involved in original peace deals passed away. For example, there was a short-lived coup, in mid-September, against the chairman of the NDA-K (New Democratic Army-Kachin), an armed group that entered into a ceasefire in December 1989 and that comprised ethnic Kachins, also known as "Red Shan" from the defunct Maoist Burma Communist Party or BCP War Zone 101. The chairman was away in Yangon when his headquarters was taken over by a minority loyal to the general secretary. The coup collapsed in two weeks because of a counter-coup by troops loyal to the chairman, backed by government authority.

In November the splinter group from the KIA (Kachin Independence Army which is the military arm of the ceasefire group Kachin Independence Organization, or KIO) that broke away in 2004, after being accused of attempting to stage a coup, further split when some of its members refused to follow their leader Colonel Lasang Aung Wa when he moved to a new area designated as their quasi-autonomous territory by the government.[31] On the other hand, the Wa group — militarily the most powerful among the armed ceasefire groups — which had seemed restive in the immediate aftermath of the ouster of General Khin Nyunt (reputedly, its mentor) appeared to have arrived at a *modus vivendi* with the junta's new military and administrative hierarchy.[32] Their military campaign into SSA-S territory in April and May apparently resulted in heavy casualties without gaining much ground and seemed to fizzle out with the rainy season.

The government had also prevented the ceasefire groups from forming lobbying alliances and coalitions. The Shan groups were also facing problems of factional discord and confrontation with the government (see "Shan Affair", above). The much weaker smaller groups had leaders who were generally satisfied with the economic and financial gains from their cooperation with the military and did not wish to rock the boat. In fact, over 840 troops of the Palaung State Liberation Army (PSLA), which had entered into a ceasefire at the end of April 1991, laid down their arms on 29 April 2005.[33] All in all, the ceasefire groups attending the NC were in no position to effectively bargain with the junta for their rights and privileges and usually toed the junta's line.

International Pressures

Narcotics issues

Since the early 1990s, the junta has been accused by its opponents and the Western media of not tackling the narcotics issue effectively, especially the alleged involvement of those ethnic groups, Wa in particular, that had entered into ceasefire arrangements with the government. In fact there were many allegations that the junta was reaping benefits from the huge sums of money generated by the narcotics trade. In 2005, as in recent years, there were also accusations that the junta had been unable to prevent the deluge of "speed" pills or methamphetamine tablets into Thailand and other neighbouring countries.[34] On 24 January the US Federal Court in Brooklyn, New York, indicted, *in absentia*, eight UWSA (United Wa State Army, the military arm of the Wa ceasefire group) members including Wei Hsueh-kang, a top leader who carried a US$2 million reward for his capture. The Myanmar government was unfazed and the indictment remained unenforceable.[35]

The junta has been introducing legislative, institutional, administrative, and interventionist measures in its war against narcotic drugs and sought regional cooperation to counter the drug trafficking. These measures continued in 2005 and a new opium-free zone was set up with the cooperation of ceasefire groups in the Wa region. Nevertheless, the US President's "Memorandum for the Secretary of State: Presidential Determination on Major Drug Transit or Major Illicit Drug Producing Countries for Fiscal Year 2006", released on 15 September 2005, listed "Burma" (Myanmar) as one of the "major drug transit or major illicit drug-producing countries" alongside 19 other countries that included Afghanistan, India, Laos, and Pakistan from Asia. It also designated Myanmar as one of the two countries "that have failed demonstrably during the previous 12 months to adhere to their obligations under international counternarcotics agreements".[36] Myanmar's Ministry of Foreign Affairs issued a public statement on 23 September refuting the US Presidential Memorandum's allegations and pointing out that US-DEA (Drug Enforcement Agency) had assessed from the annual US-Myanmar joint opium survey that in 2004, poppy cultivation actually declined by 34 per cent and opium production by 39 per cent as compared with 2003.[37] Most outside observers opined that there had been a declining trend in opium production in recent years and Myanmar deserved to be removed from the infamous list in the annual US "Presidential Determination" memorandum. Many concurred that the United States had disregarded, for political reasons, real progress in Myanmar's opium-eradication efforts in the past several years and 2005 was no exception.

ASEAN and Myanmar

ASEAN had always stood by Myanmar in its engagement with the EU (European Union) and the United States of America, which have attempted to ostracize Myanmar even in dealing with the grouping as a whole. The regional grouping generally refrained from commenting publicly on Myanmar's political situation, regarding it as an "internal affair", while quietly trying to persuade the regime to speed up the political transition and seek reconciliation with the legal opposition.

However, in recent years, concerns increased within ASEAN that the grouping's collective image would suffer from the Western perception that Myanmar was not making political progress and that the "Myanmar issue" had become a point of contention in ASEAN's dealings with other groupings and with its major dialogue partners. This led ASEAN to be more explicit about its discomfort over Myanmar's handling of its internal problems.

The issue came to a head in 2005 when anti-regime lobbies in the West campaigned to deny Myanmar the ASEAN chair due to it in mid-2006 (by way of the traditional rotation in alphabetical order). The US, British, and EU authorities also expressed disapproval of Myanmar having its turn, on account of what they regarded as continued absence of meaningful democratization and the incarceration of Daw Aung San Suu Kyi. They also hinted that they might boycott the annual meeting with ASEAN if Myanmar assumed the chair. There seemed to be some split within ASEAN states on this matter: authorities in some ASEAN states conveyed privately and even publicly their preference for Myanmar to "voluntarily" give up its turn in order to preserve ASEAN unity and integrity; others, however, voiced their support for Myanmar to take its turn in line with past practices. Eventually, despite having undertaken costly preparations to host the ASEAN meeting in Yangon as the next chair, Myanmar decided to give up its prerogative, much to the relief of some ASEAN governments. In the statement by the ASEAN Foreign Ministers released in Vientiane on 26 July 2005, it was stated "Myanmar had decided to relinquish its turn to be the Chair of ASEAN ... because it would want to focus its attention on the ongoing national reconciliation and democratisation process". It was further elaborated, "2006 will be a critical year and the Government of Myanmar wants to give its full attention to the process".[38] However, despite the deferment of an impending crisis over the chair issue, ASEAN was still left with the broader Myanmar problem which drew incessant pressure from influential members of the international community.

On the other hand, ASEAN still demonstrated its willingness to stand by Myanmar whenever the group's integrity was compromised by discriminatory practices of the West. An example was the 6th Asia-Europe Meeting of economic ministers at Rotterdam in mid-September, which ASEAN's economic ministers refused to attend "as a matter of principle" (only senior officials represented the ASEAN states) because the Netherlands denied visa to the Myanmar economic minister.[39]

At the 11th ASEAN Summit held at Kuala Lumpur in December, Myanmar's Prime Minister came under quiet pressure from some member states and finally agreed to allow an ASEAN envoy to visit Myanmar in the near future to assess the situation firsthand and report back to the grouping. This task fell on Malaysia's Foreign Minister. No date had yet been agreed for the visit. The summit's declaration also contained an unprecedented call for the release of political prisoners.[40]

The ASEAN Inter-Parliamentary Myanmar Caucus (AIPMC), initially formed in November 2004 and chaired by a Malaysian parliamentarian from the ruling party (a caucus dedicated to lobbying for the release of Daw Aung San Suu Kyi and all political prisoners, honouring the results of the May 1990 elections, and restoring liberal democracy in Myanmar) emerged as a vocal critic of Myanmar's rulers. In the first half of the year it pushed for denying the ASEAN chair to Myanmar. Thereafter, it continued to agitate for its stated objectives and in December issued a statement calling for the suspension of Myanmar from ASEAN if its members failed to act upon the following three goals in the next 12 months: not to allow Myanmar to chair ASEAN until it achieved "meaningful reforms"; to endorse Philippine's support for the initiative to "raise Myanmar [issue] to the agenda of the UN Security Council"; and to include "Myanmar on the agenda of the ASEAN Summits and ASEAN Ministerial Meetings" as well as to stipulate that the ASEAN Secretary-General make "regular reports on Myanmar" to the members of ASEAN.[41]

Havel-Tutu report and the UN Security Council

The Myanmar government continued its running battles with the International Labor Organization (ILO) over forced labour issues and with the United Nations over its refusal to allow both Professor Pinheiro, the Special Rapporteur of the Commission for Human Rights and Tan Sri Razali Ismail, the Special Envoy of the UN Secretary-General to visit Myanmar during the year. There were a host of other controversies over a broad spectrum of human rights issues, including with many non-governmental organizations (NGOs) and advocacy groups such as Amnesty International, Human Rights Watch, Earth Rights International, Global Witness, and Global Fund to Fight AIDS (acquired immune deficiency syndrome), Tuberculosis and Malaria, among others. But a more a serious challenge that quickly became a sort of a cause célèbre arose on 20 September when the so-called Havel-Tutu Report came out.[42] This report advocated referring "Burma" (Myanmar) to the UNSC because the prevailing situation in the country constituted "a threat to peace". The 70-page report, formally known as "Threat to the Peace — A Call for the UN Security Council to Act in Burma", was commissioned by former Czech President Vaclav Havel and Nobel Peace Laureate (1984) South African Bishop Desmond Tutu (both have been sympathizers of Daw Aung San Suu Kyi) and compiled by the global law firm DLA Piper Rudnick Gray Cary.[43] Despite many inaccuracies, dated information and misrepresentations, as pointed out by many knowledgeable observers and Myanmar specialists, including some who are sympathetic towards democratic reforms, the report set off a chain of endorsements for the call to table Myanmar's case at the UNSC — from the US government and its allies, legislators, NGOs, anti-regime organizations, insurgent groups and prominent individuals.[44] Interestingly, the NLD came out with a vaguely worded statement that could be interpreted as welcoming the report for its principles but not going so far as to explicitly endorse the call for the UNSC action. Played up by the anti-regime media and fuelled by the bandwagon effect, the report assumed a life of its own and provided a basis for punishing the junta beyond the usual cacophony of blaming and shaming. The fact that the main argument to support the so-called "threat to peace" claim would not hold in the face of serious analysis, that China and Russia, among the Big Five in the UNSC, would not allow the Myanmar case to be discussed even if it were tabled, did not deter its proponents from trying the long shot. Finally, the United States and its allies managed to lobby the 15-member UNSC to agree to a briefing by a senior UN Secretariat official on the Myanmar issue on 16 December 2005. By the end of the year nothing substantive seemed to have come out of initiative and even long-standing democracy advocates were sceptical about the value of the process for bringing about political change in Myanmar.[45] Perhaps it might even backfire by hardening the resolve of the generals, forcing them to withdraw inwards and giving false hope to people hoping for a positive change.[46]

Meanwhile, Myanmar's military government responded with a barrage of measures against the report and its two sponsors that included official rebuttals, media commentaries, mass rallies, refutations/denunciations by business and social organizations, and a letter-writing/petition campaign that lasted several weeks.[47] Meanwhile, some ASEAN member states also took sides on the issue under US pressure and Myanmar's foreign minister was reported to have urged his ASEAN colleagues to "maintain a common stand", in order to "prevent Myanmar from being singled out" at the UNSC for criticism.[48]

Regional support

Despite relentless pressures from the West and anti-regime forces in the international community, Myanmar appeared to have been able to garner continued support from China, India, Laos, and Vietnam premised on the principle of "non-interference in internal affairs". National interests of these countries related to issues such as regime security, security cooperation, energy security, trade and investment, and raw materials supply that undergird this solidarity with Myanmar continued to be relevant in 2005 and would remain so in the short term at least.

Economy

The government's target for the growth rate in the real GDP in fiscal year 2005/2006, the last year of the third five-year plan beginning 1 April, was 12.6 per cent.

Claiming an average growth rate of 12.4 per cent for the first four years of the plan, it appeared confident that the target could be achieved. On the other hand, the London-based Economist Intelligence Unit (EIU) estimated that Myanmar's economy would grow by only 1.5 per cent in the same period. The International Monetary Fund (IMF) estimate was reported to be 3.7 per cent.[49]

According to official statistics (which lagged by about 9 months), inflation eased to single-digit rates during the first quarter of 2005 because of price stability in staple food and essential commodities but anecdotal evidence suggests that it rose to double digit levels in the second half of 2005. In particular, urban transport charges in Yangon and other cities quadrupled after the government, on 20 October, raised the heavily subsidized prices of petrol and diesel fuel from K180 and K160 per gallon, respectively, to a uniform price of K1,500 per gallon.[50] Meanwhile the authorities continued to crack down on the supply of fuel in the black market in a campaign that was launched months before the fuel price hike. Consequently, there was a knock-on effect on commodity prices leading to increased inflationary pressures.

After the first quarter of the year, the market value of the US dollar in relation to the local kyat as well as the gold price fluctuated sharply on an upward rising trend mainly due to speculative pressures fuelled by rumours of political instability. The unprecedented triple bombing in Yangon and the government's closure of the private Myanmar Universal Bank (allegedly for money laundering) in late August apparently dampened the business climate and aggravated the volatility of the free-market exchange rate of the local currency and the gold price. The closure of the Myanmar Universal Bank followed the closure on 1 April of two major private banks — the Asia Wealth Bank and Myanmar Mayflower Bank — blacklisted by the US Treasury Department as "primary money laundering concerns". Their operations had been suspended in the wake of a bank run in early 2003. The Myanmar currency, officially pegged at around K6.7 per dollar to the IMF Special Drawing Rights, gradually fell from about K880 per dollar in January 2005 to some K950 in May and to K1,170 in August. It fell further to a record low of K1,360 to the dollar in late September but recovered to around K1,200 by mid-October and remained just below that level till the end of the year. The price of the highest-quality gold, which stood at around K213,000 per tical (0.525 troy ounce), peaked at over K350,000 in early October before settling back to around K300,000 in the last quarter of the year.

However, external trade is likely to maintain its positive balance for the fourth consecutive year in 2005/2006 with an estimated surplus of several hundred million dollars over a total volume of some US$5 billion compared with US$4.9 billion in 2004/2005. Exports were expected to reach US$3 billion, which is slightly more than the US$2.9 billion attained in the previous fiscal year, which saw a trade surplus of some US$950 million. Natural gas exports to Thailand, which accounted for more than one-third of total export earnings in 2004/2005, would most likely be the highest-earning export item, surpassing other major items such as timber, garments, marine products, and beans and pulses by a large margin.[51]

The annual value of approved foreign direct investment (FDI) in Myanmar, which hit rock-bottom at some US$19 million in fiscal year 2001/2002 had been rising in the following years to reach US$128 million in calendar year 2004. A US$62 million Chinese commitment in the oil and gas sector in January 2005 brought the cumulative total of FDI approved by the government since 1989, when Myanmar began to allow FDI, to US$7.76 billion as at 31 January 2005, though the actual inflow could be less due to time lag, delays, and deferments. The oil and gas sector retained the largest share, comprising one-third of the total approved amount (see Table 1). Further investments in the offshore gas exploration sector by Chinese, Indian, Korean, and Thai companies could boost the total value of approved FDI for 2005 to a new high in recent years.

TABLE 1
Sectoral shares of approved FDI, 31 January 2005

Sector	Percentage Share
Oil and gas	33.6
Manufacturing	20.7
Real estate	13.6
Hotels/tourism	13.3
Mining	6.9
Others	11.9

Source: Ministry of National Planning and Economic Development.

Energy emerged as the most promising growth industry in 2005, with new business ventures in offshore natural gas and hydroelectricity launched during the year. The production-sharing contract (PSC) between the Myanmar government and Daewoo International of Korea for exploration in Block A-1 off the Rakhine coast opposite Bangladesh resulted in the discovery in 2004 of a huge natural gas deposit estimated to hold 2.88 to 3.56 trillion cubic feet (tcf; equivalent to about 0.6 billion barrels of crude oil).[52] Later, a consortium was formed with Daewoo (60 per cent), Korea Gas Corporation (10 per cent), and two Indian firms ONGC

Videsh (a subsidiary of Oil and Natural Gas Corporation, 20 per cent) and Gail (India) (Gas authority of India Ltd., 10 per cent), to develop this new gas field named Shwe. On 13 January 2005 after a two-day tri-nation meeting of energy ministers from Myanmar, India, and Bangladesh in Myanmar's capital Yangon, a memorandum of understanding (MoU) was signed with all parties pledging to cooperate in a project to pipe A-1's natural gas output to India across Bangladesh. Further negotiations appeared stalled in the following months as the two South Asian countries could not agree on the terms and conditions of the project. India was caught unaware when news broke that Myanmar had agreed in early December 2005 to sell 6.5 tcf of gas from the A-1 block to Hong Kong–listed PetroChina over 30 years.[53] This left the future of the tri-nation pipeline, to transport gas to India from the A-1 field, in doubt as India's options to carry through the project came under additional pressure.[54]

In other developments in the oil and gas sector, it was reported, in January, that a China-Singapore consortium had secured the rights to explore onshore blocks C-1 in the Indaw area of Kachin state, C-2 in Shwebo-Monywa area within Sagaing Division, and offshore block M-2 in the Gulf of Moattama (Martaban). The consortium comprises CNOOC or China National Offshore Oil Company [Myanmar], China Huanqiu Contracting and Engineering Corporation, and Golden Aaron of Singapore. The government also signed a PSC with India's Essar Oil Ltd., in early May, to exploit two adjacent blocks, one offshore designated as A-2 and the other onshore known as L, both off the Rakhine coast. This came as a surprise to industry watchers as Myanmar had announced in early April that all onshore blocks would be held in reserve for domestic investments only.[55] In late July, Thailand's PTT Exploration and Production Plc. (PTTEP), which had already secured four offshore exploration blocks, was granted exclusive rights to explore the M-11 block off the Gulf of Moattama.

Electricity shortages in urban Myanmar manifesting as brownouts and daily rationing of supply continued in 2005 despite the government's efforts to increase output. New initiatives for large hydroelectric schemes were announced. They included a US$125 million equipment deal struck in mid-July with China International Trust and Sinohydro as well as a US$46 million dam contract given in early August to China's Gezhouba Water and Power Company, both for the 790-MW (megawatts) Yeywa Hydropower Project on the Myitnge River in central Myanmar.[56] An agreement was also reached in December with Thai government's EGAT Public Company Ltd. to jointly implement the 600-MW Htoogyi Hydropower Project on Thanlwin (Salween) River in Kayin state,[57] which could be the first of a series of five plants along Thanlwin planned to produce up to 10,000 MW.[58] Another was the MoU signed in November between Myanmar's Ministry of

Energy and Yunnan Machinery Equipment Export-Import Corporation (YMEC) to cooperate in developing a three-dam cascade on the Ruili (Shweli) River by the YMEC under the build-operate-transfer (BOT) scheme. The river's potential yield of hydropower was reported to be as high as 10,000 MW.[59]

The year also saw the first ever inter-governmental agreement between Myanmar and Thailand to allow Thai businesses to invest in contract farming in Myanmar. In line with the cooperative agreement concluded in November at the Second ACMECS (Ayeyawady–Chao Phraya–Mekong Economic Cooperation Strategy) Summit in Bangkok, a MoU was signed between the two agriculture ministers in early December to facilitate Thai contract farming of cash crops such as corn, rubber, sugar cane, tapioca, and palm oil.[60] Two weeks later, another MoU was signed between Sutech Engineering Company of Thailand and Myanmar's state-owned Myanmar Sugarcane Enterprise to allow the Thai company to plant 2,000 acres of sugar cane in Bago Division in lower Myanmar.[61]

In the face of high oil prices and inadequate domestic production of crude oil, Myanmar authorities began promoting, in the second half of the year, the cultivation of physic nut plants extensively throughout the country to harvest biodiesel from the nut. Eventually, in mid-December on the occasion of a meeting with officials from two states and four divisions, the junta chairman Senior General Than Shwe "gave guidance on putting 500,000 acres under physic nut plants in each state and division in three years". Theoretically, such a scheme, if successful, would yield, over a five-year cycle, more than 500 million gallons of biodiesel (700 million in a six-year cycle) that can be used as a diesel substitute, thereby plugging the decades-old gap between domestic production and consumer demand.[62]

Conclusion

Three major political issues remain unresolved in Myanmar: the power-sharing dilemma, the consolidation of national unity among the indigenous national races, and the legitimacy of the regime in power. The SPDC now claims that it has gone further than all its predecessors who had governed Myanmar towards resolving these critical issues and only the political opposition, led by Daw Aung San Suu Kyi, and the hostile West (governments, NGOs, and multilateral international institutions) stand in the way of rapidly achieving its goal of a united, strong, peaceful, and prosperous Myanmar. On the other hand, the issue of human rights and democracy still haunts the military rulers and the junta's claim that it was on the right track in resolving these three interlinked issues was hotly disputed, as in previous years, by the loose coalition of the NLD and its allies at home and abroad.

The political space in Myanmar, which has been significantly circumscribed by perceived imperatives of national security since the upheaval of 1988, remained as such in 2005. On the other hand, the regime seemed to tolerate critical comments by old politicians, literati, and former student leaders who spoke to foreign radio stations, appeared in foreign publications (even the *Irrawaddy*, which was denounced by General Khin Nyunt) and attended events organized by opposition figures and political parties throughout the year.[63] However, the government had not lowered its guard yet and, time and again, came up with exposé of conspiracies and plots against the state hatched by domestic and external enemies.

In 2005 the regime seemed to be as strong and as determined as ever to have its way on its own version of economic and political transition towards a market economy and parliamentary democracy as exemplified by the continued infrastructure building and the NC process. It faced many challenges to its legitimacy and authority from both domestic and foreign detractors but remained defiant and unfazed throughout. Despite the sound and fury from the opposition camp and many assaults with the help of powerful players in the international community the opposition failed to score significantly during this year.[64] One could say that the playing field was not level but the brutal truth was that nothing could be done to redress that either. Far from being a failed state, as labelled by some observers, Myanmar in 2005 appeared to represent the apex of state power in relative terms in the nearly six decades of political independence since 1948.[65] In that context, the move to Pyinmana may be interpreted as an attempt to further enhance the state's autonomy and power *vis-a-vis* societal actors in line with the regime's belief that the *Tatmadaw* is the embodiment of the Myanmar state.

Notes

[1] Lieutenant General Myo Nyunt's speech, *New Light of Myanmar* (hereafter cited as *NLM*), 8 June 1993.

[2] *NLM*, 31 August 2003.

[3] Rumours circulating at that time indicated that the main reason was the arrest of Major-General Sao Hso Ten, who was a leader of the SSA-N by the military government.

[4] Kaytu Nilar, "Implementing the Seven-Point Road Map for the Future Nation", *NLM*, 28 December 2005.

[5] Associated Press, "Myanmar to Resume Drafting Constitution Amid Simmering Discontent", 4 December 2005.

[6] Kaytu Nilar, op. cit.

[7] The SSPC formed in 1996 combining SSA-N and SSNA (Shan State National Army) and was not recognize by the government. The SSIAC was formed in November 2004

with representatives form the SNLD, SSA-N, SSNA, and an unregistered group of Shan nationalists called New Generation Shan State. The government claimed that SSPC and SSIAC had established links with the insurgent group known as SSA-S (Shan State Army-South) or SURA (Shan United Revolutionary Army, a name used by the government) and its aims and objectives entailed setting up a federal union that could eventually lead to national disintegration through secession of some constituent states. For details of the government's exposé, see the Press Conference 2/2005 of the Information Committee of the State Peace and Development Council held on 15 March 2005 (*NLM*, 16 March 2005).

8 *Irrawaddy*, December 2005, p. 2.

9 Another identified as U Shwe Ohn, an octogenerian leader of the deregistered Shan Nationalities League for Democracy, was placed under house arrest and was still in custody at the year's end (ibid.).

10 Mizzima News, 4 October 2005, http://www.mizzima.com.

11 It was also reported that SSA-South's Lieutenant Colonel Moengzuen, military leader of the 758th Region (renamed Shan State Army-Central), supported the ISG and his unit had become estranged from Yawdserk's group (SHRG [Shan Human Rights Group] News, 6 February 2006, http://www. shanland.org/).

12 For details, see the Information Committee's Press Conference 3/2005, 21 April 2005 (*NLM*, 22 April 2005) and Press Conference 4/2005, 15 May 2005 (*NLM*, 16 May 2005).

13 It was reported that in late December Colonel Sai Yee was elected to the vice-chair of the Restoration Council of Shan State (RCSS), which is SSA-South's political wing and chaired by Ywet Sit (DVB [Democratic Voice of Burma] News [in Myanmar], 28 January 2006, http://burmese.dvb.no/b_news/).

14 It was preceded by two bombing incidents in Yangon in which nobody was injured. The first explosion occurred on the morning of 17 March in the compound of Parami bus terminal in South Okkalapa Township. The small blast was on a bus of the Magway-Yangon-Pathein bus-line that was parked for the night in the bus-line compound. The second was in the small hours of the morning of 19 March at the Panorama Hotel on Pansodan Street in Kyauktada Township, Yangon. A small explosion also occurred in front of the Traders Hotel in Yangon's central business area at dusk on 21 October with no casualties. On 26 April 2005 a bomb exploded on the ground floor of the historic Zegyo market in Mandalay (Myanmar's second largest city) that resulted in several fatalities.

15 For details, see Press Conference 4/2005, 15 May 2005 (*NLM*, 16 May 2005).

16 A radical fringe group of militant ex-students who were involved in the seizure of Myanmar Embassy in Bangkok in October 1999.

17 An organization formed in November 1988 in rebel-held areas by students who fled to escape the crackdown when the 1988 uprising collapsed. It resorted to armed struggle against the junta for more than a decade.

18. For details, see Press Conference 6/2005, 28 August 2005 (*NLM*, 29August 2005).
19. For details, see Press Conference 4/2005, 15 May 2005 (*NLM*, 16 May 2005). Thai premier Thaksin Shinawatra expressed "surprise" at accusations that alluded to his country as a sanctuary for alleged terrorist acts against Myanmar. He reiterated his government's policy of not allowing "anti-government groups" to use Thai territory to launch attacks at neighbouring countries and suggested using "existing channels, including the diplomatic channel, to settle any misunderstanding" (*The Nation*, 18 May 2005).
20. Irrawaddy, 6 July 2005, http://www.irrawady.org.
21. For details, see Press Conference 6/2005, 28 August 2005 (*NLM*, 29 August 2005).
22. Associated Press, 23 July 2005.
23. Agence France-Presse, 17 October 2005.
24. It was rumoured that the exchange of positions between the Chief of Military Training and the Chief of Special Operations Bureau (both junta members) was for health reasons.
25. Apparently, long convoys of military trucks carried the personnel and office equipment to a sprawling complex, parts of which were still under construction by Myanmar's leading private construction companies believed to be involved in many government infrastructure projects in the past decade.
26. Time and again since 2001, rumours surfaced that a huge self-contained military complex, complete with an airfield, a hospital, underground bunkers, and a tunnel complex incorporating the most modern fibre-optics links and secure water and electricity supplies (from Myanmar's first and only underground hydroelectric power station built on the nearby Paulaung River with Chinese technical and financial assistance — US$170 million of supplier credit — and designed to produce 280 megawatts of electricity), was being built for use as the military headquarters. In early 2005, rumours of an imminent move of the defence military to the new headquarters resurfaced but there was virtually no indication of the involvement of civilians and line ministries. See, for example, Aung Zaw, "Dreams of a Rat Hole", Irrawaddy, April 2005, http://www.irrawaddy.org; and Aung Zaw, "Pyinmana: The Long Arm of the Law", Irrawaddy (online commentary), 14 November 2005, http://www.irrawaddy.org.
27. See, for example, "Myanmar", in *Regional Outlook: Southeast Asia 2006–2007* (Singapore: Institute of Southeast Asian Studies, 2006), pp. 44–45).
28. *Irrawaddy*, March 2005, p. 3.
29. See, for example, Toby Hudson, "The Fading Promise of Youth", *Irrawaddy*, July 2005, pp. 17–18.
30. See, for example, Kyaw Yin Hlaing, "Myanmar in 2004: Why Military Rule Continues", in *Southeast Asian Affairs 2005* (Singapore: Institute of Southeast Asian Studies, 2005), pp. 241–44, for a succinct discussion on the NLD's apparent mistakes and weaknesses.
31. Irrawaddy, 15 November 2005, http://www.irrawaddy.org.
32. Anecdotal evidence suggested that some of their special privileges that allowed for egregious behaviour outside their territory and use of unlicensed vehicles might have been withdrawn after General Khin Nyunt's demise.

33 *Irrawaddy*, May 2005, p. 2.
34 See, for example, the section on Burma (Myanmar) in the International Narcotics Control Strategy Report-2005 (INCSR), released by the Bureau for the International Narcotics and Law Enforcement Affairs of the U.S. Department of State, in March 2005, http://ncgub.net/Int'l%20Action/INCS%20Report%202005.htm.
35 *Irrawaddy*, February 2005, p. 2.
36 For details, see White house Press Release, Office of the Press Secretary, 15 September 2005, "Presidential Determination No. 2005-36", http://www.state.gov/p/inl/prsrl/ps/53327.
37 *NLM*, 24 September 2005.
38 "Statement by the ASEAN Foreign Ministers, Vientiane, 25 July 2005", http:://www.aean.org/17590.htm. On hindsight the government's move to Pyinmana as the new administrative capital, which began in November, suggested that this relocation of the entire central executive apparatus might have been one of the principal reasons behind the relinquishing of the ASEAN chair.
39 Xinhua News Agency, 17 September 2005.
40 See, for example, Sharon Vasoo, "A Foot in Myanmar's Door", *Today*, 13 December 2005.
41 AIPMC Statement: Conference on Good Governance, Democracy and ASEAN, 3 December 2005, http://www.aseanmp.org/.
42 For a summary of the assortment of contentious issues see, for example, "Situation of Human Rights in Myanmar", UN General Assembly, 60th Session, 3rd Committee, Agenda item 71(c), Report A/C.3/60/L.53, 2 November 2005.
43 The report is available at http://www.freedom-now.org/documents/FinalReportforDistribution.pdf.
44 See, example, the letter from Jean-Luc Lemahaieu, Representative in Myanmar for the United Nations Office of Drugs and Crime (UNODC) and Chair, Joint Programs for HIV/AIDs, dated 28 September 2005, addressed to Jared Genser of the law firm DLA Piper (personal communications).
45 See, for example, Harn Yawnghwe, "Will the United Nations Act on Burma?" Shan Herald News Agency, 3 December 2005, http://www.shanland.org.
46 See, for example, Amyotheryei U Win Naing/Rangoon, "Burma Needs More Than False Hopes", 7 October 2005, Irrawaddy (online commentary), http://www.irrawaddy.org.
47 See, for example, Ministry of Foreign Affairs Statement, "Myanmar Poised at Threshold of New Era", 29 September 2005 (*NLM*, 30 September 2005); and Associated Press, "Criticism of Distinguished Author's Report on Myanmar Takes a Turn for the Verse", 13 October 2005.
48 Kyodo News, 11 December 2005.
49 *Regional Outlook: Southeast Asia 2006–2007* (Singapore Institute of Southeast Asian Studies, 2006), p. 119.
50 The airfare charged by private carriers for domestic routes more than doubled in early December. This increase in fuel prices probably resulted in an additional gross annual

income of K250 billion to K300 billion for the government (estimated on the basis of the total volume produced in fiscal year 2004/2005 together with possible imports). Though the net income could be less, given that the civil administration and the military consume a substantial portion of such fuels, it is still a significant sum when compared with the government's total tax revenue, which amounted to only K257 billion in 2004/2005. This price hike, which placed the official price nearer to the (then) prevailing black market price, virtually put a stop to the widespread practice among private car owners of diverting part of the monthly quota (maximum 2 gallons per day for Yangon and much less for other cities) to the black market at a handsome profit.

51. In 2004/2005, natural gas was the top export item valued at K5.81 billion, followed by timber at K2.24 billion, garments at K1.24 billion, beans and pulses at K1.18 billion, and marine products at K1.03 billion. Rice, the traditional export earner, was way down the list at K0.18 billion. See *Selected Monthly Economic Indicators* (Yangon: Central Statistical Organization), April 2005.

52. The figure was reportedly confirmed by a US-based oil industry consultancy Ryder Scott. See Ko Kyoung-tae, "Daewoo Secures Giant Gas Reserve in Myanmar", *Korea Herald*, 28 December 2005.

53. This amount exceeds the estimated commercial yield of the Shwe field. The premise seems to be that other fields, like Shwephyu being delineated in the same A-1 block, would have substantial deposits to augment Shwe's output. In fact, it had been estimated that entire block's reserves could be as high as 20 trillion cubic feet (*EIU Country Report*, May 2005, p. 22).

54. See, for example, Anand Kumar, "Myanmar-PetroChina Agreement: A Setback to India's Quest for Energy Security", SAAG Paper No. 1681 (19-01-2006), http://www.saag.org/papers17/paper1681.html.

55. *EIU Country Report*, May 2005, p. 23

56. *EIU Country Report*, August 2005, p. 23.

57. *NLM*, 10 December 2005.

58. *The Nation*, 6 December 2005.

59. *Yunnan Daily*, 1 December 2005.

60. BurmaNet News, 6 December 2005, http://www.burmanet.org. Initiated by Thai Prime Minister Thaksin Shinawatra, in Bangkok, during the special ASEAN (SARS) Summit in April 2003, ACMECS was formally endorsed by the leaders of Cambodia, Laos, Myanmar, and Thailand at the Bagan (in central Myanmar) Summit in November 2003. Vietnam joined the group in May 2004.

61. Xinhua General News Service, 21 December 2005.

62. Kyaw Swa Ngei, "Physic Nut Oil Will Shape Brighter Future of Farmers", *NLM*, 3 February 2006. The figures are premised on ideal conditions for both cultivation and processing of the nut. In practice the output may vary and some fuel would be consumed in the production process and the net yield may be less.

63 Individual or even collective actions seemed to be overlooked so long as there was no incitement or mobilization of the polity against the regime, personal attack on the military leadership, attempt to split the military, and no linkage with insurgents or foreign organizations or unfriendly governments.

64 See, for example, Reuters, 12 January 2006, Ed Copley, "World Raises Volume on Myanmar, but Does Junta Care?"

65 However, this does not mean that the Myanmar state (conflated with the regime by its miliary rulers) possessed a high state capacity in the Fukuyaman sense (Francis Fukuyama, *State-Building: Governance and World Order in the 21st Century* [Ithaca, NY: Cornell University Press, 2004]). It could be weak in its capacity to manage change towards democratic governance and wealth creation while still be relatively strong compared with the past when measured against its opponents. For a brief explanation of the term "failed state", see, for example, "Failed state" at the following URL: http://www.sourcewatch.org/index.php?title=Failed_state.

Myanmar's Human and Economic Crisis and Its Regional Implications

Bruce Matthews

> *"Quite so!"*, *said one of the retired professors from behind a cloud of cheroot smoke. "My Western friends always ask me, 'Why are the Burmese so cynical?' I reply that there isn't any* single *reason to be cynical. But in these prevailing conditions there is absolutely* no *reason for optimism."*
>
> (Emma Larkin, *Secret Histories: Finding George Orwell in a Burmese Teashop* [London: John Murray, 2004], p. 30)

Myanmar is a leading example of what represents, at least by some definitions, a failed state: tyrannically governed by a military junta whose sullen leaders are seldom seen in public, with a downtrodden, impoverished, and dispirited citizenry — most of whom struggle to survive, at best with the most basic standard of living.[1] Except for the swollen hierarchy of the State Peace and Development Council (SPDC), upper elements of the armed forces (*SitTat* or *Tatmadaw*) and crony businessmen (including an increasingly self-evident resident Chinese population), the people of Myanmar experience few of the comforts and advances of the modern world. The unloved governing military junta, in absolute power under one name or another since 1962, prevails only because of the authority of the gun, and obliging neighbours on all sides eager to partake of Myanmar's still abundant natural resources at fire-sale prices.

But Myanmar's internal situation has deep geopolitical ramifications. Emanating from this wounded nation are huge and problematic challenges for the region. There is evidence to suggest that despite periodic state efforts to eliminate the production of opium poppies, Myanmar remains one of the world's largest producers of heroin and amphetamines — most of which is consigned for

---

BRUCE MATTHEWS is Dean, Faculty of Arts and C.B. Lumsden Professor of Comparative Religion, Acadia University, Nova Scotia, Canada.

international delivery through India, China, and Thailand. This, combined with what amounts to an uncontrolled HIV/AIDS epidemic, arguably makes Myanmar a threat to regional security.[2] Perhaps even more destabilizing is the steady wave of despairing people aiming to escape, particularly through the border region with Thailand, a phenomenon which will only increase as Myanmar's economic and political instability continues unabated.[3] This has become a serious problem for Myanmar's five neighbouring countries, and for the Association of Southeast Asian Nations (ASEAN), to which Myanmar has belonged since 1997. ASEAN has met with no success in persuading Myanmar to reform its polity, to free Nobel laureate Daw Aung San Suu Kyi, and to make a reasonable attempt to join the modern world.[4] Likewise, the United Nations has failed in its efforts to bring about human rights reform. Elsewhere, in the European Union, the United States, and Canada, economic embargos remain in place, though with little consequence.[5]

This article sets down the background for what confronts the international community as it comes to grips with Myanmar's increasingly maverick — and dangerous — situation. I first focus on Myanmar's internal situation. I review something of the command structure of government and the armed forces, which is crucial to an understanding of Myanmar's domestic state of affairs. I reflect as well on the much-diminished prospects of the National League for Democracy (NLD) and on the role of Buddhism as it finds its place in a frayed society and troubled polity. Second, I examine current geopolitical ramifications that flow from Myanmar's internal struggles. This includes the mission of ASEAN as it now wrestles with the dark side of its unfortunate partnership with Yangon; the challenge before the United Nations as fresh attempts are made to bring Myanmar's human rights crisis before the Security Council; and the economic and strategic concerns of China and India, which help keep an unreformed SPDC in power. In conclusion, I ask what might be the prospects for a future Myanmar if its conditions become so intolerable that they provoke insurrection, political implosion, and a breakup of the state — or, less likely, international intervention.

The Internal Situation

Turning to the first point, Myanmar's population (currently 52 million, and growing at an estimated 2 per cent per annum) remains 65 per cent BaMa (Bamar or Burmese) and 25 per cent ethnic minorities.[6] To reflect this ethnic division, the country is divided into seven "divisions" for the Burmese people and seven "states" for the ethnic minorities. Some minorities are demographically substantial in size (for example, the Karen/Karenni in Kayin state, the Shan and Kachin in states bearing their name, and the Rohingya in the Rakhine state). As well, sometimes large communities of ethnic minorities live amongst the Burmese in the heavily populated southern divisions (for example, the Pokaran or "delta Karen" in Ayeyarwady Division). Regional demographers do not consider Myanmar to be an over-populated country. Myanmar's population is only one-third that of neighbouring Bangladesh, but its geographic size is four times larger (677,000 sq. km. compared with Bangladesh's 144,000 sq. km.).

Economically, Myanmar remains dependent upon a subsistence agriculture, consistent with five other regional "least-developed countries" (Bangladesh, Laos, Bhutan, Nepal, and Cambodia).[7] Myanmar's agricultural and industrial infrastructure is not much different from what it was 60 years ago (though for internal "food security", Yangon has since 1992 successfully introduced a second or "summer" high-yield paddy crop and some limited mechanization). With such reliance on agriculture (57.2 per cent of the GDP in 2002), industry (however defined) has remained subdued (7.8 per cent of GDP in 2002).[8] Natural gas has replaced rice as the primary export, with garments second (this industry perilously depends on imported materials). But Myanmar's entire export economy remains stunted — only the equivalent of 2.6 per cent of Malaysia's export economy.[9] This inability to foster new industrial initiatives indicates that Myanmar will not be able to benefit much from economic cooperation with its ASEAN partners who are in the first and second tiers of the so-called newly industrialized economies (NIEs). Further, Myanmar's chaotic approach to economic development remains burdened with arbitrary, constantly changing rules and regulations. The junta has little understanding of market forces. It continues to print money at whim, operates with two and sometimes even three exchange rates, producing an economy which is recognized as one of the most distorted in the world. Everything is in short supply, particularly electrical power. The key lack of electricity — only one-twentieth of neighbouring Thailand's — paralyses the daily economy and leaves whole cities — like Mawlamyaing (Moulmein) — in virtually total darkness after nightfall. Cars, telephones, machines of any kind are endlessly repaired for lack of parts. This situation clearly "restricts the ability of local producers to compete on an equal footing with foreign firms in the domestic and foreign markets".[10] The governing junta remains in total denial, claiming a growth rate of 10 per cent on an average annual basis. But an IMF (International Monetary Fund) mission to Myanmar in September 2003 could find no evidence of this, and averred that Myanmar is experiencing zero growth. Although, as thinkers such as Vaclav Havel and John Ralston Saul rightly warn us, GDP growth statistics do not tell the whole story of the quality of life in any given country, nonetheless, with a GDP per capita per year of about US$285, Myanmar has the lowest gross national income per capita in ASEAN.[11] Furthermore, only 3 per cent of the national budget goes to health and 8 per cent to education, compared with 30 per cent to the armed forces.[12]

Arguably the most serious threat to the authority of the junta is availability of rice and cooking oil. An estimated 15 per cent of the population face immediate "food insecurity", and one out of three children is chronically malnourished and/or physically stunted.[13] Rural peoples have the modest advantage of access to some agricultural products from their own fields, but in the first half of 2005, based on widespread anecdotal evidence, I estimated that K100,000 per month (US$75) was required for an urban family with two children to have a moderate standard of living (US$1 = K1,330). Average public sector (state) salaries are far from approaching this level (the urban mean is about US$24 per month), forcing moonlighting, double work loads, selling of possessions, and so forth.[14] About 70 per cent of an average income (compared with 11 per cent for the average Canadian expenditure on food) goes to food.[15] Inflation has been between 36.6 and 57 per cent for the past three years, compared with as low as 1.7 per cent in the developed parts ASEAN.[16]

At present some of the costs involved in Yangon and Mandalay for foodstuffs are, first, for rice: high-quality *aindaw san,* 1 *pyi* (eight condensed milk tins), K1,000; *emata* (middle grade, most commonly consumed), 1 *pyi*, K500 to K700; lower grades of rice (*nga sein*) cost K350 per *pyi*, but avoided if possible except by the utterly destitute and prisoners. 16 *pyi* comprise one basket, the normal consumption of one individual in one month.[17] These prices are actually lower than what is available in Thailand, but they are also five times the cost of the same commodities in Myanmar in 1997 (for example, K200 for 1 *pyi* of *aindaw san*). State salaries have hardly kept pace. The other essential item is cooking oil, also dangerously exposed to inflation (1 *viss* edible oil, 1.6 kg, now K2,000, up from K800 in 2001). Even a cup of roadside tea or a bowl of *mohingya* (fish gravy and noodles) is K150 in 2005 (up from K120 in one year).[18] Because rice and cooking oil are absolute requisites for everyone, effort is made to bring these particular prices under some kind of control. Not unexpectedly, the hoarding of rice, oil, and other staples is rampant, contributing to a steady inflation. Meanwhile, official development assistance from various governments and multilateral agencies (for example, United Nations Conference on Trade and Development, or UNCTAD) usually available to states in such fearful subsistence conditions, has shrunk from US$342 million per annum in 1988 to US$150 million. The exception is periodic special humanitarian initiatives by Japan and the European Union for specific ventures — for example, to the largely forgotten 850,000 refugees on the Thai border or elsewhere in Thailand, whose conditions are often reported as parlous.[19]

For an internal perspective on contemporary Myanmar, an important theme is the military command structure and its relationship to "government". Although normal rotations of senior military personnel are to be expected in any country, when these occur in Myanmar, they are closely watched as precursors of cracks in the system. Such "cracks" are in evidence, but they have not precipitated a breakdown of the junta. The most significant "crack" occurred on 19 October 2004 when Secretary 1, Lieutenant General Khin Nyunt, was unexpectedly arrested and charged with corruption and insubordination by the reclusive and inflexible Chairman, Commander-in-Chief of Defence Services and Senior General Than Shwe (now 72 years of age). This had major ramifications. Khin Nyunt's Directorate of Defence Services Intelligence unit (National Intelligence Bureau, or NIB — 10,000-strong) was dismantled, its personnel dispersed or jailed.

The former NIB is now called the Office of Military Affairs Security. All ambassadors were recalled to Yangon and a major shake-up occurred, with ripple effects through the entire apparatus of government and armed forces. The once-powerful Khin Nyunt, English-speaking pragmatist and competitor to Deputy Senior General Maung Aye, was known for his relatively accommodating attitude towards NLD leader Daw Suu Kyi, to ASEAN, to the People's Republic of China (PRC), and to the international community in general. Khin Nyunt represented a known rivalry between his intelligence wing and that of the combat forces of the *SitTat*. He also likely underestimated the continuing hazard of his association with the deposed former dictator Ne Win, who died in 2002. Notwithstanding this, an unchallenged accomplishment of Khin Nyunt was his ability to secure peace with over a dozen armed ethnic rebel groups.[20] He was also the architect of the 2003 so-called seven-point "Road Map to Democracy". His subsequent sentence to 44 years in prison has, however, been commuted to house arrest, a subtle sign that Khin Nyunt is not without a possible political future.[21]

Thus as of October 2005, five powerful generals rule Myanmar: Senior General Than Shwe (who arguably sees himself up as a kind of monarch in the style of the last dynastic Konbaung kings), Deputy Senior General Maung Aye, Prime Minister General Soe Win (in charge of the infamous "Depayin-Sagaing" incident in May 2003, which saw the assault on and subsequent arrest of Daw Suu Kyi), Defence Services Chief of Staff General Thura Shwe Mann, and Secretary 1, General Thien Sein (in charge of the so-called National Convention). Rumours abound about the activities of this cabal, with some suggesting that Maung Aye does not want Than Shwe to feel openly threatened or confronted, and that

Than Shwe wants to balance Maung Aye's influence by endorsing Thura Shwe Mann (though the latter lacks the necessary prestige, especially with the junior officers).

Key to the survival of the junta is the *SitTat* or armed forces. It remains one of the largest in Southeast Asia, an estimated 380,000 to 400,000 personnel (largely light infantry units, with a small naval and air sector).[22] Since there are no serious prospects of invasion, and there are now only moderate ethnic insurgencies to combat, this huge force is in place specifically to control Myanmar's population — at which it is undeniably successful. The army is divided into four corps, each overseeing three of the twelve command regions. Thus the commanders of the regions (*taing hmus*) — formerly virtual warlords in their own fiefdoms with access to graft and corruption opportunities — are now theoretically linked to a more centralized system. Though the *taing hmus* remain powerful, and clones of a system that throws up new senior officers for each emerging generation, they are no longer members of the SPDC.

Clearly, however, over time the *SitTat* does not meet the standards of a professional armed force. Favouritism, nepotism, and loyalty-based promotions have all degraded command structures. The morale of the officer corps is low, caught between autocratic leadership and rampant corruption. The other ranks are not particularly well-armed, some pressed into service, and not infrequently exposed to brutal treatment by superiors. Any observant visitor to Myanmar with opportunity to walk or drive past military compounds or roadblocks will also be aware of the relative youth of the rank and file, some of whom are mere teenagers not averse to impertinent behaviour towards ethnic minorities, senior citizens, and women, the latter not infrequently targets for assault. In a wholly peculiar way, the armed forces have become a kind of "caste" in Myanmar society, comprised almost completely of BaMa soldiers. Ethnic minority troops are uncommon, and it is not possible for a non-Burmese or a non-Budddhist officer to rise above the rank of a Major. Even for the lowest ranks, belonging to the *SitTat* has significant privileges for the soldier and his family, including subsidies, access to education, housing, and health care. A soldier's entire family (remarkably, up to 60 people) is technically part of an ancillary militia, obliged to undergo some form of fundamental infantry training.[23] With approximately four million Burmese associated with the *SitTat* (both personnel and family members), this represents a significant sector of the population with an interest in seeing itself empowered and with continuing access to perquisites.

Recent evidence shows, however, that Than Shwe and other senior officers have a mounting concern for their own survival. In particular, this is evident in late 2005 by the bizarre construction of a new "capital" deep in the hinterland, with government ministries, a military headquarters, "parliament", hospital, large airstrip, tunnels, bunkers, supermarkets, shopping malls — even "luxury hotels" — at Pyinmana, 350 km. north of Yangon.[24] This is a kind of return to the isolationism of the past, suggestive of the Konbaung period (1752–1885 CE) when Bagyidaw, Mindon Min, and other monarchs built their capitals (Ava, Amarapura, Mandalay) in the interior, far from the coast (unlike neighbouring Siam, which understood the need to communicate with the emerging power — and technology — of the outside world, keeping their capital at Krung Thep close by the seacoast). The withdrawal could be anticipated as far back as October 2004, with the arrest of Khin Nyunt. Not surprisingly, Pyinmana's new names are Nay pyi daw ("place of the kings"), and Yan Lon ("secure from strife"). The Pyinmana complex has been described as many things: a bunker within a bunker, a redoubt from invasion or uprising, a more central location to control ethnic minorities — and even to control the spread-out armed forces. But Pyinmana is also a symbol for what the modern state of Myanmar has become — reclusive and paranoid.[25]

An issue closely related to the structure of government is the so-called National Convention, set up in 1994 to establish a new Constitution for Myanmar. The Convention reconvened in May 2004 for three months after an eight-year hiatus, and in 2005 met for only five weeks. Boycotted since 1995 by Daw Suu Kyi and the NLD (a controversial strategy), the National Convention is currently comprised of 1,076 hand-picked representatives, including 90 delegates from 28 "cease-fire" groups. Most delegates have connections to either the *SitTat* or to the United Solidarity Development Association (USDA, or Khaing Yea Hnin Hpyint Hpyo Yea). In any future national "election", however defined, the USDA, as the pro-government party of choice (backed by an ancillary Myanmar Women's Affairs Federation, Ahmyothani Asiayone, which claims a membership of 1.5 million), will have an obvious role. If the move to Pyinmana does not postpone a national election in the near future, it is not beyond possibility that Than Shwe may involve himself in such an election and find himself a "civilian" president for life.

A final feature pertinent to Myanmar's internal stress concerns the role of Buddhism, the religion of the majority and a continuing factor in the self-identity of the country. The faith has not been a catalyst for mobilizing public demands for reforms. On the contrary, the junta has succeeded in compromising some sectors of the vast clerical body (*sangha*).[26] The junta hosted the December 2004 Fourth World Buddhist Summit, and although this was considered a sham by many Buddhist prelates — and the leading financial patron and supporter for previous summits (Japan's Nembutsushu Association) backed out — the event went ahead with 2,600 representatives from 17 countries, some with prime ministers in attendance (for example, Thailand, Laos, and Sri Lanka). Although an important wing of the *sangha* (for example, the outlawed *yahanpyo* or Young Monks Association) would unquestionably side with a future "people power" uprising, the chances for wide-scale civil disobedience are too remote for this to have any serious meaning.[27] The question has been asked whether Burmese Buddhism is so inherently passive — or has it become so under Myanmar's brutal conditions — that the brave confrontations of earlier Buddhist activists such as Venerable U Ottama and Venerable U Wissera (both of whom stood up to British colonial rule in the 1920s) are no longer emulated. Elsewhere in the region consumer prices and exchange rates are the cause of street protests, even riots. The Burmese appear to accept such fluctuations with a certain resignation. The commentator Amyotheryei U Win Naing takes this one step further, arguing that religion, like any mature sense of "nationalism", has been seriously damaged by the severity of life in an uncompromising police state:

> Is such tolerance the product of religion, or has it become something of a national characteristic? The current air of submission in Burma has gone much deeper. Survival is the only thing that most Burmese care about. Moral and ethical considerations have been sacrificed for the sake of family and livelihood. Even religious belief has been conditioned by social problems. ... Nationalism — once the rallying cry of all Burmese — has also withered. In a society where the gap between privileged and disadvantaged has become chasm-like, nationalism can never flourish. This is the present reality of daily life in Burma.[28]

To sum up: Myanmar's internal social, economic, political, and even spiritual life remains problematic, much as it has since the military takeover in 1962. The all-powerful SPDC has always had leadership fractures and cliques, and these continue. By strange irony, the example of earlier British rule has influenced armed forces allegiance to a strict chain of command. Further, unlike other contemporary examples of authoritarian regimes (North Korea, Cuba) where there appears to be more public acceptance of the dictatorship, in Myanmar there is no doubt about the widespread public discontent. Yet the citizenry remains unable to express its want and painfulness either through democracy or through protest. This state of affairs does not end at the borders of Myanmar, however. It has far-reaching international implications.

The Regional Implications

The geopolitical impact of Myanmar's suffering is foremost brought into perspective with the issue of the chairmanship of ASEAN in 2006. Decided solely by its place in an alphabetical rotation, as early as 2004 Myanmar's looming chairmanship became problematic for ASEAN's international reputation. Some ASEAN spokespersons were reluctant to strip Myanmar of its claim because, in the opinion of Singapore's Foreign Minister George Yeo and ASEAN Secretary-General Ong Keng Yong, this would set a bad precedent. It was argued that by permitting Myanmar the chairmanship it would keep the country "within the radar" of the international eye, and provide leverage for the release of Daw Suu Kyi. Other ASEAN officials disagreed, pointing out that the chair has to be capable of handling a complex agenda, including drug trafficking, international crime, mass migration, sectarian conflict, and disease epidemics, all of which Myanmar suffers from acutely but does little to combat. Datuk Zaid Ibrahim, head of the "ASEAN Pro-Democracy Caucus on Myanmar" (comprised of six member states), averred that ASEAN "must have more self-respect than to accept leadership by a regime that rules not by people's voice but by the gun".[29] Then suddenly, on 9 August 2005, the Myanmar government relinquished its proposed chairmanship, saving face with the claim that it wanted to focus attention on the country's process of national reconciliation. (There are those who maintain that loss of the ASEAN chair was a relief for the junta, saving them from likely unending external criticism.) The loss of the chair was nonetheless arguably a major humiliation. The junta urgently needed the chair's prestige. It would have added to the junta's legitimacy, and help stimulate Myanmar's moribund economy. Much physical preparation was already under way, with airport and downtown improvement in Yangon to give it a modern look.[30] Arguably, the surrender of the ASEAN chairmanship provides its own danger — that of a lonely Myanmar. Even a democratic Indonesia cannot now be as close to Yangon as it might have been in a time of mutual dictatorship. Some ASEAN countries, notably Singapore and Malaysia, have extensive investments in Myanmar, and worry about increased economic isolation. Although the government of Myanmar does not have much regional respect, there is a case to be made that the situation would be even more destabilizing and hazardous if Myanmar did not have at least membership in ASEAN.[31]

A second geopolitical issue focuses on the inability of the United Nations to have any meaningful reforming role over Myanmar's frightful human and civil rights record, and no success in agitating for democratic transformation. On the occasion of the United Nation's sixtieth anniversary, a hopeful headline in the *International Herald Tribune* (19 September 2005) opined, "Threat to the Peace:

A Call for the UN Security Council to Act on Burma". But this appears virtually impossible. Desmond Tutu and Vaclav Havel's recently commissioned *Report on Burma* (based in large part on UN data and statistics) claims that Myanmar's situation is far worse than that of seven other failed states where the UN has intervened because of internal conflicts and the transnational issues involved (for example, Afghanistan, Rwanda, Haiti).[32] The *Report* recommends a Security Council resolution compelling Myanmar to work with the Office of the Secretary-General in implementing a plan for national reconciliation and restoration of democracy. In early December 2005, the Security Council agreed to at least discuss the human rights issue in Myanmar. But the inability of the United Nations to reform its Human Rights Commission in September 2005 accentuates the fact that neither the long-term presence of UN "special envoys" to Yangon, nor the spectre of possible UN-sponsored interventions or sanctions, have made any impact on the military government. UN representatives have been refused visits to Myanmar for two years, and with Khin Nyunt's fall from grace, the two current UN envoys are not soon likely to resume their role.[33] These are UN Special Raporteur for Human Rights Paulo Sergio Pinheiro (denied entry to Myanmar since November 2003) and Razali Ismail, Kofi Anna's Special Envoy (denied entry since March 2004). This has important media consequences and brings the discredited regime into the international public eye.[34] There are UN agencies at work in Myanmar, notably the UN World Food Programme, but most agencies have never met with top junta officials, and have limited access to their various projects. The World Food Programme buys hundreds of tons of rice from the government of Myanmar to distribute in specific internal areas within the country, aimed at about 750,000 marginalized people, but the distribution process is notoriously delayed by state bureaucracy and lack of infrastructure.

Thirdly, India and China continue to cosset Yangon's SPDC as they eye Myanmar's untapped natural resources and its strategic geographic location. This is perhaps the more surprising for India, which until four years ago was a vociferous critic of the junta. The "new" attitude is represented by Ambassador R.K. Bhatia's recent observation: "I wish to reassure my Myanmar friends that while India is proud to be a democracy, we are not in the business of exporting it."[35] Clearly India's aim is to secure access to some of the new offshore natural gas resources in Myanmar's Rakhine state (a proposed US$1 billion pipeline from Sittwe to Kolkata), and open possible land links by road through Myanmar to Southeast Asia. Border security concerns in Manipur and Assam justify some military cooperation between Delhi and Yangon, but it is disappointing for supporters of the NLD to witness the extent of India's complicity with the regime. In all of this, Sonia Gandhi's heart is at least in the right place — she sent Daw Suu Kyi sixtieth birthday greetings, expressing the Indian people's admiration for Suu Kyi's selflessness and determination. There is also the matter of the People's Republic of China's major outreach to Myanmar. China's search for energy resources is aggressive and worldwide. Ready access to Myanmar's natural gas, mineral, and forestry reserves requires better access from Yunnan and new roads are under construction. Chinese commercial investment is also greatly accelerating. Perhaps more disturbing are Chinese naval and military "listening posts" on the Bay of Bengal at Sittwe (Akyab) and Coco Island in the Andaman archipelago.

Concluding Observations

In conclusion, five observations might be made. First, the SPDC (16 powerful senior generals) and the 12 *taing hmus* (regional commanders) are arguably more entrenched than at any point in the 17 years since the military took formal power as a ruling "Council". As David Steinberg has argued, "the military leadership has reinterpreted history to reinforce belief that only they can save the country and have done so to a degree that they believe it".[36] An obsession that the West is contriving to expedite assassinations or even invasion has long been in place and provokes the junta to avoid the daily realities confronting the general population. Internal and external criticism makes little difference. The life of the ordinary Burmese is harsh and unbearable.[37] There have been incidents pointing to unrest (the detonation of three bombs in Yangon and Mandalay in May 2005 indicates a clear anti-government message from any one of a dozen potential sources), but a sense of resignation prevails and no wide-scale public protest has an opportunity to emerge. The border areas are particularly tragic, brutal, and neglected places, and its people subject to relocation and abuse. Factions within the armed forces are not sufficiently divisive to sponsor change. The junta knows that the most ominous weak point for its continued rule is severe food shortage, resulting in careful state husbanding of rice and cooking oil availability.

Second, the NLD remains in crisis. Daw Suu Kyi's continued detention under house arrest (extended for another year on 27 November 2005) has added to this paralysis. Organized support for democracy has atrophied. Most citizens to whom I have spoken about the NLD and prospects for democracy in Myanmar are sceptical. Sadly, many now equate the NLD with suffering and retribution. As a local saying goes, "If you died once you should know the cost of the coffin", referring to the devastating defeat of opposition forces in 1988–90. Others will ask: "If it doesn't work, why try again?" There is a fear of change — any change — lest it bring more tyranny and hardship. Should the present junta suddenly collapse due to internal implosion or as the result of a successful "people power" uprising, the possibility of Myanmar breaking up into ethnic enclaves would be high. Burmese citizens know this. Many fear becoming another Iraq. But Daw Suu Kyi remains a powerful international symbol, and her eloquent plea "Please use your liberty to promote ours" clearly resonates with a wide international community.

Third, it is important to note that Myanmar has made no attempt to fit into the "commercial norms" which have triggered Asia's economic progress, and which even authoritarian states such as Vietnam are attempting to embrace. Myanmar is not just an economic disaster in its own right, but a major barrier to close cooperation between South and Southeast Asia. For example, apart from a road between Myanmar's northern city of Myitkyina and Kunming in Yunnan, China, no highway from the outside appears likely to soon be constructed — for example, one connecting India, and Thailand through Myanmar.[38] Further, Myanmar's internal situation affects regional security as it spills over into other nations, marked by refugee migration and a wide-scale narcotics trade. Lee Kuan Yew notes: "To stay frozen in time means the SPDC are building up problems for themselves and those problems will overflow into ASEAN."[39] ASEAN, India, and China are likely to be regularly reminded that support for Myanmar's military government is no longer in their interests, economic or otherwise.

Fourth, the July 2005 relinquishment of Myanmar's turn for the 2006 rotating chairmanship was a particularly painful rebuke for Yangon. Perhaps it was easier to give up the chair than to adopt reforms, despite its warm invitation to join ASEAN eight years before. Had Myanmar assumed the chair, the United States and the European Union would likely have boycotted ASEAN — a harbinger of this prospect was seen in US Secretary of State Condoleeza Rice's refusal to attend the July 2005 Vientiane ASEAN meeting. But does ASEAN's role in persuading Myanmar to withdraw from the chairmanship indicate a readiness to shift from "non-interference" to "constructive intervention", especially when the problems of one maverick state threatens regional stability? Singapore's Prime Minister Lee Hsien Loong avers that adopting a confrontational stance with threats to Myanmar's expulsion from ASEAN will not solve the problem. Notwithstanding this widely endorsed point of view, without reform Myanmar will continue to remain problematic for ASEAN's international credibility.

Fifth and finally: what might the international community's response be to Myanmar's stalemate? Constructive engagement? Embargos? Isolation? Even Daw Suu Kyi argues that an "absolutist" approach will not work, and that there must be continued private negotiation with the SPDC. There are high-profile spokespersons who argue for "constructive engagement", notably Robert Taylor, Morten Pedersen, David Steinberg, Helen James, and Michael Aung Thwin. The latter also argues that the Burmese prefer strong centralized rule, are used to "voluntary labour", and are innately resistant to Western values and to the "cultural jihad" of the democracy movement.[40] Should a pardon to groups and individuals accused of atrocities and human rights abuse be offered, possibly by the United Nations, with no insistence that power be transferred to any political party until stability is achieved? Given important changes in command, can such strategies have any real opportunity of success, in the short or long term? When I asked a retired economist in Yangon who has carefully analysed economic and social data over the last two decades about the chance for meaningful political change, his answer was something I might have expected, but still quietly shocking: about 3 per cent — and no higher.

Notes

[1] Observations and arguments in this article are based on fieldwork conducted in Myanmar in July 2005.

[2] An estimated 400,000 to 500,000 Burmese have HIV/AIDS. The spread of AIDS from one country to another is arguably a security issue. Thailand in particular is affected by the unregulated transmigration of Burmese workers in the sex trade, diffusing the deadly disorder the more so into Thai society and bringing with it serious elements of social destabilization.

[3] An estimated 526,000 internally displaced people remain in Myanmar (*Burma Issues* 15, no. 6 [August 2005]). New refugee arrivals from Myanmar in Thailand come at the rate of 300 per month, down from 800 five years ago. "However, the new arrivals relate familiar stories of forced village relocations, forced labour and other human rights abuses. The reasons for reduced numbers is probably due to the fact that there is now a much reduced population living in the immediate border area than in former days and it is more difficult for displaced people to travel to Thailand than before due to ever-increasing Burmese Army presence." (*Thailand Burma Border Consortium Programme Report*, January to June 2006, p. 3).

[4] Daw Aung San Suu Kyi was under house arrest from 1989 to 1995, November 2000 to May 2002, and from May 2003 up to the present. She has no telephone or access to communicating with the outside world and no visitors except an attending physician.

[5] The US government continued its ban on all Burmese imports for another year, from July 2005.

[6] Government of Myanmar website, Ministry of Foreign Affairs (http://www.mofa.gov.mm/aboutmyanmar/population.html). Other statistics indicate a population that

is 70 per cent rural with 30 per cent under 14 years of age (*Xinhua*, 16 July 2005). In my opinion the 2005 CIA *Report on Burma* underestimates the total population of Myanmar at 42 million (http://www.cia.gov/cia/publications/factbook/geos/bm.html).

[7] 2005 UN statistics, http://www.un.org/special-rep/ohrlls/ldc.list.htm.

[8] *The Europa World Year Book 2005*, vol. II (London: Routledge, 2005), p. 3072.

[9] Myanmar produces 23 million tons of rice per year on 6.75 million cultivated hectares. In 2004 it exported 106,000 tons, which was a relatively small amount.

[10] "Structure of GDP", Yangon, December 2004 (private circulation). "Just as it is not possible to build a modern army based on traditional Burmese weapons system and traditional concepts of warfare, it is not possible to build a modern economy by relying on traditional commodities such as rice and beans and on traditional approach to development such as building public works. To modernize the economy, Myanmar as a least developed country must avail itself of the opportunities and must have adequate and fair access to the technology, knowledge, expertise and resources that are available in the rest of the world".

[11] Vaclav Havel, "I don't understand why the most important deity is the increase of the GDP. It is not about GDP. It is about the quality of life, and that is something else." (as quoted in John Ralston Saul, *The Collapse of Globalism and the Reinvention of the World* [Toronto: Viking, 2005], p. 24).

[12] There are conflicting per capita GDP and income statistics. Those based on unverified Government of Myanmar statistics are assumed to be unreliable.

[13] UN World Food Programme Director James Morris, 4 August 2005, http://www.reliefweb.int/rw/RWB.NSF/db900SID/FPRI-6EYBJK?OpenDocument.

[14] In March 2005, state salaries were adjusted upward, with the lowest skilled employee receiving K17,000 per month (US$14) and the highest (a Director-General) K56,000 (US$43). Former benefits in terms of rice and petrol subsidies have been abandoned. Note as well that schooling is by no means free. It costs an estimated K6,500 per child per month for tuition and "contributions".

[15] Canadians in the lowest economic quintile (poorest 20 per cent of the population) spend 17.5 per cent of their income on food, the highest (the richest 20 per cent) spend 8.5 per cent on food (*Statistics Canada*, Tables 2030001 [Survey of Household Spending], and 2020409 [2001 Census]).

[16] See Asian Development Bank statistics, http://www.adb.org/Documents/Reports/Annual_Report/2002/mya.asp, as well as http://en.wikipedia.org/wiki/Economy_of_Malaysia.

[17] The price of rice in Arakan sky-rocketed in July 2005, in part because the government will not permit rice transport between regions. One bag of rice (24 *pyi* or small tins) in Buthidaung cost three times the average monthly salary.

[18] For those with vehicles, diesel petrol is K3,300 per gallon, though the official rate is K180. Automobiles are hard to come by and exorbitant in cost, and new vehicles unavailable to non-SPDC-sponsored individuals.

19 Other independent aid is periodically noted, such as OPEC's 2004 contribution of US$10 million to help Myanmar upgrade its oil crop production for edible oils self-sufficiency. But there are more examples of international aid pulling out than going in to Myanmar, as indicated by the withdrawal of the Global Fund to help with AIDS in August 2005 (*Bulletin of the World Health Organization* [Geneva] 83, no. 10 [October 2005]).

20 The Wa, Kokang (Chinese), Chin, and Kachin were all permitted reasonable control of their territory in return for truce and for the right of the *SitTat* to enter these autonomous regions as it pleases.

21 Although his once-vast military intelligence apparatus has been disbanded (with 300 arrested, including 26 high-ranking colonels and above), it would not be impossible for Khin Nyunt to stage a comeback should conditions deteriorate. Khin Nyunt's two sons, businessman Ya Naing Win (Bagan Cybertech) and Major Zaw Naing Oo were also arrested and subject to secret trial.

22 *The Europa World Year Book 2005* cites 485,000 men, 350,000 in the army, 13,000 in the navy, and 15,000 in the air force, as well as a "Paramilitary People's Police Force" of 72,000, and "People's Militia" of 35,000 (p. 3061).

23 "The Reserves are aimed at serving as part of the defensive strategy against foreign invasion, to defend the base areas when the normal troops are in the front line and to engage in the economic activities of the military establishments." (*Narinjara*, India, 4 August 2005).

24 The date and time of the move to Pyinmana was determined astrologically at 6.37 p.m. on Sunday, 6 November 2005, which may explain the abruptness of the departure. Somewhat ironically, Pyinmana was also General Aung San's headquarters in his struggle against the Japanese towards the end of World War II.

25 Another secret project is the construction of a nuclear facility at Kyaukse, an isolated generally mist-shrouded valley near Mandalay. Most Asian countries have a research reactor (only Myanmar, Sri Lanka, Laos, and Cambodia do not).

26 The state has tried to use Buddhism to its advantage in several ways. Unfortunate examples of anti-Christian and anti-Muslim activities are collaterally related to this. Churches in ethnic locations are often open to desecration, possibly as a way to provoke ethnic minority folk to seek vengeance and get them to fight. Religious freedom, at any rate, is seen to be a threat to national unity. See Mooke Hlee, "People's Faith: A Toll of War", *Burma Issues* 15, no. 8 (August 2005).

27 Apart from an estimated 1,400 political prisoners in Burma's jails, 300 monks (*pongyi*) remain incarcerated. But in 2005 two important Buddhist prelates have emerged asking for flexibility on the part of the junta and Daw Suu Kyi. These are the *sayadaws* U Zawtipala, abbot of Kyakhatwaing Kaung, Pegu, and Ashin Kundalebiwuntha of Mahagjandharon Kaung, Mandalay.

28 *Irrawaddy*, 7 October 2005.

29 *Bangkok Nation*, 13 July 2005.

30 Including, somewhat remarkably, the renovation of the Anglican Holy Trinity Cathedral at its key location beside the historic Scott or Bogyoke Market.

31 According to Rodolfo Severino, former Secretary-General of ASEAN, "The only thing worse than having Myanmar inside ASEAN is to have it outside ASEAN" (Agence France Presse, 17 July 2005). Severino also said that ASEAN would be the foundation of East Asian economic regionalism, presiding over the East Asia Summit in Malaysia in December 2005.

32 The *Report on Burma* was written for Vaclav Havel and Desmond Tutu by Jared Genser of the Washington law firm, DLA Piper Rudnick Gray Cary, in September 2005.

33 Since 1988, other UN envoys have included Sadako Ogata (former head, UNHCR), Yozo Yokoto, and Alvaro De Soto. Ali Alatas, former Indonesian Foreign Minister and now UN representative, has met with Than Shwe in 2005, but with no known constructive results.

34 On 19 August 2005, Burmese Head of State Than Shwe met with former UN envoy Ali Alatas at a military guest house, but nothing has been reported of their conversation.

35 *Hindustan Times*, 3 June 2005.

36 *South China Morning Post*, 6 August 2005.

37 José Ramos, East Timor's Foreign Minister, and other recent visitors to Rangoon, remark on the sad look of citizens' faces in their isolation and poverty.

38 A "South Asian highway" from Bangladesh, linking up with a repaired World War II Ledo Road from India, with both continuing on to connect with Kunming in China, is not infrequently referred to. "The reality is that commercial demand for such road(s) will remain minimal while Burma itself is divorced from the trade-centred development of its neighbours and discriminates against minorities (including Indian and Chinese) ... a private sector economy would long ago have developed the sort of trans-border linkages for which much of South East Asia is renowned." (*Irrawaddy*, 25 July 2005).

39 *Straits Times*, 12 August 2005.

40 *Reconciling Burma/Myanmar: Essays on U.S. Relations with Burma*, edited by John Badgely (Seattle: National Bureau of Asian Research, March 2004), vol. 15, no. 1, p. 10. "The West took a dangerous turn when it focused solely on human rights and democracy in its relations with Myanmar, leaving other strands of policy unattended. As a result, the landscape of Myanmar's external relations has been altered by its growing dependence on China for assistance, both military and economic, as well as for investment and trade."

Philippines

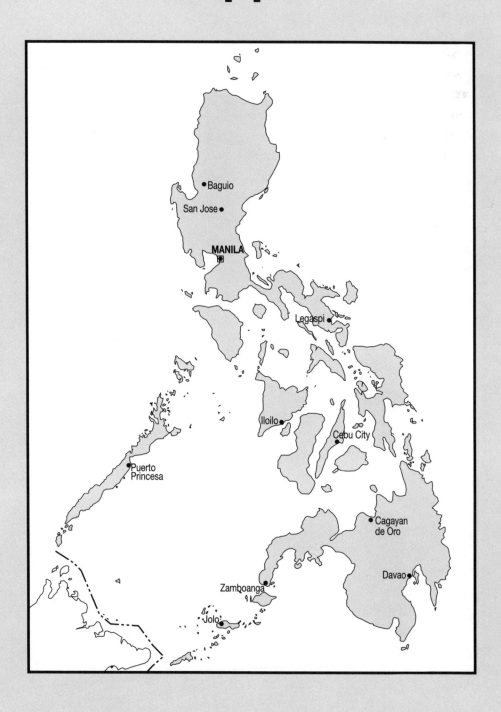

THE PHILIPPINES
Crisis, Controversies, and Economic Resilience

Lorraine C. Salazar

For a country known for both its strong commitment to democracy and its weak political institutions, the year 2005 was full of intrigues and challenges for the Philippines. In July the Arroyo administration almost collapsed amidst rumours of coups, political controversies, and another People Power movement, sidelining efforts towards economic reform. Yet, despite this crisis and the ensuing policy setbacks, the economy displayed unexpected resilience.

The analysis of the events of 2005 will be divided into three sections. The first deals with the country's main political events, the second with the state of the economy. The final section concludes by reflecting on the country's economic and political prospects in the short term.

Political Developments

Crisis and controversies

The year 2005 saw the Filipino President almost toppled by street protests — yet again. Despite being impeached and facing considerable public opprobrium, the Arroyo administration narrowly survived. However, at the end of the year, the controversies surrounding the President's mandate were far from settled. These issues threaten to resurface in 2006 as her administration endeavours to push for changes in the Constitution as a way of solving the gridlock that besets the Philippine political system.

Mrs Arroyo won the 2004 elections by a margin of about 1 million votes over her closest rival, actor Fernando Poe. This entailed a six-year term for Arroyo,

---

LORRAINE C. SALAZAR is Visiting Research Fellow, Institute of Southeast Asian Studies and Assistant Professor, University of the Philippines, Diliman, Quezon City.

who rose to the presidency in January 2001.[1] The new presidential term evoked promise, as questions of Arroyo's mandate and legitimacy seemed to be resolved by her electoral victory.[2] Yet, the optimism was short-lived as economists from the University of the Philippines warned of an impending fiscal crisis. In her July 2004 State of the Nation Address (SONA), President Arroyo declared that the country's "most urgent problem" was solving the government's worsening fiscal and debt condition. Eight new revenue measures were announced as a legislative priority but Congress took its time legislating them. Because of this, credit rating agencies downgraded their ratings of the Philippines.

Rumblings early in 2005

Faced with an uphill battle getting the unpopular tax measures passed, Arroyo's public approval rating fell. In early March, rumours of coups circulated as a former general called for the establishment of a transitional government, declaring that the Arroyo government had failed to respond, thus far, to the problems of poverty, economic development, and social justice.

In May Mrs Arroyo's popularity dipped further when the Senate investigated claims that her husband and son had been receiving pay-offs from *jueteng* (an illegal numbers game), which had led to former President Estrada's political demise.

In June Manila was abuzz with a more explosive topic. This time it involved President Arroyo herself, supposedly caught on record giving instructions to cheat to ensure her victory in the May 2004 polls. The records consisted of phone conversations allegedly between President Arroyo and a top Commission on Elections official, Virgilio Garciliano, on various occasions during May and June 2004.

The government claimed that the release of the illegal recordings was part of a "grand destabilization plan". Arroyo disputed allegations by the opposition of foul play. She argued that her victory was such — over 40 per cent of all ballots cast and a margin of one million votes — that it could not have been achieved by cheating. She also reiterated her commitment to focusing on the economy, in particular addressing the hike in oil prices, tackling unemployment, and investing in infrastructure.

Meanwhile, copies of the taped conversation flooded the streets, selling for about 5 pesos (S$0.15) each. The wire-tapped conversation became the number one mobile phone ringtone and jokes about the President rigging the elections proliferated, leading to further erosion in the public's respect for Arroyo.

On 27 June, after three weeks of silence, Arroyo finally admitted on live television that she called a senior official of the Commission on Elections to "protect" her votes. She apologized for a "lapse in judgement" and for not immediately addressing revelations of the taped conversations. In a ten-minute speech, the ostensibly remorseful Arroyo promised to redouble her government's efforts to implement its reform agenda and to leave behind all the divisive politicking.

Because of the controversy, Arroyo's net satisfaction rating fell to −33 per cent in the Social Weather Station (SWS) survey for the month of May 2005 — the lowest for a president since 1986. The public's disenchantment with the President was heightened by rising oil prices, inflation, new taxes, and a perceived increase in corruption. Opposition politicians hoped that these issues would have a "snowball" effect, ultimately leading to another "People Power" movement.

While dissatisfaction was high, there was really no mass support at the grassroots level or among the military for another "People Power" uprising. The majority of the urban middle class, while finding the President's actions distasteful, were equally disgusted by the composition of the anti-Arroyo coalition, an assortment of opportunistic and strange bedfellows: supporters of deposed President Joseph Estrada, old Marcos loyalists, retired military officers, and legal organizations of the Communist Party of the Philippines (CPP). One analyst called them "a cabal of communists and clowns", which neither aroused passion among the middle class nor offered a viable leadership alternative. Deposing Arroyo would not have solved the country's structural problems of poverty and weak institutions.

Tumultuous July

On 8 July the ante was upped and the Arroyo government nearly collapsed, as various sectors withdrew support from the increasingly beleaguered President.

First, ten of Arroyo's most trusted economic team members, led by Finance Secretary Cesar Purisima, resigned from the cabinet. In a publicized event, they read out a prepared statement claiming the erosion of "the ability of our President to continue to lead and govern our country with the trust and confidence of our people". They urged the President to resign, which they argued was the "least disruptive and painful option that can swiftly restore normalcy and eventually bring us to prosperity".

Their move was followed by a similar call from the Makati Business Club (MBC), the country's premier big business organization and previously a strong supporter of Arroyo. A few hours later, former President Corazon Aquino joined the fray and asked Arroyo "to make this supreme sacrifice" of resigning. Finally, members of the Liberal Party, led by Senate President Franklin Drilon, formerly coalition allies of Arroyo, also called for her to step down.

It is not difficult to realize that the unfolding of events, while occurring separately, were well coordinated and clearly related, and were intended to pressure Arroyo to resign in the name of the "national interest". The withdrawal of support from within Arroyo's camp added fuel to the calls for resignation from the opposition, the left, some civil society groups, and academia. Indeed, the perception created was of a cauldron near boiling point that could spill over at any time into massive street protests, leading to yet another president dismissed via "People Power".

The market reacted immediately to these developments. The peso neared its record low of 56.45 to the US dollar while the stock market suffered. The top three rating agencies, Fitch, Standard and Poor, and Moody's, changed their outlook for the Philippines from stable to negative. In addition to the raging political crisis, the rating agencies pointed to the Supreme Court's suspension of the expanded value added tax (EVAT), a key component of the government's fiscal reform agenda.[3]

It seemed that Arroyo's days were numbered and her resignation inevitable. Yet, those who thought that a transition was in the offing did not expect that the calculated staging of events was no match for the President's stubbornness. Arroyo went on live TV affirming that she would not resign. She had already apologized for a "lapse in judgement" but firmly believed she won the May 2004 elections. Indeed, she dared her political foes to bring their grievances to Congress and impeach her.

More importantly, two strategic sectors did not join the bandwagon. First, the military declared neutrality and adherence to the Constitution. Second, the Catholic Church, through the Catholic Bishops Conference of the Philippines (CBCP), issued a pastoral letter stating "like Pope Benedict XVI, we do not believe in the 'intrusion into politics on the part of the hierarchy'". These decisions blunted the clamour for Arroyo to step down and gave her breathing space.

Before that long Friday ended, Arroyo received a further boost from former President Fidel Ramos. Ramos, who enjoys much respect from the military, proposed a swift revision of the Constitution within ten months, changing the form of government from presidential to parliamentary and holding a federal election by May 2006. This, according to Ramos, would provide a "graceful exit" for Arroyo and at the same time resolve the crisis and deadlock-prone political system.

The opposition, intending to sustain the pressure, held a demonstration on 13 July along Ayala Avenue, the country's central business district. The event failed to generate enough public support. Some observers pointed to the public's exhaustion with "People Power". Others were underwhelmed by the leadership alternatives. Still others believed that while Arroyo was very unpopular, she remained innocent until proven guilty. The alleged smoking gun — the wire-taps — was damning. Yet, its authenticity and, more importantly, its source were not established.

In her much-awaited SONA speech on 25 July, Arroyo remained silent on the controversies haunting her. Departing from the usual recitation of projects and priority bills, Arroyo called for "the opening of the great debate on Charter Change" as the best way to reform a political system that had degenerated over the years and become "a hindrance to progress". The call for Charter Change, via a Constituent Assembly,[4] was the most applauded part of the President's short 23-minute speech. Congressmen and local government officials who have long been critical of "imperial Manila" were the most enthusiastic supporters of the proposed move towards a federal, parliamentary government to replace the current presidential system.

Thus, while Arroyo barely survived the political onslaught on her administration, she successfully deflected calls for her resignation by putting the spotlight on political reforms, in particular changing the Constitution.

Impeachment hearings

When the option of street protests did not materialize, the opposition, which initially rejected impeachment as a trap (given that the President's party controls the majority of the Lower House seats), changed its tack. On 25 July, 42 opposition lawmakers filed an impeachment complaint claiming that Arroyo was guilty of "cheating, lying, and stealing". Lacking the required 79 signatures for automatic transmittal to the Senate, the complaint was sent to the House Committee on Justice, which had 60 days to assess its merits.[5]

During August and September the House Committee on Justice deliberated on the merits of the impeachment case against President Arroyo. Partisan bickering on a range of trivial and procedural issues bogged down the hearings. During the deliberations, the opposition failed to present credible and sufficient evidence beyond hearsay (testimonies of people of questionable credibility and suspicious financial status) or potentially inadmissible evidence (such as the "Hello Garci" tapes).

On 6 September the political turmoil engulfing the Arroyo administration reached a plateau when the Lower House threw out the impeachment case against her. After an intense 23-hour debate, Members of the House voted 158 to 51 to dismiss the impeachment complaint. The complaint, which alleged that Mrs Arroyo had rigged the 2004 elections, was declared insubstantial and based on illegally obtained evidence. Thus the Lower House, where allies of the President held the majority of seats, effectively gave her a one-year protection from ouster via impeachment.

The opposition acknowledged that the impeachment case against the President was dead, but warned that the issue will continue to "haunt and hound" her. With its defeat in Congress, the anti-Arroyo coalition threatened massive street protests to force the President's resignation. They claimed that the killing of the impeachment initiative signalled the move to the streets for "the search for truth". Yet, as it had been for past months, public support for street protests was meagre.

Various anti-Arroyo personalities, including former President Aquino, made pronouncements that military intervention was needed for a regime change. Despite such thinly veiled prodding for military involvement, the military hierarchy reiterated that it would respect the constitutionally mandated civilian chain of command. In addition, the Catholic Church, through the CBCP, reaffirmed that it would not join calls for the President's resignation. The Church called on the people to "move on forward and address the more important and urgent problem of grinding poverty". These two key sectors, as in July, blunted the pressure on Arroyo to step down.

Charter Change

On 25 July 2005 Arroyo appealed for political reforms through Charter Change. Mrs Arroyo acknowledged that it is Congress that would decide on the mode of Charter Change, but endorsed the idea of a Constituent Assembly, composed of the Lower House and the Senate, as the quickest means to do so. This call was consistent with the initiatives of the President's allies in the House, who proposed to fast-track the constituent assembly project with the goal of presenting a draft of a new constitution and of holding a referendum by mid-2006.

The sudden attention to constitutional change in the midst of the President's crisis of legitimacy was interpreted by regime opponents as a bid for a "graceful exit" rather than as a fundamental constitutional reform designed to avoid stalemates that had become more pronounced during the 2005 crisis.

Arroyo's detractors (some of whom have been steadfast supporters of amending the Constitution) dismissed the move as diversionary. Also, members of the Senate, across party lines, expressed opposition. The senators' vehement opposition can be attributed to the fact that the constitutional changes would entail the creation of a parliamentary system with a unicameral legislature, which would lead to the abolition of the Senate. Nonetheless, members of the Lower House as well as local government officials expressed their fervent support for constitutional change.

Changing the Charter has been a long-standing issue in the Philippines. All post-1986 Presidents from Ramos to Estrada and Arroyo have made it part of their policy agenda to amend the Constitution. In 2004 the House passed a resolution calling for a Constituent Assembly but the Senate threw out a similar measure. Senators disagreed with the House of Representatives over how and when to amend the 1987 Charter. They prefer that a Constitutional Convention, whose delegates would be elected by the people, draw up the amendments to the Constitution.[6] The current attempt to change the form of government is perhaps the most serious so far when viewed in the context of solving the deadlocks facing the Philippine presidential system.

Proponents of a parliamentary form of government argue that it is better than the current presidential system. The main reason cited is that under a parliamentary system, the legislature combines the role of an elected assembly responsible for passing laws and granting government the right to levy taxes with that of providing the executive ministers of government. The executive and legislative branches of government are fused together, leading to a more responsive rather than an adversarial system. Second, to win election to parliament, one would have to be a member of a distinctive party — sheer popularity alone would not suffice. Finally, with a parliamentary system, the country would no longer need to resort to extra-constitutional means to remove an erring chief executive at mid-term. The head of the government and the cabinet are chosen from among the majority bloc in parliament. The government, collectively, and the cabinet ministers, individually, are directly responsible to parliament. Once ministers lose parliament's confidence, they are compelled to resign to allow a new government to be formed.

Consultative Commission

In September President Arroyo appointed 55 people to form a Consultative Commission (ConCom) to recommend amendments to the 1987 Constitution. The ConCom was given three months to consult the public and come up with a draft constitution to be submitted to the President and Congress. The Commission was headed by former University of the Philippines President Jose Abueva, a staunch campaigner for a shift to a parliamentary and federal form of government. Other members included representatives from business, academia, civil society, and local government.

In a record two-and-a-half months, the ConCom submitted its proposals to President Arroyo on 16 December, which the President transmitted to Congress for its consideration and action. The ConCom's main proposals in revising the 1987 Constitution included the following:[7]

1. Change in the form of government, from presidential with bicameral congress to a parliamentary system with a unicameral parliament.
2. Change in the structure of government from a highly centralized unitary structure to a decentralized structure of autonomous territories and eventually a Federal Republic.
3. Removal of unnecessary economic restrictions on foreign investors to allow them to fully own corporations, utilize natural resources, lease agricultural and reclaimed lands, and engage in education, advertising, mass media, and public utilities.
4. Electoral reforms:
    - Abolish national elections and extend officials' term of office from three to five years, with no term limits.
    - Elect members of parliament in parliamentary districts and through proportional representation of the political parties in parliament.
    - Enable voters to vote not only for candidates but also for political parties to emphasize the importance of political parties.
    - Urge parliament to empower overseas Filipinos and those with dual citizenship to vote for members of parliament.
    - Rationalize and modernize the Commission on Elections.
5. Political party reforms:
    - Promote the development of a two-party system, with checks and balances of power for healthier party competition, and political stability.
    - Promote political party responsibility and accountability for policy and performance in parliament and in autonomous regional governance.
    - Encourage party solidarity, loyalty, and commitment to its programme of government.
    - Punish political turncoats who shall lose their seats in parliament if they switch allegiance from one party to another while being members of parliament.
    - Provide state funds to political parties to help counter money politics.

6. Implement judicial reforms to strengthen the independence of the judiciary and its capacity to render justice more efficiently and expeditiously.
7. Establish a transitional presidential-parliamentary government from 1 June 2007 to 31 May 2010:
    - The current president and vice-president serve their full term to May 2010 according to the 1987 Constitution.
    - An interim parliament comes into existence in 2007, formed from the existing bicameral houses of Congress, which will elect an interim prime minister.
    - The interim prime minister will be the senior-most member of the cabinet, next to the president.
    - The president appoints at least one-third of the members of her cabinet from among members of the interim parliament, and 30 more members who are experts in their respective fields.
    - The president is not vested with the power to dissolve the interim parliament.
    - The interim parliament shall enact laws of the republic which shall be approved by the president.
    - The president and vice-president are subject to the same disqualification and manner of removal as provided in the proposed constitution.
    - Because of their interdependence, there will be substantial power sharing between the incumbent president and the interim parliament led by the interim prime minister.

The first six proposals were generally acceptable. However, the last point, with regard to transition from a presidential to a parliamentary form of government, created a ruckus. At the heart of the controversy were two proposals: first, the suspension of the May 2007 local and national elections and extension of the term of office of these officials until 2010; and second, that Mrs Arroyo and the Vice-President, Noli De Castro, would continue their term, side by side with the interim prime minister, until the national elections to be held in May 2010.[8]

Detractors of the President and opponents of the move to change the Charter criticized the ConCom report as a ruse to keep President Arroyo in power, and the scrapping of the 2007 elections a way of buying the support of senators, congressmen, and local government officials who were up for re-election in May 2007.[9] One congressman called the proposal "not only undemocratic but ... also a shameless political, self-preservation ploy to avoid an election disaster that is expected in 2007 due to the President's record-low ratings".[10]

On another front, the country's major political parties agreed unanimously to support the Charter reform, including an urgent shift to a parliamentary government, and to formulate an economic action plan to revitalize the economy, foster development, and address poverty. In a meeting of the Conference of Philippine Political Parties in December, heads of the major parties agreed "to push the momentum for constitutional reform and set the stage for approval of a unicameral parliamentary system".[11] The heads of major political parties approved in principle the first six recommendations of the ConCom. Nevertheless, they deferred decision on the proposed scrapping of the May 2007 elections and agreed to consult with their respective parties further, emphasizing that the proposal "should not benefit legislators".[12]

However, former President Ramos, who proposed Charter Change as a "graceful exit" for President Arroyo in July, described the ConCom's transitional provision as a "monumental blunder". His statement pointed to a possible rift with Mrs Arroyo and a potential waning of support for Arroyo. Ramos reiterated his suggestion that Arroyo use the crisis as an opportunity to change the form of government from presidential to parliamentary, initiate such a shift by voluntarily stepping down in 2007, and stand in parliamentary elections to end the political crisis.

In a five-hour directorate meeting on 16 January 2006 at the Malacañang Palace, the political party that Ramos established, the ruling Lakas-Christian Muslim Democrats party rejected Ramos' call for Arroyo to resign by the middle of 2007. The party unanimously agreed that President Arroyo must serve out her six-year constitutionally mandated term until 2010 and threw its support behind Arroyo amidst persistent calls for her to resign. The party also approved the seven core amendments aimed at shifting to a parliamentary government and a unicameral parliament and sustaining economic growth and fighting poverty:

- Transformation from the presidential to the parliamentary system.
- Establishment of a unicameral legislature and abolition of the Senate.
- Lifting the term limits of elected officials.
- Providing for a five-year term of office for all elective officials.
- A ban on political "turncoatism".
- Creation of autonomous regions towards the establishment of a federal system.
- Easing of restrictions on foreign investments in the country.

The party resolved to let Congress and the public decide on the contentious issue of whether to hold elections in 2007 through a national plebiscite. De Venecia, the Lower House Speaker, proposed a Charter reform timeline, recommending that a national plebiscite be held in June and, upon ratification of the amendments, a shift to a parliamentary system and a unicameral parliament be made in July 2006.[13]

Political analyst Amando Doronilla opined that the Lakas' meeting indicated that the party was prepared to push for Charter Change in much the same way it smothered the impeachment case against the President in September. He argued that Lakas, it seemed, was engineering a "historic transformation of the political system, without public participation, as though constitutional change is the exclusive concern of a majority coalition". In addition, it appeared that the party was preparing to change the constitution with or without the cooperation of the Senate.[14] Indeed, the Senate's assent to convening a Constituent Assembly to jumpstart the process of constitutional change is crucial. Yet, given the Senate's opposition, it looked like the Arroyo administration was planning ways to bypass the Senate such as through the campaign for a people's initiative to amend the constitution. Local government officials led by the Union of Local Authorities of the Philippines (ULAP) have already initiated efforts towards the collection of the signatures of 12 per cent of the registered voters (roughly 5 million).[15] These moves on the part of the President and the House leadership point to their persistence and commitment to push for Charter Change.

At the public opinion level, it is clear that the people do not know enough about the Constitution to make an informed choice at this point. A May 2005 poll by the Social Weather Station (SWS) found that seven out of ten adult Filipinos believe that there are no provisions in the 1987 Constitution that need to be changed at the moment. Yet the same survey found that 73 per cent of the 1,200-sample admitted to having little or no knowledge of the Constitution. In another survey in August 2005, the SWS found that only 22 per cent know enough about parliamentary systems. The 22 per cent were divided on whether it would work for the country. Both of these surveys point to the need for a nationwide information campaign to inform people of the benefits of a shift to a parliamentary system.

At the end of the day, it is really the public who will decide whether or not to change the Constitution. Thus, the Arroyo government and supporters of Charter Change would greatly benefit from focusing their energy on public education on the issue. From this vantage point, the road towards Charter Change seems long and difficult, littered with power struggles among elites, an uncooperative Senate, and a public needing more information on the matter.

Peace talks with the MILF and the CPP

The political controversies surrounding the Arroyo presidency have also affected the progress of peace talks between the government and the Moro Islamic Liberation Front (MILF) and the CPP. The MILF has expressed commitment to the peace talks while the latter has stated that it would wait for the next government to resume negotiations.

In July the Malaysian government, which was mediating the peace talks with the MILF, served a notice of temporary suspension — pending resolution of the political crisis in the country. Despite this, MILF spokesperson Eid Kabalu reiterated that the MILF was committed to peace.[16]

During the ASEAN Leaders Summit in December, President Arroyo and Malaysian Prime Minister Abdullah Badawi announced that the peace talks would resume in 2006. The MILF is hoping that a peace agreement would be signed within the year, ten years after exploratory talks started in 1996. Formal talks bogged down in the year 2000 following strong disagreements on contentious issues such as ancestral domain, as well as on who shall manage the proposed Bangsamoro rehabilitation and development package. Despite the suspension of formal talks, technical-level discussions continued and MILF negotiators were reportedly ready to submit several proposals for self-rule.[17] These developments bode well as concrete steps towards solving the decades-old conflict in Mindanao.

On the other hand, the government's relations with the CPP turned for the worse. With the CPP's legal members in Congress leading the opposition to Arroyo, it has declared that it will wait for the next administration to resume peace talks. The Arroyo administration responded to this provocation by withdrawing the immunity of 97 rebel negotiators and their staff, exposing those with pending criminal cases to possible arrest.[18] The CPP's armed wing, the New People's Army (NPA) retaliated by intensifying their attacks on government targets and telecommunications relay sites. In December the military recommended that the traditional two-week ceasefire for the Christmas season be cut down to two days and announced that it will step up its military campaign against the CPP-NPA in 2006. Despite these events, Philippine officials said Manila would continue to press for a resumption of negotiations to end the 35-year-old communist insurgency, though a resumption does not seem likely in 2006.

Relations with the United States, China, and ASEAN

With respect to the diplomatic ties, in particular with the United States, China, and ASEAN, 2005 was also a year of changes and positive developments for the Philippines.

Since July 2004 the Bush administration has been slightly cool towards the Philippines because of its decision to withdraw its small contingent from Iraq. This move was a response to the demands of Iraqi insurgents who had kidnapped Filipino truck driver Angelo De la Cruz. At the cost of alienating the Bush administration, Arroyo took this bold step to avoid a potential domestic backlash from Overseas Filipino Workers (OFW) and their family members whose repatriated income comprises a substantial chunk of the GDP. Angelo De la Cruz became the epitome of the modern-day Filipino who has to leave his country in order to provide for his family's needs. Sacrificing his life for a commitment to a war that most Filipinos do not relate to and have not expressed support for would have been too damaging at the start of the President's new six-year term.

Nonetheless, the Philippines continued to be a major front in the "war against terror" in Southeast Asia, with the US government expressing commitment to military support and exercises in Mindanao. In addition, US Embassy officials in the Philippines voiced their preference for a constitutional resolution to the ongoing political crisis, thumbing down suggestions of using extra-legal means of removing the president.

Due to the slight chill in relations with the United States in 2004, the Arroyo administration turned its attention to cultivating ties with China. During a three-day state visit in September 2004, five government and business agreements were signed, signalling improvement in bilateral relations. Arroyo signed a confidential protocol with the Chinese government on cooperation to exploit oil and fishing resources of the South China Sea. China provided a loan for the construction of a railway project aimed at easing congestion in Metro Manila. China also offered the Philippines US$3 million for the establishment of a Chinese language-training programme for the Philippine military, donated engineering equipment, and invited the Philippines to participate in naval exercises. Further, the two governments agreed to facilitate visa-issuing processes to encourage Chinese tourists to visit the Philippines.[19]

The Philippines agreed to take over the chairmainship of ASEAN when Myanmar bowed to international pressure not to lead the organization. Again, concerns were raised over the Philippines' domestic political turmoil and how it might affect Manila's leadership of ASEAN. Foreign Affairs Secretary Romulo, however, has assured that the Philippines has a firm commitment to the regional grouping. A possible issue, however, is how, given the country's fiscal problems, the administration will deal with domestic requests to slow down tariff cuts on goods as part of the country's commitments to the ASEAN Free Trade Area.

The Not So Bad State of the Economy

As 2005 ended, many analysts of the Philippines were puzzled over why the economy performed well despite the political turmoil. To the disappointment of the political opposition, the expected economic fall-out from the near downfall of the Arroyo presidency did not happen. Indeed, the economy grew more slowly from July to September, at a rate of 4.1 per cent — down from 6.2 per cent in the same period in 2004 — but it grew nonetheless, even at the height of the impeachment challenge to Mrs Arroyo. For 2005 the country's gross domestic product grew 5.1 per cent compared with its performance of 6.0 per cent in 2004. This growth was lower than the government's goal of 5.3 per cent, but slightly higher than market projections of 4.7 to 5 per cent. Despite domestic political troubles, high oil prices, weak global demand for electronics, and middling agricultural growth, the Philippine economy performed comparatively well. Thus, it defied predictions of a meltdown made by some observers.

The role of overseas Filipino workers

A large part of the answer to this puzzle lies in the efforts of 8.4 million Overseas Filipino Workers (OFWs). Their remittances contributed US$8.5 billion to the economy in 2004 — equivalent to 9.2 per cent of the country's GDP. In 2005 the Bangko Sentral ng Pilipinas (Central Bank of Philippines, or BSP) estimated that remittances would hit over US$12.3 billion, or about US$15 billion if money sent through informal channels such as friends, relatives, or other unlicensed couriers were accounted for. This meant that, next to electronics, OFW remittances were the second biggest foreign exchange earner and contributor to the economy.

There are about 8 million OFWs working in about 200 countries worldwide, equivalent to 10 per cent of the country's population. Of these, 3 million are permanent residents while 5 million are temporary workers. What was seen a temporary means of alleviating unemployment in the 1970s has now become a solution for the lack of opportunities for a highly skilled and educated population. It is thus not surprising that almost every opinion poll finds that one in three Filipinos looks towards migration or overseas employment as a means of improving their families' economic well-being.

The huge inflow of remittances explains why the economy has been growing, driven by a strong consumption demand — despite record-high oil prices, inflation, and pessimism among the populace and investors alike because of political uncertainties. Hal Hill argued that there appears to be a "firewall" developing between the Philippine economy and its politics, which protects the latter from burning up from the heat generated by power struggles among the political elite. A big part of this "firewall" is made up of OFW remittances, cushioning the economy from a meltdown.

The strong inflow of remittances has provided many positive macroeconomic benefits. At the end of the year, the peso emerged as one of the strongest currencies in the region, buoyed against the US dollar. Remittances sustained the country's international reserves, reaching US$18.1 billion in November 2005. Strong remittances inflows have also led to a balance of payments surplus, which reached an estimated US$2 billion at year-end. In addition, because of strong inflows of foreign exchange, the government could borrow more from domestic sources and lessen its dependence on external debt, and in the process also lower the cost of borrowing.

Remittances also fuel domestic consumption growth as low-income levels were compensated by the inflow of remittances from family members working abroad. Many Filipino families receive income from abroad. Six out of ten of these families live in urban areas and are relatively better off, creating a new middle class that helps generate a consumer-led economic growth in the midst of recession and high unemployment.

Indeed, the role of remittances in economic development and poverty reduction is increasingly being recognized. The World Bank has recently focused on the subject in its 2006 Global Economic Outlook (GEO). Today the debate on international migration is no longer focused simplistically on "brain drain" from a country. The GEO estimated that in 2004, developing countries received about US$160 billion in remittances — more than twice the size of official aid.[20] This figure still underestimated the full scale of remittances because of unrecorded payments made through informal channels. The GEO argued that migration has enormous growth and welfare implications for both origin and destination countries. A major finding of the study was that overseas migration can reduce poverty as remittances improve people's lives at the micro level.

Remittances are also useful for their counter-cyclical nature. They rise in times of need during natural disasters, financial crises, or conflict. They are a stable source of foreign currency in comparison to foreign direct investment (FDI) or overseas development assistance (ODA) — especially in countries that are considered unstable or below investment grade. Yet, the GEO cautions that remittances are fundamentally private funds or household incomes and thus should not be viewed as a substitute for development aid or for policies aimed at improving a country's overall investment climate.

The OFWs now comprise an evolving middle class, which would hopefully demand more accountability of the country's political leaders. However, while the economic benefits of migration are positive, the phenomenon is coupled with high social and familial costs. The breakdown of traditional family structures and roles, an increase in sexually transmitted diseases among certain types of OFWs, and dependence on remittances are among the many high social costs that migrant families face. Yet, most of them undertake these risks in order to provide for their families and, indirectly, save their nation from economic collapse.

Fiscal reforms and the Expanded Value Added Tax

Another factor that can help explain the positive economic developments is the Arroyo government's pursuit of fiscal reforms, which is commendable, given the unpopularity of introducing new taxes in the midst of a political crisis and global oil price hikes.

As early as July 2004, President Arroyo identified the country's perennial fiscal deficit as the major problem facing her administration. The long-winded legislative debates and posturing finally ended in May 2005, when Congress passed a compromise law on expanding the coverage and rate of the EVAT.

On 24 May, President Arroyo quietly signed the law, which is the biggest revenue-raising measure in the fiscal reform package. Along with the EVAT, new taxes on alcohol, tobacco, and petroleum products, increased corporate income tax, as well as a Lateral Attrition Law (a law providing incentives and sanctions to officials and employees of revenue agencies to improve their revenue collection performance) were passed. On the implementation side, the Bureau of Internal Revenue's (BIR) and the Bureau of Customs (BOC) have been improving their revenue collection performance and reversing their reputation for corruption and inefficiency.

Yet, on 1 July 2005 the Supreme Court (SC) — acting on a petition questioning the legality of the EVAT law — issued a temporary restraining order (TRO) to stop its implementation. Under the Philippine Constitution, only Congress has the power to raise taxes. While Congress passed the law, it has a provision that grants the President power to raise taxes from 10 to 12 per cent in January 2006 if either VAT collection as a percentage of GDP of the previous year exceeds 2.8 per cent, or the national government deficit as a percentage of GDP of the previous year exceeds 1.5 per cent.[21] The petitioners claimed that the law was tantamount to Congress abdicating its exclusive power to tax, given the provision that allows the President to raise taxes by an additional 2 per cent by 2006.

On 1 September the Supreme Court upheld the constitutionality of the EVAT law. The Court ruled that the intent and will to increase the tax rate came from Congress, and Congress only delegated the power to implement the law.

Yet, given the rising oil prices in the world market, two bills were filed in both Houses of Congress to defer the EVAT on oil and power for at least a year. Congressman Joey Salceda, Presidential Adviser on Economic Affairs and a major proponent of the EVAT, argued that levying tax on oil and power at this time could do more harm than good as it would led to economic contraction and consumer pessimism as prices of goods soar. However, Finance Secretary Margarito Teves opposed delaying implementation of the law. He argued that without the implementation, the country would lose an estimated P500 million (about US$9 million) a day in revenues, worsening its fiscal situation. Yet, aides of the President have signalled her willingness to postpone the EVAT on oil and electricity *only* if Congress initiates the deferment.

With the EVAT, the Department of Finance anticipated collecting an additional P80 billion (US$1.45 billion) a year. About P28 billion (US$500 million) was expected to come from the oil and power sectors. Such revenues were central to the goal of lowering the budget deficit to 3.4 per cent of GDP (P180 billion, or US$3.27 billion) in 2005 and 2.1 per cent of GDP in 2006 (P125 billion, or US$2.27 billion). Finance officials argued that rising oil prices had already been factored into forecasts used during the EVAT deliberations. They were worried that any suspension on the tax law would mean another credit downgrade. In the face of popular pressure, critics of the government predicted that Arroyo would suspend the implementation of the EVAT to help replenish her extremely low political capital.

Defying the odds, the government started implementing the EVAT in November 2005 and announced that it will increase the tax rate from 10 to 12 per cent on 1 February 2006, as mandated by law. This tough decision has earned the government some applause from both the domestic and the international community, signalling its commitment to achieving its fiscal goals. With the passage of the EVAT, the BIR's vigilance in revenue collection, and cuts in government spending, the budgetary deficit was expected to hover around P140 billion, falling below the P180 billion ceiling for 2005.

Conclusion

The year 2005 was full of twists and turns, as the country moved from an unresolved fiscal crisis to a deeper political crisis which overshadowed, if not held back, some positive developments in the economy.

A 2004 survey of 120 chief executives of multinationals and leading Filipino companies by Wallace Business Forum found that the Philippines continues to be an attractive investment location because of its English language proficiency; labour availability, quality, and reliability; adaptability to Western culture and practices; market potential, size, and quality; positive Filipino attitudes; educational attainment and literacy; low costs, including labour; availability of quality and quantity of middle management and technical people; and comfortable lifestyle.[22] These advantages give the Philippines competitive advantages in five key economic sectors, namely, information technology (IT) and business process outsourcing; tourism; health, wellness and medical tourism; logistics; and transport.[23]

The economy has coped well despite the strains that the political controversies have placed on it. Hal Hill argues that the economy's resilience is proof of its growing independence from the conflicts among the political elites, and is due to the OFWs and competitive economic sectors that operate independently of government or require little in the way of public facilities such as IT, call centres, and medical tourism. These sectors keep the economy moving even as politicians bicker bitterly, acting as an "economic firewall" against the volatile political situation.

Arroyo is struggling to rebuild her credibility after a determined push for her ouster by the opposition. The President is weakened but not immobilized. She faces real economic and social pressures and has little room for manoeuvre in the face of the fiscal deficit and escalating oil prices. Given these limitations, her administration would not find it easy to make the tough decisions necessary for economic recovery.

Before 2005 ended the President and her political party have initiated a determined effort to push for Charter Change as a way out of the political gridlock that the country finds itself in. Thus, the issue of Charter Change will be a defining issue for 2006. This means that the economic reform agenda will take a backseat, as political reforms would be given priority.

Notes

1. Arroyo, the Vice-President in 2001, was the constitutional successor to Joseph Estrada, who was forced to step down from the presidency through popular pres-

sures, known as "People Power 2". Estrada is currently being tried for plunder and corruption.

2. However, losing presidential and vice-presidential candidates Fernando Poe Jr. and Loren Legarda filed election protests regarding the outcome of the 2004 election, claiming foul play. The Supreme Court threw out Poe's petition in December 2004 when he died of a heart attack. Legarda's petition is still being heard.

3. See the article's economic section for more discussion on the Expanded Value Added Tax.

4. The 1987 Constitution provided three modes of changing the charter: first, through a Constitutional Convention that is popularly elected; second, a Constituent Assembly composed of both Houses of Congress; and third, via a People's Initiative, which needs the signature of 12 per cent of registered voters and at least 3 per cent of the voters in each district.

5. If at least one-third of the Lower House members vote that the case has substance, the impeachment articles would be transmitted to the Senate, which will then convene into an impeachment court to try the President. The senators would act as judges.

6. *Philippine Star*, 17 January 2006.

7. "A Report to the Filipino People by the Constitutional Commission", 16 December 2005, http://pcij.org/blog/wp-docs/concom-report-highlights.pdf.

8. It should be noted that of the 55 ConCom members, 22 submitted a two-page dissenting opinion objecting to these transitional provisions.

9. Scheduled for re-election in 2007 are 12 senators, and all congressmen, governors, mayors, and other local government officials. Those who are on their third and last term are not qualified to run for the same post in 2007. At least one-third of the present House members fall in this category. Their stay in Congress would be extended if the coming elections are scrapped See *Philippine Star*, 20 December 2005.

10. *Philippine Daily Inquirer*, 19 December 2005.

11. They were Senator Edgardo Angara of the LDP; Rep. Jesli Lapus of the Nationalist People's Coalition; Manila Mayor Lito Atienza and Rep. Rolando Andaya Jr. of the Liberal Party; Rep. Luis Villafuerte of Kampi; and Secretary Norberto Gonzales of Partido Sosyalista-Demokratiko ng Pilipinas. Other political leaders in attendance included Secretary Heherson Alvarez, Rep. Roque Ablan Jr. of Lakas, and Rep. Constantino Jaraula.

12. *Philippine Star*, 20 December 2005.

13. *Manila Times*, 16 January 2006.

14. *Philippine Daily Inquirer*, 16 January 2006.

15. This effort is reminiscent of the work of the People's Initiative for Reform and Amendments (PIRMA, meaning signature in Filipino), which tested the waters to change the Constitution via a People's Initiative during the twilight years of the Ramos administration. The Supreme Court rejected their efforts by arguing that there was no enabling law that guides People's Initiative in changing the constitution. Currently,

ULAP officials are not deterred and were keen on collecting signatures to show that the people at the grassroots want a change in the Charter, if the Senate remains obstinate and resist their efforts towards change.

16. See *Philippine Daily Inquirer*, 4 July 2005, and *Philippine Star*, 24 July 2005.
17. *Philippine Star*, 4 January 2006.
18. *Philippine Daily Inquirer*, 10 August 2005.
19. http://english.people.com.cn/200409/07/eng20040907_156212.html.
20. The Philippines is the third largest remittance receiver, next to Mexico and India.
21. *Philippine Star*, 9 June 2005.
22. Peter Wallace, "Some Good Things about the RP Economy", *Manila Standard*, 22 October 2004.
23. Jaime Augusto Zobel De Ayala, "Doing Business in the Philippines: Opportunities and Challenges", Breakfast Talk at the Tower Club of Singapore, 24 May 2005.

THE ABU SAYYAF GROUP
From Mere Banditry
to Genuine Terrorism

Rommel C. Banlaoi

Since the Philippine government joined the global war on terrorism, it has been in hot pursuit of the Abu Sayyaf Group (ASG). Though government and media sources continue to describe the ASG as a mere bandit group because of the many kidnap-for-ransom activities (KRAs) it perpetrated in the past, the series of bombings that the ASG carried out in 2004 and 2005 were hallmarks of terrorism rather than banditry. Is the ASG mutating from a mere bandit group to a genuine terrorist organization?

Much has already been written about the ASG. But there is still little understanding of its exact origin, ideological inclination, organizational structure, leadership dynamics, operational capabilities, and recruitment strategies. This article aims to add value to the ongoing discussions on the ASG by focusing on such issues. It also aims to update the reader on the terrorist attacks conducted by the ASG in 2005 and to describe the Philippine government's counter-terrorism response.

The Genesis of the ASG

Though it is widely known that Ustadz Abdurajak Janjalani founded the ASG, there is no uniform account of its exact origin.[1] According to media reports, the military allegedly formed the ASG in early 1990s to penetrate the ranks of Muslim radicals in Southern Philippines. The ASG reportedly acted as an agent provocateur of the Armed Forces of the Philippines (AFP).[2] Edwin Angles (aka Ibrahim Yakub), who

---

ROMMEL C. BANLAOI is a Professor of Political Science at the National Defense College of the Philippines, where he previously served as Vice President for Administrative Affairs and Assistant Vice-President for Research and Special Studies.

is believed to be Janjalani's co-founder of the ASG, was said to be the deep cover agent for the Defense Intelligence Group (DIG).[3] Some sources even said that the National Intelligence Coordinating Agency (NICA) facilitated the establishment of the ASG[4] with the prodding of the Central Intelligence Agency (CIA).[5] A Moro National Liberation Front (MNLF) leader in Basilan even confessed that the ASG enjoyed the support of the military assigned to the area.[6] The International Peace Mission that went to Basilan on 23–27 March 2002 found that there were "consistent credible reports that the military and the provincial government are coddling the Abu Sayyaf".[7] But the AFP, the Department of National Defence (DND), and NICA have denied all these allegations. ASG leaders too have denied that the Group was a creation of the military. On 18 November 1994 Abu Abdu Said, then known as the ASG Secretary-General, issued an important document entitled "A Voice of Truth" to describe the origin of the ASG. In this document, the ASG strongly denied that it was created by the military. It argued that the ASG was a radical movement aimed at pursuing the establishment of an Islamic State in Southern Philippines.

According to intelligence records, the ASG can be traced to disgruntled members of the MNLF who joined the International Islamic Brigade that fought the Soviet forces in Afghanistan from 1980 to 1988.[8] After the Afghan war Janjalani and his followers formed a still unnamed group in 1988 to advance the idea of an Iranian-inspired Islamic State in Southern Philippines. In 1989 Janjalani called this group the Mujahideen Commando Freedom Fighters (MCFF), which became the forerunner of the ASG. With the formation of the MCFF, Janjalani officially broke away from the MNLF in 1991. The MCFF was known in Mindanao as "Janjalani's group". Because the *nom de guerre* of Janjalani during the Afghan war was "Abu Sayyaf", in honour of Afghan resistance leader Professor Abdul Rasul Sayyaf, the MCFF eventually became known as Abu Sayyaf's group. Some scholars and journalists mis-translated ASG to mean "bearer of the sword".[9] But ASG really means in Arabic, "Father of the Swordsman".[10]

It was in August 1991 that Janjalani first publicly used the name ASG in connection with the bombing of *M/V Doulos*, a Christian missionary ship docked at the Zamboanga port in Southern Philippines.[11] The bombing of *M/V Doulos* was a watershed event in the history of the ASG as it received international media attention for the death of two foreign missionaries and the wounding of 40 others. The ASG gained further international notoriety on 20 May 1992 when it assassinated Fr. Carzedda, a foreign Catholic missionary in Mindanao. Janjalani wrote an open letter claiming responsibility for the killing of the priest and warned of more violence to pursue its radical Islamist goals.

The ASG officially established its headquarters in Isabela, Basilan in 1992 and called it Camp Al-Madinah Mujahideen. The Philippine Marines captured this camp in May 1993, prompting the ASG to transfer its base to Patikul, Sulu. There, Janjalani closely cooperated with Ghalib Andang (aka Commander Robot), who headed the Sulu-based unit of the ASG. With the assistance of Commander Robot, the ASG embarked on vigorous manpower build-up, arms acquisition, and a series of fund-raising activities that involved primarily kidnapping for ransom.

To attract foreign funding, Janjalani renamed the ASG as Al-Harakatul Al-Islamiya (AHAI), or Islamic Movement, in 1994. The ASG reportedly received financial and logistical support from like-minded organizations in Iran (Hezbollah), Pakistan (Jamaat-I-Islami and Hizbul-Mujahideen), Afghanistan (Hizb-Islami), Egypt (Al Gamaa-Al-Islamiya), Libya (International Harakatu'l Al-Islamia), and Algeria (Islamic Liberation Front). But the largest assistance allegedly came from the International Islamic Relief Organization (IIRO) operated by Mohammed Jamal Khalifa, Osama bin Laden's brother-in-law.

The ASG reportedly established links with Al Qaeda through Khalifa. But it was Ramzi Yousef who was said to have deepened the ASG's ties with Al Qaeda. The ASG's relationship with Al Qaeda was also facilitated by the personal friendship between Janjalani and bin Laden. Both stayed in Peshawar, Pakistan in the 1980s. Though Jason Burke argues that bin Laden did not directly provide funding support for Janjalani during the mid-80s,[12] what is clear is that the ASG played a supporting role in Yousef's Bojinka Plot, which was foiled in 1995.[13]

From 1991 to 2000, the ASG reportedly engaged in 378 terrorist activities, which resulted in the death of 288 civilians.[14] During the same period, the ASG ventured into 640 kidnapping activities involving a total of 2,076 victims. Because of its kidnappings the Philippine government preferred to describe the ASG as a mere bandit group. There was even a view that "the ASG is a mere homegrown criminal gang that employs terror tactics as its modus operandi".[15] But the United States has listed the ASG as a Foreign Terrorist Organization.

Dr Samuel K. Tan of the University of the Philippines' Department of History provided a more scholarly discussion of the ASG's origin. He said that the ASG started as a movement called Juma'a Abu Sayyaf.[16] Dr Tan documented Janjalani's own account of the origin of ASG and wrote that Janjalani formed the ASG in 1991 as an alternative group of Filipino Muslim radicals who were disappointed with the secular leaderships of the MNLF and the moderate Islamist position of the MILF. In fact, most of the original founders of the ASG were disgruntled members of the MNLF and the MILF. In his undated public proclamation, presumably written between 1993 and 1994, Janjalani aptly stressed what he called the "Four Basic Truths" about the ASG, to wit:

1. It is not to create another faction in the Muslim struggle, which would be against the teaching of Islam, especially the Quran, but to serve as a bridge and balance between the MILF and MNLF, whose revolutionary roles and leadership cannot be ignored or usurped;
2. Its ultimate goal is the establishment of a purely Islamic government whose "nature, meaning, emblem and objective" are basic to peace;
3. Its advocacy of war is a necessity for as long as there exist oppression, injustice, capricious ambitions, and arbitrary claims imposed on the Muslims;
4. It believes that "war disturbs peace only for the attainment of the true and real objective of humanity — the establishment of justice and righteousness for all under the law of the noble Quran and the purified Sunnah".[17]

Zachary Abuza also provides his own historical account of the ASG. He divides the evolution of the ASG into the following periods: Founding Years (1988–91), Anti-Christian/Islamic State Terrorism including Deepening Ties with Al Qaeda (1991–95), Degeneration (1995–2001), Post-9/11 Global War on Terror (2001–2003), and Regeneration (2003 to the present).[18] Though this periodization reveals Abuza's deep understanding of the ASG's history based on intelligence sources he consulted, his citation of police intelligence documents claiming that Ramzi Yousef encouraged the formation of the ASG did not stand unchallenged. There is a view that Janjalani formed the ASG not because of Yousef's prodding but as a result of the trend in political fundamentalist movements in the Philippines that began in the late 1980s.[19] MILF founder Hashim Salamat commented that the emergence of the ASG "is caused by the oppression and the continuous usurpation of the powers within our homeland".[20] Salamat also argued that "as long as the region and the Bangsamoro people are still under the control of the Philippine government, and oppression continues, we should expect more Abu Sayyaf style of groups to come to existence".

Ideological Inclination

The ASG's original ideology was anchored on Janjalani's religious and political thoughts. ASG followers recognized Janjalani not only as their leader but also as their ideological beacon.[21] As an ideologue, Janjalani was well-informed of the historical, religious, economic, political, and social conditions in which Muslims in the Philippines found themselves.

At the early stage of world Islamic resurgence in the late 1970s and early 1980s,[22] Janjalani travelled to different Muslim countries where he received training and education in radical Islamic thought. He received a very good Islamic education in Saudi Arabia in 1981 and went to Ummu I-Qura in Mecca where he studied Islamic jurisprudence for almost three years. There, Janjalani was deeply attracted to the concept of "jihad". Armed with radical Islamic ideology, Janjalani returned to his homeland in Basilan in 1984 to preach initially in various mosques before formally organizing the ASG. In 1988 Janjalani went to Peshawar, Pakistan, where he conscientiously studied the Islamic revolution in Iran. It was also in Peshawar that he reportedly met and befriended Osama bin Laden, who helped him organize the ASG.

When Janjalani formed the ASG, his original intention was to create a group of Muslim Mujahideen committed to *Jihad Fi-Sabil-lillah,* a "struggle in the cause of Allah" or "fighting and dying for the cause of Islam". Before Janjalani died in December 1998, he delivered eight radical ideological discourses called *Khutbahs*, which may be considered as primary sources of Janjalani's radical Islamic thought. These discourses explained Janjalani's Quranic perspective of *Jihad Fi-Sabil-lillah,* which he lamented was misinterpreted by many Muslims. He even denounced the *ulama* (Muslim scholars) for their poor knowledge of the Quran and lamented that most Muslims in the Philippines calling themselves Moros were not really practising the true meaning of Islam compared with their counterparts in West Asia. These eight discourses also revealed Janjalani's deep grasp of Wahabi Islam. Indeed, the Islamic theology of Wahabism greatly informed Janjalani's radical ideology.

In his analysis of Philippine society, it is clear that Janjalani was aware of the injustices committed against Muslim communities. Thus he purportedly founded the ASG to vigorously seek *kaadilan* or justice for Muslims through jihad. For Janjalani, jihad was the highest form of struggle for justice or for a cause. He classified jihad into two forms: *jihad al-akbar* (greater jihad) and *jihad al-asgar* (lesser jihad), but did not elaborate. He only argued that they "are the same in Divine assessment but are merely differentiated in human terms and conditions".[23] He contended that the "surest guarantee of justice and prosperity for Muslims" is the establishment of a purely Islamic state that can only be achieved through jihad. Janjalani even urged Muslims in the Philippines to pursue their jihad to the highest level in order to fulfil their paramount duty of martyrdom for the cause of Allah. His appeal for martyrdom also means endorsement of suicide terrorism. Though there had been no recorded incident of suicide terrorism in the country at the time, Janjalani was aware of the value of suicide terrorism as a favoured tactic of radical Muslims pursuing jihad. Some years later, the bombing of Superferry 14 on 28 February 2004 was originally planned by the ASG as a suicide mission.[24]

One of Janjalani's *Khutbahs* revealed his deep resentment against Christian missionaries in Mindanao, particularly those maligning Islam. Janjalani said that the aggressive preaching of Christian missionaries in Mindanao gravely insulted Islam and provoked Muslims to respond violently. The bombing of *M/V Doulos* in August 1991 was the ASG's retaliation against Christian missionaries who used derogatory words against Islam and called Allah a false God.

Organizational Structure and Leadership Dynamics

Janjalani's original plan when he established the ASG was to form a highly organized, systematic, and disciplined organization of fanatical secessionist Islamic fighters in Southern Philippines.[25] Towards that end, he conceptualized the formation of the Islamic Executive Council (IEC) to serve as the main planning and execution body of the ASG. He chaired the IEC with 15 other Amirs supporting him. The IEC was intended to have two special committees: (a) the Jamiatul Al-Islamia Revolutionary Tabligh Group to pursue fund-raising and Islamic education; and (b) the Al-Misuaratt Khutbah Committee to pursue agitation and propaganda activities.[26]

Janjalani also planned for the ASG to have a military arm called Mujahidden Al-Sharifullah with three main units to carry out the terrorist activities of the group: (a) the Demolition Team, (b) the Mobile Force Team, and (c) the Campaign Propaganda Team.[27] But Janjalani's organizational plan for the ASG did not fully materialize because of his untimely death in December 1998. His demise led to the disarray of the ASG and resulted in the creation of two major factions in Basilan and Sulu. Janjalani's younger brother, Khadaffy Janjalani, headed the Basilan faction while Galib Andang (aka Commander Robot) headed the Sulu faction. Though intelligence sources identified another faction in Zamboanga City headed by Hadji Radzpal, other intelligence sources also said that Radzpal actually belonged to the Sulu faction. In July 1999 these two major factions agreed to appoint Khadaffy as their new Amir.

Khadaffy, however, did not have the leadership quality of his elder brother to assert full control of the two factions. The Basilan group itself was factionalized, with ten armed groups in 2002 acting independently of each other. The Sulu faction, on the other hand, had 16 armed groups. All these groups carried the name of ASG. In Basilan, Khadaffy was not even in control of his own faction because he was overpowered by his deputy, Aldam Tilao (aka Abu Sabaya), who was then acting as the ASG spokesperson. There were also small bandit groups in Basilan and Sulu that wanted to be associated with the ASG for prestige. Thus the ASG became a very heterogeneous organization of factions and individuals with varying interests from radical Islamism to mere banditry.

Being heavily factionalized, the ASG quickly degenerated. The ASG went on a series of high-profile kidnapping sprees, prompting the Philippine government to label the group a "criminal gang". While there is no doubt that some ASG members continued to uphold the radical Islamist agenda, there are members, particularly in Sulu, who are just interested in KRAs. In 2000-2001 alone, the ASG was involved in 140 KRA incidents that resulted in the death of 16 victims.[28] Some members see KRAs as a means of raising funds to finance their weapons purchase and ASG recruitment activities.

After 9/11, the ASG was very much on the run as a result of intensified military and police operations of the Philippine government. The conduct of the joint Philippine-American military exercise in 2002, dubbed "Balikatan 02-1", led to the neutralization of many ASG members, which included the death of Abu Sabaya in June 2002. The death of Abu Sabaya provided Khadaffy Janjalani the opportunity to take full control of the ASG, but only initially in the Basilan area. The Sulu faction continued under the control of Galib Andang. The capture of Galib Andang in December 2003 and his subsequent death in a bloody jail break attempt in March 2005 finally allowed Khadaffy to consolidate his leadership of the ASG and "bring the organization back to its roots".[29]

ASG Strength and Capabilities

The ASG started with no more than 1,000 members in 1991 and the number rose to almost 1,300 in 1998. According to the Philippines' Anti-Terrorism Task Force (ATTF), ASG strength as of the last quarter of 2005 was no more than 350 members, very close to the figure of 380 during the second quarter of 2005 but well above its August 2005 figure of 250. An undersecretary of the DND estimated the current strength of the ASG to be around 500, close to the military intelligence figure of 409. Abuza has said that the current size of the ASG is around 250 to 300 "hard-core militants". In fact, there is no certainty about its current strength because some ASG members are also members of the MILF and the Misuari Breakaway Group (MBG) of the MNLF. Other ASG members are even associated with the Rajah Sulaiman Movement (RSM), a group of Muslim converts in the Philippines believed to be funded by the ASG.[30]

While its exact strength is unclear, what is certain is that the ASG remains a very small but very lethal armed group of Muslims in the Philippines. Despite its small number, it draws its strength from a huge local support base. Most ASG members are relatives, friends, classmates, and neighbours of local folks. ASG members even buy their foodstuffs from local stores and get "early warning signals" from local communities during military offensives. The Philippine military has said that religious and political propaganda, financial compensation, and even coercion are the ASG's primary means of gaining local support in the form of manpower, intelligence, and sometimes logistics.[31]

Local support enhances the capability of the ASG. The AFP has reported that the ASG has the capability to stage "high impact terrorist attacks against civilian targets not only in Basilan and Sulu but also in other parts of the country".[32] When ASG members fight, they "can pin-down up to a company size unit" and during military engagements, they are capable of "reinforcing beleaguered members in a short period of time", particularly in areas "near a Muslim village of an MNLF and MILF camp".[33] There are even some "enterprising Muslims who join the fight purposely to acquire firearms and ammunitions left by government casualties".[34]

As of the last quarter of 2005, Philippine military intelligence estimated that around 480 weapons were in the ASG's possession. In previous encounters with the ASG, the military had seized night-vision devices, thermal imagers, sniper scopes, various types of commercial radios, satellite and cellular phones, and high-speed sea craft. Military intelligence assessments also indicate that some ASG members have enhanced their bomb-making capabilities as a result of joint training with JI members operating or hiding in the Philippines. Before his death in October 2003, Roman Al-Ghozi, known to be "the bomb maker" of the JI, admitted during interrogation that he shared his bomb-making expertise with ASG members. Rohmat Abdurrohim (aka Zaki), known as "the bomb trainer" of the ASG, confessed that he trained ASG members in bomb-making, including the use of mobile phones as detonating devices and the use of toothpaste tubes as among the bomb paraphernalia. Dulmatin and Umar Patek, wanted for the 2002 Bali bombing, reportedly trained some ASG members in bomb attacks. As stated earlier, Dulmatin and Umar Patek also prepared ASG members for future suicide missions. National Security Adviser Norberto Gonzales was quoted as saying, "What we are looking for now is suicide terrorists, not (only) suicide bombers."[35]

The ASG has also developed the capability to use car bombs. Khadaffy Janjalani has boasted that he allowed training in 2004 of a long line of bombers who could hit targets in major cities in the Philippines. The ASG reportedly formed an Urban Squad in 2005 to stage bombing operations in the cities. It has also developed the ability to wage maritime terrorist attacks. Almost all ASG members have deep familiarity with the maritime domain, having belonged to families of fisher folks with a long seafaring tradition.[36] The Superferry 14 bombing in February 2004 was a clear demonstration of the ASG's maritime terrorist capability. The group also conducted some maritime training activities in Sulu and Tawi-Tawi in June 2005. In July 2005, ASG and JI fighters received underwater training in Sandakan, Malaysia to attack maritime targets such as ports and commercial vessels.[37] In August 2005, military intelligence disclosed that ASG leaders and some foreign terrorists met in Patikul, Sulu, to plan an attack on some beaches in Palawan. This prompted the Philippine government to intensify the security of major ports and beaches in the country to prevent any planned maritime terrorist attacks.

Because of the small size of the ASG, the Office of the President has belittled its capability by describing the group as a spent force. This is strongly resented by the ASG leadership. In an official statement, ASG spokesperson Jainal Sali (aka Abu Sulaiman) argued that government officials are "belittling us, but they are exaggerating the problem of terrorism in the country".[38] In a telephone interview pertaining to the Superferry 14 bombing, Abu Sulaiman also taunted the Philippine government by saying, "Still doubtful about our capabilities? Good. Just wait and see. We will bring the war that you impose on us to your lands and seas, homes and streets. We will multiply the pain and suffering that you have inflicted on our people."[39]

Though the membership of the ASG continues to be small at present, it is embarking upon vigorous recruitment drives to recover from the loss of its members who were killed, neutralized, and arrested after 9/11. It has various techniques to recruit members. Apart from religious propaganda and agitation, the ASG motivates recruits through financial rewards. It also pays local recruits to serve as second and third security layers at their makeshift camps. Some members start their recruitment process by initially befriending potential recruits through ball games or pot (marijuana) sessions. The ASG also utilizes deception to recruit members. ASG leaders allow young Muslims to bring their firearms and take pictures of them and then use the pictures to blackmail them into joining the group.[40] The ASG also uses marriages to expand its membership. At present, the ASG is paying attention to younger and more idealistic MILF members who regard the ongoing peace process with the Philippine government as a sham. ASG leaders think that if the MILF makes peace with the government, they will inherit some of the MILF firebrands in Southern Philippines. MILF leader Al-Haj Murad Ebrahim warned that a great deal is needed quickly "before younger Muslims in the region succumb to the greater radicalism of the Abu Sayyaf".[41]

Reviving Radical Islamism, Returning to Terrorism

From mere banditry, Khadaffy Janjalani has been reinvigorating the ASG to be a "genuine" Islamic Movement that resorts to terrorism as a political weapon. Abuza is correct when he says that since the capture and subsequent death of Galib Andang in 2004, the ASG has not conducted KRAs. Instead, the ASG has waged a series of high-profile terrorist attacks, the most lethal of which, so far, was the blasting of Superferry 14. The explosion on Superferry 14, which carried more than 899 passengers, resulted in the death of 116 persons and injury to 300 others.

On the eve of Valentine's Day in 2005, the ASG masterminded three simultaneous bombings in Makati City, Davao City, and General Santos City. The bombings resulted in the death of at least ten persons and the wounding of 136 others. Abu Sulaiman said that the three bombings were ASG's Valentine gift to President Gloria Macapagal Arroyo and warned that "we will not stop until we get justice for the countless Muslim lives and properties that you people have destroyed". Shortly after the 2005 Valentine's Day terrorist attacks, detained ASG members at Camp Bagong Diwa in Taguig City conducted a jail-break attempt in March 2005, which was foiled. The attempt resulted in the death of five ASG members, including Galib Andang. In August 2005 the ASG waged another terror attack when it bombed the Dona Ramona ferry in Lamitan, Basilan. At least 30 people, including several children, were injured. Two weeks before the bombing, the ASG staged small bombing attacks in Zamboanga City, Koronadal City, and Cotabato City in Mindanao.

All these bombing incidents in 2005 were hallmarks of terrorism rather than mere banditry. They show that the ASG has already transformed itself from a bandit group to a genuine terrorist organization. There are indications that Khadaffy Janjalani is reactivating the Islamic Executive Council (IEC) of the ASG to advance the original Islamist agenda of Al-Harakatul Al-Islamiya,[42] centred on establishing an Islamic State in Mindanao.

The Philippine Government's Counter-Terrorism Response

On 12 October 2001 the Philippine government announced its 14-point approach to combat terrorism. It also formulated in November 2001 the National Plan to

Address Terrorism and Its Consequences. To coordinate all efforts of the national and local government in the fight against terrorism, the government formed the Anti-Terrorism Task Force (ATTF) on 24 March 2004. This was followed by the adoption of a 16-point counter-terrorism programme to operationalize its 14-point anti-terrorism policy.

The ATTF serves as the government's anti-terrorism super body that aims to establish an extensive anti-terrorism information system and accelerate intelligence exchange among all the intelligence units in the Philippines to identify terrorism personalities, cells, groups, and organizations in various local government units.[43] The ATTF is strongly pushing for the passage of an Anti-Terrorism Law.[44] In November 2005 the House of Representatives started plenary discussions on the anti-terrorism bill and approved it on 14 December 2005. According to Speaker De Venecia, "approval of the anti-terrorism bill reflects our resolve to fight head-on the threats of terrorism".

But with the current political crisis facing the Arroyo administration and the call by some sectors for constitutional amendments, it is unlikely that an anti-terrorism law would be passed soon. The Philippine Senate does not even regard such a bill as urgent. Moreover, opposition leaders and cause-oriented groups have expressed apprehensions that such a law might be used as a pretext to curtail human rights and civil liberties.

The absence of an anti-terrorism law, however, weakens the Philippine government's hand in its fight against terrorism. There have been several instances of suspected terrorists being arrested but only to be released on bail because of the absence of a law permitting continued detention. The Department of Justice (DOJ) reported in 2005 that it had filed 156 cases against suspected terrorists and named 867 for committing criminal acts related to terrorism. Ten have been sentenced to death. In November 2005, an Indonesian national (Zaki) believed to be a JI member, and two ASG members (Abu Khalil Trinidad and Gammal Baharan) were sentenced to death for multiple murder and multiple attempted murder in connection with the Superferry 14 bombing. But the DOJ admitted difficulties in prosecution because of the absence of an anti-terrorism law.

To add teeth to its anti-terrorist efforts, the government had passed the Anti-Money Laundering Act in 2001.[45] In December 2005 the US Treasury Department was reported to have frozen the assets of three ASG leaders: Radullan Sahiron, Isnilon Totoni Hapilon, and Jainal Antel Sali. The Philippine government has also been intensifying military operations against the ASG. Combined military and the police raids led to the seizure of ten sacks of explosive devices in March 2005 in Quezon City. These explosives were intended to be used during the 2005

Lenten season to bomb soft targets in Metro Manila. The military and police establishments were also able to arrest, neutralize, or kill several ASG members during encounters. The efforts of the two services significantly reduced the strength of the ASG from its peak of 1,269 fighters in 2000 to approximately 250 fighters in 2005, though as stated earlier, the current strength of ASG remains disputed. As 2005 closed, the ASG was conducting a vigorous recruitment drive in Mindanao to recover from the losses it had suffered.

On 11 November 2005, the AFP began its offensive operations against the ASG in Sulu. Using Italian made S-211 jets and two US-made OV-10B ground assault planes, the military dropped bombs on suspected ASG lairs in Indanan and Maimbong towns of Sulu. The Philippine Marines and Scout Rangers were also deployed to hunt down ASG fighters in these towns. By 20 December, 25 ASG members had been killed. But according to some in the Muslim communities, the military had targeted MNLF rather than ASG camps in Sulu. The clashes also resulted in the death of six soldiers, while 33 were wounded. Hundreds of local residents caught in the crossfire were displaced. Though the AFP utilizes military action to fight terrorism, it recognizes that a military approach alone cannot defeat the ASG.[46]

Conclusion

Despite its nebulous beginning and small number, the ASG continues to be the most lethal armed Muslim group in the Philippines. From mere banditry, the ASG has rapidly mutated into a post-modern terrorist group that can operate militarily, politically, and ideologically.[47] It is reorganizing itself to pursue its radical Islamist agenda. It has enhanced its capability to wage traditional bombing activities, and developed new capabilities to conduct maritime terrorist attacks and suicide terrorist missions. Only time will tell when the ASG will use these new capabilities.

Because of the virulence of the threat posed by the ASG, the AFP is intensifying its military operations against the group while being fully aware that the problem of terrorism cannot be solved by military means alone. There is no doubt that the problem of terrorism needs to be tackled through a comprehensive long-term approach that takes cognizance of the social, religious, ideological, political, and economic contexts in which ASG members operate. Unless the government recognizes the contexts that give rise to terrorism, the threat will continue to menace not only Philippine national security but also regional security.

Notes

This article does not represent the official position of the Department of National Defense, the National Defense College of the Philippines, or any agency of the Philippine government.

1. For earlier attempts, see Rohan Gunaratna, "The Evolution and Tactics of the Abu Sayyaf Group", *Janes Intelligence Review*, July 2001; Glenda Gloria, "Bearer of the Sword: The Abu Sayyaf Has Nebulous Beginnings and Incoherent Aims", *Mindanao Updates*, 6 June 2000; and Mark Turner, "Terrorism and Secession in the Southern Philippines: The Rise of the Abu Sayyaf", *Contemporary Southeast Asia* 17, no. 1 (June 1995): pp. 1–19.
2. Eusaquito P. Manalo, "Philippine Response to Terrorism: The Abu Sayyaf Group" (MA thesis, Naval Post Graduate School, Monterey, California, December 2004), p. 3; Mark Turner, "The Management of Violence in a Conflict Organization: The Case of the Abu Sayyaf", *Public Organization Review* 3, no. 4 (December 2003): 394.
3. Dorian Zumel Sicat, "Transcript of Interview with Elmina Abdul, Widow to Edwin Angeles Taken at Basilan Community Hospital General Ward Isabela City, Province of Basilan Republic of the Philippines", 10 March 2002, http://www.okcbombing.org/News%20Articles/deathbed_confession.htm (accessed 14 November 2005).
4. Mirian Coronel Ferrer, ed., *Peace Matters: A Philippine Peace Compendium* (Quezon City: University of the Philippines Center for Integrative and Development Studies, 1997), p. 218.
5. Jose Maria Sison, *US Terrorism and War in the Philippines* (Manila: Aklat ng Bayan, 2003), p. 37.
6. Marites D. Vitug and Glenda M. Gloria, *Under the Crescent Moon: Rebellion in Mindanao* (Quezon City: Ateneo Center for Social Policy and Public Affairs, Institute for Popular Democracy and Philippine Center for Investigative Journalism, 2000), p. 217.
7. For a complete copy of the report, see "Basilan: The Next Afghanistan?" (report of the International Peace Mission to Basilan, Philippines, 23–27 March 2002), http://www.bwf.org/pamayanan/peacemission.html (accessed 30 August 2004).
8. Department of National Defense, "Info Kit on the Abu Sayyaf Group" (presentation before the hearing of the Senate Committee on National Defense and Security at the Philippine Senate, Pasay City, 30 August 2001).
9. See, for example, Graham H. Turbiville, Jr., "Bearer of the Sword", *Military Review*, March/April 2002, pp. 38–47.
10. Jose Torres, Jr., *Into the Mountain: Hostages by the Abu Sayyaf* (Quezon City: Claretian Publications, 2001), p. 35.
11. "Special Report on the Abou Sayaff" (briefing of MIG9 during the Southern Command Conference, 19 January 1994).

12. Jason Burke, *Al-Qaeda: Casting a Shadow of Terror* (London: I.B. Tarus, 2003), p. 101.
13. For a detailed account of the Bojinka Plot, see Rommel C. Banlaoi, *War on Terrorism in Southeast Asia* (Quezon City: Rex Book Store International, 2004); Maria Ressa, *Seeds of Terror: An Eyewitness Account of Al-Qaeda's Newest Center of Operations in Southeast Asia* (New York: Free Press, 2003); Zachary Abuza, *Militant Islam in Southeast Asia: The Crucible of Terror* (London: Lynne Rienner Publishers, 2003).
14. Office of the Deputy Chief of Staff for Operations, *Knowing the Terrorists: The Abu Sayyaf Study* (Quezon City: General Headquarters of the Armed Forces of the Philippines, 2002), p. 1.
15. Carlyle Thayer, "Political Terrorism in Southeast Asia", *Pointer: Quarterly Journal of the Singapore Armed Forces* 29, no. 4 (October–December 2003): 58.
16. Samuel K. Tan, "Beyond Freedom: The Juma'a Abu Sayyaf (Assessment of Its Origins, Objectives, Ideology and Method of Struggle)", in *Internationalization of the Bangsamoro Struggle* (Quezon City: University of the Philippines Center for Integrative and Development Studies, 2003), revised edition, p. 94.
17. Ibid., p. 96.
18. Zachary Abuza, *Balik-Terrorism: The Return of the Abu Sayyaf* (Carlisle, PA: Strategic Studies Institute, US Army War College, 2005), pp. 2–11.
19. Julkipli M. Wadi, "Philippine Political Islam and the Emerging Fundamentalist Strand", in *Cooperation and Conflict in Global Security*, edited by Carmencita C. Aguilar (Quezon City: International Federation of Social Sciences Organization, 1996), p. 210.
20. Salamat Hashim, *The Bangsamoro People's Struggle Against Oppression and Colonialism* (Camp Abubakre: Agency for Youth Affairs — MILF, 2001), p. 36.
21. Nathan G. Quimpo, "Dealing with the MILF and Abu Sayyaf: Who's Afraid of an Islamic State?" *Public Policy* III, no. 4 (October–December 1999): 50.
22. For a detailed discussion on the rise of Muslim radicalism in the Philippines, see Rommel C. Banlaoi, "Radical Muslim Terrorism in the Philippines", in *Handbook on Terrorism and Insurgency in Southeast Asia*, edited by Andrew Tan (London: Edward Elgar Publishing, 2006).
23. Tan, *Internationalization of the Bangsamoro Struggle*, p. 98.
24. Because of continuing radicalization of Muslim communities in the Philippines, the ASG may employ suicide terrorism in the near future. Dulmatin and Umar Patek, key suspects in the 2002 Bali bombings that killed more than 200 people, have reportedly established their base in the Philippines to prepare ASG members for future suicide missions. In his speech to the Foreign Correspondents Association of the Philippines in Manila on 11 August 2005, National Security Adviser Norberto Gonzales warned that up to ten Indonesian militants, including Dulmatin and Umar Patek, were on the loose in the Philippines and plotting suicide attacks. See Joel Francis Guinto, "10 Indonesian suicide bombers hunted in RP", *Philippine Daily Inquirer Breaking*

News, 11 August 2005, http://news.inq7.net/breaking/index.php?index=2&story_id=46552 (accessed 26 December 2005).

25. This particular section is largely based on Rommel C. Banlaoi, "Leadership Dynamics in Terrorist Organizations in Southeast Asia: The Abu Sayyaf Case" (paper presented at the international symposium "The Dynamics and Structures of Terrorist Threats in Southeast Asia" organized by the Institute of Defense Analyses in cooperation with the Southeast Asia Regional Center for Counter-Terrorism and the US Pacific Command held at Palace of Golden Horses Hotel, Kuala Lumpur, Malaysia, on 18–20 April 2005). Also in *Proceedings of the International Symposium on the Dynamics and Structures of Terrorist Threats in Southeast Asia*, edited by John T. Hanley, Kongdan Oh Hassig, and Caroline F. Ziemke (Alexandria, VA: Institute for Defense Analyses, 2005).

26. To know more about the strategy of the ASG, see Office of the Assistant to the Chief of Staff for Intelligence, *Field Handout: Doctrinal Extract for the Abu Sayyaf Group* (Headquarters of the Philippine Marine Corps, 21 January 2002).

27. For detailed discussions, see Banlaoi, "Leadership Dynamics in Terrorist Organizations in Southeast Asia: The Abu Sayyaf Case", p. 4.

28. Abuza, *Balik Terrorism: The Return of the Abu Sayyaf*, p. 8.

29. Ibid., p. viii.

30. For a detailed analysis of the RSM, see Rommel C. Banlaoi, *Urban Terrorism in the Philippines: The Rajah Solaiman Movement* (forthcoming, 2006).

31. Office of the Deputy Chief of Staff for Operations, *Knowing the Terrorists: The Abu Sayyaf Study*, p. 13.

32. Ibid., p. 14.

33. Ibid., p. 15.

34. Ibid.

35. Michael Punongbayan, "DOJ to Expose Terrorists' Financiers, Media Handlers", *Philippine Star*, 7 November 2005.

36. For more discussions on the maritime terrorist capability of the ASG, see Rommel C. Banlaoi, "Maritime Terrorism in Southeast Asia: The Abu Sayyaf Threat", *Naval War College Review* 58, no. 4 (Autumn 2005): 63–80. Also see Rommel C. Banlaoi, "The Abu Sayyaf Group: Threat of Maritime Piracy and Terrorism", in *Violence at Sea: Piracy at the Age of Terrorism*, edited by Peter Lehr (London: Routledge, forthcoming 2006).

37. National Security Council Briefing, 7 September 2005. Also see Rommel C. Banlaoi, "Is the Philippines the Next Target? The Second Bali Bombing Brings Terror Closer to Home", *Newsbreak*, 7 November 2005, p. 33.

38. Cited in Abuza, *Balik-Terrorism: The Return of the Abu Sayyaf*, p. 11.

39. Marco Garrido, "After Madrid, Manila?" *Asia Times*, 24 April 2004, http://www.atimes.com/atimes/Southeast_Asia/FD24Ae01.html (accessed 28 August 2004).

40. Office of the Deputy Chief of Staff for Operations, *Knowing the Terrorists: The Abu Sayyaf Study*, p. 41.

41. Simon Elegant, "The Return of the Abu Sayyaf", *Time Asia*, 30 August 2004.
42. Angel M. Rabasa, "Southeast Asia: Moderate Tradition and Radical Challenge", in *The Muslim World After 9/11*, by Angel Rabasa et al. (Santa Monica, CA: RAND, 2004), p. 402.
43. For a detailed analysis of local government response, see Rommel C. Banlaoi, "Local Government Response Against Terrorist Threats in the Philippines: Issues and Prospects", in *Security Managesment in Asian Cities*, edited by C. Durkop (Singapore: Konrad Adenauer Foundation, 2005), pp. 29–54.
44. For an early interest on the subject, see Lauro Patiag, "Towards a National Legal Counter Measure to Combat Terrorism in the Philippines" (MA thesis, National Defense College of the Philippines, 2002).
45. Noel B. Mianos, *An Assessment of Government Efforts at Dismantling Terrorist Financing* (MA thesis, National Defense College of the Philippines, 2004).
46. ASG Combat Research and Study Group, "After Action Report" (submitted to the Commanding General of the Philippine Army on 19 September 2001 by the Training and Doctrine Command of the Philippine Army).
47. The case of ASG is not an isolated one. Terrorist groups elsewhere are also undergoing profound changes. See Rohan Gunaratna, ed., *The Changing Face of Terrorism* (Singapore: Eastern University Press, 2004).

Singapore

Singapore

SINGAPORE
Globalizing on Its Own Terms

Terence Chong

Lee Hsien Loong's succession of Goh Chok Tong as Prime Minister (PM) in August 2004 was long anticipated. It was thus unsurprising that political analysts spent 2005 dissecting the new PM's every public utterance for clues as to the character of his new administration. These analysts have endeavoured to describe and define the new Lee administration perhaps not just to distinguish it from the long shadow of Minister Mentor Lee Kuan Yew and the highly popular Senior Minister Goh, but also to decipher the People's Action Party (PAP) government's visions for Singapore at the dawn of the 21st century. In a one-party state with only three prime ministers since independence, it is tempting to see each transition as epochal even if the PAP government takes pains to spread the message of ideological continuity and political stability. It was thus inevitable that Lee's widely publicized inaugural "open and inclusive society" slogan would be contrasted with Goh's own "kinder, gentler society" tagline as though a national paradigm shift had quietly occurred between administrations. Given the growing demands of an increasingly cosmopolitan citizenry, Lee's slogan was interpreted by some to be a hint at further political liberalization, even prompting the *Straits Times* to herald in a "brave new Singapore"; one that was moving away from a "one-size-fits-all paradigm" in terms of government policies.[1]

Initial expectations of greater political liberalization have, however, at the close of 2005, been replaced by a more sober appreciation of the fact that the proposed "open and inclusive society" was never intended to signal democratic openness but, rather, societal acceptance of different personal and social achievements. By celebrating individuals who have wandered off the beaten track and achieved success in non-academic fields and non-mainstream careers, the message of the new Lee administration was that society no longer

---

TERENCE CHONG is Fellow at the Institute of Southeast Asian Studies.

recognized just one peak of excellence but an entire mountain range, even as the traditional out-of-bounds markers continue to remain firmly installed. This of course begs the questions: Just how is an "open and inclusive society" different from a "kinder, gentler society"? Is it not the nature of a kinder, gentler society to be inclusive and embrace difference? Who decides on the acceptable level of openness and inclusiveness? What are we open to, and who do we include?

Selective Globalization

These open questions point to Singapore's policymaking challenges. If Singapore's policymaking style had to be summed up in a phrase, it would be the practice of selective globalization; that is, the conscious effort to encourage certain forms of globalization and to discourage others. For example, the government, on the one hand, encourages economic globalization through the synchronization of local financial regulations and polices with international standards while, on the other, energetically protects an Asian "conservative" society from the ills of satellite dishes, pornographic magazines, and other unwholesome global commodities.

This constant oscillation between being globally open and locally particular has given rise to the Singapore paradox. The city-state enjoys its status as one of the most globalized countries in the world in terms of migration, global finance, and telecommunications, and yet regularly garners criticism from international human rights institutions for its insistence on practising its own brand of politics, whereby certain civil liberties are curtailed in view of local multiethnic and multireligious realities. The practice of selective globalization expresses the need to remain globally connected for the sake of nothing less than national survival, and the desire to retain certain notions of tradition and conservatism that protect specific dominant interests.

2005 has been a lesson in selective globalization. It has been a year in which the city-state duly served as a site for global events such as the Shangri-la Dialogues (3 to 5 June); Asia-Middle East Dialogues (20 to 22 June); and the International Olympic Committee meeting (6 July). The economic pact — Comprehensive Economic Cooperation Agreement (Ceca) — signed between Singapore and India in June set the stage for the city-state's accelerated involvement in the second fastest-growing economy in the world. Conversely, it has also been a year that saw a police investigation into a political film; the government's withholding of an entertainment licence for a gay party; and finally, PM Lee's announcement that a Western model of democracy was not for Singapore. As the events of 2005 unfolded, and as the government's responses to them crystallized, it became clear that Lee's new administration seeks to globalize selectively and at its own pace.

A Socially Conscious Budget

The 2005 Budget, unveiled on 18 February, was the Prime Minister's first real opportunity to materialize his visions for Singapore. It was not a dramatic Budget by many accounts, but one dedicated to fine-tuning existing policies and regulations. The 2005 Budget was designed to ease the social and economic burdens of Singaporeans, while, unlike past Budgets, doing relatively less for local businesses and entrepreneurs. The foreign domestic maid levy, for instance, was lowered substantially. This move was an implicit government acknowledgement of the fact that many Singaporean families rely on foreign maids to care for their young and elderly, thus freeing up parents to join the workforce. Furthermore, the lowering of the maid levy was in keeping with the government's concern over two groups of people — babies and older Singaporeans — both of whom received special mention in the PM's 2004 National Day Rally speech.[2] In contrast, the levy for foreign labour employment in other industries was increased. This increase is seen as a necessary first step towards the "re-designing" of low-skilled jobs. Job "re-designing" usually entails partially mechanizing or computerizing traditionally menial jobs in order for them to command higher wages and to, ultimately, make them more attractive to Singaporeans who may otherwise shy away from them. The Budget also included provisions for skills upgrading for older and lower-educated sectors of the workforce, all of which was part and parcel of the ongoing national effort to restructure the economy. In keeping with the government's long-running health campaign, the duties on tobacco products were also increased. Continuing from the previous Budget, top personal income tax was also to be reduced from 22 to 20 per cent over the next two years.

Another noteworthy feature of the 2005 Budget was the decision to expand the definition of "charitable purposes" for Institutes of Public Character to promote volunteerism and philanthropy. In effect, this meant that more local non-profit and voluntary organizations were now eligible for tax-exemption status. It is hoped that the extension of tax-exemption status to voluntary welfare organizations would encourage the proliferation of community-based and citizen-driven welfare in order to meet the challenges of structural unemployment and an ageing population. The carefully crafted message is that though the government will not succumb to a welfare mentality, it is not blind to the plight of the needy or the victims of a maturing economy; and will endeavour to help Singaporeans to care for fellow Singaporeans.

On the whole the 2005 Budget was a socially conscious one that offered qualified assistance to those in need, as well as to encourage higher fertility rates. It managed to dispense necessary financial aid without promoting a welfare mentality. With regard to the external world, the Budget was designed to nurture a vibrant national economy, one that could absorb shocks while offering a safety net for Singaporeans who found themselves sidelined by the capricious processes of globalization. The effects of these "socially conscious" policies are trickling down and would put the PAP government in good stead for the coming general elections.

The Signs of a Recovering and Maturing Economy

Another factor that would favour the PAP government in the coming general elections is the national economy's better-than-expected growth. The Singapore economy delivered a strong performance and ended the year with a 5.7 per cent growth spurt.[3] This was well above an earlier 4.5 per cent revised projection.[4] With jobs uppermost in the minds of many Singaporeans, the job market expansion that followed this growth was welcome news indeed. It was reported that the number of jobs created reached a four-and-a-half-year high in the first half of 2005, with 49,500 jobs added.[5] This was double that of the 24,600 jobs created in the same period in 2004. The industries that enjoyed significant job creation were the service, manufacturing, and construction sectors, which saw 18,400, 9,300, and 3,400 jobs created in April, May, and June, respectively.

Meanwhile the tourism and financial sectors both displayed outstanding performances in the second quarter of 2005.[6] Tourist figures have shown steady increase, suggesting that the economic aftershocks of the 2004 Asian tsunami have subsided. The influx of tourists and development of the MICE (meetings, incentives, conventions, and exhibitions) industry has left a trail of happy hotels, restaurants, and retailers along Orchard Road. Down in Shenton Way, the financial sector benefited from the growth of private-banking services targeted at the region's rich. Other factors that drove the finance industry were robust stock market activity, specifically with regard to oil- and gas-related counters, as well as property shares.

Nonetheless, despite the generally optimistic economic outlook, local economists expected the unemployment rate to hover at around 3.2 per cent because of structural unemployment. Bearing the brunt of this were the older and less-educated workers. The unemployment rate for those aged 40 and above, and those with below secondary education soared from 5.9 per cent to 6.8 per cent by June 2005. This brought issues of ageism to the fore. Many of these older and less-educated workers were thought to face discrimination from employers, many of whom preferred to hire younger workers or fresh graduates. This trend is reflected in the relative ease with which the better educated and those below the age of 30 secured employment. To keep older citizens employed the government is considering Japanese-inspired retiree-employment laws where local companies would be required to offer to retain workers who have passed their retirement age. Nevertheless companies are not bound to offer them the same job or similar wages under this legislation.[7] Given the increasing population of senior citizens the success of such retiree-employment laws would have political consequences at the ballot boxes.

Another symptom of globalization is the widening wage gap in Singapore. The Household Expenditure Survey, released by the Department of Statistics in June, revealed that the bottom 20 per cent of households suffered a 3.2 per cent income drop between 1998 and 2003. In contrast, it was reported that the average income of all households rose by 1.1 per cent a year.[8] This widening wage gap was framed more starkly by a survey that showed that there were nearly 50 000 millionaires in Singapore.[9] This survey, conducted by Merrill Lynch, defined millionaires as those with financial assets worth over US$1 million, excluding primary residential property. More interesting is that Singapore posted the biggest leap in the number of millionaires — a whopping 22.4 per cent — for the 68 markets surveyed.

With a broad lens one can begin to identify the signs of a maturing capitalist economy. Structural unemployment, the disappearance of low-skill jobs, the economic marginalization of the old and less educated, and the widening income gap between the haves and the have-nots, all suggest that neo-capitalist processes are deeply embedded in the national economy and are, consequently, making the domestic workforce and industries vulnerable to the capricious forces of globalization. The character of the 2005 Budget was an explicit recognition of this vulnerability while other government initiatives like ComCare, launched on 28 June 2005, seeks to help individuals become self-reliant and to enable children from needy families to break out of the poverty cycle. As Singapore links itself ever more intimately to world markets for survival, it would be interesting to measure the political and social consequences of a growing number of Singaporeans who find themselves missing out on the Singapore dream.

Global Threats, Local Precautions: Terrorism and the Avian Influenza

Besides countering the ill effects of economic globalization, Singapore has had to actively address two very different global security threats. The London bombings on 7 July came a day after the International Olympics Committee's (IOC) announcement in Singapore that the English capital had won the bid to host the 2012 games. Three bomb explosions on the London Underground and one on a double-decker bus left over 30 people dead and around 700 injured. News that the bombers were British Muslims sent shockwaves through the country. Closer to home, and barely two months later, on 1 October, three bomb attacks shook the Indonesian tourist island of Bali. About 26 people were killed and more than 50 others injured as the blasts ripped through three restaurants — two in the Jimbaran beach resort, the third in Kuta.

Singapore has spared little effort in heightening national security. From the middle of August 2005, officers from the newly set up Police MRT (Mass Rapid Transit) Unit were deployed to patrol MRT stations and trains. The unit aims to increase armed police presence and to conduct high visibility patrols and security checks. In October, Deputy Prime Minister and Coordinating Minister for National Security Professor S. Jayakumar announced that the newly set up National Security Coordination Secretariat would be developing the Risk Assessment and Horizon Scanning System, an early warning system that identifies new and emerging threats to national security.[10] Various government agencies will be connected in a data-sharing and assessment network called the Sensemaking System Architecture. This network will connect the Ministry of Home Affairs, Ministry of Defence, and the policy and intelligence services, as well as the cyber and bio-chemical surveillance units, in order that they may tap on each other's expertise for strategic planning, intelligence, research, and surveillance.

On an international strategic level, Singapore and the United States signed the Strategic Framework Agreement (SFA).[11] The agreement was described as a formalization of the "special relationship" between the two countries. However, it was not a treaty and did not require either country to come to each other's defence. Instead, it reinforced the way both countries had become "major security cooperation partners" and their cooperation on a range of mutual security issues and humanitarian efforts.

A different but no less deadly global threat is the avian influenza. The fatal H5N1 strain of the avian flu had been endemic in East Asia since 2003, when it first spread to humans and caused deaths in Hong Kong. By mid-November 2005, the virus had infected at least 125 people in Vietnam, Thailand, Indonesia, and Cambodia, killing about half of them. In Singapore, several public health measures are already in place. They include the upgrading of disease surveillance capabilities, maintenance of essential public services, stockpiling of anti-viral drugs, and the implementation of border control measures to detect imported cases.[12] The Ministry of Health has also come up with an Influenza Readiness and Response Plan, one that will be reviewed periodically to incorporate new developments and vaccines.

Gambling on Casinos

Though it actively seeks to mediate globalization's side effects such as structural unemployment and terrorism, the PAP government has also made bold strides towards opening up the city-state. One of the main talking points of 2005 was PM Lee's 18 April announcement that two casinos, both incorporated in larger "Integrated Resorts" (IRs), were to be built by 2009. One located in the southern island of Sentosa, and the other in downtown Marina Bay, these two casinos, though taking up no more than 3 to 5 per cent of the total floor area of the IRs, have polarized Singaporean society. Although the government had stoically opposed casinos in the past because it was thought that their ill effects outweighed their economic advantages, it was now believed that casinos, and the larger IRs, could help to boost tourist figures, which have been generally declining over the years. Both the casinos and the IRs were necessary, it was also argued, to combat the strait-laced and sterile reputation that the city-state had garnered. Another argument presented to the public was that Singaporean gamblers often flocked overseas, and sometimes to the high seas, to gamble, which resulted in an estimated S$1.8 billion to S$2 billion loss in potential revenue.

The idea to build a casino on Singaporean soil was floated to the public in 2004. The later half of 2004 witnessed an island-wide debate on the casino issue with the national newspapers, government policy institutions, and other feedback organizations providing ample space for the airing of views from both the pro- and anti-casino camps. The issue stirred up strong views from conservative groups, religious organizations, and economic pragmatists alike, and it is hard to think of another national issue that has generated the same amount of public interest and participation. Eventually the public debate congealed into a simplistic contest between the conservative moralists and economic pragmatists with the former associated with softness and dogmatism, and the latter with hard-headed rationalism. Little attention was given to questions as to why and how the strategies of the Singapore Tourist Board (STB) over the years had failed. Not many wondered if the replicating of the IR concept in Singapore would result in IR fatigue, or if Chinese tourists, which constitute a target group, would prefer travelling to America, Australia, or Europe, instead of Singapore, for the IR experience. Lastly, aside from the IR, no other tourist, leisure, or entertainment concept was presented to the public.

Interestingly, Minister Mentor (MM) Lee noted that the cabinet was itself spilt over the issue. And while ministers who made public statements on the casinos were largely for it, none emerged to argue publicly against it. Beyond a moral issue, the casino decision also impacted perceptions of the public consultation process. Many felt that the casino debate was less of a consultation exercise than a purposeful device of the government to gauge the possible political consequences of building the casinos. To some, in cynical terms, the *raison d'être* of the debate was to allow the airing of anti-casino views in order for the government to identify and counter them. Another popular conclusion was that the government placed greater importance on economic opportunities than on public sentiment, a charge as old as the country itself.

Sensitive to such criticisms and constantly alert to threats to social order, the government has, in its usual efficient manner, announced several safety net features. Firstly, to dampen the gambling appetite of locals, Singaporeans will be charged an entrance fee of S$100 per day, or S$2,000 per year. Foreigners and tourists will enter free of charge. The government's initial suggestion to allow only Singaporeans of a requisite income in was quietly dropped after charges of elitism were levelled. Secondly, gambling on credit will be prohibited. Thirdly, Singaporeans will be able to exclude themselves or their family members from entry. Those on financial assistance programmes will be automatically barred. Fourthly, the Casino Control Bill will be ready as early as 2006 to spell out the operational and regulatory ground rules, while in 2007 or the year after, a regulatory body for the casinos will be born. The decision to cap casino revenue at 50 per cent of total IR earnings was rescinded after protests from potential IR operators. Fifthly, the government has promised assistance to counselling and rehabilitation centres in the combat against gambling addiction.

The lesson of the casino issue is that the PAP government is willing, and capable, of forsaking long-held ideological principles for economic gains. Unprecedented levels of regional competition and a worrisome economy have paved the way for this ideological U-turn. This seemingly cold, pragmatic stance has its critics, but the more important point here is that the government may be less ideologically dogmatic than it used to be. This is not to say that it has become more consultative or democratic in the liberal vein, but that the government's desire to show to the world that the city-state is indeed changing, becoming more vibrant, and ready to discard its cloak of sterility, suggests that the demands of globalization are indeed forcing open previously authoritarian mindsets. More crucially, it reinforces the belief that the PAP government's political legitimacy is linked to its economic delivery given that it is willing to defy its conservative and religious constituents for the promise of more jobs.

Civil Society: Local, Vocal, and Disobedient

If the casinos demonstrated the government's ability to make U-turns, other events highlighted its ability to refuse to accede to certain global trends and politics. On 13 May 2005, 38-year-old Singaporean Shanmugam Murugesu was hanged for trafficking 1 kilogram of cannabis from neighbouring Malaysia into Singapore. The run-up to 13 May saw a campaign conducted by various groups and individuals from the arts and academic communities to save Murugesu from the gallows. It is not entirely clear as to why this case aroused civil society's interest given the numerous executions prior to Murugesu's. Murugesu was financially desperate, a victim of drug abuse, and had a profile that did not vary greatly from other drug runners before him. His lawyer, however, was able to create public awareness and, subsequently, public sympathy for a man who was a former regular in the Singapore Armed Forces and Singapore's representative at the 1995 World Championship Jetski Finals. Pretty soon, vocal anti-death penalty activists began to organize themselves, predominantly through Internet newsgroups, and, with the help of occasional reporting from the international media and human rights groups, the campaign started to gain momentum. Among the events organized to promote awareness of Murugesu's plight were candlelit vigils, press conferences, petitions, prayer sessions, and an appeal to the President for clemency, which was rejected. Last-minute publicity stunts also failed. Murugesu was duly hung on 13 May. The police only permitted an anti-death penalty concert at the Substation to go ahead on 18 August after the organizers removed all images of Murugesu; presumably because the government did not want him turned into a martyr.

A similar case that had international dimensions was that of Australian citizen Nguyen Tuong Van. Nguyen, of Vietnamese descent, was arrested on transit at Changi Airport in December 2002 with 396 grams of heroin. Throughout his trial Nguyen claimed that he was only carrying the drugs in order to pay off debts owed by his twin brother. Nguyen, who had no previous criminal record, admitted in his police statement that he knew he was transporting heroin to Australia but said that he had feared for the safety of his family and that prevented him from rejecting the assignment. Nguyen's case came to public attention when his appeal to the President for clemency was rejected in October. Sections of the Australian liberal media played up the story while some Australian politicians predictably indulged in Singapore-bashing with "Chinese rogue port city" among the more colourful descriptions of the city-state.[13] Meanwhile, on a more constructive note, local civil society activists sought to raise debate over the death penalty. All these, however, were to no avail. Even letters from the Australian Foreign Minister Alexander Downer to his Singapore counterpart George Yeo failed to change the government's mind.[14] Nguyen was hung on 2 December 2005.

According to PM Lee, this uncompromising stance is to, firstly, protect citizens from drugs and, secondly, to ensure the country does not become a transit centre.[15] Such resistance to external pressures wins the government legitimacy from many Singaporeans, who believe in the direct link between capital punishment and low crime rates. Nonetheless, there is a growing section of vocal Singaporeans who oppose the death penalty, ensuring that the issue will be re-visited over and over again.

Other examples of resistance to external pressures include the government's defence of Singapore's press. In a global survey on press freedom, Singapore was ranked 140 out of 167 countries by an international NGO, Reporters Without Borders. The ranking itself was of little consequence but the minor debate it stirred provided the government the opportunity to reiterate that "an unfettered press that acts irresponsibly can be destructive", and to conclude that "Singapore's model of government and the media has given our country a clean government, social equity and harmony, and, as a result, a strong economy".[16]

Another seemingly trivial matter that grew into a *cause célèbre* was the white elephant saga at Buangkok MRT Station. The MRT station was initially slated to open in 2003 but it remained closed because the transport authorities believed it would not be commercially viable due to the lower-than-expected number of residents living in the station's vicinity. Residents' repeated appeals and petitions did not result in a satisfactory outcome and the consequence was eight cardboard cartoons of white elephants lined along a road to greet a minister on his visit to the area. Although the "white elephant" saga will go down in local history as an act of civil disobedience, it reveals other truths about local politics.

Firstly, it demonstrated to some the relatively limited powers of MPs to broker deals between their constituents and the relevant authorities they represent. PAP MP Charles Chong had repeatedly tried to convince the transport authorities of the viability of the station but was rebuffed. Secondly, the readiness of the press to see the cardboard elephants as a "national issue" with "political intentions",[17] amounted to an exercise in political policing. Describing a harmless protest as a "national issue" was to make it more serious than it actually was, thus justifying a strong governmental reaction. This led a local scholar to comment that such a reading was "paranoid" and that the reason it was not seen as a "municipal" matter, as it should have been, was because of the "single-tier government" in Singapore.[18] Lastly, for all the available feedback channels — newspapers, Meet the People sessions, Feedback Unit, petitions — the white elephant saga clearly shows that Singaporeans, or Buangkok residents at least, do not think such channels produce the desired results. Transport Minister Yeo Cheow Tong's subsequent announcement that Buangkok would be open by mid-January 2006 only seemed to reinforce the popular belief that a bunch of cartoon elephants was more effective than any available institutional consultation process.[19] The fact that the General Elections had yet to take place no doubt hastened the opening of the station. This saga, however, places the project of public consultation under harsh focus and it will not be long before the government has to re-assert its wholehearted commitment to it.

Finally, on 11 August, four individuals planted themselves outside the Central Providence Fund (CPF) Building to protest against the perceived lack of transparency and accountability in certain institutions such as the National Kidney Foundation, CPF, Government of Singapore Investment Corporation (GIC), and the Housing Development Board (HDB). The number of protesters was kept to only four individuals in order to circumvent the law that interprets the congregation of five people or more as an "illegal gathering". This protest, together with the white elephants, prompted the Minister of Home Affairs to reiterate that all acts of civil disobedience, whether peaceful or not, were illegal.[20] Whether or not civil disobedience takes off in Singapore depends not only on how the government responds to concerned individuals, but also the variety of ways in which ordinary citizens can find creative means to bend but not break the law. This mode of resistance may embed itself in local civil society given that it leverages on an educated citizenry's competence with legalese and statutes in order to navigate the shoals of state reprisal.

Singapore Rebel, the Sedition Act, and the Trial of the Golden Taps

With the various restrictions on political activities in Singapore, it was not surprising that local documentary-maker Martyn See was hauled up by the police for making what was deemed to be a "political film". *Singapore Rebel*, a short documentation of opposition politician Chee Soon Juan, was withdrawn from the Singapore Film Festival in 10 May 2005 after censors judged the documentary to be too "political". A police investigation followed this withdrawal. The Films Act prohibits the production and distribution of "party political" films, defined as those "made by any person and directed towards any political end in Singapore".[21] See was questioned several times by the police over a period, along with some of his acquaintances.[22]

Another headliner was the charging of three Singaporeans under the Sedition Act. Two bloggers, 21-year-old Nicholas Lim and 27-year-old Benjamin Koh, were charged under the act for promoting ill-will and hostility between races in Singapore on 12 September 2005. Lim had posted derogatory comments about Malays and Islam on an Internet forum for dog lovers. His comments were triggered by a discussion about whether taxis should refuse to carry uncaged pets out of consideration for Muslims, whose religion considers dogs unclean. Koh, Lim's friend, meanwhile, advocated the desecration of Islam's holy site of Mecca in his blog. In an unrelated case, 17-year-old Gan Huai Shi was also charged on 16 September 2005 with sedition for making racist comments on the Internet about Malays, and later sentenced to 180 hours of social service within the Malay community.[23] First introduced by the British colonial administration in Malaya, the Sedition Act was primarily a weapon against communist insurgents. It was later incorporated into Singaporean law just ahead of independence and has broad provisions against inciting hostility among races. The reason the act was used so sparingly in the past was probably because the government was wary of having court proceedings turned into public platforms for racist views. In such cases an acquittal could potentially inflame ethnic feelings. Hence, it is not completely clear as to why the three bloggers were charged under the Sedition Act. The Media Development Authority (MDA) is the traditional censorship apparatus in Singapore. Websites that discuss local politics have to be registered with MDA; which also decides if racial and religious content on such websites are objectionable. One reason why the act was used could be because the government, sufficiently confident of the harmonious state of interethnic relations, calculated that the sheer seriousness of the sedition charge would be more effective than MDA censure in sending a clear message to the public.

Perhaps the most talked about event of 2005, aside from the casinos, was the National Kidney Foundation's (NKF) libel suit against the *Straits Times* (*ST*). The salacious affair began on 19 April 2004 when *ST* journalist Susan Long published an exposé on NKF. In her article, Long described how an anonymous plumber was asked to install, among other things, a glass-panelled shower, a pricey German toilet bowl, and gold-plated taps in the office of NKF CEO T.T. Durai. When contacted for a response, NKF replied that it was difficult to give an answer since *ST* would not reveal the identity of the plumber. Four days after the article appeared, NKF served a writ on *ST*. At the trial, which commenced on 11 July 2005, NKF argued that the article suggested that it had misused public funds and that it had mismanaged public donations. *ST* counter-argued that the article was not defamatory but a fair comment on the lack of transparency in NKF. During the well-publicized and well-attended trial, Durai was subjected to two days of cross-examination and, in the end, admitted that the article was not defamatory and, consequently, withdrew the defamation lawsuit.[24]

The trial threw up several talking points. Firstly, the court was told of NKF's S$262 million reserves. NKF had initially told *ST* that this reserve would only last three years. But Durai later admitted on the witness stand that the three-year estimate was not accurate. Secondly, it was revealed that Durai was paid a total of S$600,000 in salary and bonuses for 2003 and 2004. He received a total of nearly S$1.8 million from 2002 to 2004. Public outrage stemmed from the fact that, unlike CEOs of private companies, whom Durai compared himself to, Durai's salary was not a reflection of company profits but derived from public donations meant for kidney patients. Thirdly, Mrs Goh Chok Tong, wife of the Senior Minister (SM) and NKF's patron, fuelled public outrage by claiming that the S$600,000 Durai earned was "peanuts" for someone who ran a multi-million-dollar organization. Mrs Goh stepped down as NKF's patron on 14 July 2005. SM Goh later said his wife regretted her "peanuts" remark.[25] An independent audit later found NKF guilty of poor corporate governance.[26]

The NKF saga left us with a few salient points. Although *ST* won some measure of goodwill from many local readers for its "investigative journalism", its self-assigned responsibility in the nation-building process and its public eschewment of a Fourth Estate role narrows its investigative scope. For example, it remains highly improbable that *ST* would, if the opportunity arose, run a similar exposé on a government organization or ministry. Any possible information that the local press may have on inappropriate behaviour within government organizations would most likely be submitted discretely back to the government for internal handling. Secondly, much of the public discontent was aimed at the way in which NKF was T.T. Durai personified. There is little doubt as to the nobility of NKF's *raison d'être* but more stringent checks and balances would have been in place if Durai's personality and influence had not permeated every level of the charitable institution. Lastly, given the local press's deference for the government, the scope of "investigative journalism" may only be confined to private corporations, other charitable or volunteer institutions, or prominent but not politically connected individuals.

The (Non-)Elected Presidency

In comparison with the NKF saga, the Elected Presidency (EP) was a damp squib. S.R. Nathan, who first took office in 1999, was returned unopposed on 1 September 2005. The EP was implemented in 1991, and was intended to transform the office of the president from a purely symbolic institution into one vested with certain executive powers. It is an institutional mechanism designed to safeguard national reserves should a rogue government ever come into power. In addition to this, the president's power includes the ability to reject key civil service appointments if nepotism is suspected and to act against corruption. As such, even against the wishes of the prime minister, and upon the president's instructions, the Corrupt Practices Investigation Bureau can investigate a minister on suspicion of corruption.

Eyebrows were raised when Andrew Kuan, a relatively unknown figure and former Group Chief Financial Officer of Jurong Town Corporation (JTC), announced his intention to contest the presidential elections. In response to the Presidential Elections Committee's (PEC) request for an appraisal of Kuan's performance, the government-linked corporation submitted an "unsatisfactory" verdict.[27] Kuan was consequently denied the right to contest the elections by the PEC. The overriding concern in this year's presidential elections was the lack of qualified candidates willing to throw their hats into the ring. To be sure, the PEC's stringent selection criteria — such as the need for candidates to have a minimum of three years executive and financial experience in government, statutory board, or a company with a paid-up capital of at least S$100 million — makes only just over 400 Singaporeans eligible for the post.

We can infer two points from the presidential walkover. Firstly, Singapore's elite is relatively publicity-shy, preferring to wield influence in the background. They are also less prone to open conflict given their reluctance to stand against a PAP government-endorsed candidate. Secondly, the absence of elections harms the institution of the EP. As a local scholar has suggested, only an election can endow the EP with the legitimacy and the moral authority it needs to check the government. The fact that the presidency was made elective is itself a recognition that this legitimacy and moral authority can only be won through the ballot box. Moreover, as she goes on to write, "Singaporeans can vote only for PEC-vetted candidates, which seems to indicate a paternalistic concern that the electorate cannot be trusted to evaluate candidates and select the right person for the job. Furthermore, PEC decisions are unaccountable as they are not subject to judicial challenge. Where the PEC states a candidate lacks good character, it cannot, in the absence of malice, be sued for libel. Who then guards these unelected guardians?"[28] On a more sombre note, 2005 also saw the deaths of two former presidents. Wee Kim Wee, who held office from 1985 to 1993, passed away on 2 March; Devan Nair, president from 1981 to 1985, passed away on 6 December.

Conclusion: Can a City Globalize on Its Own Terms?

At the beginning of this chapter, it was suggested that the PAP government practises selective globalization. On the one hand, it is open to economic globalization; on the other, it shuts its doors to liberal democratic processes and organizations. For the most part, the government has succeeded in negotiating global forces, and has, generally, mediated the external influences and pressures on the local. Nonetheless, three events in 2005 suggest that this negotiation and mediation may have ramifications for its global city ambitions.

In June 2005 the Singapore government denied Fridae.com, a gay portal, the entertainment licence to hold its annual Nation Party. Fridae.com responded by moving its annual bash to Phuket. For a government that already acknowledges that there are homosexuals in the civil service, the licence withdrawal looked like a step backwards. Fridae.com's pull-out may have mollified the majority of conservative Singaporeans but it does little to show the international community that the city-state is culturally exciting. Or, in the words of MM Lee, "To remain only as the cleanest, greenest, safest, most efficient and healthiest city in Southeast Asia, the "with it" world will pass Singapore by."[29]

There was also an unexpected poke in the eye. In his farewell speech on 11 October 2005, the out-bound US Ambassador Frank Lavin mildly criticized the Singapore government for its repression of political expression.[30] The ambassador also recounted his embarrassment at being asked by the local police if he wanted to press charges against local demonstrators protesting outside the US Embassy over the Iraq war.[31] These remarks were surprising in a post-Clinton era, and are significant in the light of the Singapore government's strong support for the Bush administration's "War on Terror" campaign and the Iraq war.

Lastly, but no less surprising, was Warwick University's decision not to set up campus in Singapore.[32] According to reports, the Economic Development Board invited the British university, on account of its vibrant research culture, to set up campus on the island. After months of deliberation and feasibility studies, the university turned down the invitation, citing its concern over both financial costs and the lack of academic freedom in Singapore. Predictably, it was the latter issue that dogged the headlines. Whether overblown or not, the perceived lack of academic freedom has had economic consequences for Singapore. This is the first time that a potential investor has publicly cited Singapore's famed OB-markers, its emphasis on non-confrontational academic analysis, and the government's intolerance for dissent, as reasons for not coming. The consequences of this on the city-state's education hub ambitions will only unfold later.

These three incidents suggest that a nation-state and a global city require different management ethos. Conventional arguments for cultural and ideological protectionism may sit well with the character of nation-states, but are increasingly incongruent with the functions of global cities. And since a global city cannot be willed into being but becomes one only when others recognize it as such, all global cities require cultural legitimacy from the international community of transnational professionals, creative classes, and international opinion-shapers who have the power to confer it recognition. The competition to distinguish oneself as a global city is, in reality, the competition to win legitimacy and recognition from this international community. The fact that Singapore's survival as a nation-state depends on its status as a global city means that the government has little choice but to constantly shift gears between the national and the global when it comes to policymaking, thus compelling it to send mixed signals to this international community. Casinos are allowed but satellite dishes are not, topless cabaret shows are permitted but civil disobedience is not, and the list goes on. These discrepancies are at the heart of the dilemma facing Singapore at the dawn of the 21st century — globalizing at one's own pace and terms may be prudent for a small nation-state, but how much of this prudence can an aspiring global city afford?

Notes

[1] Chua Mui Hoong, "One Size Fits All? That's No Longer the Way to Go", *Straits Times*, 17 November 2004.
[2] National Day Rally Speech 2004, http://www.gov.sg/nd/ND04.htm (last accessed 1 November 2005).
[3] "S'pore Growth 7.7% in Q4, Betters Forecast", *Straits Times*, 3 January 2006.
[4] Aaron Low, "MM's Take on the Economy: We've Never Had It More Promising", *Straits Times*, 8 November 2005.
[5] Sue-Ann Chia, "Job Creation Rate Highest in 4½ Years", *Straits Times*, 13 September 2005.

[6] Bryan Lee, "Tourism and Financial Sector Buoy Up Services", *Straits Times*, 12 July 2005.
[7] Aaron Low and T. Rajan, "Firms Lead the Way by Re-hiring Retirees", *Straits Times*, 21 November 2005.
[8] Leslie Koh, "Bigger Wage Gap Can't Be Avoided: Boon Heng", *Straits Times*, 20 June 2005.
[9] Alexandra Ho, "Singapore's Millionaire Ranks Swell to Almost 50,000", *Business Times*, 11–12 June 2005.
[10] "S'pore to Develop Terror Risk Assessment and Scanning System", *Channel News Asia*, 25 October 2005, http://www.channelnewsasia.com/stories/singaporelocalnews/view/175366/1/.html (last accessed 6 November 2005).
[11] Chua Mui Hoong, "S'pore, US Deepen Security Partnership", *Straits Times*, 13 July 2005.
[12] Ministry of Health, Press Release: "Singapore Prepares for Flu Pandemic", 29 June 2005.
[13] Michelle Grattan, Michael Gordon, and James Button, "Whitlam Hits Out at 'Chinese Rogue Port City'", *The Age*, 25 November 2005.
[14] *Channel News Asia*, "S'pore Unable to Change Its Decision in Australian Drug Trafficking Case", 3 November 2005, http://www.channelnewsasia.com/stories/singaporelocalnews/view/176743/1/.html (last accessed 10 November 2005).
[15] Paul Jacob, "PM: 2 Reasons for S'pore's Firm Stand on Drugs", *Straits Times*, 18 November 2005.
[16] Stanley Loh, Press Secretary to the Senior Minister, "S'pore's Model of Govt and Press Has Worked" (Forum Page), *Straits Times*, 9 November 2005.
[17] Chua Lee Hoong, "Hold That Cynicism, Please", *Straits Times*, 12 September 2005.
[18] Chua Beng Huat, "White Elephant Saga Isn't a National Issue" (Forum Page), *Straits Times*, 14 September 2005.
[19] "Buangkok Station to Open in January 2006", *Straits Times*, 11 November 2005.
[20] Sue-Ann Chia and Pei Shing Huei, "Don't Throw the Baby Out with Bathwater", *Straits Times*, 12 September 2005.
[21] Films Act (Chapter 107), http://statutes.agc.gov.sg/non_version/html/homepage.html (last accessed 10 November 2005).
[22] For See's account please see http://singaporerebel.blogspot.com.
[23] Chong Chee Kin, "Not Jail But Immersion in Malay Community", *Straits Times*, 24 November 2005.
[24] *Channel News Asia*, "NKF Withdraws Defamation Suit Against SPH and Journalist", 12 July 2005, http://www.channelnewsasia.com/stories/singaporelocalnews/view/157556/1/.html (last accessed 13 November 2005).
[25] *Channel News Asia*, "Ex-NKF Patron Mrs Goh Chok Tong Regrets Remarks about TT Durai's Pay: SM Goh", 16 July 2005, http://www.channelnewsasia.com/stories/singaporelocalnews/view/158246/1/.htm (last accessed 13 November 2005).

[26] Bertha Henson, "Old NKF Slammed for Poor Practices", *Straits Times*, 20 December 2005.
[27] *Channel News Asia*, "JTC Says Presidential Hopeful Andrew Kuan's Work Unsatisfactory", 11 August 2005, http://www.channelnewsasia.com/stories/singaporelocalnews/view/162697/1/.html (last accessed 14 November 2005).
[28] Thio Li-Ann, "Is Singapore Headed towards a Selected Presidency?" *Straits Times*, 19 August 2005.
[29] Lee Kuan Yew, Speech in Parliament on the Proposal to Develop Integrated Resorts, Ministry of Information, Communication and the Arts, 19 April 2005.
[30] Frank Lavin, "Foreign Policy: No Islands Anymore", 11 October 2005, http://singapore.usembassy.gov/101105.html (last accessed 10 November 2005).
[31] *Today*, "Sealed Lips in the Age of Blogs?" 12 October 2005.
[32] Ho Ai Li and Sandra Davies, "Warwick Says 'No'", *Straits Times*, 19 October 2005.

Thailand

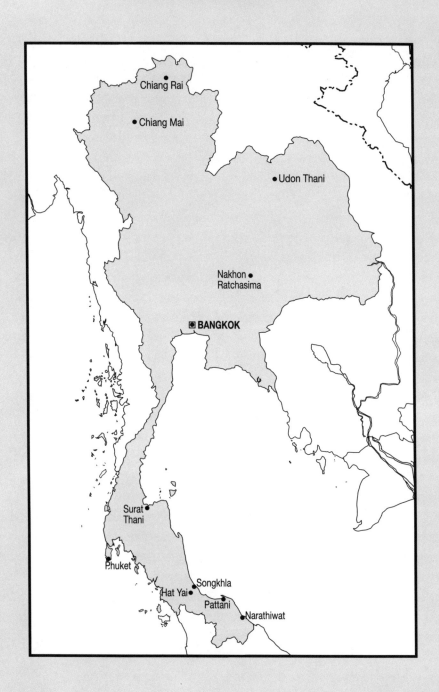

Thaksin's Political Zenith and Nadir

Thitinan Pongsudhirak

The year 2005 is likely to be remembered as extraordinary, even peculiar, in the history of Thailand's evolving democracy since 1932. Within the year Prime Minister Thaksin Shinawatra soared to unprecedented political heights and then descended steeply into a political abyss. His Thai Rak Thai (TRT) party secured a thumping victory in the February 2005 General Election. Yet less than a year later, he faced a virulent Bangkok-based insurrection that called for no less than his resignation and permanent banishment from Thai politics. How did Thailand's most popularly elected prime minister who had risen so meteorically decline so precipitously?

This article sheds some light on key episodes following Thaksin's re-election triumph in February 2005. It begins with the significance of the re-election and the factors that led to the TRT's overwhelming victory. In the immediate aftermath of his re-election, Thaksin exhibited uncharacteristic signs of magnanimity and benevolent statesmanship, which lasted just several weeks. By mid-2005, his authoritarian streaks returned in full force, fanning the flames of discontent over his governance. By September an anti-Thaksin movement broke out into the open, spearheaded by a disgruntled media tycoon who had been an erstwhile ally of the Prime Minister. While this movement was initially confined to the Bangkok-based intelligentsia, middle classes, and civil society groups, it expanded into a mass movement to topple Thaksin when his family-owned Shin Corporation (Shin Corp) was sold to the Singapore government's Temasek Holdings in January 2006. The Prime Minister's political standing appeared untenable as long as he remained unable to convincingly explain the controversial sale of Shin Corp. The article concludes with the implications of

---

THITINAN PONGSUDHIRAK is Assistant Professor of International Political Economy, Department of International Relations, Faculty of Political Science, Chulalongkorn University, Bangkok, Thailand.

TABLE 1
Thailand's 6 February 2005 Elections: A breakdown by region

Political Party	Bangkok	Central	Northeast	North	South	Total Constituency Seats	Party-list Seats	Total No. of MPs
Thai Rak Thai	32	80	126	71	1	310	67	377
Democrat Party	4	7	2	5	52	70	26	96
Chart Thai	1	10	6	–	1	18	7	25
Mahachon	–	–	2	–	–	2	–	2
Total	37	97	136	76	54	400	100	500

Source: The Election Commission of Thailand. The Thai Rak Thai lost two constituency seats to Chart Thai and Mahachon in subsequent re-runs.

these developments for the post-Thaksin era, including Thailand's near-term prospects.

Overwhelming Election Victory

In line with widespread expectations, Thaksin and the TRT scored a crushing victory in Thailand's general election on 6 February 2005. Despite claims of vote-buying and fraud, the election was relatively clean by Thai standards. The TRT garnered more than 75 per cent of the 500 seats for members of parliament (MPs), including 67 party-list seats. With 25 party-list seats, the Democrats mustered just under 100, less than the 129 seats they won in the January 2001 election. Chart Thai Party remained relevant with 25 MPs. Mahachon Party, a newcomer from a Democrat breakaway faction, managed to win just one constituency, further testifying to a new era of Thai politics in which only existing parties with established voter bases can survive. The other two dozen-odd parties proved insignificant. For Thaksin, the TRT's result was well above his optimistic pre-election prediction of 350 seats. Consequently, his control over Thailand's political environment was rock-solid, unsurpassed by any elected leader in Thailand's history.[1]

Key revelations from election results included the TRT's overwhelming support in the Bangkok metropolitan area. Of the 37 contested seats in the capital, the ruling party took 32, negating previously held views that the Democrats had regained the urban vote when it won the gubernatorial election in August 2004. This suggested that the Democrats had won the Bangkok governor's race partly because the TRT had fielded a weak candidate. Having carried almost all of the constituency seats in the south but just a handful elsewhere in the country, the Democrats became "regionalized", lacking nationwide appeal. Tellingly, of the 11 MP seats in the three southernmost provinces dominated by the Malay-Muslim insurgency, the Democrats won ten, Chart Thai one, and TRT none. The Muslim communities in the southernmost provinces evidently did not find political appeal in Thaksin and the ruling TRT.

A Brief Change of Mindset?

Surprisingly, Thaksin began his second term in a very different fashion from his first. He exhibited uncharacteristic modesty and humility, apparently trying to make amends for some of the mistakes and controversies of the previous four years. His policy statement in parliament on 23 March 2005 was in marked contrast to the picture of pandering to the grassroots with state funds, conflicts of interest, state-sponsored violence, suppression of dissent, and virtual authoritarian rule that were the hallmarks of his first administration. There were reasons to view the outset of his second term as kinder, gentler, and more tolerant. His apparent change of mindset was conducive for achieving domestic political consensus, and represented a more promising approach towards addressing the southern violence.[2]

The policy statement was comprehensive and conspicuously less populist. The new focus was on inclusiveness and good governance. He pledged to give more political space to civil society groups who had been marginalized in his first term. Thaksin promised to reconsider his handling of the raging violence in the southern border provinces of Yala, Pattani, and Narathiwat, where the death toll in the year to March 2005 neared 600. To this end, he appointed Anand Panyarachun, Thailand's esteemed former prime minister and elder statesman who recently headed a UN reform panel, to pick and direct a national blue-ribbon commission aimed at reconciliation with southern Muslims. Thaksin acknowledged the need to revamp the entire conflict resolution and management process in the three southern provinces in accordance with the "understand, relate, and develop" concept promoted by the King. This was a departure from past blustery, vindictive, and heavy-handed tactics used in dealing with the southern unrest.

Industrial upgrading and competitiveness-boosting programmes to cultivate a knowledge-based economy also featured in the policy statement. Thaksin's economic restructuring centred on the planned 2.35 trillion baht expenditure on infrastructure over five years, although the government announced an outlay of 1.55 trillion baht to assuage fiscal concerns. This massive investment was to be funded by state-owned enterprises, the government's budget, the private sector through state enterprise listings on the stock market, and foreign borrowings, including supplier credit and barter trade. The government's future budget outlays were not to exceed 50 per cent of the total investment costs. Thaksin banked on this infrastructure boost as a principal driver of GDP growth in the medium term, and he appeared committed to a massive infrastructure overhaul. As Thaksin presided over Thailand's first one-party government, having become its first prime minister to complete a full four-year term and to be re-elected, he apparently felt much more secure in power. By having lasted to this point, he had proved his critics wrong. He felt confident enough to promote a kinder, cleaner administration more in line with democratic values. Thaksin seemed to be eyeing a lasting legacy much like that of a few other eminent statesmen in the region.

Thaksin Consolidates the TRT

Following the landslide re-election victory in February, the ruling TRT was beset with internal wrangling and infighting. The internal party rifts were understandable. As the TRT comprised several factions based on patronage networks, the faction leaders were lining up for post-election political rewards. However, Thaksin did not fully oblige. He left out key faction leaders from cabinet appointments in favour of his personal associates and policy experts close to him. The faction leaders protested in a war of words in the press. The conflict between Thaksin and faction bosses came to a head at a party conference on 24 April 2005. In the event, Thaksin cleaned house and reconsolidated his authority over the TRT, thereby ensuring that unruly factions would not be able to destabilize his second term in power.[3]

In the past, Thai political parties had always been weak because their internal factions were too strong. Splintered and wayward factions could hold an entire party hostage, and indeed had brought down many a coalition government. The only party that has maintained its cohesion is the 60-year-old Democrat Party. Still, the Democrats have weathered many splits, including the breakaway of a small faction in 2004 that created the Mahachon Party. Although it had been around for only seven years, the TRT represented a new phenomenon in Thai politics. Never before had such a large party been able to keep a tight rein on its factions. That the TRT was able to do so was attributable to Thaksin's ingenuity. He kept key factions on board by a divide-and-rule strategy. Thaksin relied on three bases of support to keep the provincial barons at bay. He commanded the northern Wang Bua Ban wing, headed by his sister Yaowapa Wongsawat, and the Bangkok camp under Sudarat Keyuraphan. In addition, Thaksin stacked the TRT's party list of 100 MPs with his loyalists, many of whom were elected to the Lower House. These three core bases gave Thaksin a critical mass to discipline misbehaving provincial factions. As long as the Thaksin government can withstand the threat of factional defections, the Prime Minister can maintain overall control of the TRT's various factions.

Yet the post-election clamouring by the provincial faction leaders was fierce. Thaksin was attacked in the press for his dictatorial style. Pramual Rujanaseri, a lieutenant of the eastern Wang Nam Yen faction, a sizeable group of old-style MPs headed by Snoh Thientong, published a book criticizing Thaksin directly. The party conference thus gave Thaksin an opportunity to settle scores, reconstitute the TRT hierarchy, and further institutionalize the party. In a master stroke, Thaksin resigned from the party leadership, a move that automatically retired the entire executive board. Thaksin was then re-elected as party leader, and then Transport

Minister Suriya Jeungrungruangkit re-elected as party secretary-general. The 95-member board was expanded to 119, and appointments to it were strictly along factional lines. Included in the new line-up were 21 deputy party leaders, also evenly divided among the factions. To maintain control of party policies, Thaksin reduced the deputy secretary-general posts from seven to five and filled all of them with his trusted aides. Pramual was ostracized and left out of all party posts. The return of the Thaksin-Suriya team also extinguished doubts about personal rifts between the two leaders.

Thaksin also streamlined party processes and decision-making mechanisms, placing greater emphasis on the TRT as an institution. He pledged to gradually reduce the role of money in internal party politics, and to make the TRT something greater than himself. With sufficient institutionalization of the party, Thaksin could then choose a successor. In the light of its new look, the TRT coalesced into a stable big party in a one-party-dominant political system, much like Malaysia's United Malays National Organisation, with Thaksin firmly at its helm. Having deepened his authority over the factions, Thaksin's position in the TRT and his second-term administration appeared secure.[4]

Post-censure Cabinet Reshuffle

Because of the TRT-led government's overwhelming parliamentary majority, the outcome of the censure motion against then Transport Minister Suriya Juengrungruangkit on 27 June 2005 was a foregone conclusion. The government's 377 TRT MPs were instructed by the Prime Minister before the debate to show their loyalty with a vote for Suriya. In the event, Suriya carried the day with 367 votes, excluding abstentions by the parliament speaker, his two deputies, and a handful of rebellious MPs.[5] Yet the vote of confidence failed to put to rest questions about Suriya's involvement in a corruption scandal over the new airport's purchase of CTX explosives-detection machines. As the censure debate ended, another scandal emerged focusing on stock fraud and embezzlement of family-owned companies belonging to Deputy Commerce Minister Suriya Lapwisuthisin, who resigned from the cabinet on 6 July 2005 to avoid further adverse publicity. The post-censure political landscape thus turned up the heat on Thaksin to reshuffle his cabinet and remove Suriya from the transport portfolio.

The reshuffle was thus designed to address the scourge of corruption following the censure debate, to overhaul the economic team, and to improve the management of the affairs in the three southernmost provinces where violence was raging. As it happened, the reshuffle became a prolonged game of musical chairs dominated by Thaksin's personal confidants and the ruling TRT party's barons. As an exercise in revamping the government's corruption-tainted image and improving policy efficiency, the reshuffle was a disappointment. It swept corruption-related problems under the carpet, and failed to tackle economic and southern challenges head-on. The reshuffle also showed that Thaksin was running out of ideas and human talent to beef up his cabinet.

Of the three main concerns, corruption was the most immediate, as the censure debate damaged the credibility of Suriya Jeungrungruangkit who had been Transport Minister until then. Opinion polls after the censure debate indicated new lows for the government and were abysmal on Suriya's performance relating to the procurement of equipment and construction of the US$3.2 billion new airport. As Suriya was the TRT's No. 2 man, his political future tested Thaksin's mettle. The Prime Minister opted for a compromise to save his secretary-general's face. Suriya became Industry Minister and Deputy Prime Minister, holding two posts concurrently instead of the lucrative and graft-prone transport portfolio. As Deputy Prime Minister, Suriya was given broad jurisdiction over the Transport Ministry, an outcome that did not put public criticisms of government corruption to rest. Thaksin's manoeuvring was intended to appease Suriya's powerful Wang Nam Yom faction of close to 100 MPs. In place of Suriya, Pongsak Raktapongpaisal, Thaksin's troubleshooter and confidant was made Transport Minister.[6]

The reshuffle took several weeks to finalize because Thaksin could not find a suitable finance minister. A small number of old hands were approached but all turned down the premier's offer. Overtures to new faces who might have inspired investor confidence were unsuccessful. No one wanted to join the Thaksin government as its popularity began to plummet and the economy slowed. As Somkid Jatusripitak pleaded to be shifted elsewhere from his finance portfolio, Thaksin was forced to swap his finance and commerce ministers. Somkid took over as commerce minister and retained a deputy premier slot overseeing overall economic management, while the finance portfolio was passed to Thanong Bidaya, another Thaksin confidant. Thanong once worked for Thaksin's family businesses, and later became president of Thai Military Bank, which granted loans for Thaksin's business financing needs. Thanong was also the finance minister during the baht crisis in 1997. Many observers still questioned how the Shinawatra conglomerate emerged from the baht flotation virtually unscathed. When Thaksin became prime minister, Thanong soon found himself on a number of plum state enterprise boards. The choice of Thanong reflected trust, first and foremost. It also revealed Thaksin's lack of candidates of sufficient stature, expertise, and experience for the finance portfolio. Thanong and Somkid both hailed from Thaksin's inner circle, and both have known each other for three decades harking back to their days as lecturers.

The reshuffle offered an opportunity to improve the management of the crisis in the southern provinces. Here Thaksin's choices may have increased the stakes. Jaturon Chaisaeng was moved to the education portfolio. Soon afterwards, he announced plans to reform the education curriculum in the three predominantly Muslim provinces to reflect their Malay heritage, including the teaching of Jawi, the local Malay language written in Arabic. Jaturon's heightened role in resolving the southern conflict boded well. Yet Thaksin also put in Air Chief Marshal Kongsak Wantana as interior minister. Kongsak, along with Defence Minister General Thammarak Israngkul and the new Justice Minister and Deputy Prime Minister Police General Chidchai Wannasathit formed a hawkish trio managing the southern violence. Their conflict with the civilian-led and dovish faction led by the likes of Jaturon intensified and undermined conflict resolution in the deep south. Putting the untested Kongsak in charge of internal security boded ill for resolving the southern unrest. This choice merely reflected Thaksin's personal ties with Kongsak, whose wife was close to Thaksin's.

The Southern Violence[7]

The spiralling violence in Thailand's three southern border provinces of Pattani, Yala, and Narathiwat was a frustrating conundrum for Thaksin throughout 2005. On the one hand, the violence intensified markedly over the year with almost daily killings of Thai state officials and Muslim and Buddhist civilians carried out by a shadowy Malay-Muslim separatist insurgency. On the other hand, the intensification of the violence did not palpably affect economic conditions such as the stock market, foreign investment, and the baht. By late 2005, Thailand seemed to be just a bomb away from security risk ratings on par with Indonesia. A few factors indicated that the risk of escalation and external involvement was mounting.

First, the southern Muslim insurgency was able to establish the wherewithal to carry out violent attacks at will, aimed at selected targets ranging from local leaders and informants to Buddhist monks, soldiers, policemen, and bureaucrats. The campaign of violence had been sustained with growing sophistication. Although it has decidedly kept its identity under a cloud of mystery, academic research, investigative journalism, and official intelligence and military data suggested that the insurgency movement drew its strength from the Pattani United Liberation Organization (PULO), the New Pulo, the Gerakan Mujahideen Islam Patani (GMIP), the Barisan Revolusi Nasional (BRN), and the BRN Coordinate — separatist groups that had been in operation for decades. The organization, coherence, and objectives of these separatist groups remained unclear. The subgroup known as the BRN Coordinate was believed to have been behind the most violent and coordinated attacks. It was also unclear to what extent the personnel, plots, and tactics of these groups were based out of southern Thailand as opposed to across the border in Malaysia's Kelantan state.

What appeared certain was that the insurgency had a command and control system and could dictate outcomes on the ground. Observers were focused on whether these insurgent groups, whose aims range from greater administrative autonomy within Thailand to a separate homeland on the basis of the pre-1902 Patani kingdom, can coalesce into a unified, organized, and coherent movement with stated political objectives. Such a movement could then demand a dialogue with the Thai authorities, much akin to the peace process in Aceh. There was also the real danger that these insurgent groups would be infiltrated by other Muslim extremist elements operating in the region, particularly Jemaah Islamiyah. No such connection was evident to date. Yet, the likelihood of external and/or regional jihadist involvement increased as the insurgency progressed, especially given the insensitive responses from Bangkok.

Second, the Thaksin government increasingly mishandled the southern crisis. Several key incidents have exacerbated Muslim grievances in the deep south. In early September 2005, 131 Thai Muslims fled to Malaysia for fear of their safety, creating a refugee crisis that elicited the attention of the United Nations High Commissioner for Refugees (UNHCR) and soured Thailand-Malaysia relations. Shortly thereafter, Thaksin made acerbic remarks about the United Nations aimed at the UNHCR and the Malaysian government, further internationalizing the issue that the Thai government was trying to keep within its domestic realm. Just days later, an incident at Tanyonglimo village in Narathiwat marked another escalation in the level of violence. Two Thai marines were stabbed to death by unknown assailants after being taken hostage by villagers who were outraged by the gangland-style shooting of several local Muslims earlier in the day. Thaksin quickly condemned the deaths of the marines but failed to redress the anger and grievances of local villagers. He also promised to go on the "offensive" against the insurgents. In mid-October 2005, the insurgent killings of a Buddhist monk and two attendants at a temple further infuriated Thaksin. Around the same time, the Thaksin government renewed the emergency decree governing the three southernmost provinces for another three months, virtually designating them as a war zone. The pattern of insurgent attacks, met by harsh government responses, was discernible. It was viewed as an unconventional, limited war between the southern insurgency and the Thaksin government.

It appeared that the southern crisis had to get worse before it could get better. Thaksin could be counted on to keep up his nationalist rhetoric against the aims of separatism and to continue the harsh crackdown, while the insurgents kept up their attacks. The long road ahead may well involve a negotiations process if the insurgents can organize themselves. But the government under Thaksin was not predisposed to negotiations. A settlement of any kind, it seemed, was difficult to come by as long as Thaksin was in charge.

The Return of Street Politics

Street politics returned to Bangkok in full force by the end of 2005. Not since May 1992 had tens of thousands of people assembled in Bangkok as a show of force against the incumbent government. The May 1992 mass movement against the military-backed government led to a violent confrontation and produced a five-year political reform process that culminated in the drafting and promulgation of an eclectic constitution designed to promote transparency and accountability in the political system and stability and effectiveness of government. The similarities between the two events were compelling. This time the crusader attempting to bring down the Prime Minister was Sondhi Limthongkul, a media mogul who owns a media conglomerate anchored around the Manager Group, with extensive interests in telecommunications, real estate, hotels, and publishing, including the *Manager Daily* and the Hong Kong–based *Asia Times* newspapers. The 1997 economic crisis was disastrous to Sondhi's over-leveraged finances and he was eventually declared bankrupt and his media group nearly disintegrated. As Thaksin and Sondhi had been business associates prior to 1997, it was during Thaksin's rule from January 2001 that Sondhi was able to revive his flagging media empire with capital injections and debt reductions from state-owned Krung Thai Bank and with lucrative time slots on state-run television.[8]

Although the campaign against Thaksin on charges of corruption, cronyism, and disloyalty to King Bhumibol Adulyadej,[9] Thailand's revered monarch, resonated with many Bangkokians, Sondhi's motives and timing were unclear. No one knew why he turned against Thaksin so vociferously in the latter half of 2005. Unlike May 1992 when the movement to oust the military-backed government was spearheaded by Chamlong Srimuang, who had been the most popular governor of Bangkok and founder of the influential Palang Dharma Party, Sondhi's self-pedalled heroism on the back of another "people's power" did not sit well with even the most trenchant of Thaksin's critics. Yet Sondhi succeeded in providing a voice for an electorate whose dissent had been suppressed by Thaksin's virtual authoritarian rule and apparent usurpation of independent institutions and checks-and-balance mechanisms under the constitution.

The political climate in late 2005 was in stark contrast to that of May 1992. Thaksin had been elected twice by an overwhelming margin over the previous five years, having gained more electoral ground in all-important Bangkok with 32 of 37 MP seats in the election of February 2005. Corruption under his administration had been mostly disguised as apparent conflicts of interest. Charges of a parliamentary dictatorship did not carry weight given his invincible democratic mandate. Civilian meddling with the military elicited Thailand's last *coup d'état* in February 1991 in the lead-up to the popular uprising a year later. However, as a former police officer who attended the elite military preparatory school, Thaksin had shrewdly put his classmates in key command positions and in the high command.

The Prime Minister's contentious relationship with the king, whom the Thai people increasingly looked to as an institutional check on Thaksin's runaway power, did not appear to be at a breaking point. Sondhi's vendetta against Thaksin reached a critical point on 9 December 2005 when Thaksin's critics of all stripes massed at Lumpini Park in central Bangkok. The event proved well attended but remained insufficient to rock Thaksin's power. It was in need of a spark to fan the simmering public discontent against Thaksin.[10]

The Shin Corp Scandal[11]

Although the deal had been in the pipeline for weeks, Thaksin's sell-off of his family-owned Shin Corp to Singaporean government's Temasek Holdings was shrouded in mystery. The largest share sale in Thai corporate history netted the Shinawatra and related Damapong families a whopping 73.3 billion baht as Temasek acquired 49.3 per cent of Shin Corp, a business empire Thaksin built over three decades that straddled mobile phone and satellite services, television, and a budget airline. Thaksin's explanation was that getting rid of Shin Corp would enable him to rule with a free hand without the conflicts-of-interest allegations that had hounded him from the outset of his administration in 2001. Another popular explanation was that the Shin Corp sale was purely a shrewd business strategy, as Thailand's telecommunication sector was set to open up to fiercer competition as old concessions run out. However, the most plausible explanation was that Thaksin might have known that the opposition to his rule was mounting and that he was unlikely to complete a second term. The sale thus made his assets liquid and mobile. If he had to depart office, as many suspected, the Prime Minister could find a safer place for his money, possibly abroad. The sale of Shin Corp therefore had to be seen as a political insurance in the event of a disgraceful downfall whereby his allegedly ill-gotten assets could be seized and confiscated.

The first explanation of dumping Shin Corp to reduce political liability was unconvincing. If Thaksin was intent on clearing up his conflicts of interest and promoting transparency, he would have unloaded Shin Corp five or six years earlier before he took power or even in early 2005 prior to his re-election landslide. Instead, the Shin Corp deal generated greater scrutiny of his business transactions, not less. His political opponents monitored the after-sale money trail closely. Thaksin also came under intense pressure for pocketing the sale proceeds virtually tax-free. Legal questions abounded, as a telecommunication law enabling foreign entities to own 49 per cent as opposed to the old ceiling of 25 per cent was enacted just a few days before the deal was clinched. Notwithstanding Thaksin's transparency claims, the Shin Corp sale did not reduce his political liability. The murky and questionable circumstances surrounding the controversial sale instead undermined him and ignited Thailand's political crisis in February 2006.

The second explanation pointing to astute business decision-making was also unpersuasive. According to this argument, competition in the local telecommunication sector was set to intensify as previous concessions were expiring and new players were about to enter the fray, and substantial investments would be required for 3G technology as the telecommunication sector matured. Thaksin may have wanted to cash out before he had to face a more level playing field. This explanation in part assumed that the price of Shin Corp had more or less maxed out and faced an inevitable slide as competition increased and Thaksin's political strength eroded. However, Shin Corp had exploited monopoly power from concessionary agreements with spectacular success. For example, its mobile phone unit, Advanced Info Service (AIS), commanded more than half of total market share. AIS could continue to yield lucrative revenue even as its profit margins gradually declined. Its lopsided market power also made future technological investments such as 3G worthwhile. The market power of AIS, in fact, was a primary motivation in Temasek's buyout. Shin Corp's privileged market position, including its satellite arm, was so entrenched and fortified that existing competitors would have difficulty making inroads and new entrants may be deterred from competing. Shin Corp remained attractive, as Temasek Holdings' buyout decision attested.

To grasp the rationale of the Shin Corp deal, it is instructive to look at its timing and accompanying circumstances. In view of a full-fledged Bangkok-based movement to overthrow him, Thaksin must have realized that his political standing might soon become untenable. Past politicians facing corruption allegations as blatant and extensive as Thaksin had seen their assets seized and confiscated. Selling Shin Corp therefore represented a political insurance policy for Thaksin and his family members at a time of growing political uncertainty.[12]

A Political Brinkmanship

After the sale of Shin Corp in late January 2006, Thailand entered a tumultuous period of political brinkmanship. Arrayed on one side was the anti-Thaksin coalition led by Sondhi of the Manager media group. On the other side was Thaksin, his TRT party lieutenants and cabinet associates. The Sondhi-led forces, comprising the Bangkok-based social activists, NGOs, the intelligentsia, the disaffected middle class, and disgruntled businessmen held a huge rally in the capital on 4 February that drew more than 100,000 street protestors who demanded Thaksin's resignation. They perceived the dubious sale of Shin Corp to Temasek Holdings as the last straw in a long trail of corruption and conflicts of interest. To them, Thaksin had lost all political legitimacy following the Shin Corp deal.

In the face of this opposition, Thaksin rallied forth from his northern hometown of Chiang Mai, backed by tens of thousands of supporters. He was adamant that he still had the right to rule, having been re-elected by a landslide just a year earlier. Elsewhere around the country, pro- and anti-Thaksin forces showed their strength in large numbers. The balance of forces clearly illustrated a divided Thailand between those who were for Thaksin, mainly comprising rural folk and the urban poor, and those against, consisting mostly of the urban intelligentsia, NGOs, and civil society groups in the major cities. While the Bangkok-based forces against him were stacking up, with another anti-Thaksin gathering called for 11 February 2006, Thaksin hunkered down for the long haul. As the anti-Thaksin coalition would apparently stop at nothing short of the Prime Minister's resignation, events appeared headed for an impasse and heightened political uncertainty.

Such an impasse was reached in late February 2006. The coalition to topple the Thaksin government continued to gather steam. More broad-based, large-scale, and spontaneous, it took on a new name, the People's Alliance for Democracy (PAD), comprising virtually all stripes of civil society groups. The PAD became much larger and broader than what media firebrand Sondhi had started when he launched his personal anti-Thaksin crusade in September 2005. On the other hand, Thaksin was not going away quietly. He opted to weather the storm by trying to outflank and outlast his opponents. The protracted struggle between the two sides resulted in a prolonged standoff, bringing the country's political and business environments almost to a standstill.

In alliance with like-minded parliamentary forces intent on ousting Thaksin, the PAD scheduled a major street rally for 26 February. Its efforts to bring down Thaksin were extra-parliamentary and extra-constitutional. Outside parliament, but within the constitutional framework, Thammasat University students organized a 50,000-signatures drive to impeach the Prime Minister. Civil society groups, particularly university lecturers, held almost daily debates and campaigns to demand Thaksin's resignation. That the Thammasat University students in particular and the Students Federation of Thailand (SFT) in general became involved was noteworthy. In past political catharses in October 1973 and May 1992, university students were the foot soldiers of the people's movements to destroy the military dictators of the day. The advent of the PAD was also ominous for Thaksin because it represented a broader base of Thai society and gained more credibility from Sondhi's decision to become just one rally organizer among many.[13]

The Prime Minister tried to reduce the public pressure against him by calling for a public referendum on amending the constitution in conjunction with the upcoming senatorial elections on 19 April. However, this suggestion was quickly withdrawn after Thaksin was reminded of the 90-day requirement before referendums can be called. Instead, the government offered to listen to public views on constitutional amendments on its websites. Around the same time, Thaksin's TRT lieutenants announced a plan to hold counter-rallies across the country in support of Thaksin. The government also attempted to deprive the PAD of the use of Sanam Luang public grounds near the Grand Palace on 26 February 2006 by scheduling government-sponsored events there. Lest the TRT factions try to jump ship at this critical time, Thaksin tried to keep them in line by brandishing his authority to kick them out of the party and dissolve the Lower House. These MPs would then need 90 days of party membership before they could contest an election.

A Political Dead End[14]

Thaksin's outflanking manoeuvres were intended to keep the PAD and the anti-Thaksin forces in parliament off balance. For a while, it seemed as if Thaksin was holding his ground while the coalition against him widened and deepened, especially since the Prime Minister failed to adequately address the shadowy sale of his family-owned Shin Corp conglomerate to Temasek. Thailand's political crisis thus deepened and headed towards a dead end. Thaksin succumbed to public pressure for his ouster by dissolving the Lower House on 24 February. The House dissolution abruptly brought the curtains down on his second-term administration three years ahead of schedule. Following the house dissolution, with a snap election set for 2 April 2006, Thai politics became fluid, volatile, and increasingly polarized and confrontational. By dissolving the Lower House and calling a snap election, Thaksin intended to release the pressure from street protesters led by the PAD who had been demanding his immediate resignation. To ensure another landslide re-election victory at the polls, the Prime Minister exploited incumbency advantages by increasing salaries for civil servants, publicizing a one-sided open letter to his constituents to clear his name from the Shin Corp scandal, and putting a tight time-frame on the snap election. These manoeuvres maximized the element of surprise and left the opposition with an insufficient interval to field candidates, mobilize funds, and prepare campaign platforms.

Faced with certain overwhelming defeat and with the lack of funds and preparation time, the Democrat, Chart Thai, and Mahachon parties of the opposition initially announced an outright boycott of the election. However, fear of public criticism and reduced credibility from their boycott decision, opposition parties later hedged their position by issuing an ultimatum to Thaksin demanding his agreement to a set modality and an agenda for constitutional reform in exchange for their electoral participation. Thaksin ostensibly agreed but on his own terms, with his own modality and reform agenda. Viewing Thaksin's countermove as disingenuous and sinister, the opposition proceeded with the boycott, sending Thai politics into a tailspin.

The unprecedented boycott was widely perceived as undemocratic and uncharacteristic of professional politicians. Above all, it ruled out the possibility of the opposition's takeover of government in the event Thaksin managed to hold and win the election on 2 April 2006 but is forced to resign thereafter, as only sitting MPs are eligible to lead the government. On the other hand, the boycott robbed Thaksin of electoral legitimacy as his TRT party would be the only major party in the contest. With the snap election in limbo, Thaksin proposed to extend the election timetable to allow for more preparation time, but the opposition baulked in response. The parliamentary process and electoral prospects were in disarray. The parliamentary opposition's rejection of the snap election reinforced the PAD's street-based opposition. The PAD ominously pegged 5 March 2006 as their next "D-Day" for Thaksin to resign. The anti-Thaksin coalition did not reveal what precisely it would do in the event Thaksin stayed on in office past the deadline. A host of senators also rounded up signatures to call for Thaksin's immediate resignation. Other pressure groups such as women's rights advocates and university students came out to demand Thaksin's resignation as well. Notwithstanding Thaksin's continuing support among grassroots electorate and the urban poor, he was unable to extricate himself from the escalating crisis because of his inability to clear his involvement in the scandalous sale of his family-owned Shin Corp to Temasek in a deal worth US$1.9 billion. All avenues of dissent thus appeared to be converging on his immediate resignation.

Conclusion: Implications for the Post-Thaksin Era

As Thailand's crisis escalated, it is instructive to recapitulate the crux of the matter. At issue was the minority's right to take Thaksin to task for lacking political legitimacy versus the majority's preferences for a populist leader who had both redressed the long-neglected needs and grievances of the rural grassroots and engaged in widely perceived corruption. To be sure, Thaksin exploited the long-standing income divide between Bangkok and the countryside to spectacular success by implementing a plethora of populist policies over his five-year rule, from universal health coverage and business start-up funds for rural villages to debt suspension for farmers. He promoted a visionary economic policy platform that included the targeting of growth industries such as automobiles, fashion, food, healthcare, and tourism. He displayed assertive leadership abroad by carving out his own space on the international stage with regional cooperation initiatives and counter-terrorism efforts, the latter contributing to Thailand's new-found status as a major non-NATO ally of the United States.

However, at the same time, there were serious shortcomings in governance and accountability. To his political opponents, anchored around the PAD, who were massing in the streets of Bangkok in February 2006 to demand his immediate resignation, Thaksin was an authoritarian leader dressed up as a democrat through the ballot box. He had abused power by usurping constitutional mechanisms, marginalized the parliamentary opposition, mishandled the violence in Muslim-dominated southern Thailand, intimidated civil society groups, turned state-owned electronic media into agencies for government propaganda for rural consumption, and converted power into profit for his family-owned business empire. To Thaksin's domestic critics, political legitimacy in Thailand required more than just electoral victory. It also should incorporate morality, ethics, and integrity, which had been absent from Thaksin's rule.

While public discontent with Thaksin's authoritarian tendencies and disguised corruption had been incubating for months, it burst to the fore after the Shin Corp scandal. The sale was the last straw that brought out anti-Thaksin protesters of all stripes, including the intelligentsia, middle classes, and civil society forces. The anti-Thaksin coalition thus broadened into a mass movement to eject the Prime Minister from office. The charges against Thaksin from this mass movement were constitutional violations, corruption, and even treason. To uphold accountability and minimize conflicts of interest, the reform-driven 1997 constitution barred holders of political office from owning or operating businesses. In cashing out on the family's telecommunications conglomerate, Thaksin insisted that his children were the signatory parties, an unacceptable explanation to his opponents. As the Shin-Temasek transaction involved labyrinthine share transfers and a nominee company in the British Virgin Islands, Thaksin was alleged to have taken advantage of domestic tax loopholes and insider information. Because Shin Corp's assets involved state concessions in sensitive and protected sectors, such as satellites, a mobile phone service, a television station, and a budget airline, the widely held perception is that their sale to a foreign company may have breached indigenous ownership laws and impinged on national security considerations. Ironically, the nationalist sentiment that Thaksin shrewdly cultivated in his rise to power was turning against him, his family, and associates.

What next for Thailand is a matter of conjecture. However, Thaksin's continuation in power appears untenable as long as he remains unable to explain the Shin Corp deal convincingly. With the opposition parties' boycott of the April 2006 snap election, Thaksin and the TRT could be deprived of post-election legitimacy. Thai politics is reaching a dead end as the PAD piled pressure on the recalcitrant Thaksin to resign. A power vacuum following Thaksin's likely departure would probably lead to intervention by Thailand's revered monarch. A caretaker government appointed by the King could oversee constitutional amendments to pave the way for new elections and the restoration of political order and legitimacy.[15]

As they are poised to overthrow Thaksin in the streets of the capital, the urbanite minority should not lose sight of Thailand's fledgling democratic rule and Thaksin's enduring legacy of focusing on the downtrodden countryside. They must do their utmost to shore up the provisions and institutions enshrined in the constitution and pay more attention to their rural brethren. They should not propel the likes of Mr Thaksin into power and overthrow him in the streets five years and two electoral triumphs later, and then rely on their ageing monarch to save the day. The rights of the minority to topple Thaksin came with a responsibility to bolster constitutional rule and to bridge the urban-rural divide, which brought Thaksin to power in the first place. A review of Thailand in 2005 demonstrates that Thaksin was in the business of power to promote both Thaksin Inc. and Thailand Inc.[16] By selling Shin Corp, whose price more than trebled during his time in power, Thaksin has cashed out on Thaksin Inc. The explosive political fallout from the Shin Corp scandal was also forcing Thaksin to abandon Thailand Inc., leaving subsequent governments to deal with the consequent policy disarray, social polarization, unfinished foreign policy ventures, and income and regional divisions exposed by the 2006 political crisis.

Notes

[1] For more details, see Thitinan Pongsudhirak, *Thai Politics After the 6 February 2005 General Election*, Trends in Southeast Asia series (Singapore: Institute of Southeast Asian Studies, March 2005).

[2] *Matichon sudsapda*, 1–7 April 2005, p. 10; Thitinan Pongsudhirak, "Thaksin's Second Chance in Thailand", *Straits Times*, 26 March 2005.

[3] "Annual Convention: Thaksin Calls for Reform of TRT", *Nation*, 25 April 2005.

[4] *Matichon sudsapda*, 29 April–5 May 2005, pp. 11, 13–14.

[5] "Easy Win for Suriya as 'Rebels' Hide", *Nation*, 30 June 2005.

[6] "Cabinet Reshuffle Announced", *Nation*, 2 August 2005.

[7] This section draws on "Thailand's Emergency Decree: No Solution", *International Crisis Group Asia Report*, October 2005; Rohan Gunaratna, Arabinda Acharya, and Sabrina Chua, *Conflict and Terrorism in Southern Thailand* (Singapore: Marshall Cavendish, 2005).

[8] *Matichon sudsapda*, 25 November–1 December 2005, pp. 9–12.

[9] One prominent case of the alleged tensions between Thaksin and the King concerned Jaruvan Maintaka, the Auditor-General whom the Senate tried to replace in vain because the King did not countersign to approve the new candidate. Many believed the Senate was doing Thaksin government's bidding in its failed attempt. See "Committee Agrees to Reinstate Jaruvan as Auditor-General", *Nation*, 16 February 2006.

[10] See http://www.nationmultimedia.com/specials/sondhi/.

[11] *Matichon sudsapda*, 27 January–2 February 2006, pp. 9–16.

[12] Thitinan Pongsudhirak, "Thaksin's Political Insurance Policy", *Bangkok Post*, 26 January 2006.

[13] *Matichon sudsapda*, 3–9 March 2006, pp. 9–12.

[14] This section draws on the *Nation*, various issues during 25 February–15 March 2006.

[15] Thitinan Pongsudhirak, "Thailand: Thaksin's Challengers Have Responsibilities, Too", *International Herald Tribune*, 14 March 2006.

[16] Thitinan Pongsudhirak, "Thailand: Democratic Authoritarianism", *Southeast Asian Affairs 2003* (Singapore: Institute of Southeast Asian Studies, 2003).

THAILAND'S INDEPENDENT AGENCIES UNDER THAKSIN
Relentless Gridlock and Uncertainty

Alex M. Mutebi

Present-day Thailand has a more stable and transparent political system than in the past, when frequent changes in government, often by military intervention, seemed to be the leitmotif of the Thai polity. The last coup in 1991, followed by events in May 1992, where security officers killed at least 50 unarmed civilians during street confrontations in Bangkok, shocked the Thai political system and stimulated a marked change in the kingdom's democratic consolidation. Since then, not only have the armed forces kept out of the operation of the civilian government, but there have also been five successful elections with peaceful transitions. In addition, Thailand's political party system has grown increasing stable over time. In January 2001, Thaksin Shinawatra's Thai Rak Thai (TRT) party almost won an absolute majority in the first general election under the new charter, and subsequently absorbed a variety of factions and parties into its fold.

During the February 2005 General Elections, TRT established the first-ever popularly elected single party administration as it convincingly defeated four other parties. The 2005 elections were a watershed in Thailand's democracy, as TRT's victory ensured the Prime Minister's hegemonic control over parliament and other key state institutions without the need for coalition partners, legitimizing his seeming insolence towards democratic consultation.[1] Whether one labels his regime as "semi-authoritarian", "soft-authoritarian", "diminished democracy", or simply "delegated democracy", there is little doubt that Thaksin's administration has shown greater authoritarian tendencies in comparison to his immediate

---

ALEX M. MUTEBI is Assistant Professor in the Lee Kuan Yew School of Public Policy, National University of Singapore.

predecessors. Thaksin's tenure has been characterized by frequent violations of Thailand's democratic institutions, so much so that his administration has been criticized as close to failing to meet conventional minimum standards for a true democracy.[2] Levitsky and Way coined the term "competitive authoritarianism", which is the most apt term to describe Thaksin's type of regime.[3] In this type of regime, violations of democratic criteria are both frequent and serious enough to give the incumbent unfair advantage over the opposition. The incumbent routinely abuses state resources, harasses the opposition, and denies them media coverage, and spies on, threatens, harasses, or even arrests government critics.[4]

This article examines one of the most significant consequences for Thai democracy of Thaksin's hegemonic control over the country's political institutions: the alleged manipulation of independent watchdog agencies by influential interests said to be aligned with the Prime Minister. It examines key milestones regarding four key agencies as examples in which the Thai legislature and judiciary — weak as they may be in the face of a powerful executive — have occasionally become focal points of opposition activity. Despite the fact that Thaksin's TRT enjoys a large majority in the Lower House, opposition and progressive forces, particularly in the Upper House, have used some institutions as arenas of democratic contestation. Likewise, judges in some parts of the judiciary have exploited the combination of their judicial independence and incomplete control by the executive to frustrate actions by the Prime Minister and those around him.

High Hopes for the Independent Bodies of the 1997 Constitution

A generally non-partisan assembly, selected in January 1997, re-wrote the nation's constitution, which was put into force in October of that year.[5] The document, which included 33 articles, contained the standard provisions one might find in the constitutions of Western polyarchies and, in some cases, even more. The constitution also restructured many aspects of both public and non-public sectors such as the legislature, electoral system, judiciary, cabinet, bureaucracy, and so on.

One of the main reforms of the new constitution was the establishment of a number of independent agencies to provide checks and balances in the political system. Among the most notable were those aimed at balancing and controlling administrative power (including a Constitutional Court, Administrative Courts, a National Committee on Human Rights, a State Audit Commission, and an

Ombudsman), as well as others aimed at balancing and controlling political power (including a national Election Commission [EC] and a National Counter Corruption Commission [NCCC]). Of all the new independent agencies, the latter two, that is, the EC and the NCCC, were the most controversial. In theory the government had no control over their work. Their members were to be appointed by a process intended to lessen political meddling, and they would exercise powers that had rarely been granted to unelected officials.[6]

The Election Commission, whose main function was to conduct elections and regulate political parties, was tasked with eliminating vote-buying. Among other duties, the Commission would investigate all alleged electoral fraud and disputes. In cases where its judges were convinced that fraud had occurred, the Commission was granted the power to order new elections or referendums in any or all polling stations. Likewise, the Commission was given the power to order re-elections, ban cheats from running again, or dissolve political parties that did not stick to regulations. Its rulings would not be subject to appeals.[7]

Politicians who made it past the Election Commission, along with most senior bureaucrats, were made accountable to the National Counter Corruption Commission through mandatory annual disclosures of their assets and liabilities. The Commission was granted the power to inquire and decide whether a public official had become "unusually wealthy", demonstrated corruption, or made a false or incomplete declaration.[8] The Commission could then bar the offender from office for up to five years, subject to the approval of the Constitutional Court.

The State Audit Commission, under the leadership of an independent and impartial Auditor-General, was to examine state expenditures for evidence of misappropriation of funds. Some its more specific duties included auditing all public receipts and payments each fiscal year; auditing the country's currency reserve account; and examining fees and other income of audited public agencies in connection with the collection of taxes. The Auditor-General was given commensurate search and seizure powers in the exercise of these duties.[9]

For its part, the Constitutional Court was to oversee and decide on all organic laws, bills, decrees, and ordinances under the new constitution.[10] Likewise, the new constitution established a completely new institution — the Administrative Court (with two subordinate courts: a Supreme Administrative Court and a Central Administrative Court) — to rule on cases between government departments or officials and private organizations or ordinary people, and between government departments or officials.[11]

The new constitution also created the Ombudsman's Office, which would oversee administrative problems by considering cases where state officials were accused of either failing to comply with the law, exercising powers beyond their authority, or failing to perform their duties — transgressions that would trigger independent recommendations to the Constitutional Court or the Administrative Court for further action.[12] Likewise, a National Human Rights Commission (NHRC) was established to safeguard human rights, primarily through examining allegations of violations and reporting findings to the National Assembly.[13]

Elsewhere, the constitution mandated two new independent bodies: the National Broadcasting Authority (NBA) and the National Telecommunications Authority (NTC), charged respectively with regulating the media and telecommunications sectors.[14] These agencies were supposed to reduce the domination of media, broadcasting, and telecommunications by a small number of small agencies and private owners.[15]

During Thaksin's tenure in office, most of the watchdog agencies have found themselves mired in seemingly endless leadership and operations struggles, due in large part to differences between the legislature, the judiciary, and the executive on the qualifications and legal process of appointing Commissioners. Although the Prime Minister has generally tried to stay publicly clear of these quarrels regarding appointments to these various watchdog agencies, his critics allege cronyism and political interference, particularly in the Senate.

Diminished Expectations under Thaksin: Four Recent Cases

While it is beyond the scope of this article to fully discuss all the ways in which independent agencies have been undermined during Thaksin's tenure, four agencies beset by problems critics claim are symptomatic of the cronyism, manipulation, political interference, and even outright capture by influential governmental figures will be examined.

State Audit Office

Perhaps no other political contest in recent years has involved progressive forces within the bureaucracy and civil society pitted against formidable vested interests both in and outside government quite like the so-called "Jaruvan affair". The Jaruvan affair not only symbolized a coordinated rearguard effort by vested interests to oust an honest and principled bureaucrat, Khunying Jaruvan Maintaka, from a top government post, but also exposed the diminishing integrity of key institutions in the Thai polity.[16] For her part, Jaruvan stoically challenged the network of influential governing politicians, well-connected civil servants, and business interests, many very close to Prime Minister Thaksin, who had managed to stall her appointment — and in turn, the full-functioning of the State Audit Office — for over four years.

The seeds of this particular saga were laid in July 2001 when State Audit Commission (SAC) chairman Panya Tantiyavarong submitted a list of three candidates for the Auditor-General post to the Senate. Jaruvan emerged as the preferred candidate, and subsequently received royal endorsement. By all accounts, Jaruvan was a formidable and well-respected graft-busting career bureaucrat who had unearthed some major shady political dealings, several concerning some of the biggest names in politics.[17]

Almost two years later, in June 2003, Senator Surapong Painual filed a rather unexpected petition with the Constitutional Court challenging the constitutionality of Jaruvan's appointment. A year after that, the Court returned a highly controversial ruling agreeing that the process leading to Jaruvan's appointment had been technically unconstitutional. The Court reasoned that Thailand's Constitution allowed the SAC to nominate only the person who had garnered the highest number of votes from a simple majority, not three people as had been the case when Jaruvan was nominated. The SAC suspended payment of Jaruvan's salary the following day and appointed a deputy Auditor-General as caretaker Auditor-General the day after. However, Jaruvan surprised everyone by vowing to remain in her post, reasoning that she had been legitimately appointed by royal decree and would only step down on royal command — thereby triggering one of the most intractable political contests in recent years. Not ducking from a fight, the SAC nominated Visut Montriwat, a former Deputy Finance Permanent Secretary, as the new Auditor-General in October 2004, and six months later, on 10 May 2005, voted to accept his nomination, with 107 senators in favour. The SAC subsequently announced on its website that Jaruvan was no longer Thailand's Auditor-General, citing the Constitutional Court ruling that her appointment had been unconstitutional.[18]

However, several months later, the speaker of the Senate, Suchon Chaleekrua, disclosed that he had in fact stealthily submitted Visut's nomination for Royal endorsement earlier in June. Some 60 ruling party members of parliament (MPs) under the veteran power-broker Snoh Thienthong's Wang Nam Yen's faction then upped the ante by protesting Suchon's move, only to back down and withdraw their signed petition following a stern warning from the Prime Minister. Even so, the warning apparently did not stop one former cabinet member and disgruntled

Wang Nam Yen faction MP, Pramuan Rujanaseri, from writing a local bestselling book, *Phra Ratcha-amnat* ("Royal Powers"), about the powers of the King in relation to the constitution and history. The book, thought to be an attempt to embarrass the government over the palace's long delay in sending back Jaruvan's nomination, prompted a group of TRT members to try and oust the rebel MP from the party's ranks over what they saw as his attempt to embarrass the Prime Minister by questioning his loyalty to the Thai royalty.[19]

In an attempt to quiet insinuations that the situation was only benefiting vested interests close to his administration, Thaksin was compelled to break his silence on the "Jaruvan Affair" when he indirectly denied any government involvement by emphasizing his unqualified allegiance to Thai royalty:

> This government serves under HM the King. We are more than 100 per cent loyal to His Majesty. We do everything to make His Majesty happy. … I graduated from the Pre-Cadet School and the Police Academy. … I went through a process that instilled in me a great sense of loyalty to the country and the monarchy.[20]

By all measures, this was a clever — some would say cynical — move timed to keep the Prime Minister's many critics at bay, at least for a while. However, Visut further muddied the political waters by unexpectedly asking that his nomination as the new Auditor-General be withdrawn.[21] Six days later, a group of 22 senators led by Kaewsan Atibhodi filed an urgent motion demanding that the Senate reaffirm Jaruvan's job status, paving the way for her reinstatement as Auditor-General.[22]

In the end, the State Audit Commission (SAC) unanimously agreed to restore Jaruvan to her position following the King's principal private secretary's communication to the SAC expressing the King's advice on this issue.[23] By unanimously agreeing that the King's appointment of Jaruvan was still in effect and that there was no resolution stripping Jaruvan of her position, the SAC essentially backed down. Indeed, the SAC was not only compelled to cease trying to find a new Auditor-General, but was also charged with informing Jaruvan and Senate Speaker Suchon about this resolution, and considering compensation for Jaruvan.[24]

The National Counter Corruption Commission

Much like the State Audit Commission, the NCCC has not been spared from various delays in properly setting up shop to carry out its mandate during Thaksin's administration. The delays have been due to alleged political interference and cronyism in various institutions, resulting in a seriously flawed selection process for NCCC Commissioners. Most of the backroom manipulation and contestation was done through the selection and confirmation process in the Senate. Often, progressive forces within the Senate used the democratic space the law accorded them to stave off the selection of close associates and friends of Thaksin to serve on the Commission.

To be sure, the very first NCCC, under the leadership of Klanarong Chantik, had won widespread accolades and public trust for its handling of alleged corruption cases. Its most memorable ruling occurred in January 2001, when it convicted Thaksin of concealing his assets.[25] In May 2005, however, the work of the NCCC came to a grinding halt after a historic ruling that found all Commissioners guilty of abusing their authority. This eventually prompted resignations — an ironic development given that the Commissioners were supposed to be the country's leaders in the fight against corruption.[26]

Months earlier, a judicial tribunal had found cause to suspect wrongdoing on the part of the NCCC following a charge by 203 senators and MPs that the Commissioners had awarded themselves substantial salary increments.[27] The tribunal then suspended the Commissioners and ordered prosecutors to initiate a trial. Based on the tribunal's ruling, prosecutors built a case under Article 157 of Thailand's Criminal Code, which deals with malfeasance. In March 2004 the NCCC Chairman General Wutichai Srirattanawuth and the eight Commissioners were summoned to appear at the Supreme Court for corruption and abuse of authority. They were subsequently suspended from duty and each given a suspended two-year jail term — a verdict that essentially put them under immediate pressure to resign.

The unanticipated termination of General Wutichai's Commission was significant for several reasons. First, the verdict against the NCCC Commissioners boded ill for members of the other watchdog agencies including those on the Constitution Court, Office of Parliamentary Ombudsman, and Election Commission (EC) — virtually all of whom had earlier raised their own salaries.[28] Citing the precedent of the NCCC case, lawmakers called for members of the other agencies to resign or face being dragged to court. Second, and more interesting, is that all this occurred at a time when the opposition was trying to set in motion a censure bid against the scandal-plagued Thaksin government. Indeed, the NCCC had about 7,000 pending corruption cases, including 20 against powerful political office-holders such as Education Minister Adisai Bodharamik and former Interior Minister Wan Muhamad Noor Matha. Other big cases included the Klong Tan water-treatment plant scandal and a high-stakes entrance-exam leak. Delays in setting up the NCCC invariably meant that some of those cases would eventually lapse (which they did) under the country's statute of limitations. Besides, the 1997 constitution required that any graft-related censure motion be accompanied by an impeachment motion — which must go through the Senate and the NCCC — the very organs in and around which democratic contestation between various political forces was unfolding.[29]

Following months of wrangling about which the Prime Minister said surprisingly little, the government spearheaded a controversial decision to change the composition of the NCCC as specified by the constitution. Under this decision, a legislative selection panel would second 18 new candidates from 80 nominated applicants for consideration by the 200-member Senate. Most of the short-listed candidates had close ties to senior government figures or their families, and in some cases, to the Prime Minister.[30] Five of these candidates were widely perceived as likely to take seats on the NCCC because of their extremely close ties with senior figures in the ruling TRT.[31]

On 1 November 2005, following hours of heated debate and a walkout by some protesting senators, the Senate predictably voted for nine nominees closely associated with senior government figures.[32] During the first round of voting, seven of the candidates won support from a majority of the Senate.[33] In the second round of voting, Sompote Kanchanaporn, Deputy Director of the National Intelligence Agency, and Naengnoi na Ranong, Deputy Secretary to the Prime Minister (and a relative of an aide to the premier's wife Pojaman), won the highest tallies.

The broadcasting and telecommunications commissions

In November 1997 the Thai government adopted a comprehensive Master Plan for the National Telecommunications Commission (NTC), which provided guidelines for the establishment of an independent and impartial regulatory body. However, no one could have predicted that the much-needed Commission would still not be up and running almost nine years later.[34] In January 2000, the government enacted the Organization of Frequency, Wave Allocation, and Supervision of Radio Broadcasting, Television, and Telecommunications Enterprises Act ("Frequency Law"), which paved the way for the creation of the NTC along with a sister agency, the National Broadcasting Commission (NBC). The two agencies were to supervise and regulate telecommunications and broadcasting activities. The NBC was given a constitutional duty to ensure and oversee the even-handed distribution of airwaves to all parties. The NBC was charged with drafting broadcasting laws that would help set national broadcast media plans, allocate frequencies, and grant licences. For its part, the NTC was to be responsible for regulating licensing, spectrum management, and supervision of the telecommunications sector. Thus the NTC would tackle such controversial issues as interconnection, competition, tariff rebalancing, and standards development.

For a while the implementation of the various institutional reforms in the telecommunication and broadcasting sectors seemed to be on track; however, the economic downturn in 1997, combined with the landslide election of Thaksin's populist TRT party, triggered what has since become an unending delay in the completion of critical reforms, including the establishment of the NTC and the NBC. Once again, a lack of transparency in the selection methods seems to have provided opportunities for certain government agencies and influential politicians to manipulate (or even capture) the policy directions of both telecommunications and broadcasting sectors. This prompted various progressive forces both within and outside the state to challenge the interests of various influential politicians — contestation that partly explains the delays in setting up the two commissions.

That the process of selecting the NTC's members started in August 2000 when about 70 people from all walks of Thai society filed applications to be NTC members is a case in point. A panel, appointed by the Prime Minister, was to select 14 applicants, seven of whom would then be chosen by the Senate to eventually run the NTC. One of the failed candidates for the NTC, Pramut Sutrabutra, brought the entire process to a halt when, in January 2002 the Administrative Court agreed with his claim that the selection process had been conducted unfairly.[35] The re-selection of the NTC proceeded in December 2003 when the Prime Minister's Office once again provided a short list of 14 names from which the Senate was to pick seven. However, the process (along with that of the NBC) was stalled again.[36]

Thaksin's government has long been suspected of manipulating the selection of the panellists of the NBC and the NTC. Several nominees for these independent agencies were well-known sympathizers or supporters of the government — a fact that Thaksin's critics point to as evidence of government manipulation.[37] Thus, when in January 2003 eight of the 17-member selection committee tasked with finding candidates for the NTC resigned *en masse*, the remaining committee members, who represented civic groups, tried to fight against Thaksin-led machinations favourable to big business.[38]

To be sure, the delays in the inception of these two independent bodies were but the first in a long series of postponements in implementing key institutional reforms in media and telecommunications. This postponed the need for the government to deal with controversial issues in these lucrative sectors. The delays meant that the planned telecommunication concession conversion process, launched under former Prime Minister Chuan Leepkai's administration, proceeded very slowly. Critics saw the process as having been designed to favour private telecommunication firms while generating huge losses for the then state-owned telecommunication agencies: Telephone Organization of Thailand (TOT) and the Communications Authority of Thailand (CAT).[39] Consequently, the stalled process postponed the government's original plan to list the TOT and CAT on the stock market by April and June 2002, respectively.[40] Separately, behind-the-scenes disputes also stalled the Telecommunications Business Operations Bill, which was meant to set guidelines and control the NTC's powers. The controversial Bill, which would repeal the 1934 Telegraph and Telephone Act, abolish the Post and Telegraph Department's monopoly rights in the market (rights which were transferred to CAT and TOT), and regulate licence distribution to private operators, then languished in the long wait for the Senate's consideration.

A fully constituted NTC was also supposed to deal with the controversial but critical article in the telecommunication law, which capped foreign ownership of local telecommunications firms at 25 per cent. Predictably, the large local telecommunications firms, many of them with foreign ownership in excess of that figure, were not in favour of such a cap. During Prime Minister Thaksin's first term, the Thai cabinet approved an amendment to that article in principle, but made little progress with its implementation. Whereas an army general, Chuchart Promprasit, was eventually elected as the first chairman of the NTC in September 2004, crucial time had passed that allowed for various vested interests to gain from the delay. The company believed to gain the most from the NTC deadlock, and in turn, the slow liberalization of the industry, was none other than Advanced Info Service (AIS), the cellular phone flagship of Shin Corporation, founded by the Prime Minister and controlled by his family until early 2006. The longer liberalization was delayed, the longer telecommunication giants such as AIS could exploit their favourable concessions and maintain an advantage over their rivals.[41]

Similar delays in staffing the NBC and the resultant policy vacuum also created opportunities for vested interests in broadcasting to exploit the state media. Under the media liberalization plan, the NBC was to supervise frequency allocation for community radio operations to producers to promote local service. Yet a number of so-called "community" radio stations began commercial operations without making concession payments to the state, notably in the Chiang Mai region, the Prime Minister's hometown.[42] The absence of any government clampdown on such operations suggests that powerful and well-connected interests controlled these radio outlets. After all, all terrestrial free-to-air television services were still in the hands of government agencies, the army, or well-heeled and politically well-connected business interests.

In June 2004 the Public Relations Department (PRD) of Thailand, a body under the Prime Minister's Office which, along with the Mass Communication Organization of Thailand (MCOT), controlled Thai broadcasting until very recently, launched three plans that came under virulent opposition by democracy activists, press freedom advocates, and campaigners for greater consumer protection. Critics claimed that the government was rushing these plans to allow vested interests to take advantage of the policy vacuum created by the absence of a fully functioning NBC.[43] The first of those plans called for privatizing the MCOT despite Article 40 of the constitution, which required the establishment of the NBC to regulate and distribute broadcast frequencies. In the end the MCOT was privatized and now trades on the Stock Exchange of Thailand (SET). The second plan called for awarding several satellite channels under the PRD's control to several politically connected firms, again, before the NBC had been set up to distribute or regulate public airwaves. The third plan called for allowing the early listing of a company controlled by army-run Channel 5. The firm, RTA Entertainment Plc, was owned by Channel 5 and a group of wealthy businesspeople and some military officers. General Chaisit Shinawatra, the then army chief and a cousin of the Prime Minister spearheaded this initiative, which included adjusting the company's balance sheet before floatation on the SET by transferring its debt to Channel 5 — itself a quasi-state enterprise and thus public property, and allowing RTA Entertainment to keep all the revenues from the sale of the TV station's services.[44] Following a huge outcry from activists, sections of the public, and parliamentary opposition, the Prime Minister was forced to intervene and suspend this particular plan. However, he also played for time by initiating a Commission of Inquiry instead of reprimanding the army commander who was in clear violation of the constitution. The fourth controversial but unsuccessful plan called for the creation of six additional satellite TV channels. This followed on the heels of another heated political tempest over two other channels previously created by the PRD.[45]

Members to staff the NBC were ultimately selected in 2005, only to be followed by an Administrative Court order later in the year nullifying the selection process because a member of the selection panel was not qualified. The chaos in the broadcasting sector brought to the fore questions about the willingness of the Prime Minister to do what was right, follow the rule of the law, and abide by the spirit of the constitution.[46] Some of the obvious beneficiaries from the delay included TV channels that were able to split their frequencies into more channels via satellite technology; Channel 11 which interpreted outdated regulations and laws in its favour; investors who bought shares in TV channels floated on the SET; agents and programme producers with political connections; and the Prime Minister's family-controlled Thaicom Satellite, which rented satellite transponders to TV channels. On the other hand, among the obvious losers from the delays were independent TV and radio programme producers, some of whom lost their licences or failed in their bids to acquire new ones — a move clearly designed to preclude the eventual NBC takeover on grounds that they did not handle their own production. Other losers included Thai taxpayers by virtue of their collective ownership of state-owned TV stations; legitimate but politically unconnected agents and programme producers; the local media industry which would be ill-prepared in a fully liberalized market following WTO requirements; and the country's reputation, as the media sector became polarized and corruption continued unchecked.[47]

Whither the Constitutional Checks and Balances?

Thailand's 1997 constitution married the aspirations of various competing reform forces in the Thai polity.[48] On the one hand, liberal activists sought not only legislation to keep pace with rapid social changes in the country, but also a complete overhaul of Thailand's dictatorial past where authorities were rarely responsive to the people. On the other hand, enlightened conservatives — disillusioned by corrupt politicians and governments toppled by military coups, the absence of political continuity, and expertise in managing the economy — mostly sought more government stability, albeit with more checks and balances on politicians.

The result was a comprehensive document reflecting this whole range of aspirations. The constitution set out to establish a system of checks and balances on government power, support the decentralization of authority to better empower the people, and encourage greater public participation in the political process. It explicitly emphasized a strong mistrust of those in authority and a commensurate determination to spread power thinly and scrutinize its exercise closely. In particular, it included major political, social, and economic reforms to help break powerful and long-entrenched special interest groups, give a greater voice to the disenfranchized and underprivileged, and establish a system of rules and regulations equally applicable to all. As part of the efforts to increase accountability and transparency and place limits on the power exerted by the key branches of the Thai state, notably the executive, the new constitution established a series of independent agencies with separate and independent powers and areas of responsibility. The constitution also included a Charter of Rights, provisions for impeachment, a Freedom of Information Act, and plans for liberalizing the state-dominated broadcasting, telecommunication, and electronic media.

In reality, however, the new constitution paved the way for the TRT government to subvert the original intention of the drafters of the constitution. For whereas the constitution aimed to balance the government's and the opposition's influence by having each party nominate representatives, in practice the TRT government used its majority to outweigh the opposing Democrats' influence. Thus, the power of some of the most influential of the purportedly independent bodies meant to balance government power has slowly eroded under the TRT. The Prime Minister's critics allege that various fledgling independent institutions have struggled to establish both their authority and their credibility largely because of undue influence of vested interests bent on maximizing their rewards at public expense.[49] In particular, critics allege that since coming to power in 2001, the TRT party has not only quietly built a majority in what is supposed to be a politically neutral Senate, but has also filled the various political parties and their factions with close acquaintances and relatives. The Senate has shown little hesitation in using its power to appoint political affiliates, relatives, and friends to various independent agencies.

However, despite Prime Minister Thaksin's attempts to put an authoritarian stamp on Thailand's institutions, various democratic institutions have offered important channels through which the opposition has continued to challenge his regime. Any authoritarian enterprise, the Thai Prime Minister's included, almost always comes up against important domestic obstacles including elite fragmentation, high costs in co-opting opponents, state weakness, and so on.[50] Indeed, various progressive forces in Thailand have regularly used the few remaining arenas such as the legislature, the judiciary, and the media to challenge, undermine, and even occasionally defeat various Thaksin initiatives that undermine the country's democratic ideals. For example, the opposition (which is outweighed by the TRT's majority in parliament and thus precluded from initiating censure motions against government politicians) has used the little political space available to it to call for amendments to the constitution as its lone recourse.[51] Elsewhere, members of civil society have tried to use the media to express their displeasure about the alleged shenanigans by the Senate, which they complain have only accelerated the decline in the credibility of the country's system of checks and balances.[52] For example, when the Senate erred by installing NCCC Commissioners who turned out to be lacking in principles, it not only did nothing to find better qualified nominees, but instead went ahead with the selection and confirmation of a new set of Commissioners who, because of their debatable backgrounds, won little trust from an increasingly disillusioned public.

Outside the media, the other significant arena of democratic contestation in Thailand has ironically been the Administrative Court, one of the independent agencies created by the 1997 constitution. In contrast to other watchdog bodies, the Administrative Court's Justices have been lauded for their probity, their rigour, constitutional values, and flexibility in implementing secondary laws that might infringe on public liberty or well-being.[53] These principles have all too often been overlooked, or virtually derided in some instances, by other constitutionally mandated watchdog agencies including the Constitutional Court, the NCCC, and the EC. From the moment the Administrative Court handed down a historic ruling in June 2002 on a scandal involving the Prime Minister's use of the Anti-Money Laundering Office (AMLO) for an illegal investigation into the banking transactions of journalists critical of his government, the Court has proven to be a key arena for questioning the abuse of state power.[54]

Conclusion

Using the examples of the National Counter Corruption Commission (NCCC), the State Audit Office, the National Broadcasting Commission (NBC), and the National Telecommunication Commission (NTC) this article has examined the consequences for Thai democracy of the ruling party's hegemonic control over the country's political institutions. The article has also highlighted how various arenas in Thailand's democratic fabric have become the focal points of opposition activity and democratic contestation.

To the extent that they continue to exist, the various arenas of political contestation in Thailand will bring out the contradictions in Prime Minister Thaksin's authoritarian project, forcing him to choose between egregiously violating the 1997 reformist constitution at the cost of both domestic conflict and international condemnation, and allowing challenges to his leadership style to proceed even at the cost of possible defeat.

Notes

1. Erick Kuhonta and Alex Mutebi, "Thaksin Triumphant: The Implications of One-Party Dominance", *Asian Affairs: An American Review* 33, no. 1 (2006).
2. Duncan McCargo, "Democracy under Threat in Thaksin's Thailand", *Journal of Democracy* 13, no. 4 (2002): 112–26; Pasuk Phongpaichit and Chris Baker, "Thaksin Dismantles the Opposition", *Far Eastern Economic Review*, 168, no. 3 (March 2005).
3. S. Levitsky and L. Way, "Elections Without Democracy: The Rise of Competitive Authoritarianism", *Journal of Democracy* 13, no. 2 (2002): 52–65.
4. Ibid., p. 53.
5. Led by Uthai Pimchaichon and Anand Panyarachun, the Constitution Drafting Assembly (CDA) comprised some 99 representatives: 76 delegates from each of Thailand's provinces, eight public law experts, eight political and public administration experts, and seven officials with experience in both drafting constitutions and laws, or in bureaucratic regulation.
6. *The Economist*, 28 February 2002.
7. Articles 136–48, Constitution of the Kingdom of Thailand BE 2540 (1997).
8. Articles 297–307, Constitution of the Kingdom of Thailand BE 2540 (1997).
9. Article 312, Constitution of the Kingdom of Thailand BE 2540 (1997).
10. Articles 255–70, Constitution of the Kingdom of Thailand BE 2540 (1997).
11. Articles 276–80, Constitution of the Kingdom of Thailand BE 2540 (1997).
12. Articles 196–98, Constitution of the Kingdom of Thailand BE 2540 (1997). The Organic Law on Ombudsmen came into force on 15 September 1999.
13. Articles 199–200, Constitution of the Kingdom of Thailand BE 2540 (1997). For more on the roles of the various bodies, see Pichet Soontornpipit, "Is a Culture of Accountability Developing in Thailand?" (paper presented at a conference hosted by the Center for Democratic Institutions (CDI), Canberra, Australia, 23 April 2002).
14. Article 40, Constitution of the Kingdom of Thailand BE 2540 (1997).
15. Duncan McCargo and Ukrist Pathmanand, *The Thaksinization of Thailand* (Copenhagen: Nordic Institute of Asian Studies Press, 2005), pp. 23–69.
16. "Thailand's Iron Lady: Jaruvan", *Nation*, 31 August 2005.
17. Ibid.
18. "Jaruvan 'Relieved of Duties'", *Bangkok Post*, 27 June 2005; and "OAG Says Jaruvan No Longer at the Helm", *Nation*, 27 June 2005.
19. Anand Panyarachun, "The King's Constitutional Powers and Beyond ...", *Nation*, 6 September 2005.
20. Jintana Panyaarvudh, "Thaksin Won't Have His Royalty Questioned", *Nation*, 9 September 2005.
21. "Impasse Eased After Surprise Move by Visut", *Nation*, 24 September 2005.
22. "Request to Reinstate Jaruvan", *Nation*, 30 September 2005.
23. "SAC Restores Khunying Jaruvan's Status", *Bangkok Post*, 5 February 2006.

24 Ibid.
25 For details on this conviction, see Paskuk Phongpaichit and Chris Baker, *Thaskin: The Business of Politics in Thailand* (Chiangmai: Silkworm Book, 2004); pp. 1–7.
26 "Graft-busters Guilty of Abuse of Malfeasance", *Bangkok Post*, 27 May 2005.
27 The chief prosecutor, Atthapol Yaisawang, alleged that the nine commissioners approved a monthly allowance of 45,500 baht for Wuthichai and 42,500 baht for the eight others, on 29 July 2004.
28 Suphon Thanukrit, Kornchanok Raksaseri, "NCCC Ruling Bodes Ill for Other Bodies", *Nation*, 27 May 2005.
29 Ibid.
30 Some of the more prominent names included Army Chief General Pravit Wongsuwan, who was soon scheduled to retire, Attorney-General Khampee Kaewcharoen, former Supreme Court Judge Prasert Khiannilsiri, former Supreme Court Judge Thiradet Meepian, Provincial Administration Department Director-General Siva Saengmanee, Agricultural Land Reform Office Secretary-General Adisak Srisanpakit, Auditor-General Office Deputy Governor Sajja Sasanavin, former National Intelligence Agency Director Pumarat Thaksadipong, former Defence Adjutant Department Director-General Chuchart Suksa-nguan, and Third Army Commander Lieutenant-General Picharnmet Muangmanee. Other, less well-known, names included Food and Drug Administration Secretary-General Pakdi Pothisiri, NESDB Deputy Secretary-General Santi Bang-aw, Foreign Ministry Deputy Permanent Secretary Chalermpol Ekuru, Tourism and Sports Ministry Deputy Permanent Secretary Pirom Simasathian, Finance Ministry Deputy Permanent Secretary Prakob Tantiyapong, former Land Transport Department Director-General Preecha Awprasert, Higher Education Commission Deputy Secretary-General Suchart Muangkaew, National Police Deputy Commissioner-General Police General Piya Jiamchaisri, National Police Assistant Commissioner-General Police Lieutenant-General Wanchai Srinualnid, Supreme Court Chief Justice Kulpat Ithithamwinit, and Criminal Court Deputy Chief Justice Santi Wongrattananond.
31 These are the outgoing Army Chief General Prawit Wongsuwan; the Provincial Administration Department Director-General Siva Saengmanee; Attorney-General Kampree Kaewcharoen; former adviser to the Prime Minister's Office Darun Sothibandhu; and a former judge, Prasert Khiennilsiri.
32 To be sure, some senators had felt that their colleagues in the majority had seriously erred when they rushed through the nomination and confirmation of the nine new commissioners even though the law required that 18 be considered. The eighteenth candidate, retired Army Chief General Prawit Wongsuwan, had withdrawn his candidacy just before the nomination process was finalized but the Senate inexplicably failed to comply with the law by replacing him with a new candidate.
33 In addition to Darun (one of the Prime Minister's former teachers at the police academy) and Siva (who had been promoted to one of the most coveted positions in

the Interior Ministry following TRT's victory in 2001, and had been a big defender of the government's handling of the Tak Bai incident in the deep south), Wanchai Srinualnad, a former assistant police commander (and a classmate of Thaksin at the police academy); Surapol Ekyokha, a Supreme Court judge; Sawai Janthasri, a senior Criminal Court judge; Kasemchat Naretseni, Chairman of the Defence Ministry's advisory board; and Somsak Kaewsutthi, Governor of Ayutthaya province (and a close confidant of Deputy Interior Minister Sermsak Pongpanit) were all elected to the Commission. Wanchai obtained 130 votes, the highest among the nominees, followed by Sawai (128), Siva (125), Somsak (116), Darun (112), Surapol (111), and Kasemchat (108). See Prapasri Osathanon, "NCCC List Full of PM's Friends", *Nation*, 2 November 2005.

[34] The Master Plan also called for the privatization of two state enterprises, the Communications Authority of Thailand (CAT) and the Telephone Organization of Thailand (TOT); the conversion of existing build-transfer-operate concessions into licences; and the gradual liberalization of Thailand's telecommunication market to competition.

[35] Separately, the court would later similarly rule against the selection process of the NBC, following another appeal from disgruntled NBC candidates. The original 17 members of the NBC selection panel were elected from representatives of groups registering for the contest. Six of them later resigned in response to complaints that the election was unfair. Three academics later filled some of the vacant seats on the nominating panel, but the delays continued in part because the election of those to fill the slots for non-governmental organizations (NGOs) was stalled. See "Judge Backs Lower Court", *Nation*, 14 January 2003, and "NBC Candidate Choices Nullified", *Nation*, 5 March 2003.

[36] The December 2003 nominees by the Prime Minister included General Songkram Tanavora, Deputy Supreme Commander; Paiboon Seingkong, Deputy Permanent Secretary, Ministry of Education; Ms Tananuj Tritipbutr, Deputy Permanent Secretary, Information Technology and Telecommunication Ministry; Worarak Chansamart, Legal Consultant to the Commerce Ministry; General Winai Pattiyakul, Secretary to the Security Council; Kobchai Dejharn, Telecommunication Engineering Division Chief, Institute of Technology Prachomklow Lad Krabang; Somchai Jitapankul, Electrical Engineering Division Chief, Chulalongkorn University; Ekachai Sangin, Dean of Faculty of Engineering, Chulalongkorn University; Narong U-thanom, Dean of Faculty of Engineering, Sri Pratum University; Chamnan Hokiat, Engineering Association of Thailand; Vallop Surakampoltorn, Electrical Electronic Computer Telecommunication and Information Technology Association; Sayant Chowpreecha, Information Technology Network Association; Anan Voranitipong, Telecommunication Association of Thailand; Ms Saree Ongsomwang, Comsumer Protection Foundation; Pairoj Polpetch, People's Right Protection Association; Ms Chantana Bansirichoti, Child Development Foundation and Torpong Selanont, Thai Association for the Blind.

37 Parista Yuthmanop, "Thaksin 'Weakening' Charter's Institutions", *Bangkok Post*, 28 January 2005; Veera Prateepchaikul, "Thaksin's NCCC Flip-flop Worrying", *Bangkok Post*, 6 June 2005.

38 Prior to the 12 January 2003 mass resignation, the NTC selection committee had consisted of 17 members from four groups (a) appointed representatives of state agencies: General Songkhram Thanaworn, Deputy Supreme Commander; Paiboon Siangkong, Deputy Permanent Secretary for Education; Chalor Khacharat, Inspector-General of the Transport Ministry; Wararak Chansamart, Legal Adviser to the Commerce Ministry; and General Winai Pattiyakul, National Security Council Secretary-General; (b) elected representatives of institutions of higher education that offer telecommunications courses: Thawil Puengma, of King Mongkut Institute of Technology, Lat Krabang; Athikom Kritsabutr, of Mahanakorn University of Technology; Chanin Wong-ngamkam, of King Mongkut Institute of Technology, Thon Buri; and Pisit Chankiatkong, lecturer at Rangsit University; (c) elected representatives of telecommunication or IT-related professions: Amarit Phumirat, of the Engineering Institute of Thailand; Kraisorn Pornsuthi, of the Telecommunications Association of Thailand; Anan Worathitipong, of the IT Network Association; and Manu Oradeedolchet, of the Thai Computer Industry Association; (d) elected representatives of non-profit telecommunication consumer groups: Pakdi Sirichanthakul; Sawaeng Boonruang; Visit Chavalitnititham; and Pratuang Yankoses. It was the members of the second and third groups that resigned in their entirety, while members of the fourth group tried to resist resigning. See "Mass Resignation from Telecom Panel", *Nation*, 13 January 2003.

39 Under concession conversion — which was a crucial aspect of market deregulation — existing concession payments would be turned into licence payments to level the playing field between existing telecommunication firms with new entrants.

40 One of the conditions of the conversion process was that the private telecommunication concessionaires would have to buy back their networks from the TOT and the CAT — something that the concessionaires stubbornly delayed, thus making it impossible for the TOT and CAT to value their assets for listing purposes.

41 "Indecisiveness Stalls Reforms", *Nation*, 13 February 2002.

42 Ibid.

43 "Battle Shifts to MCOT", *Nation*, 15 March 2004.

44 Chang Noi, "Tradition of Turning State Assets into Crony Wealth", *Nation*, 21 June 2004.

45 "Furore Kills New Channels", *Nation*, 23 June 2004.

46 "NBC Selection Process Was Against Law", *Nation*, 24 November 2005.

47 "Academics: PM Must Act", *Nation*, 28 June 2004.

48 Borwonsak Uwano and Wayne D. Burns, "The Thai Constitution of 1997 Sources and Processes", *University of British Columbia Law Review* 32, no. 2 (1998): 227–47.

49 "Insidious Threat to Democracy", *Nation*, 4 November 2005.

50 Levitsky and Way, op. cit., pp. 62–63.

51 "Democrats Seek Help to Amend Charter", *Nation*, 25 April 2005.
52 "Public's Been Cheated", *Nation*, 3 June 2005; "Watchdogs Weakened in Crisis", *Bangkok Post*, 21 November 2005; Somroutai Sapsomboon and Kornchanok Raksaseri, "Cash Is King in the Upper Chamber, Senators Say", *Nation*, 11 February 2006.
53 See "Somroutai Sapsomboon, "An Island of Prosperity", *Nation*, 6 November 2005; and Opas Boolom, "The Country's Last Truly Independent Organization?" *Nation*, 6 November 2005.
54 Kesinee Taengkiew, "'Nation' Wins Key Battle over AMLO", *Nation*, 21 June 2002; and "The 'Thaksingate' Verdict Is a Victory", *Nation*, 26 June 2002.

TIMOR LESTE

TIMOR LESTE
On a Path of Authoritarianism?

Jacqueline Siapno

Scholars, journalists, and political analysts observing East Timor for the past 20 to 30 years and visiting East Timor in 2005 comment that things seem to have become more "disheartening": the local people are more angry towards the *malaes* (foreigners), more disillusioned with the government, the political elite, and emerging Timorese capitalists; members of civil societies and non-governmental organizations (NGOs) are more worried about the narrowing of spaces for pluralistic visions, opposition, and dissent; ex-Falintil[1] veterans are feeling more betrayed by the lack of acknowledgement of their contributions to the independence resistance struggle; armed forces soldiers have abandoned their barracks in Metinaro claiming discrimination and inequality; and citizens genuinely are concerned that the path to nation-building and democratization is increasingly signalling an authoritarian Mozambique-style suppression of opposition and freedom of speech.

Politically, East Timor is a fascinating study of democratization processes in a conflict/post-conflict context, in addition to being a paradoxical case study of the United Nation's mixed performance and most extensive involvement in nation-state building and peacekeeping in Asia and the Pacific. The country is currently undergoing serious challenges to freedom of speech and judicial sector reform, with a centralistic and rather insecure state trying to control, censor, and regulate NGOs, civil society, media, and opposition parties. As an example, one of the most widely discussed issues between the government, the judicial sector, and civil society at the moment is the re-introduction of the defamation

---

JACQUELINE SIAPNO is a Joint-Lecturer in Political Science and the Asia Institute, University of Melbourne. She has been living and working in East Timor and Australia since July 1999 and has worked for political movements and women's groups in East Timor — as Lecturer in Universidade da Paz, as former Vice-Rector I in Universidade Dili, and as consultant and adviser to local and international NGOs.

law in the East Timor Penal Code. A defamation law (somewhat akin to the "Internal Security Act" in Singapore and Malaysia), which was criminalized by the Indonesian occupation and used under the "Subversion Law" to imprison independence resistance leaders, and was de-criminalized by the United Nations Transitional Administration in East Timor, or UNTAET (Executive Order No. 2000/2) under Sergio de Mello, is being reinstated by the Prime Minister Mari Alkatiri and the Council of Ministers in a move seen within opposition circles as intended to silence opposition in the country prior to the 2007 legislative and presidential elections. Under Indonesian occupation, it was better known as *pasal-pasal penghinaan*. These "elastic laws" (*pasal karet*) — so-called because they were so wide-ranging, arbitrarily applied, and elastic — included "engaging in an act or an activity which indicates sympathy for the enemies of the Republic of Indonesia ..." (Article 13 UU No. 11/PNPS/1963); "whoever defames, insults or intentionally deviates from the State Ideology of Pancasila or discredits the authority of the State or the Head of State or any apparatus of the State"; or "spreads, gives rise to and perpetuates enmity, separatism, conflict, disorder, a state of unrule, or anxiety among the population" (Article 13 UU No. 11/PNPS/1963).

The United Nations subsequently de-criminalized this law.[2] However, at the seventy-second meeting of the East Timor Council of Ministers on 7 May 2004, the following decision was made in relation to the re-criminalization of defamation in East Timor, reversing Executive Order No. 2 by UNTAET:

> Following the decision of 19 February 2004, the Council of Ministers renewed their discussions about the proposed law on the criminalization of defamation presented by the Minister of Justice. This objective of the proposal is to end the situation of impunity, for whoever commits defamation or injures someone's reputation, and to reinstate the law set out in Articles 310–321 of Chapter 16 of the applicable Penal Code. The Council of Ministers partially approved the substance of the law, and decided to improve on the preamble.

While President Xanana Gusmao has yet to promulgate the defamation law, Prime Minister Mari Alkatiri is already using it as a threat, summoning opponents for interrogation via the Prosecutor General's office, in an apparent attempt to silence opposition. The first opposition leader to be subjected to the controversial defamation law making it a crime to criticize the Prime Minister is Fernando de Araujo, President of Partido Democratico (PD), the second largest political party in East Timor, and a former clandestine resistance leader of the Resistencia Nacional dos Estudantes de Timor Leste (RENETIL), who was tried and imprisoned for almost seven years under the "Subversion Law" during the Indonesian occupation.[3]

This article provides a historical background before reviewing the developments in East Timor in 2005. It investigates the government's increasing authoritarian tendencies and its attempts at foreclosing public space for democratic discussion. Next, issues with regard to foreign relations with its two immediate neighbours, Indonesia and Australia, are examined. The article then looks into the efforts on poverty reduction, and human security. Finally, the article examines the in-between spaces in the politics of culture, memory, and identity, and the resilience of the East Timorese.

Historical Background

East Timor is the world's newest country, gaining its official independence on 20 May 2002, after a UN-sponsored referendum to integrate or separate from Indonesia in 30 August 1999, in which the majority of East Timorese voted for independence. A country of less than one million people, it shares the tropical island of Timor with a province belonging to Indonesia (West Timor). The island of Timor was divided between the Portuguese, who first came to the island in the 16th century and stayed on to colonize the country up to 1975. The Dutch took over West Timor, which became part of newly independent Indonesia in 1949.

East Timor is a unique country in the sense that indigenous belief systems and practices, especially in the central mountain highlands, have been highly resilient, but it is also adaptive to a mix of migrations from Ceylon, China, Arab, Papua, Pacific, and the Malay peninsula, and to colonization and occupation by the Portuguese and Indonesians. There are numerous local languages spoken in Timor, the more dominant ones being Tetum, Indonesian, Portuguese (declared as the official language by the current Republica Democratica de Timor Leste or RDTL government), and English (used primarily by the development organizations, donor communities, and urban elite diaspora Timorese educated in Australia, England, and America). East Timor extends over 14,610 km.² covering 12 districts, plus the enclave of Oecussi-Ambeno, the island of Atauro, and the island of Jaco near Tutuala in Lautem. Contrary to colonial perspectives that it is "too small a country" to be significant, in fact in terms of physical geography it is larger than dozens of other countries in land mass, including Brunei, Hong Kong, and Singapore.

While it may be the world's newest nation-state, according to more recent significant archaeological explorations and findings by Australian, American, and Indonesian scholars, the Lene Hara and Ilik kere-kere caves near Com and Tutuala in Lautem and other excavations reveal that East Timor holds the oldest evidence of human civilization in Southeast Asia, dating back 35,000 years.[4] Local Timorese guardians of the caves in Tutuala argue that while Portuguese and Indonesian archaeologists have known about these historical cultural heritages, it was not in their interest to make it public. On the contrary, they did their best to keep it secret as it went against their justification to colonize East Timor for it was supposedly "uncivilized". Yet another myth is that East Timor is "isolated". While this might have been true during the Indonesian occupation from 1975 to 1998, the French historian and geographer Frederic Durand argues that in examining European, Chinese, Arab, and Malay documents since the 11th century, he found that Timor had been at the crossroads of trade in sandalwood and spices, different migrations to the island (from Ceylon or present-day Sri Lanka, Papua, and the Malay peninsula), and of travellers going to and from Australia.[5]

East Timor had been on the United Nations General Assembly agenda for 24 years before agreement was reached between Portugal and Indonesia on a process of self-determination. After the overwhelming vote for independence in 30 August 1999, there followed an orgy of violence and severe destruction of property, leading to East Timorese fleeing their homes, setting up refugee camps, and becoming internally displaced persons (some temporarily, others permanently) within the country (in Dare and elsewhere) and outside the country (in West Timor, primarily in Atambua and Kupang). Others were evacuated to a temporary refugee shelter in Darwin on 11 September 2001, along with the last United Nations Transitional Mission in East Timor (UNAMET) officials evacuating the country. Indonesia was pressured to consent to an Australian-led, UN-mandated, multinational force, the International Force for East Timor (INTERFET) of about 8,000 soldiers, to restore order. Since UNAMET, which oversaw the East Timor Popular Consultation in 1999, the Security Council mandated a subsequent mission, the UNTAET, to administer the territory pending elections and the installation of a sovereign independent government. When the first government of Timor Leste was installed on 20 May 2002, the United Nations remained to assist in the form of the United Nations Mission of Support in East Timor (UNMISET).

An article by Ian Martin, former Head of UNAMET, on the role and performance of the United Nations in East Timor is much more critical than mainstream UN analysis. He acknowledges, for example, that in the UNTAET-sponsored elections for the Constituent Assembly in 2001, "the timescale for the transition process was short, civic education was limited, and new political parties had little time to establish themselves".[6] Opposition parties and independent analysts have been arguing for a long time that the 2001 elections were not a "level playing field". On the contrary, they claim that the United Nations supported the pre-determined victory of one dominant ruling party majority (that is, Fretilin — Frente Revolucianário de Timor Leste Independente, or Revolutionary Front for an Independent East Timor) as part of a clean exit strategy. Martin also writes: "While UNTAET secured independence in a short period, its contribution to sustainable self-government and a democratic political environment was limited."[7]

Timor Leste's structure of government involves a semi-presidential system, with the principle of separation of powers between the executive, judiciary, and legislature. The legislature is a unicameral system where members of the national parliament are elected for five years through a proportional representation system. While the president is the commander-in-chief of the armed forces, in practice most executive power is in the hands of the prime minister (as approved by the national parliament in the Constitution of the Democratic Republic of Timor Leste in 2002), with the current president having mostly ceremonial roles and moral authority. The prime minister, ministers, vice-ministers, and secretaries of state constitute the executive government. A civil service has been established, with 12,000 civil servants, half of them teachers, subject to the Statute of the Civil Service Act 2004 setting out their duties and responsibilities as civil servants.

Lack of Space for and Acknowledgement of Critical Problems

A recent UN report to the Security Council states that "time will be required for democratic governance ... to take root in the country".[8] The report notes that a "major challenge facing Timor Leste in the near future will be the forthcoming presidential and parliamentary elections in 2007".[9]

While there were more than 13 political parties that participated in the first Constituent Assembly elections for members of parliament in August 2001, the multi-party system is rather weak. The ruling party, Fretilin, controls 55 out of 88 seats in parliament. The rest of the seats went to opposition parties including the Partido Democratico, seven seats; Social Democrat Party of East Timor (Partido Social Democrata Timor Lorosa'e) six seats; and Timorese Social Democratic Association (Associação Sosial Demokrata Timorense), six seats.[10] The opposition parties hardly have any power in terms of number of votes to enact important legislation, but have a lot of moral authority in providing checks-and-balances, enlivening critical debate, and making sure the space for dissent in the public sphere is not totally annihilated.

Contrary to more sanitized official reports put out by the UNMISET to the UN Security Council on the "peacefulness" and "orderliness" of UN-monitored nation-building, reconstruction, and development in East Timor,[11] the *suco* elections[12] from December 2004 to September 2005 administered by Technical Secretariat for Election Administration (STAE) and the Ministry of State Administration, provoked surprise among independent foreign electoral observers, including UNMISET Political Affairs officers, who did not predict a landslide victory by Fretilin.[13] Due in part to poor electoral administration,[14] and in several cases alleged rigging of ballots and corruption, the Commission on Elections ordered re-election in several districts. As for the *suco* elections 2005 data: Fretilin received 56.98 per cent of the votes, the majority from Dili; PD garnered 10.75 per cent, the majority from Dili. PSD got 6.62 per cent, majority of which were also from Dili. The smaller parties received less than 2 per cent of the votes each. Meanwhile, individual candidates got 22.10 per cent of the votes.[15]

Mainstream media reports, opposition parties' submissions to the Commission on National Elections (CNE), press conferences by the CNE, international observers' documentation and reports (for instance, by the National Democratic Institute), and NGOs and civil society reports provide a plurality of perspectives on the 2005 *suco* elections process. These perspectives are not captured in the STAE's and UNDP Support to Suco Elections reports. In a press release on 20 September 2005 on the *aldeia* elections in Dili and Liquica, for example, STAE reported that "election day has largely been a success". Similarly, the Security Council Progress Report (for the period 13 May to 15 August 2005) provided by Mr Hasegawa to the UN Secretary-General states under section II "Recent Political and Security Developments in Timor-Leste" that "the elections were conducted in a peaceful and orderly manner".[16] Alternative sources of information, on the other hand, including alternative media, civil society, NGOs, and opposition parties involved in the elections, provide very different accounts of intimidation of rural villagers by Fretilin, manipulation of the number of votes, tampering with ballots, switching photos of candidates on the ballot boxes, conducting a disinformation campaign against opposition leaders and parties, and allegedly the use of huge numbers of civil servants and government facilities under the Ministry of State Administration to "administer" the elections, with a key target of ensuring that the ruling party (Fretilin) wins.

For truly democratic societies to develop, it is highly important to allow, create, or generate a plurality of discursive spaces, including "non-state spaces" for citizens to articulate their political perspectives. In various analyses of democratization and reconstruction in newly independent, regime transition, conflict/post-conflict societies, it is "normal" for citizens to have differences in opinion and views different from those of the ruling party. It is part of the process of democratization to allow these to be generative, rather than producing a mono-culture of one-perspective only, which the Indonesian New Order regime nurtured and which many continue to hope will not be repeated again in East Timor.

Foreign Relations

In 2005 the most pressing foreign affairs issues in East Timor related to its two immediate neighbours — Indonesia and Australia.

At the end of 2005 the Commission for Reception, Truth and Reconciliation[17] (CAVR) completed its final report. The East Timor Parliament set up the CAVR with the mandate of establishing the truth about the human rights violations committed in Timor Leste between 25 April 1974 and 25 October 1999, facilitating community reconciliation, and reporting on its findings. The final report is made publicly available on the website of the International Centre for Transitional Justice, at http://www.ictj.org. The President, Xanana Gusmao, initially refused to circulate the report, which provoked severe criticism from civil society groups, opposition political parties, and former members of the CAVR itself. In favour of a more conciliatory approach to Indonesia, the President and government of RDTL instead founded a "Truth and Friendship Commission" (TFC) to be based in Bali, and composed of both Indonesian and East Timorese "reconciliation" experts. Critical foreign observers, scholars, and local and international NGOs have dubbed the commission the "truth and fried chicken commission", commenting on the lack of will from the TFC to follow up on the CAVR's recommendations. Historians and scholars who painstakingly worked on conserving the historical archives and testimonies of hundreds of witnesses are concerned about the CAVR archives' fate, especially as the documents contain information about atrocities that were also committed by Fretilin, which is now the ruling party.

On the economic front, Indonesia continues to dominate East Timor's trade relations. Indonesian products (from infrastructure and construction materials to Supermie noodles and Bimoli cooking oil) flood the market. Smuggling in the borders (in Oecussi, Suai, and Maliana) is a common phenomenon, despite efforts by border control to prevent it.

In 2004 Timor-Leste imported goods worth US$113 million while the only offsetting export was US$7 million worth of coffee. Of its imports, US$52 million consisted of foodstuffs, including US$12 million for rice, US$9 million for livestock and fish products, and US$9 million for fruits, vegetables, and nuts.[18]

Meanwhile, Australian–East Timor historical, economic, and political relations are complex and can be gauged from divergent perspectives. Official perspectives tend to focus on Australia's role in "securing independence" for East Timor by sending INTERFET forces in September 1999, led by General Peter Cosgrove. Little is said of the Australian government's de facto or de jure recognition of Indonesia's illegal occupation during a quarter century.

> During that time, the general Canberra line was to characterize Timorese resistance to integration as perverse and absurd, and that Indonesian rule in East Timor was basically well intentioned and would in the long run benefit the population.[19]

More progressive Australians acknowledge a kind of "debt of gratitude" to East Timorese assistance to Australian troops in World War II, and a sense of ethical responsibility to return the favour by supporting East Timor's struggle for independence and nation-building process. This international solidarity, primarily initiated by the Australian individuals and civil society groups, in particular in larger cities such as Melbourne and Sydney where there are thousands of Timorese immigrant and refugee communities (in Melbourne alone there are more than 8,000 East Timorese), is perhaps best exemplified in the grassroots network of groups such as the Timor Sea Justice Campaign based in Melbourne.[20] The campaign has been committed to providing independent information on oil and gas offshore resource sharing between Australia and East Timor to ensure that the East Timorese get their fair share of the revenues.

The Timor Sea Agreement between Australia and East Timor continues to be a highly contentious economic and foreign affairs issue. On 12 January 2006, the Australian and East Timor governments signed the Timor Sea Agreement for the joint exploration of the Timor Sea. Opposition political parties in East Timor declared that the agreement "is not in the best interest of Timor Leste and its people".[21] The opposition parties expressed their concern about the postponement of negotiations on the establishment of maritime boundaries between Timor Leste and Australia, arguing that it can bring disadvantages and possible loss of Timor Leste's legitimate rights to the Exclusive Economic Zone that belongs to Timor Leste by international law. They demanded that the government of Timor Leste, and members of the national parliament, not abdicate the rights of Timor Leste in the Exclusive Economic Zone and to continue to insist on the continuation of negotiations with Australia for a rapid and just solution in the definition of the boundary of the Timor Sea. Civil society and environmental groups have made appeals to the Australian government to:

... be fair and just and fully respect the international rights and laws in existence. As a rich country, Australia does not need the resources and riches of the Timor Sea. On the other hand, Timor Leste depends on them to be able to eradicate poverty, illnesses and misery that affect our country and our people.[22]

On other aspects of foreign relations, East Timor continues to attend the ASEAN Ministerial Meetings as guest of the host country. Apparently its application to become a member of ASEAN is blocked by the Myanmar government, which claims that many of the East Timorese government leaders (in particular the Foreign Minister) are close friends and supporters of Aung San Suu Kyi.

"Poverty Reduction": Can One Truly Reduce Poverty?

"Poverty reduction" has become a paradox in an oil/gas/natural resources–rich country such as East Timor. Material poverty and food insecurity continue to be problems especially in the rural districts, aggravated by severe damages to crops caused by rainstorms and natural disasters. The country also continues to be highly dependent on foreign aid and donor money. Sustained economic growth will be a primary requirement for tackling poverty. Economic growth has fallen from 15 per cent in 2001 to 3.4 per cent in 2004. Economic growth in 2005 was negative because of lack of investment. The annual budget for 2004–2005 was US$86.96 million, which included a supplementary budget of US$3.9 million made in December 2005.[23] The total budget for fiscal year 2006 amounts to US$132.2 million split into the four categories of expenditures: US$29.4 million for salaries and wages, US$59.6 million for goods and services, US$6.3 million for minor capital, and US$36.9 million for capital and development.[24]

According to the *Timor Leste Human Development Report 2006*, "lifting all of Timor-Leste's poor out of poverty would take US$18 million per year". Around 40 per cent of the people live on less than US$0.55 per person per day. In conjunction with the United Nations pushing for its Millenium Development Goals, the government of Timor Leste's National Development Plan claims to aim to eradicate extreme poverty and hunger by reducing the percentage of poor people living on less than US$1 per day from 21 per cent in 2001, to 14 per cent in 2015.

A World Bank report states that Timor Leste is one of the poorest countries in the world:

The Gross Domestic Product per capita is US$405, with one in five people living on less than one dollar per day and two in five living below the national poverty line. Inequality is also high, with the poorest 40% of the population having an expenditure share of less than 18%. Two out of five adults are illiterate, half of the children under five are stunted and the under-five mortality rate is 83 deaths per 1,000 live births. In urban areas, around 70% of the population has access to electricity and safe drinking water, but in rural areas, access rates are only 43% for drinking water and 11% for electrification. Moreover, high fertility and population growth rates compound the challenges of improving the welfare of the poor in Timor-Leste.[25]

The Ministry of Health states that Timor Leste has one of the highest maternal mortality rates in the Southeast Asian region: an estimated rate of between 420 and 800 mothers die out of every 100,000 live births, due to complications related to the pregnancy, delivery, or early post-delivery. The high rate of infant mortality is mainly due to problems related to the low birth weights and infections.[26]

According to the *Timor Leste Human Development Report 2006*:

Children's health is especially vulnerable: out of every 1,000 live births, around 90 infants die before their first birthday and approximately 136 children die before their fifth birthday. Mortality rates are particularly high in the rural highlands: 15% of children die there before their fifth birthday, compared with around 7% in the major urban centres. Many of these child deaths are related to malnutrition: 43% of children under five are underweight, 47% are stunted and 12% are wasted. Other children die from immunizable diseases: some 58% of children under two have never been immunized and 95% of children are not fully protected. Many children also suffer from diarrhoea and acute respiratory infections. According to UNICEF's Multiple Indicator Cluster Survey, more than half of the children experienced some form of illness in the two weeks preceding the survey and very few parents followed recommended remedial curative procedures.[27]

The relationship between poverty, underemployment, and unemployment continues to be debated, as it is not so much a lack of employment that is the issue, but the fact that human resources continue to rely heavily on the rule of foreign experts and advisers who focus on "capacity building" among the Timorese, with much of the donor money going back to the donors' countries via their experts. For example, some contributions from the European Community (EC)

TABLE 1
Comparison of Timor-Leste's Human Development Index with Clusters of Countries

	Timor-Leste 2004*	East Asia Pacific 2003	South Asia 2003	Least Developed Countries 2003	Developing Countries 2003	High Income OECD 2003
Life expectancy at birth (years)	55.5	70.5	63.4	52.2	66.0	78.9
Adult literacy rate (age 15 and over, %)	50.1	90.4	58.9	54.2	76.6	—
Combined primary, secondary, and tertiary gross enrolment (%)	66	69	56	45	63	95
GDP per capita (PPP US$)	732*	5,100	2,897	1,328	4,359	30,181
Life expectancy index	0.508	0.76	0.64	0.45	0.67	0.90
Education index	0.554	0.83	0.58	0.50	0.72	0.98
GDP index	0.217	0.71	0.67	0.60	0.70	0.86
Human development index	0.426	0.768	0.628	0.518	0.694	0.911

*Estimated based on the latest data from Census 2004.
Source: UNDP, *Timor Leste Human Development Report 2006*, p. 11.

stipulate that the experts are to come from the EC. Similarly, Japanese experts also dominate Japan-funded projects.

East Timorese have begun to leave the country to look for work as factory workers in Ireland, or as unskilled labourers in Korea, Malaysia, and other countries. The Ministry of Labour and Solidarity has now hired a "labour migration adviser" to draft new regulations on what to do with increasing labour migration abroad. The current Ministry of Agriculture and Fisheries, according to one of their senior advisers, seems to have little imagination and initiative in terms of developing a more pro-active agricultural development policy in the rural sector. A World Bank Report in 2005 on youth and unemployment states that there has been an increase in the number of young people leaving the rural districts and moving to Dili to live in increasingly overcrowded neighbourhoods in the hope of finding income-generating activities in Dili.

Furthermore, the *Timor Leste Human Development Report 2006* states that:

> Each year, about 14,000 young people enter the labour force, swelling the ranks of the unemployed. In 2001, unemployment among youth (15–24 year olds) was 15% overall — and about 43% among those in the labour force in Dili and Baucau. As the economy continues to stagnate, so the employment situation has worsened; by 2004 the unemployment rate had increased to 8.9%, with 23% among the youth (2004 Census of Population and Housing). Many people are also underemployed, especially in the agricultural and informal sectors. The 2004 Census shows that 88% of the total 293,348 working population were engaged in self-employment or subsistence farming. Faced with limited prospects at home, a few of the more enterprising youth are migrating to seek their fortunes in foreign lands: according to the Ministry of Development and Environment, an average of about 800 of Timor-Leste's young people are leaving the country each year looking for opportunities abroad.[28]

The most serious threat to economic development is perhaps corruption, which threatens the more established nation-states in Southeast Asia, but in a three-year-old country such as East Timor, where the civil society and political institutions are weak and in the process of developing, its effects could seriously be debilitating. The Office of the Ombudsman and Prosecutor-General could be more independent and strengthened, and there needs to be serious accountability and transparency mechanisms on the part of the executive to tackle and prosecute corruption, not to mention stronger legislature and civil society organizations committed to fighting corrupt practices. A World Bank report states that the external audit functions are weak and that the risks of corruption in East Timor are high.[29]

TABLE 2
Selected Indicators for the Rural Population by Region, 2003

	East	Central	West	National
Demographics				
Rural households (thousands)	45	61	33	139
Subsistence households (thousands)	36	7	10	54
Average size of household	4.3	5.0	4.5	4.7
Total population (thousands)	184	290	140	614
Children under age 15 (thousands)	79	142	63	284
Poverty				
Poverty headcount (%)	32	49	48	44
Population below the poverty line (thousands)	59	143	46	268
Food Security				
Inadequate consumption (% of population)	66	68	54	64
Population (thousands)	121	197	76	394
Agricultural labour force (thousands)	72	113	55	241
Education				
Illiteracy rate (% 15 years and above)	55	58	62	58
Population illiterate	58	86	48	192
Basic Services				
Drinking water (% of population)	50	48	32	45
Sanitation (% of population)	25	39	30	33
Electricity (% of population)	16	10	9	12
Agriculture				
Total agricultural land (thousand hectares)	61	139	41	241
Total irrigated land (thousand hectares)	28	17	7	52
Agricultural land irrigated (%)	46	13	17	22
Per capita agricultural land (hectares)	0.33	0.48	0.29	0.39
Per capita irrigated land (hectares)	0.15	0.06	0.05	0.08

Source: UNDP, *Timor Leste Human Development Report 2006*, p. 26.

Most reconstruction and development consultants have tended to categorize the majority of East Timorese as "impoverished", without paying more attention to resilience, social capital, and social cohesion. Yet for an observer who has had the opportunity to travel extensively in East Timor, the social and cultural life, linguistic diversity and complexity, ritual and indigenous belief systems of ordinary villagers signify something different. East Timor has a wealth of resources and social capital: instead of being mono-lingual, it is multi-lingual, instead of a mono-culture, it is multi-cultural, both regionally and internationally (through Portuguese and Indonesian colonization and Chinese, Indian, Arab, and Malay trade).

Insecurities

Besides the official government rhetoric on "security", alternative definitions of security provide a more critical analysis of sources of insecurity in 2005. There are several internal sources of insecurity in East Timor today. Among them the April 2005 eruption of mass demonstrations organized by the Catholic Church against the RDTL government, but primarily directed against the Prime Minister Mari Alkatiri, concerning the issue of separation of church and state and whether or not religious education in schools should or ought not to be compulsory. There has been no resolution, and relations between the Catholic Church and the government have been tense, including one case where a priest, Domingos Soares Maubere, was reported in newspapers to be giving sermons telling people not to vote for Fretilin again as they were allegedly communists who planned to eradicate priests and nuns.[30]

Other sources of insecurity come from groups such as CPD-RDTL, led by Antonio Aitahan Matak, who refuse to recognize the legitimacy of the current government, and who have been banned by the President. In 2005 a new political party, UNDERTIM (Unidade Nacional Democrática da Resistência Timorense, or Timor Resistance and Democratic National Unity Party), was formed, led by Eli-sete (Eli-7), an ex-Falintil veteran whose group of ex-veterans is highly dissatisfied with the current political situation in East Timor. In February 2006 an estimated 400 to 700 FDTL[31] armed forces soldiers from the *Loro monu* abandoned their barracks in Metinaro in protest against alleged discrimination and lack of promotion possibilities in comparison to those from the *Loro sae* regions of East Timor (that is, Manatuto, Dili, Ainaro, Aileu — where higher-ranking officials come from).[32] In terms of external sources of insecurity, there have been several cross-border incidents in Maliana, Oecussi, and Suai since independence, with ex-militias infiltrating all the way to Atsabe and Dili. Most recently, in February 2006 there was a highly controversial case of an Indonesian armed forces soldier raping a Timorese woman in Oecussi, fracturing already fragile Indonesia–East Timor relations.

Contesting Memory and Remembrance

In 2005 the Timorese Resistance Archive and Museum (Resistencia Timorense Arkivu ho Muzeu) sponsored by the Portugal-based Mario Soares Foundation and supervised by Portuguese academics, officially opened to the public. The problem of power in history and historiography is immediately visible when one enters the display section of the museum. On this section you see mostly the photos of the current prime minister, foreign minister, the president, and council of ministers. Hardly on display are photos of any of the former Falintil guerrilla leaders (for example, Mau Hunu, Mau Hudo, Konis Santana), though their armaments are. No photos of students from the clandestine resistance are displayed either, except for one letter from RENETIL, which is not a very relevant letter. If one moves to the scanned historical documents and computerized archive, however, there is a multiplicity, even contentiousness in terms of perspectives. The archives capture East Timor as a politically divided society, rather than the official display of *unidade nacional* ("national unity").

In the archives, one finds a wealth of photographs of the Falintil guerrillas and letters from the clandestine movement. There is also an excellent book on "The Dignity of Konis Santana and the Timorese Resistance" by Jose Mattoso (2005). In several recent visits to Los Palos, Mehara, and Tutuala (Konis Santana's birthplace and former Falintil stronghold), ex-Falintil and clandestine leaders sadly reflected that if Konis Santana had lived and not been killed in 1998, East Timor would have more paths to choose from instead of taking the Mozambique-inspired road it is now taking.

Hope can be found in the realm of cultural production in the rural districts — the most innovative and imaginative, with numerous material culture and performing arts groups (local music bands, dance, theatre, martial arts, textiles, painting, sculpture) in the villages and in Dili emerging and generating local and national performance events and exhibits. There is a renaissance of expressive culture, having been suppressed for so many decades, and finally having the independence and space to articulate new dreams, visions, desires, and aspirations. While more conventional media (such as the print media and television) have been more politically censored and self-censored to the extent that opposition leaders have argued that the RTTL (Radio Televisao Timor Leste) is increasingly becoming primarily an apparatus and instrument for state and ruling party propaganda, indigenous local performing arts and expressive culture have really blossomed and generated innovative forms of articulating dissent, resilience, and hope.

Discourses of victimization, degradation, and destruction dominate the international aid commentary on East Timor, while the actual dynamics underlying change processes in the transition from Indonesian colonialism and war to independence are still only minimally understood. Most international solutions are geared towards "capacity building", while little attention has been paid to traditional ideas of power and cosmology. Take, for example, the programmes on "gender and development" run by the government and international NGOs, including UN agencies, many of which seem to begin from the standpoint that East Timorese women are "weak, need empowerment, are lacking in assertiveness, strategies of resilience and care of the self", and so on. It occurred to me while watching several of the traditional dances (in Mehara, Tutuala, Suai, Ermera, Ainaro) that a more effective means of "gender empowerment" would be to ask the East Timorese women to perform the traditional dances (including martial arts), to support and enable them to continue to pass on such cultural knowledge to younger children (male and female), as the body movements and gestures in themselves go a long way to teach and socialize East Timorese children on repose, composure, and strength, and at the same time also teach them to be creative, gracious, and confident — much more than any theory on gender empowerment can possibly do.

Notes

[1] Falintil stands for Forças Armadas de Libertação Nacional de Timor Leste, or the Armed Forces of the National Liberation of East Timor.

[2] According to UNTAET Executive Order No. 2000/2 "On the De-criminalization of Defamation":

"Effective immediately, the conduct defined in Chapter XVI (Defamation) of the Indonesian Penal Code, comprising articles 310 through 321, is of non-criminal nature in East Timor. Under no circumstances may said articles be the basis for criminal charges by the Public Prosecutor. Persons allegedly defamed shall be limited to civil actions and only to the extent that such remedies may be provided in a future UNTAET Regulation. This Executive Order shall apply to all pending proceedings in East Timor, regardless of the time of any alleged offense". (Signed by Sergio Vieira de Mello, Transitional Administrator, 7 September 2000)

[3] De Aruajo was called in for his first "investigation" by the Portuguese Adviser to the Prosecutor General, Joao Paulo Ferraz Carreira, on 14 February 2006, after making a statement about the Prime Minister possibly being guilty of corruption and accepting a US$2.5 million bribe from the oil corporation Conoco-Phillips (*karik nia simu ka lae, osan korupsaun mina nian hamutuk 2.5 miloens dolar Americano*). Oceanic Exploration had filed a case in the United States against Conoco-Phillips making the bribery allegations in 2004.

[4] See, for example, Peter Lape, "Does Archaeology Have a Role in Building the Nation of East Timor?" *Asian Social Issues Program* (The Asia Society), 2003, http://www.asiasource.org/asip/archeology.cfm.

5   Frederic Durand, *Timor Loro Sae: Pays au carrefour de l'Asie et du Pacifique, un atlas geo-historique* (France: Presses Universitaires de Marne-la-Vallee; and Bangkok, Thailand: Institute de Recherche sur l'Asie du Sud-est Contemporaine, 2002).
6   Ian Martin and Alexander Mayer-Rieckh, "The United Nations and East Timor: From Self-Determination to State-Building", *International Peacekeeping* 12, no. 1 (Spring 2005): 136.
7   Ibid.
8   United Nations Security Council, Progress Report of the Secretary-General on the United Nations Office in Timor Leste, 17 January 2006, p. 13.
9   Ibid.
10 Nine other opposition parties and an independent won the remaining opposition seats: Sons of the Mountain Warriors or Association of Timorese Heroes (Klibur Oan Timor Aswa'in, or KOTA), two seats; Timorese Democratic Union (União Democrática Timorense, or UDT), two seats; Timorese Nationalist Party (Partido Nacionalista Timorense, or PNT), two seats; People's Party of Timor (Partido de Povo de Timor, or PPT), two seats; Christian Democrat Party of Timor (Partido Democrata Cristão, or PDC), two seats; Liberal Party (Partido Liberal, or PL), one seat; Christian Democratic Union of Timor (União Democratica Cristão de Timor, or UDC), one seat; Socialist Party of Timor (Partido Socialista de Timor, or PST), one seat; Christian Democratic Party of Timor (PCDT), one seat; and Independent, one seat.
11 Report to the UN Security Council on East Timor, 2005.
12 Timor Leste is divided into 13 districts: Aileu, Ainaro, Baucau, Bobonaro, Covalima, Dili, Ermera, Lautem, Liquica, Manatuto, Manufahi, Oe-cusse, and Viqueque. Oe-cusse is an exclave located in West Timor. Each district is divided into sub-districts (65 in total) and these are further divided into 498 *sucos* ("villages") and 2,336 *aldeias* ("hamlets"). The *suco* elections in 2005 were conducted to elect Suco Councils and Suco Chiefs (*Chefe de Sucos*) and Aldeia Chiefs (*Chefe de Aldeias*). The local *suco* and *aldeia* elections was an ongoing process for several months, beginning in outlying districts from December 2004 and ending in Dili district in September 2005. For further details regarding the *suco* elections, please see the government website at http://www.stae.tl.
13 Author's interviews with independent international observers, including UNMISET Political Affairs officers, and other international NGO observers.
14 Tomas Cabral, the Director of STAE, himself publicly acknowledged that STAE was severely under-staffed and under-resourced.
15 UNDP Suco Elections Internal Progress Report, 2005.
16 United Nations Security Council, Progress Report, 13 May to 15 August 2005.
17 Commission for Reception, Truth and Reconciliation or Commissao de Acolhamento, Verdade e Reconciliacao (CAVR).

18. UNDP, *Timor Leste Human Development Report 2006. The Path Out of Poverty: Integrated Rural Development* (Dili, Timor Leste: UNDP, 2006), p. 27. See http://www.undp.east-timor.org.
19. Geoffrey Hull, "Current Language Issues in East Timor", public lecture given at the University of Adelaide, 29 March 2000.
20. See http://www.timorseajustice.org.
21. Partido Democratico, Social Democrat Party of East Timor, Timorese Social Democratic Association, and Socialist Party of Timor press releases, January 2006.
22. Ibid.
23. UNDP Parliament Budget Oversight Internal Report 2005. In addition, author's personal correspondence with Ms Mica Barreto Soares, UNDP Programme Officer, Governance Unit, and Mr Rui Gomes, UNDP Head of Poverty Reduction Unit, 2 March 2006.
24. Information on the Timor Leste Budget from Ms Fe B. Gaffud, Budgetary Oversight Advisor, UNDP Parliament Project. Presentation on the General Budget of the State for FY 2005/2006, UNDP, UN House, 31 August 2005.
25. World Bank Report No. 31924-TP, Democratic Republic of Timor Leste, Joint Staff Advisory Note on the Poverty Reduction Strategy Paper, vol. 1, April 2005.
26. Ministry of Health, Government of the Democratic Republic of Timor Leste, "Basic Packages of Services Policy", BPS, 2004. Unpublished policy document, Dili, Timor Leste.
27. UNDP, *Timor Leste Human Development Report 2006: The Path Out of Poverty: Integrated Rural Development*. UN House, Caicoli, Dili, Timor Leste. See http://www.undp.east-timor.org.
28. Ibid., p. 11.
29. World Bank, *Timor-Leste Expenditure Review*, vol. 1, 19 July 2004.
30. *Suara Timor Lorosae*, 26 February 2006.
31. FDTL stands for Forcas de Defesa de Timor-Leste, or East Timor Defence Force.
32. *Loro monu* refers to the western districts of East Timor (Aileu, Ainaro, Bobonaro, Covalima, Dili, Ermera, Liquica, Manatuto, Manufahi, and Oe-cusse) while *Loro sae* to the easternmost districts (Lautem, Baucau, and Viqueque).

Vietnam

VIETNAM
Laying the Path for the 10th National Congress

Danny Wong Tze Ken

The past 12 months have been a very successful year for Vietnam's foreign relations. The single most important event in Vietnam's foreign relations calendar in 2005 was Prime Minister Phan Van Khai's six-day visit to the United States from 19 to 25 June. The visit, the first by a national leader of Vietnam to the United States in 30 years, coincided with the tenth anniversary of the normalization of relations between the two countries. The event is also important as it came exactly 30 years after the end of the Vietnam War when the two sides faced off in the conflict. On his return to Vietnam, the visit was celebrated as a huge success, and the event was described by Prime Minister Khai as an event that would hardly have been possible only ten years earlier.[1]

The success of Khai's visit is significant for Vietnam in at least three ways: first, it points to the further improvements in the Vietnam-US relations; second, it reveals the unconventional Vietnamese stance on several important issues affecting the nation; and third, the government hopes to capitalize on the successes in its foreign relations to strengthen its position in domestic politics, especially in the run-up to the 10th National Congress of the Communist Party of Vietnam (CPV) in 2006.

In 2005, however, domestic issues continued to dominate much of Vietnam's politics. The ruling party, the CPV, faced challenges in pursuing its reform programme without compromising its position as the paramount party in the country. The threats posed by endemic corruption and the government's efforts to overcome it, questions relating to religious freedom and the government's handling of political dissidents continued to dominate much of Vietnam's domestic politics

---

DANNY WONG TZE KEN is Associate Professor, Department of History, University of Malaya.

as well as getting the attention of its leaders. The pace of equitization of the state-owned enterprises (SOEs), by turning them into joint stock companies, and Vietnam's pending entry into the World Trade Organization (WTO) were two of the main economic concerns. Also of great concern was the threat posed by the avian flu, as Vietnam was the worst-hit country in the region.

The Party

Since Nong Duc Manh took over as Party Secretary General in 2001, the CPV leadership has reiterated its commitment towards continued economic reform. The introduction of the *doi moi* programme during the party's 6th National Congress in 1986 has transformed Vietnam from a centrally planned to a market-oriented economy. Through the success of the reform programme, Vietnam graduated from the list of the world's 50 poorest nations to be among the most dynamic and fastest-growing economies in the world.[2] Its poverty rate went down from 60 per cent in 1990 to 20 per cent in 2005.[3] In the past three years, Vietnam consistently registered an annual GDP growth rate of 7.5 to 8 per cent. In 2005 its GDP reached an estimated 8 per cent, making the country one of the most vibrant economies in Southeast Asia. Per capita income has grown from a mere US$289 in 1995 to about US$542 in 2005.[4]

Since the 9th National Congress in 2001, the CPV has taken considerable steps to innovate the party and the government to preserve its integrity and to remain relevant and attractive to the Vietnamese people. The party also gained an overwhelming majority in the National Assembly elected in May 2002. This victory was seen by the party as an endorsement of its commitment to pursue further reform while remaining firmly on the socialist path. Another very important measure taken under Nong Duc Manh's leadership was the attempt to push through tough anti-corruption legislation over the last few years, especially in 2005.

While *doi moi* was started as an economic reform programme, the CPV leaders have never lost sight of the underlying reasons for its introduction. The reform programme was introduced top-down, which pointed to the sensitivity of the CPV leadership on the need to be constantly relevant. In this regard, the CPV leadership insisted that while Vietnam was making considerable advances in economic transformation, it had never lost sight of the larger picture of also ensuring that social equality is constantly enforced. This was reiterated by Prime Minister Phan Van Khai: "We cannot grow complacent, but must continue to accelerate the pace of reform, ensuring a greater harmony between economic growth and the resolution of social issues it generates. Economic reform may have taken one step ahead, but it must be linked to political reform."[5]

The CPV has a firm conviction that its political reform is sufficiently democratic. It envisioned *doi moi* not merely as an economic reform programme, but also a political reform policy decision. The rationale was based on what the CPV leadership considered as the right accorded to the Vietnamese to engage freely in economic activities since the transformation into a market economy. Through this, the party believes that democracy has been further promoted and improved.[6]

Even as the CPV had fallen back on its historical role to justify its paramount position in the political lives of the people, the challenge was to make the party continuously relevant and accepted by the people. More importantly, the party had to be seen as transparent and improving the quality of governance. Thus, it continues to carry out reform while empowering the National Assembly to introduce new legislation aimed at creating greater openness and transparency.

Such efforts and aspirations to ensure the party's paramount position could, however, be undermined by the very success achieved by the party's economic reform. This is especially true in relation to the declining party membership over the last five years. With new career opportunities offered by the economy and an expanding private sector, many younger Vietnamese no longer see party membership as essential to personal advancement. To this end, a likely issue to be discussed in the 10th National Congress is the proposal to officially allow party members to own private businesses.

However, despite the party's efforts, it also recognized shortcomings of corruption and inefficiency within the party and government that pose a great threat to the integrity of the party. Externally, the party faces many voices of dissent from both international organizations and Vietnamese living abroad, making demands on issues such as democracy, freedom of speech, religious freedom, and human rights. Yet, there were no similar voices from within that could constitute any form of domestic pressure on the party with regard to such issues.

Towards the 10th National Congress

The 10th National Congress, which is expected to be held in the second quarter of 2006, will be an important event for the CPV. The CPV national congresses have marked changes that had a significant impact on the direction of the party and the country. The tenth in the series will be no different, if not even more significant as the party is on the threshold of transforming Vietnam into a fully market-oriented economy. Howev2er, it can be expected that the CPV would continue to exercise political power though it may not seem as visible as it was before the introduction of the economic reforms.

The challenge for the CPV is less about how the economy and society will further evolve. What is at stake is the party's integrity as the body that continues to champion the welfare of the Vietnamese people, a role that it professes to play, and its ability to continue to be relevant and visible without putting a brake on the ongoing reforms.

While it is generally agreed that the present economic reforms will not be reversed, and have given a general sense of relief and openness within the Vietnamese society, the question is whether the ordinary citizens will feel obliged, and even indebted, to the efforts of the party.

In terms of leadership, it is most likely that the delegates to the 10th National Congress would continue with the present batch of reform-minded leaders. Nong Duc Manh, the Party's Secretary General, is likely to get a second term as the party boss. Prime Minster Phan Van Khai and President Tran Duc Luong are expected to step down since both are approaching the end of their second term in office, having been re-elected in July 2002.

As for the next echelon of party leaders, the present top CPV leaders' emphasis on impeccable quality reflects their concern in ensuring that the party will be able to "meet the emerging requirements of the new stage of development. ... These elements will play a key and decisive role in securing the success of the renewal, in both the immediate and long-term future".[7]

At the 12th Plenum of the Party's Central Committee in July 2005, the party leadership stated:

> The 10th Party's Congress [in 2006] should elect a Central Committee comprising those who have a firm political ideology, who are loyal to Marxism-Leninism and Ho Chi Minh's Thoughts and creatively apply these doctrines to reality, and who are persistently following the goals and ideology of national independence and socialism. Those who are qualified for the Central Committee have positive characteristics and ethics, should be proven as honest, and have no evidence of being aloof, wasting the State budget and being corrupt. The potential Central Committee members should be well educated, have managerial skills, and be creative in their work to meet the high demands of the national industrialization and modernization.

Umistakably, the main concern of the party leadership is to be well led and remain relevant and appealing to the people.

Party leaders were also concerned about the juggling for positions in the run-up to the forthcoming Congress. Even though the Congress will not necessarily bring about a change in the top leadership, many were hoping for future appointments and advances in their political career. The matter was highlighted as early as May 2004 when Tran Dinh Hoan, the Chairman of the Central Committee Organization Commission, revealed that he had heard talk of "bargaining power" and "buying appointments" in some branches and localities. These activities were also regarded as a form of corruption.[8] The matter is serious as there were concerns that it might jeopardize people's trust in the party leadership.

Perhaps the most important issue to be discussed in the 10th Congress would be the direction of the party with regard to economic reform. The matter is made even more significant by the fact that the Congress coincides with the twentieth year anniversary of the introduction of *doi moi*. Draft political report of the Party Central Committee released by the party in preparation for the Congress expressed satisfaction with the progress made thus far since the introduction of the policy. The report insisted that the directions taken by the party was "correct and creative". The tone of the report suggested that the party would further enhance what it describes as Vietnam's march towards socialism through the development of a socialist-oriented market economy. Hence, the Congress would likely endorse further economic reform including the opening up of Vietnam's economy.

Fighting Corruption

In 2005 the Vietnamese government appeared determined to push forward economic reforms necessary to turn Vietnam into an industrialized country by 2020. The party leadership set the target in its ten-year 2001–10 strategy.[9] While the government has not faced major opposition in pursuing this goal, progress towards attaining it had been hampered by the problem of corruption. According to a report released by the Party's Central Committee, an increase in corruption in Vietnam has discouraged foreign investors from grasping business opportunities in the country. According to the report: "Vietnam has several advantages to draw foreign investors but, together with a complex tax system and the prolonged time required for ground clearance, corruption is hindering foreign investment flows."[10]

The Vietnamese government recognized corruption as one of its biggest weaknesses. Corruption among government officials was considered a major threat to the legitimacy of the ruling Communist Party. For instance, despite the existence of the State Inspectorate under the government, 30–40 per cent of investment for infrastructure and construction disappears through corruption, embezzlement, and wastefulness.[11]

Even more alarming was the admission by the government that the problem was endemic, affecting every dimension of society, including education. As an example, in his report to the National Assembly, Nguyen Minh Hien, the Minister of Education, reported that corruption was rampant in the field of education. An investigation conducted by the National Assembly Standing Committee for Culture, Education, Youth and Children found that cheating and "over-teaching" in the country's education system had become widespread in "every locality and education level". Students cheating in examinations and bribing teachers for passing grades, once considered a disgrace, have now become the norm. These corrupt practices have, according to the report, caused "extremely serious degradation" in the social ethic and human dignity.[12] This indicates that the CPV recognized that corruption could derail the country's development.

Over the past year, one minister, five deputy ministers, and 14 chairmen of people's committees at both provincial and municipal levels were arrested due to corruption charges, illustrating the severity of the problem. The government also prosecuted hundreds of bank and treasury officials as well as business leaders for management regulation violations that resulted in the loss of trillions of dong.[13] In addition, many cases of corrupt practices have been highlighted in Vietnamese newspapers over the past 12 months. Most of these cases involved government officials who abused their position to enrich themselves.

Apart from being a hindrance to reform programmes, potential foreign investors were turned off by red tape and lack of transparency in governance. In his speech to the 100th Session of Monthly Donor Forum organized by the United Nations Development Program (UNDP) in Hanoi, Prime Minister Phan Van Khai emphasized that Vietnam needed to resort to transparency and openness to fight corruption, which he admitted remained a constant problem.[14] The reiteration was an important follow-up to Khai's opening address to the year-end session of the National Assembly in October 2004 where he also addressed the issue.[15] The government's commitment to fighting corruption augured well for international aid to Vietnam. For 2005, donors committed a record US$3.4 billion of official development assistance (ODA). A similar figure was also pledged for the year 2006.[16]

At the heart of solving the problem of corruption was the inadequacy of laws and enforcement. The government have taken steps to revise and amend existing laws, and have tabled them at the National Assembly. The existing anti-corruption law, the Ordinance on Corruption, was promulgated in 1998 and revised and supplemented in 2000. It was the key legal instrument in preventing and fighting corruption, penalizing culprits, and reclaiming state property. However, Quach Le Thanh, the Inspector-General of Police, stated, "After seven years in force, the ordinance has revealed many shortcomings and has not met the needs of the country's battle against corruption."[17] The existing enforcement agency was also deemed ineffective.

The emphasis in the new regulations being considered by the National Assembly was prevention. One major step in this direction was the passage of a law prohibiting state-owned corporations and companies from entering into economic contracts with enterprises owned by "spouses, parents, children, or other family members of general directors, deputy general directors, the chief accountant and members of the executive board". Another significant step to be introduced by the National Assembly was the declaration of assets and income by government officials. Under the bill, state officials and workers were required to declare assets worth more than 50 million dong (US$3,150).[18]

The 2005 August National Assembly also moved towards the creation of an anti-corruption agency,[19] which was realized during the November session. However, the new body was to be under the government and not under the National Assembly, as originally proposed by the National Assembly deputies, who felt that the body would not be effective under the government. Many of the deputies believed that under such circumstances, the new anti-corruption agency would be no better than the existing State Inspectorate.

The Vietnamese government is increasing its anti-corruption efforts not merely because corruption has become so entrenched and widespread, but more importantly because it could jeopardize the CPV's integrity and image, both domestically and internationally.

Religious Freedom and Human Rights Issues

Hanoi made a considerable shift in its religious policy when Prime Minister Phan Van Khai issued a special instruction in March banning the forced renunciation of religious beliefs. The problem was a long-standing issue, as many local authorities in the central highlands, where ethnic minorities were concentrated, were allegedly blocking applications by Christian churches to register as required by law. Local authorities feared that separatist political movements could emerge from these churches, as was the case of the United Liberation Front of the Oppressed Races

(FULRO) movement in the 1960s. FULRO fought for an independent state for Vietnam's ethnic minorities. The present concern also stemmed from the activities of what Hanoi calls "DeGa Protestantism", which called for the establishment of an independent DeGa State. The movement was started in the United States by a Montagnard exile who was formerly a member of FULRO.[20] The United States, however, has reiterated through its ambassador to Hanoi that it does not accept and will not support the so-called "State of DeGa".[21]

In relation to this, the Hanoi government allowed the visit of the President of the Institute of Global Engagement, Chris Seiple, to the Central Highland provinces of Gia Lai and Kontum in June 2005. Also, as a gesture of tolerating the activities of Christians, the Provincial People's Committee at Gia Lai recently permitted the Theological Institute of the Southern Protestant Church to commence its first theological classes in the province, providing training to 46 pastors and church workers.[22] The government also recognized the General Confederation of the Southern Vietnam Protestant Church, which it hoped would serve as an alternative to DeGa Protestantism for the ethnic minorities in the Central Highlands.

Representatives from the United Nations High Commissioner for Refugees (UNHCR) made a similar visit to the ethnic minorities at Gia Lai in June 2005.[23] The visit investigated the lives of recently repatriated ethnic minorities who had crossed over to Cambodia during the past two years because of alleged oppressive practices by the local authorities. The move was also aimed at examining if Vietnam was observing an agreement signed in early 2005 with the UNHCR on the plight of ethnic minority groups. Some of these refugees have since returned home.[24] Even though religious freedom and ethnic marginalization were two separate issues they were, nevertheless, linked. The June visit suggested that Vietnam was committed to upholding the principle of religious freedom.

The Roman Catholic Church also benefited from Hanoi's more relaxed religious policy. Long regarding the Vatican as meddling in its internal affairs especially in the appointment of priests and bishops, Hanoi adjusted its stand by formally greeting the appointment of the new Archbishop of Hanoi, Bishop Ngo Quang Kiet, and two bishops of dioceses in the south. These appointments were made in line with an agreement between the Vietnamese government and the Vatican.[25] During the consecration of the new Roman Catholic Pope in July 2005, a delegation from the Vietnamese Government Committee for Religious Affairs, led by its Chairman Ngo Yen Thi, met with the Vatican Secretary for Relations for States, Archbishop Giovanni Lajolo. The two parties explored the possibility of formally establishing diplomatic relations.[26] The party also prided itself in allowing the funeral of Pope John Paul II and the installation of the new

Pope to be witnessed by Vietnamese Catholics through the Internet and news reports on television and radio.[27] In a reciprocal move, Cardinal Crescenzio Sepe, Prefect of the Congregation for the Evangelization of Peoples of the Vatican, visited Vietnam from 28 November to 5 December 2005 at the invitation of the Catholic Church of Vietnam. The Cardinal's visit, the highest-ranking Vatican official ever to visit Vietnam, helped enhance the relations and understanding between the Vatican and Vietnam.

In August the CPV tried to further demonstrate its commitment to religious freedom by releasing statements on the Ordinance on Religions and Beliefs, which it believed met the basic needs of religious organizations. According to Ngo Yen Thi, Chairman of the Government Committee for Religious Affairs, religious organizations now have greater freedom in managing their personnel, including appointments and ordinations.[28]

All these steps can be seen as an attempt to placate international pressure on Vietnam's commitment to human rights and the needs of the minorities.

Indeed, Hanoi is responding to allegations of not allowing religious freedom in the country. This point was highlighted by Vietnamese leaders over the last two years, including in the joint statement made by Prime Minister Phan Van Khai and President George W. Bush during Khai's visit to Washington, DC in June 2005. According to the statement, "the two leaders agreed on the importance of continuing an open and candid dialogue on issues of common concern, including human rights practices and conditions for religious believers and ethnic minorities".[29]

In August 2005 the Ministry of Foreign Affairs released a White Paper on human rights issues entitled "Achievements in the Protection and Promotion of Human Rights in Vietnam". The White Paper, the first released by the Ministry of Foreign Affairs on human rights, provided insights into Vietnam's viewpoints and policies on human rights, its achievements in the protection and promotion of human rights, and international cooperation in the issue. The White Paper highlighted Vietnam's move towards advocating the abolition of the death penalty in the future.[30]

Despite Hanoi's efforts to respond to external pressures for greater religious freedom and respect for human rights, its handling of several cases of political dissidents and religious leaders continued to draw flak from international bodies such as Amnesty International, which raised questions on Vietnam's treatment of prisoners of conscience. On 21 September, US Ambassador Michael Marine urged the Vietnamese government to release a number of prisoners of conscience. In response the Vietnamese Foreign Ministry stated that there were no prisoners of conscience in Vietnam who were detained for their political opinions or religious beliefs. The Ministry insisted that only law violators were detained.[31]

In the celebrations to mark the thirtieth anniversary of the end of the Vietnam War on 30 April 2005, Hanoi declared an amnesty for more than 7,500 prisoners. Among those released were two well-known dissidents: Reverend Pham Ngoc Lien, a Roman Catholic priest who had been in prison for 18 years, and Le Thi Hong Lien, a 21-year-old teacher who is also a member of the Mennonite Christian Church.

In September, under an amnesty programme in conjunction with the country's national day celebration, Hanoi released two other alleged prisoners of conscience: Nguyen Hong Quang, a Mennonite pastor from Ho Chi Minh City and Than Van Truong, a Baptist pastor who was released from a mental hospital.

Despite Hanoi's seemingly improved record in dealing with religious groups, it continued to be critical and suspicious of unauthorized religious denominations. Religious organizations such as the United Buddhist Church of Vietnam, the Hoa Hao Buddhist Sect, and DeGa Protestantism continued to be on the receiving end of Hanoi's monitoring and restrictions on unauthorized religious activities.

At the end of 2005, the United States still included Vietnam on its list of "Countries of particular concern" for religious freedom. The Vietnamese Foreign Ministry protested the inclusion and insisted that Vietnam respects and guarantees its citizens' freedom of beliefs and religion. Hanoi urged the United States to adopt a more realistic view to improve the two countries' bilateral relationship.[32] Indeed, the concessions given to religious groups, as well as (to some extent) known dissidents, demonstrate a *certain* growing awareness by the Vietnamese authorities of the need to be seen to respond to international standards and concerns.

Economic Development

The year 2005 has been recognized as a successful year for Vietnam's economic development. The World Bank hailed the country as a success story and ranked it as the world's second fastest-growing economy after China. The government forecasted GDP growth in 2005 at 8.4 per cent. Foreign direct investment increased by 25 per cent, at US$5.8 billion. Total exports for 2005 were projected to reach US$32 billion.[33] The Vietnamese economy has been growing very healthily over the past five years with an annual growth rate of more than 7 per cent.[34] This encouraging growth has been coupled with a decline in poverty and improved living standards.

Industry and construction continued to experience vibrant growth, acting as a driving force behind the healthy economy. In the first six months of 2005, Vietnam's exports grew by almost 30 per cent. The main contributors were crude oil, textiles and garments, footwear, and fisheries — which constituted almost 53 per cent to the GDP. Crude oil export value rose 34.1 per cent.[35] Other major exports items included services, timber products, rice, coffee, pepper, and coal. The country's commodity exports are expected to continue to grow in 2006.

Despite these encouraging developments — Vietnam's rising trade deficit and the uneven economic development were sources of concern. While exports grew by 30 per cent, Vietnam's imports grew by 25 per cent, buoyed by the rapidly expanding private sector and rising consumer spending. This resulted in its trade deficit reaching a record US$5.5 billion. The figure is likely to rise given the current consumer-spending trend.

Another serious issue is the question of uneven economic development, which has resulted in disparity between the rural and urban areas. The rural-urban divide is best exemplified by the case of Ho Chi Minh City. In 2005, Ho Chi Minh City residents enjoyed a GDP per capita income of US$1,985, as against a national average of around US$542. Much of the ongoing development that has taken place since the introduction of *doi moi* restructuring programme has been concentrated in Ho Chi Minh City, its neighbouring provinces, and several of the major port cities. Meanwhile, the rest of the provinces stagnated.

One of the most glaring effects of the reforms since the introduction of *doi moi* in December 1986 was the fate of the SOEs and state-owned commercial banks (SOCBs). SOEs, which numbered 6,000 in 1997, were the products of the country's centrally planned economy. Most were huge in size but low in productivity and owed their survival to state-generated projects. By the time *doi moi* was in full swing, such projects were no longer forthcoming as many of the initiatives were taken up by the private sector. This left many SOEs in the red financially, forcing the government to rescue them through subsidies. Due to their state of unprofitability, these SOEs became the target for the equitization process.

The early challenge in SOE reform was the huge number of SOE employees — totalling half a million personnel in 1997 — which would be laid off. While equitization has gone beyond that phase, the challenge today is to speed up the process. Equitization, which aims at turning SOEs into joint stock companies, has entered a phase where larger state-owned companies are being targeted. An International Monetary Fund (IMF) report noted that the restructuring and reform of the SOEs and SOCBs remain slow, and called for its prioritization. The restructuring of key SOEs was necessary to alleviate their capacity and financial constraints.[36] The government's target for 2005 was the restructuring of 1,154 SOEs, including 1,024 slated for equitization.[37] The process, however, was protracted. The Steering Board for the Reform and Development of SOEs, the agency handling the equitization process, reported that, while most equitized enterprises have attained higher turnover and profits than in the pre-equitization period, the progress for 2005 was slow. In the first eight months of 2005, only about 300 SOEs were equitized, achieving only 25 per cent of the target. This was also far short of the 700 SOEs equitized in 2004 (68 per cent). The main problem had been the massive amounts of bad debts involved, estimated at US$1.8 billion. Also, the process has been concentrated on small and medium SOEs rather than the larger ones, which accounted for the majority of the SOE debts, such as Vietnam Airlines, Vinaconex, and Hanoi and Saigon Beverage and Brewery.[38] The continued presence of large SOEs in many sectors of the economy is a restrain to the further development of a vibrant private sector.

In October 2005, Vietnam made its first sovereign bond issue in New York, successfully raising US$750 million. The issuance was considered a huge success, with orders totalling US$4.5 billion (six times the amount on offer).[39] The amount raised was a clear indicator of international investors' confidence in Vietnam's economic future.

The issue of Vietnam's admission into the WTO continues to dominate its foreign relations. Apart from the assurance of support for its application from major countries such as the United States, United Kingdom, Australia, China, and the ASEAN member countries, Vietnamese officials continue to work hard, especially in holding bilateral negotiations with its 27 trading partners, including Japan and South Korea.[40] The move was important to ensure that bilateral trade issues were resolved before Vietnam's admission into the WTO. While Vietnam was eager to join the trade organization by the end of 2005, the schedule was unrealistic. By December 2005, it had only concluded negotiations with 21 countries, with six others remaining, including the United States and Australia. Several high-ranking Vietnamese officials involved in the negotiations accepted that they could not meet the 2005 deadline, as trade negotiations were tedious and extensive. In addition, Hanoi was concerned that some of the remaining negotiation partners, notably the United States and Australia, would link its record on human rights and religious freedom with the negotiations for its WTO entry. After finalizing the negotiations, the Vietnamese National Assembly would still need to pass a WTO compliance legislation and create implementing regulations to ensure that the legislation was not only legal, but also understood throughout the country. Thus, a more realistic target of June 2006 was set for Vietnam's admission into the WTO.[41]

Avian Flu and Natural Disasters

2005 was a difficult year for Vietnam's poultry industry. The country was in the frontline of H5N1 avian influenza infections, commonly known as the bird flu. It was surmised that the country could be one of the first to be affected if a pandemic breaks out. Since December 2003 when the flu was first discovered in the country, a total of 93 cases have been reported in 25 provinces and cities, resulting to 42 deaths.[42]

The Hanoi government had taken decisive steps to prevent an outbreak through mass vaccination of affected poultry. Vietnam also sought World Health Organization (WHO) permission to produce an avian flu vaccine, which is under WHO trial. When granted, the vaccine production project will cost an estimated US$50 million. Thus far, the country received a US$3 million donation from the Australian government to help counter an avian flu outbreak.

In September 2005 the governments of Vietnam and the United Nations signed an agreement to prevent and control diseases with epidemic potential, paying particular attention to the avian influenza. In addition the Prime Minister issued Prime Minister Directive No. 1450/TTg-QHQT, dated 26 September 2005, making efforts to counter avian influenza its priority.[43]

As the fear of avian flu was seriously affecting Vietnam's poultry industry, another force of nature in the form of bad weather dealt a severe blow to rice production in the country. In early October the northern and central parts of Vietnam were severely hit by Typhoon Damrey. This resulted in failed crops, massive losses suffered by the farmers, and a shortage of rice supplies, which was further aggravated by the over-export of rice.

The problem became so acute that the Prime Minister had to issue a directive aiming to reduce Vietnam's rice export from 5.1 million to 4.7 million tonnes.[44] The measure would allow more rice to be made available for local consumption, especially in the affected areas.

International Relations

On 19 June 2005 Prime Minister Phan Van Khai led a delegation of party and business leaders to visit the United States. During his six-day stay, the Vietnamese Prime Minister was feted and welcomed by a wide range of organizations and people. He also had a cordial meeting with President George W. Bush at the White House. In the joint statement, the two leaders expressed satisfaction with the progress of US-Vietnam relations. Both leaders also affirmed their intention to take their bilateral relations to a higher plane.

The main catalyst in bringing the two sides closer was the China factor. While the Vietnam War was a bitter experience, most Vietnamese today have little memory of the war and are probably more suspicious of China, a fellow neighbouring communist country in the north. More recent conflicts with China such as the 1979 war and clashes with the Chinese navy in the South China Sea served as reminders of the perceived China threat. While officials stressed the importance of maintaining good relations with both the United States and China, they were certainly wary of their powerful northern neighbour. This perception works well with the United States, which is keen to cultivate a new ally in the region to balance China's rapid economic and military modernization.

The US visit was also successful in encouraging foreign investment to Vietnam. Speaking at the gala dinner hosted in his honour by the Vietnam-US Trade Council on 21 June 2005, Phan Van Khai stated that his meeting with Bush "proves that we have together dispelled the shadow of the past so as to shed the light of our future cooperation ..." Indeed, both sides have come a long way since the end of the Vietnam War. The politics of the Cold War, which used to dominate bilateral relations, has given way to a more pragmatic relationship. The first ten years of bilateral relations have changed from suspicion and confrontation to mutual cooperation and respect, with emphasis on trade. Vietnam hopes that this framework would guide its long-term relations with the United States in the 21st century.

Bilateral trade with the United States is on the top agenda. In 2005 the United States was Vietnam's number one export market (19.8 per cent), whereas it ranked ninth (4.1 per cent) in Vietnam's list of importing countries. Total volume of trade increased from US$1.5 billion in 2001 to US$6.4 billion in 2004 after the signing of a bilateral trade agreement. This figure is 20 times greater than that of 1995.[45]

US-Vietnam trade is highly favourable to Vietnam. In 2003 the US trade deficit with Vietnam was US$3.2 billion. However, Vietnam is concerned that the United States is increasingly employing protectionism. Two recent cases involved lawsuits by American companies against Vietnam for allegedly dumping shrimps and catfish on the US market.[46]

During Prime Minister Khai's visit, he extracted a pledge from President Bush to support Vietnam's bid to join the WTO.[47] The promise from the US President was a timely boost to Vietnam's application for membership in the WTO as Vietnam had a tough time negotiating with the United States.

One of the most important developments in the Vietnam-US relations in recent years was the move to strengthen military and security ties between the two countries. Prior to Prime Minister Phan Van Khai's visit to Washington, Vietnam received visits from three US warships: USS *Vandegrift* (frigate, November 2003), USS *Curtis* (warship, July/August 2004), and USS *Gary* (frigate, March 2005). The visits, while routine in many ways, had a significant meaning for the two countries. The three ships were the first to visit Vietnam since the end of the Vietnam War in 1975. In May 2004, Commander of the United States Army Pacific Command, Lieutenant General James L. Campbell, visited Hanoi and held talks with officials of the Defence and Foreign Affairs Ministries with a view to deepening the two countries' military-to-military relationship. The high-level visit pointed to how the United States placed greater importance on strengthening its defence ties with Vietnam.

The increased Vietnam-US contacts in military terms implied that Hanoi viewed the United States as a more realistic counterweight to China compared with the Russians. This decision was probably influenced by how wary the Vietnamese naval force was of the Chinese navy, especially as regards their overlapping territorial claims.

At the moment, the more tangible and visible aspects of the bilateral military ties centred more on resolving long-standing issues from the Vietnam War — such as US prisoners of war (POWs) and missing-in-action (MIA) personnel, Agent Orange, and the clearing of unexploded ordnance and toxic chemicals. The POW/MIA issue was a constant topic on the Vietnam-US relations since the end of the Vietnam War in 1975. As of July 2005, there were still 1,393 POW/MIAs according to the US State Department.[48] Thus far the issue was not a serious hindrance to bilateral relations, and Hanoi signalled that it was willing to resolve it. US Special Envoy Gordon H. Mansfield, who is also the Deputy Secretary of Veteran Affairs, raised the issue recently during a visit to Hanoi. Mansfield was sent as President George W. Bush's personal envoy to participate in celebrations commemorating the tenth anniversary of the establishment of diplomatic relations.[49]

Two other areas of military and defence cooperation were on efforts to resolve the after-effects of Agent Orange and the clearing of landmines and unexploded ordnance and toxic chemicals. The settlement of the Agent Orange issue took on a legal perspective when Agent Orange victims filed a lawsuit against 37 American chemical companies that produced and supplied the toxic chemical for the use of the US Army during the Vietnam War.[50] The US Justice Department opposed the lawsuit, with the US government continuing to refuse to own up responsibility on the matter. The only positive development was the effort by the Office of the US Secretary of Defence to sponsor a workshop in Hanoi in August 2005 on destruction techniques for dioxins and chemicals associated with former storage sites for herbicide.⁵¹ The workshop, however, did not address the problem of human victims.

The other defence concern was the fight against terrorism. Even though Vietnam does not figure on the list of countries with a possible terrorist threat, Hanoi pledged its cooperation to the United States. As Prime Minister Khai stated, "it is imperative to rule terrorism out of human life and prevent the disasters it causes to innocent people. Asia and Vietnam are not immune from this scourge, and we pledge to work shoulder-to-shoulder with our neighbours and the United States to combat terror. ..."⁵² Such gestures would go down well with the United States.

Prime Minister Khai also stated that Vietnam-US defence cooperation should also include areas such as intelligence sharing on countering terrorism, transnational crimes and money laundering. In addition, Vietnam's defence ties with the United States also include training. In 2004, Vietnam and the United States agreed to implement the International Military Education Training (IMET), where Vietnamese military personnel would join English-language courses and training in medical and military expertise.⁵³

Vietnam has also strengthened ties with several major First World countries during 2005. Prime Minister Phan Van Khai visited Australia in May 2005. Apart from improved trading relationship, the bilateral ties covered defence and security. For the past three years, more than 100 Vietnam People's Army officers have undergone military training at the Australian Defence Force Academy or earned Masters degrees at Australian universities. Vietnamese Police officers have also received training in combating terrorism, drug, and human trafficking, as well as money laundering in Australia. Also benefiting from the growing bilateral relations were about 450 Vietnamese students who were studying in Australian tertiary institutions under Australian Development Scholarships.

On its part, Hanoi promised to help Canberra gain greater access to the Southeast Asian region. Vietnam, which coordinated the ASEAN-Australia dialogue partnership, supported Australia's participation in the 2005 East Asian Summit. The two sides also agreed to work together to prepare for the APEC Summit to be held in Vietnam in 2006 and in Australia in 2007. In return, Canberra expressed its support for Vietnam's admission into the WTO.⁵⁴

Vietnam-Russia relations took on a new dimension when Vietnam and Russia agreed to boost bilateral cooperation in nuclear energy during the second session of the two countries' Joint Coordinator on Cooperation in the Field of Nuclear Energy in May 2005. This is an important development in the light of the country's growing electrical energy consumption. The two sides will also cooperate in ensuring the safe and efficient operation of the Da Lat reactor, which is being used for nuclear research. Efforts were being made to upgrade radiotherapy in Hanoi.[55]

Vietnam-China relations have also improved during the last twelve months. In fostering these relations, many high-level meetings were held between leaders of the two countries, including an exchange of visits. In July 2005, Vietnamese President Tran Duc Luong led a delegation to visit China. Top of the agenda were negotiations over Vietnam's efforts to gain entry into the WTO, with China expressing support to Vietnam's membership of the organization.[56] The two sides also agreed to complete land-border demarcation by 2008.

In November 2005, Vietnam received a visit from Hu Jintao, the Secretary General of the Communist Party of China (CPC). During his visit, Hu became the first Chinese leader to address the Vietnamese National Assembly, claiming that Beijing-Hanoi ties had entered a new era of "all-round friendship and cooperation". Hu reiterated China's pursuit of peace, mutual benefit, and dialogue, over differences in diplomacy with neighbouring countries. At the end of the visit, the two countries released a joint statement outlining various efforts to boost cooperation to new levels, including raising bilateral trade to US$10 billion by 2010. In 2005, China was Vietnam's largest trading partner, with a total trade volume of US$8 billion, an increase from US$7.2 billion in 2004. The two countries also agreed to further a bilateral marine cooperation agreement and ensure the completion of the land-border demarcation by 2008.[57] During the visit, 14 significant agreements valued at US$1 billion, including financial aid from China to Vietnam, were concluded. Also signed was a joint oil exploration agreement between China National Offshore Oil Corp and a Vietnamese oil firm to explore oil and gas in the Beibu Bay (East Sea). More importantly, Hanoi reaffirmed its strong support for China's "One China Policy". This was a reaction to the growing concern over the perceived attempt by President Chen Shui-Bian of Taiwan and his party to take Taiwan towards independence from China.

However, there were several unresolved issues in their bilateral relations. These included the overlapping claims by China and Vietnam in the South China Sea. The most recent incident was Vietnam's protest against China's installation of an oil rig in an area that Vietnam claims as part of its territorial waters.[58] A more positive move was the willingness by both sides to discuss matters through the framework of ASEAN and China.

Another dimension gaining momentum in Vietnam's foreign policy was Hanoi's efforts to reach out to the overseas Vietnamese (Viet Kieu). This initiative was officially announced as part of the party's efforts in "promoting national unity, closing the past and looking toward the future". In this regard, the CPV's Political Bureau adopted Resolution 36 on reforming the work concerning the Viet Kieu. In 2004 a summer camp was organized for young overseas Vietnamese. Also implemented was the decision to allow a number of former high-level officials of the Saigon regime to return to Vietnam.[59] During Prime Minister Phan Van Khai's 2005 visit to the United States, the issue was mentioned. Khai insisted that it was Vietnam's policy that overseas Vietnamese in the United States were an integral part of the nation and an important resource for national reconstruction.[60] This indicates that Hanoi hopes to tap highly trained overseas Vietnamese for the country's development. The move gained strength as Viet Kieu investments in Vietnam increased substantially over the past three years from US$2.6 billion in 2003 to US$3.2 billion in 2004, and were projected to reach US$3.5 billion in 2005. Most of these investments were concentrated in Ho Chi Minh City.[61]

Vietnam's participation in the regional organizations and international forums over the past year should be considered very successful. Fresh from a successful 2004 when it hosted the ASEAN-Europe Meeting (ASEM) in Hanoi, Vietnam participated fully in the 10th ASEAN Summit held in Vientiane in 2005. The ASEAN Secretary General, Ong Keng Yong, heaped praise on Vietnam for its positive contribution to ASEAN's principles of equality and fairness since joining the regional organization in 1995.[62] Vietnam was also chosen to host the APEC meeting in 2006, barely six years after it joined the organization.

At the level of bilateral relations, several contentious issues were emerging. These include human trafficking and the growing Vietnamese labour presence in several countries. The Vietnamese government introduced a draft action in December 2004 to curb the lucrative business of trafficking women and children to China, Cambodia, Taiwan, Malaysia, Thailand, and some Eastern European countries. The action plan, which aimed to cut human trafficking by half by 2010,[63] focused on prevention, protection of victims, and prosecution of traffickers, with bilateral — even multi-lateral — cooperation between Vietnam and the countries involved. Vietnam has been exporting labour to Eastern European countries and the Gulf countries for many years. Recently, more Vietnamese workers travelled to its neighbours, including Taiwan, South Korea, Malaysia, and Singapore. Problems created by Vietnamese migrant workers in these countries include absconding from contracts and gang fighting, and resulted in several of these countries (including Taiwan and Malaysia) reducing their intake of Vietnamese workers. Tactful management of this labour exodus was required to ensure that their presence in these neighbouring countries do not cause diplomatic problems.

The past year was indeed a highly successful one for Vietnam in the international arena. The question remains as to whether these successes can be translated into more tangible and useful results for its domestic politics and development.

Conclusion

All seems to have been working well for the Vietnamese during the past twelve months. The achievements abroad in successfully cementing a vital bilateral relationship with the United States have been augmented with similar success with other major countries. Vietnam has also been doing very well at international forums. Apart from active involvement with ASEAN and the ASEAN Regional Forum, Vietnam was also honoured to be the host of the 2006 APEC Summit. While Vietnam is basking in its success overseas, successful management of its domestic issues would be central in the country attaining its development goals.

There are two main challenges facing Vietnam. The first is that the country is extremely ambitious in pushing ahead with reforms, which it hopes would transform the country into an industrialized country by the year 2020. Development strategies and efforts in foreign affairs have all indicated that the country was heading in the right direction. Related to this is the second challenge for the CPV to remain successful and acceptable to the Vietnamese people. This second challenge is tougher to achieve. Even as the reforms introduced through *doi moi* have brought success to the country and have greatly transformed the livelihood of the Vietnamese people, they have also brought about adverse conditions to many of the principles that the ruling party has stood for all these years. These include corruption, political dissent, and degradation of the quality of education, which could erode confidence in the party's rule. Thus, it should be the aim of the CPV to manage its reforms cautiously while continuing to pursue its ambitious year 2020 goals. The momentum of the party's success in foreign affairs should be further enhanced so that some of these might be translated into successes on the domestic front. The question will be whether the 10th National Congress of the CPV can make that difference.

Notes

[1] Speech of Phan Van Khai on 21 June 2005 at a Gala Dinner hosted in his honour by the Vietnam-US Trade Council, the ASEAN-US Business Council and the US Chamber of Commerce.
[2] *Thanh Nien News*, 23 June 2003.

3. *Sai Gon Giai Phong*, Spring, January 2005, p. 8. Cited in Vietnam UNDP News.
4. *Vietnam Review*, 2005, p. 31.
5. *Washington Times*, 21 June 2005.
6. *Washington Post*, 16 June 2005.
7. http://www.vov.org.vn/2005.
8. Viet Nam News Service, 4 May 2005.
9. "Strategy for Socio-Economic Development in the Period 2001–2010, presented by the Party Central Committee, 8th Tenure to the 9th National Congress", in *Communist Party of Vietnam, 9th National Congress: Documents* (Hanoi: Gioi Publishers, 2001), p. 190.
10. *Vietnam Investment Review*, no. 738, 5–12 December 2005.
11. *Vietnam Investment Review*, no. 733, 31 October–6 November 2005.
12. *Thanh Nien News*, 21 September 2004.
13. *Viet Nam News*, 10 June 2005.
14. *Thanh Nien News*, 8 April 2005.
15. Radio Voice of Vietnam, 6 December 2004.
16. *Sai Gon Giai Phong*, Spring, January 2005, p. 8. Cited in Vietnam UNDP News and *Vietnam Investment Review*, 2–4 November 2005.
17. *Vietnam News Service*, 11 June 2005.
18. *Thanh Nien News*, 12 June 2005.
19. CPV/VietNamNet, 4 August 2005, http://www.cpv.org.vn/details_e.asp?topic=59&subtopic=157&ID=BT48056287.
20. *Thanh Nien News*, 27 June 2005.
21. Vietnam News Agency, 6 March 2004.
22. *Viet Nam News*, 4 July 2005.
23. Viet Nam News Agency, 23 June 2005.
24. The more recent exodus of ethnic minorities from the Vietnamese central highlands to Cambodia began in 2001. Many accused the local authorities of being repressive, apart from the economic hardships faced. Some of these exiles moved on to certain European host countries, while others have been repatriated.
25. Viet Nam News Service, 22 February 2005.
26. *Viet Nam News*, 4 July 2005.
27. *Washington Times*, 21 June 2005.
28. Vietnam News Agency, 2 August 2005.
29. Joint Statement issued on 21 June 2005 by President George W. Bush and Prime Minister Phan Van Khai, *Viet Nam News*, 29 June 2005.
30. *Vietnam Investment Review*, no. 723, 22–28 August 2005.
31. Vietnam Ministry of Foreign Affairs Press Release, 23 September 2005.
32. Press Release of Vietnam Ministry of Foreign Affairs, 9 November 2005 and *Vietnam Investment Review*, no. 735, 14–20 November 2005.
33. *The Star*, 30 December 2005.

34 *Asian Development Outlook, 2005.*
35 *Vietnam Investment Review*, no. 717, 11–17 July 2005.
36 "Statement by the Representative of the IMF", Can Tho, Vietnam, 2–3 June 2005, http://www.imf.org/external/np/dm/2005/060305.htm.
37 Xinhua Net, 18 July 2005.
38 *Vietnam Investment Review*, no. 729, 3–9 October 2005.
39 *Vietnam Investment Review*, no. 733, 31 October–6 November 2005.
40 Vietnam News Agency, 18 June 2005.
41 *Vietnam Investment Review*, no. 736, 21–27 November 2005.
42 *Vietnam Investment Review*, no. 738, 5–12 December 2005.
43 *Vietnam Investment Review*, no. 731, 17–23 October 2005.
44 *Vietnam Investment Review*, no. 729, 3–9 October 2005.
45 *Washington Post*, 16 June 2005.
46 *Thanh Nien News*, 23 June 2005.
47 *Thanh Nien News*, 23 June 2005.
48 The 2005 figure of MIAs stood at 372 in Laos, 55 in Cambodia, and seven in the People's Republic of China territorial waters.
49 *Vietnam News*, 13 July 2005.
50 Radio Voice of Vietnam, 1 March 2005.
51 *Thanh Nien News*, 15 August 2005.
52 *Washington Times*, 21 June 2005.
53 *Washington Post*, 16 June 2005.
54 Vietnam News Agency, 5 May 2005.
55 Vietnam News Agency, 22 May 2005.
56 Xinhua Net, 18 July 2005.
57 *Vietnam Investment Review*, no. 734, 7–13 November 2005.
58 Vietnam News Agency, 19 November 2004.
59 Vietnam News Agency, 31 December 2004.
60 *Viet Nam News*, 27 June 2005.
61 *Vietnam Investment Review*, no. 719, 25–31 July 2005.
62 *Nhan Dan*, 3 August 2005.
63 *Thanh Nien News*, 19 December 2004.